Casein Painting with Stephen Quiller

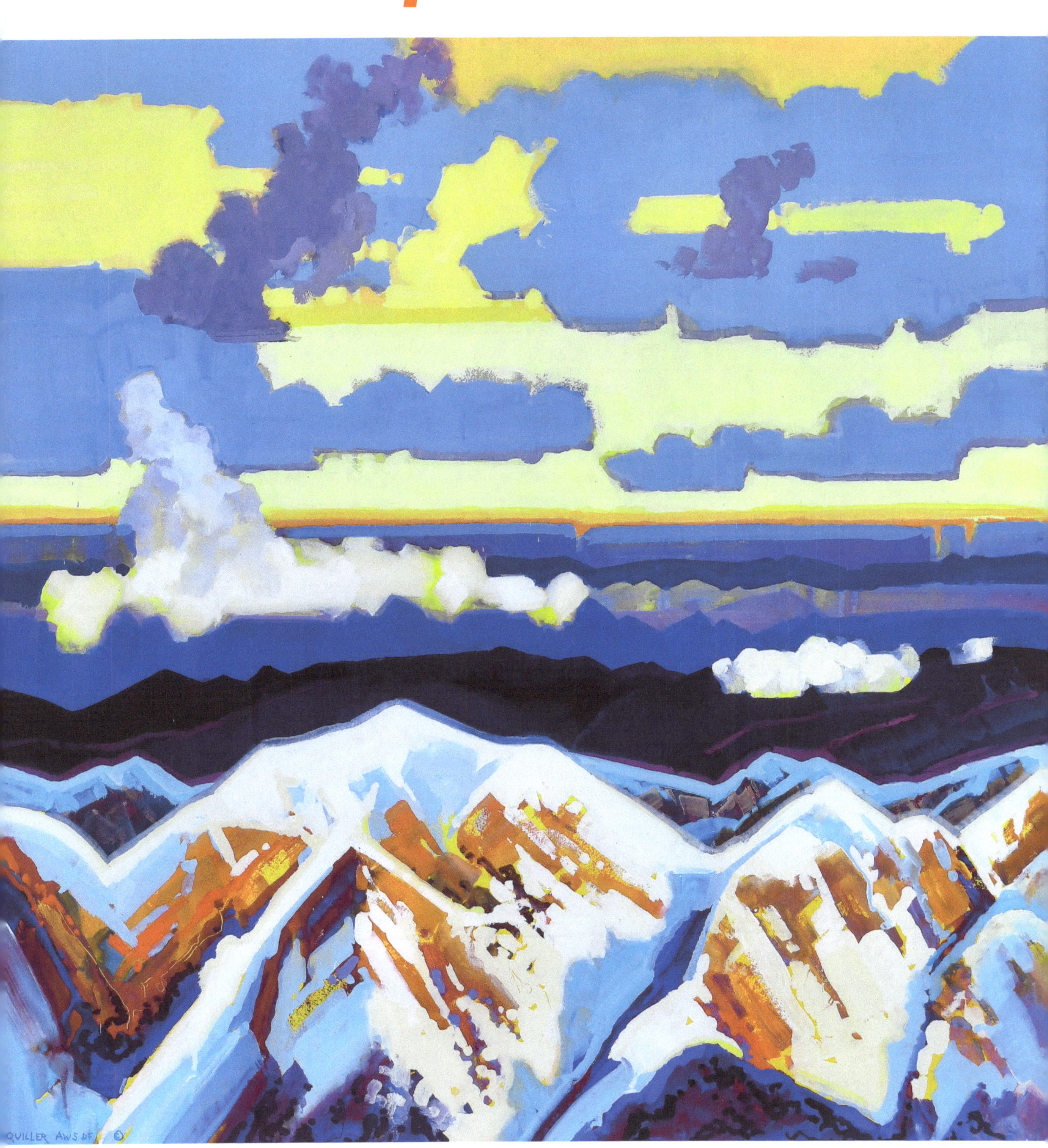

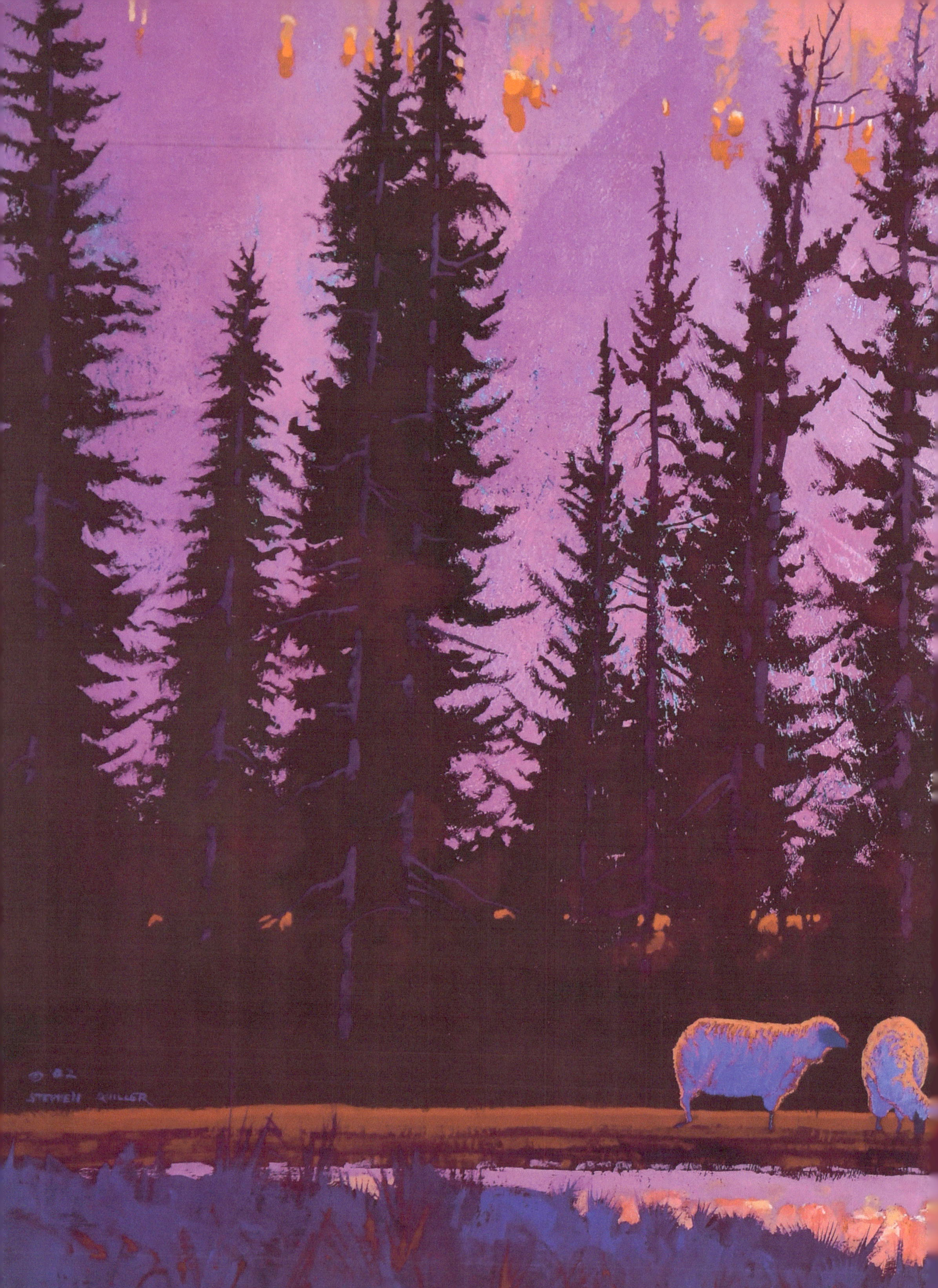

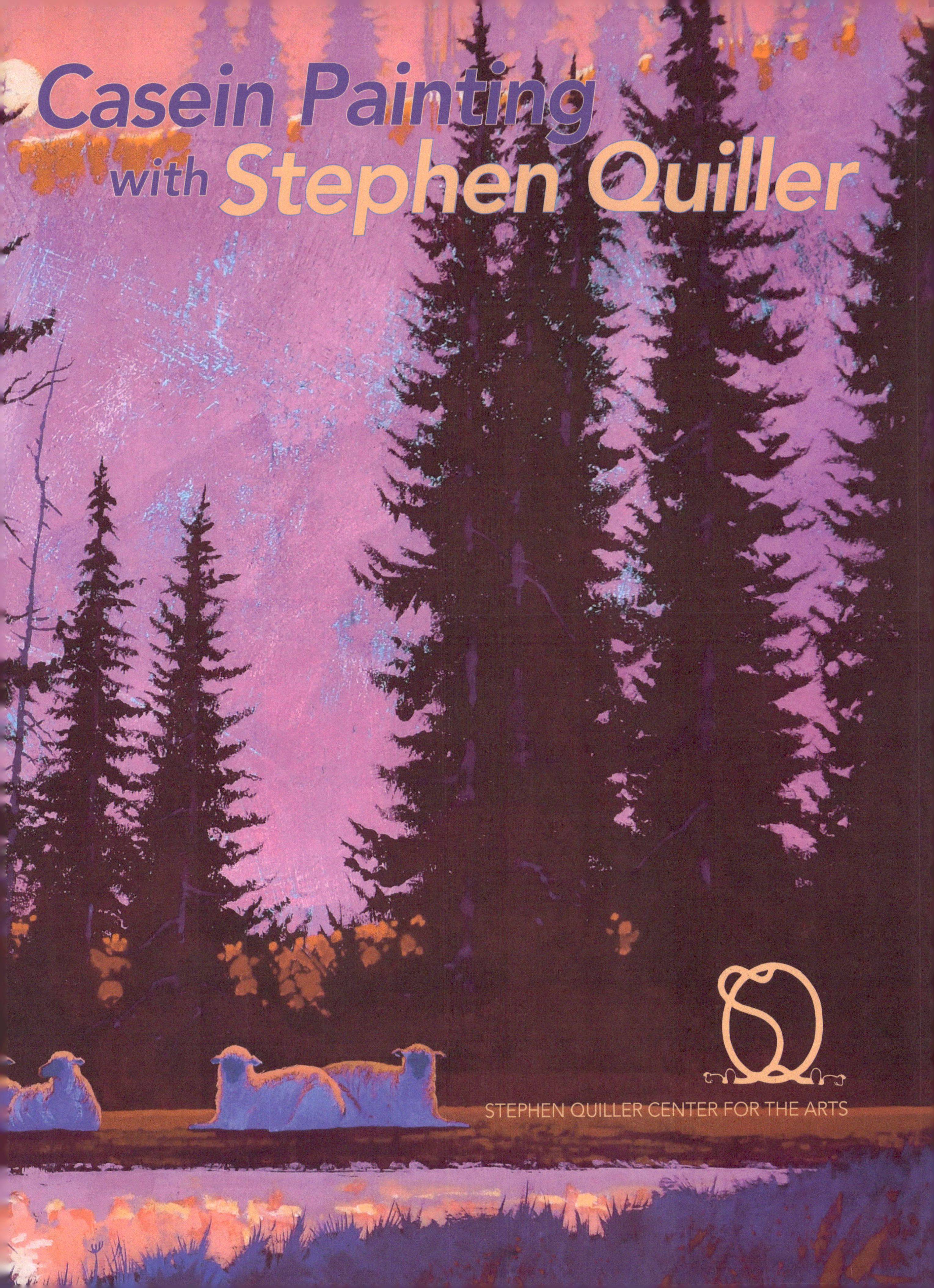
Casein Painting
with Stephen Quiller
STEPHEN QUILLER CENTER FOR THE ARTS

View from the Air #2
*(page 1) **2019***
casein, 28" x 28"
Private Collection

Sheep Symmetry, Meditation
*(pages 2-3) **1982***
casein, 21" x 29"
Collection of Bill and Teri Smith

AN ADDED HIGHLIGHT OF THIS BOOK

Allison Quiller has archived thousands of my paintings that I have done since the early 1970s. I painted many of these in casein or in combination with other water media. Since I have been working with casein for 50 years I thought it would be interesting to note the date of each painting displayed in the book. The reader can witness shifts in the development of my paintings throughout time. There will be missing information on current owners and collectors for some of the pieces, as they have changed hands over the years.

Published by Echo Point Books & Media
Brattleboro, Vermont
www.EchoPointBooks.com

Casein Painting With Stephen Quiller
ISBN: 978-1-63651-964-5 (casebound)
978-1-63651-965-2 (paperback)

Interior design by Allison Quiller

Cover design by Allison Quiller

10 9 8 7 6 5 4 3

ACKNOWLEDGEMENTS

First and foremost and with deep appreciation I thank Allison Quiller. She is the art director and layout designer for this book. It is been a joy to be able to work together on this project.

Next, thank you to Marta Quiller for her editing skills!

Christine Kraft has been most helpful with suggestions in terms of editing and layout design. She has insight that has really assisted in this publication.

Kelly Richeson is the lead paint maker of casein at the Richeson Company. She has been so helpful and easy to work with in the development of several new colors for this line.

Of course Jack Richeson, who I've come to know as a close friend, for his suggestions, thoughts and encouragement on this book.

Colleen Richeson Maxey, my compadre and leader with our Richeson International Seminars. She has been a great go between for me with the Richeson Company.

Thank you to Dyan Sublett for the beautiful heartfelt words in the epilogue.

I would also like to thank Marshall Glickman, owner and publisher of Echo Point Books and Media, Fred Lee, production manager, and Anneka Kindler, contract and royalties manager for their interest, generous encouragement, editorial advice, design tweaks and for expediting this publication.

And last, I have deep reverence for Barbara Whipple, who back in the 80s was an artist and contributing editor to American Artist Magazine and with whom I wrote my first two water media books. She and her husband Grant Heilman were also art collectors and encouraged me to continue to work in water media and especially casein.

DEDICATED TO JACK RICHESON

In the mid-80s I developed the Quiller Wheel and was looking for a company to market and distribute it in the United States. I asked a few retail art store managers in Colorado who they would recommend. The person they spoke highly of was Jack Richeson.

As divine synchronicity would have it, I had just been invited to be the guest artist for the Colorado Artist Association Conference to be held in Denver. It turned out that Mr. Richeson was one of the vendors at this event. He was able to observe two of my demonstration-presentations that weekend. We then met for breakfast and got to know each other. That afternoon in the parking lot I showed him four of my paintings and he purchased one.

Little did I know that he had been Vice President of Sales for Grumbacher and President of Morilla International Paper Company and had just decided, in his early 50s, to start his own company in Wisconsin with his wife Ruth and youngest son Darren, who was an accountant. He had a wealth of knowledge and experience in the art material industry. Today the company has grown to a family run business with over 70 employees producing, importing, and distributing the finest of high quality art supplies, furniture and easels.

What I have observed since is that Jack is an "artist" in the art material industry. He has the vision and ideas and is not afraid to take risks. Other companies sit up and take notice of his methods. He truly loves art and artists, many his closest friends. At his factory office in Kimberly, Wisconsin, he has collected and displays over 400 paintings from artists throughout the United States and abroad. This gallery is open to the public.

What I find most interesting is that when Jack was 16 years old, he began working at Sheldon's Art and Drafting Supply in Chicago. Ramon Shiva (1886-1963), who lived in Chicago, was a painter and also the leading manufacturer of casein and oil paint. Jack was a "runner" and would pick up Mr. Shiva's paint to be sold at the store. At that early age he was around painters and learned to love the smell of casein and oil paint being made. As the saying goes, "What goes around, comes around."

Today, Jack's company owns the Richeson Shiva casein line and is the sole manufacturer of this paint in the United States. And by the way, the piece that Jack purchased from me back in the late 80s was painted with casein!

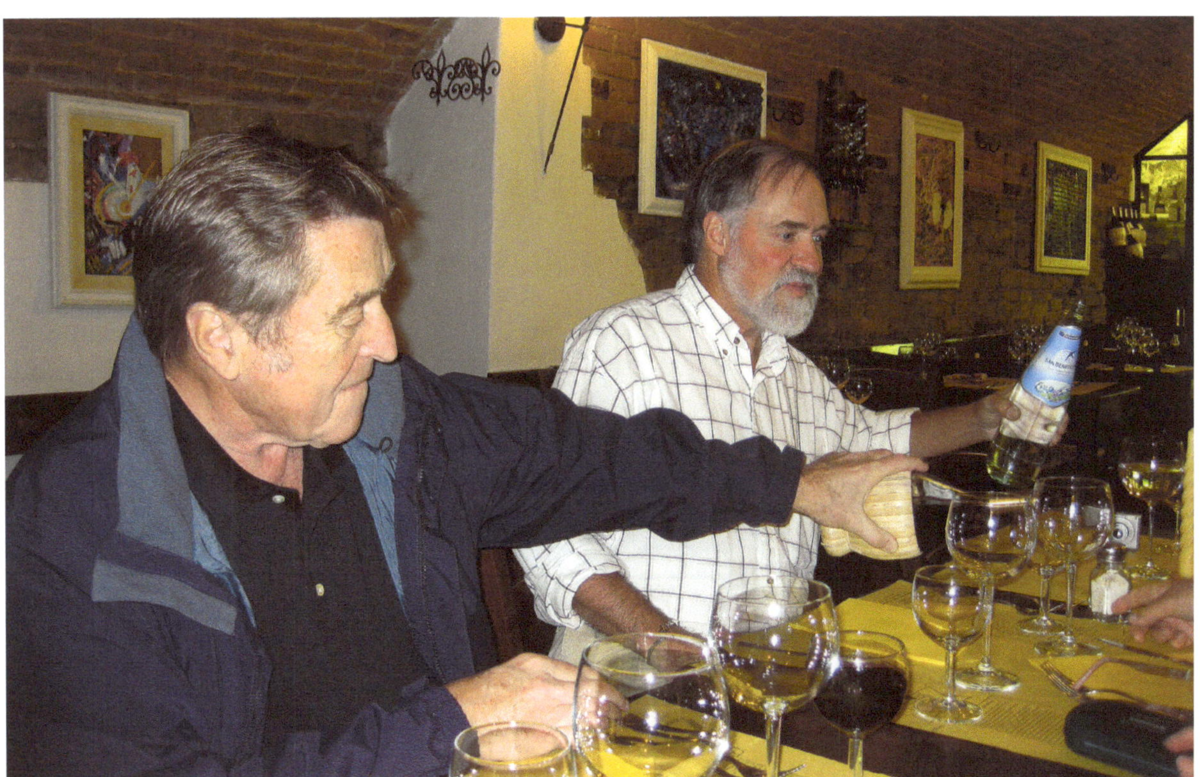

Jack Richeson & Stephen Quiller - Florence, Italy 2008

Contents

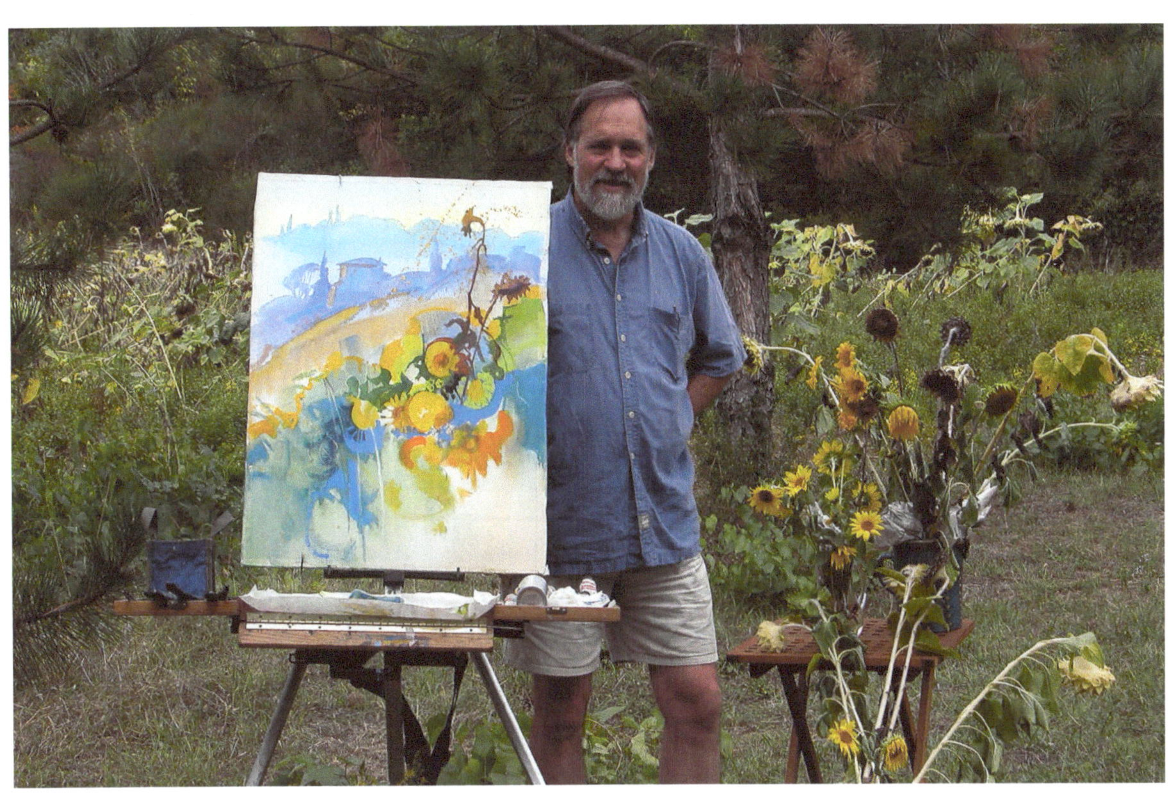

Introduction

In my early 20s I was instructing art at a high school in southern Oregon. I had been working in watercolor since I was 15 and loved the immediacy and flow of the medium. In 1969, my second year living in Oregon, I saw a notice in the local paper that the American Watercolor Society Traveling Exhibition could be viewed at Willamette University in Salem, Oregon. I decided to take a one day, 550 mile round-trip adventure to see the show.

This exhibition changed my life! There were nationally recognized painters I had read about: Dong Kingman, Chen Chee, Mario Cooper and many others. One piece in particular stood out to me, a painting of old Roman ruins by Mark Freeman. I could smell the dust and dankness of the stonework in the piece. It had a different visual quality from that of the other incredible watercolors. Later I learned that it was a casein painting and that Mr. Freeman was indeed the president of the National Society for Painters in Casein and Acrylic.

In the fall of 1972 I ended my teaching position in Oregon and moved to the small town of Creede in the San Juan Mountains of southern Colorado, and began painting full time. Close to 50 years have gone by, and I have written six best-selling books and numerous DVDs and videos on the subjects of water media and color. I have worked with watercolor, gouache, acrylic and casein and their combinations, and continue to paint daily in my studio or on location. Throughout all of these painting years I have focused frequently on casein. I love its velvety visual quality that has a look unlike any other medium.

It's important to know that every medium including casein, watercolor, acrylic or oil use the same pigments. Thus the cerulean blue pigment that is in a top-quality watercolor paint is the same pigment that is used in a top-quality acrylic. What creates the different visual qualities and handling characteristics is the binder that attaches the pigments. For instance, gum arabic from the gum of the acacia tree in Africa is the binder for watercolors. Acrylic has a poly-resin based binder. Linseed oil is the binder most used in oil paint.

Casein is a fast drying, water-soluble paint that uses the curd protein of milk as its binder. This is what gives the paint its unique and special visual quality. The word casein is derived from the Latin word "caseus" and is a medium that has been used for centuries. Etruscan tombs dating 300-800 BC were painted with casein. John Sloan, one of the Ash Can School painters, occasionally used casein as an underpainting for his oils in the early to mid 1900s. The medium was used extensively in colleges and universities in the 40s and 50s and also as a commercial art medium for illustration. However, with the invention of acrylic as a painting medium in the 50s, artists began gravitating to it. Casein seemed to almost disappear as a medium for painters.

Today casein has made a resurgence. It is a very versatile medium that can be used as a water medium both transparent and opaque, or as an easel painting medium much like acrylic, although with a very different look. The National Society for Painters in Casein and Acrylic has an annual exhibition at the Salmagundi Club in New York City. This exhibition hosts many of the top painters who use casein.

In this book I will demonstrate many of the possibilities for expression with this medium. I will begin with the Quiller Color Palette in casein colors, which will work precisely to create a universal palette of expression. I will examine each of the colors and their properties and essence. I will look at complementary color families. I will show how these color palettes can be applied to create maximum expression. This chapter will be followed by another one discussing the various visual qualities and methods of paint application: transparent, translucent, and opaque, and working light to dark or dark to light, in a juicy fluid manner.

The next chapter will discuss the various tools and surfaces that can be used for casein. I will work with watercolor paper, watercolor board, Aquabord® panels, and gessoed hardboard panels and wood panels, revealing the beauty of the medium in these various surfaces. I will discuss fixatives and emulsions and the cleaning and care of brushes. You will see finished examples of paintings using casein in combination with other media, and I will explain the development of each work. It is so exciting to see firsthand the beauty of casein used with acrylic, watercolor or drawing media, and even collage.

Last, I will display a "gallery" of my finished work where you will see my approach to this marvelous medium. Throughout the book I will have subtext of some of my thoughts about nature and painting and living a painter's life. My daughter Allison has been archiving almost all of the work that I have done since the early 70s. Along with each painting displayed in the book I will attach the year that it was done. There will be paintings spanning a 50 year period. As you look at the paintings, note the dates and see the growth and progression in my work.

It is my hope that this text will inspire you to explore this incredible medium. There are possibilities that have yet to be discovered. I hope you will take this journey and push this medium to new heights and in the process find your own voice!

—Stephen Quiller

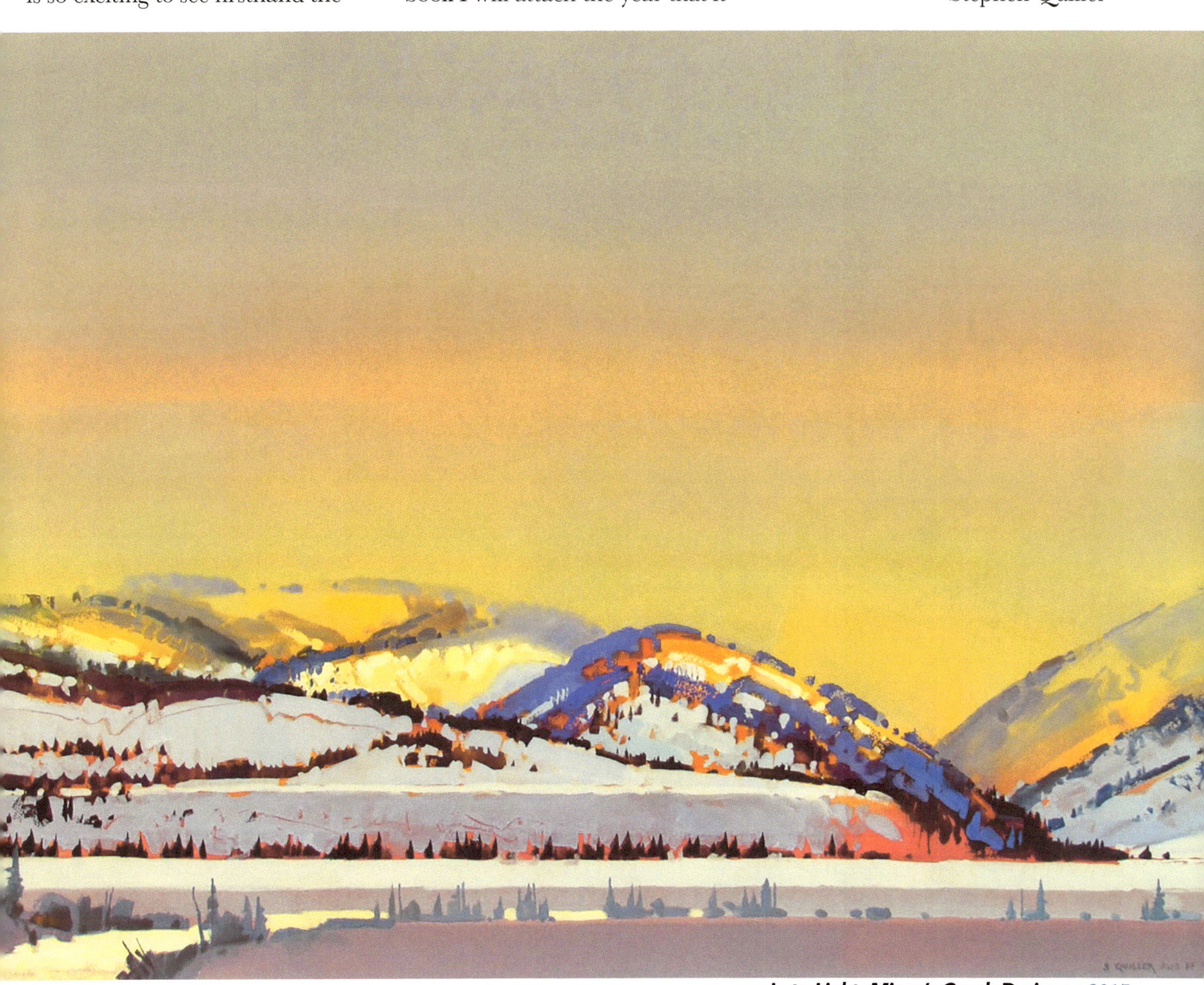

Late Light, Miner's Creek Drainage *2017*

casein, 21 ¾" x 30", Private Collection

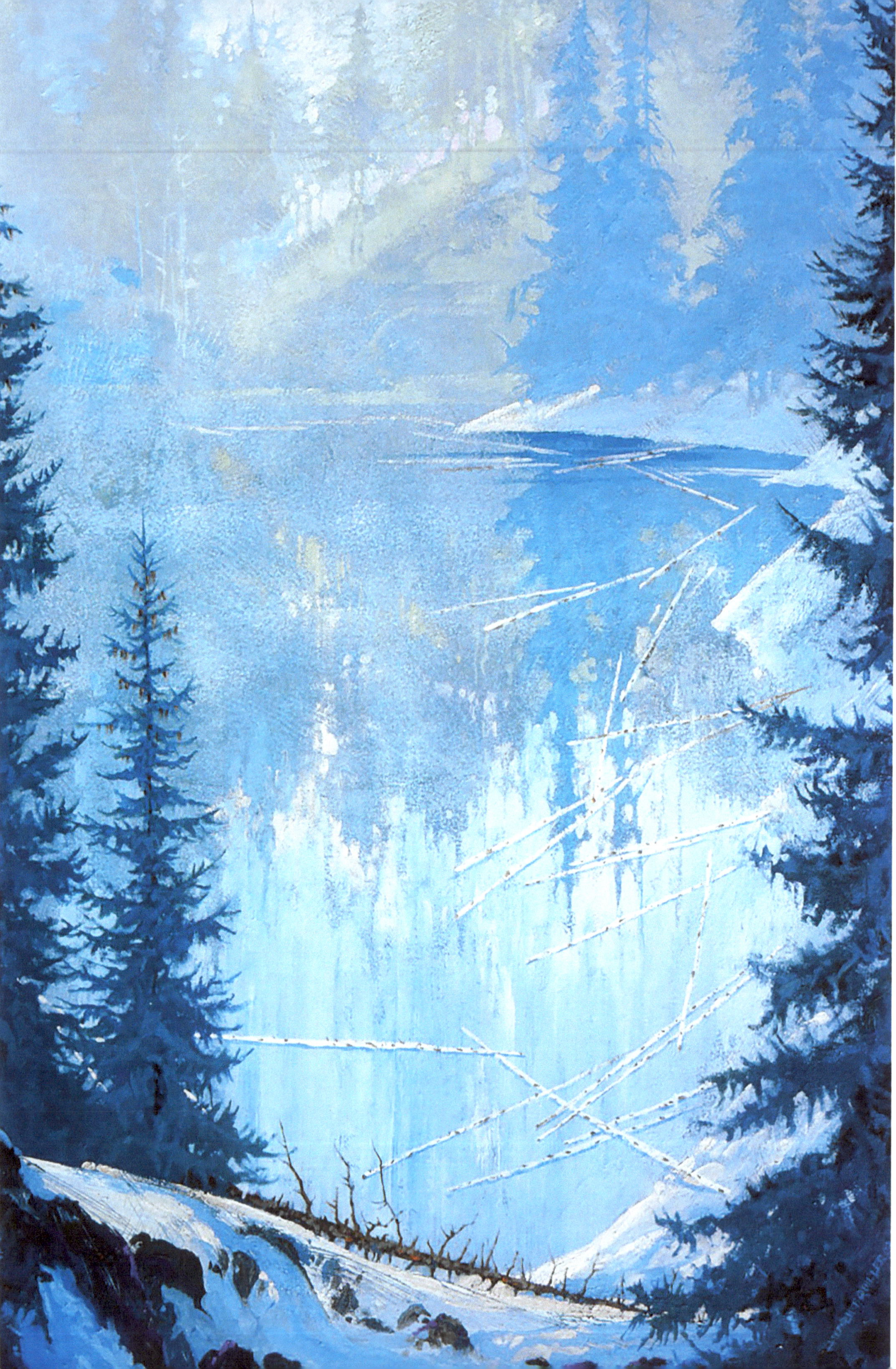

1 Quiller Casein Color Wheel and The Painter's Palette

This chapter will focus on the foundation for working in casein, and understanding the casein palette of colors with the Quiller Casein Wheel. I will begin by discussing the visual qualities and handling characteristics of casein. This will be followed by the arrangement of the primary, secondary, and intermediate colors. I will then examine each of the 36 colors. I will discuss the chemical makeup, lightfast rating, the true complementary color and the neutral that can be created from the complement, followed by my analysis of the color. I will then demonstrate the Quiller Casein Color Wheel and palette.

This chapter will also display an intensity chart of the six primary, secondary, intermediate, and complementary sets, their semi-neutral colors and true neutrals. On page 29 is a full Quiller Casein Color Wheel. This can be referenced throughout the book to achieve beautiful color relationships. I will then expand the palette, demonstrating that other colors can have not only a true complement to create the neutral, but can use near complements on either side to create warm and cool near-neutrals.

I will discuss how this palette is truly "universal." With these colors the artist can paint in Hawaii or Alaska, and capture the essence of the color. Finally, I will demonstrate different ways to create rich beautiful darks that resemble black. Not only will they seem like a black but will be full of vibrancy.

Shoalwater Bay
(left) 1979
casein, 29" x 21"
Collection of Mike Nelson

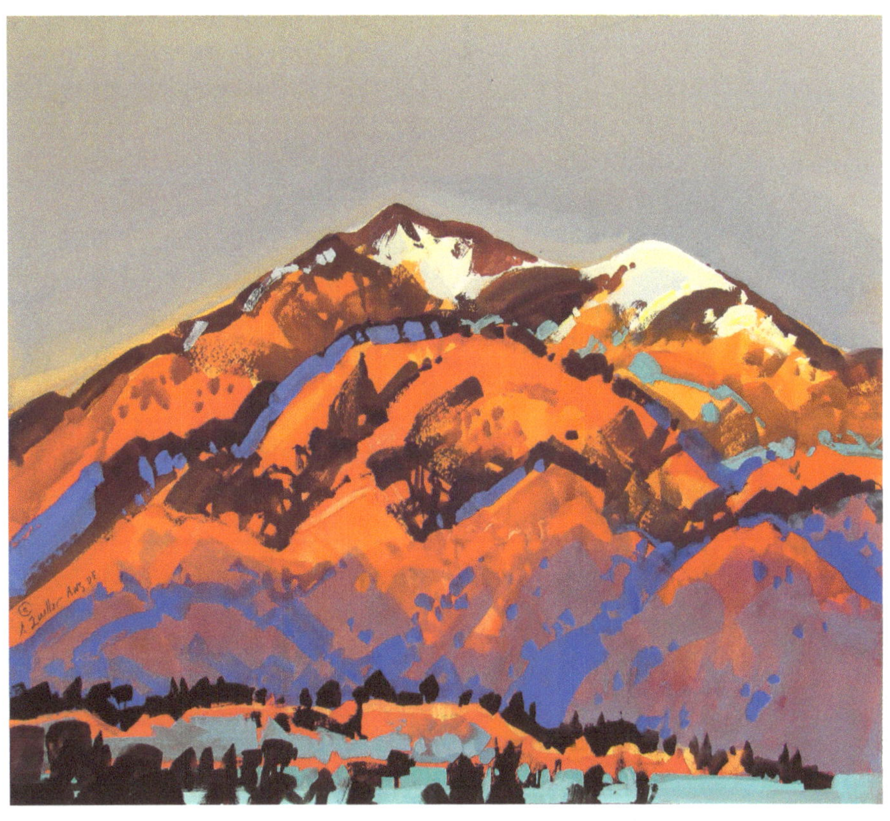

Taos Mountain
(right) 2013
casein, 11 ½" x 13 ¼"
Private Collection

Visual Qualities of Casein

The original formula used by Ramon Shiva included 20% of casein from skim milk, lime, pigments, a little oil, and chemicals. This mix is what gives casein such a beautiful, velvety visual quality. A pine oil is added to the mix, which gives it an incredibly clean smell. It has a soft visual quality that is unlike any other medium. I love to use casein to help create an airiness and earthiness in a landscape; the dryness and the aged quality of architecture and boats; and the raw earthy feel of adobe. It is truly magnificent and unsurpassed when used in this way.

Casein has a very high concentration of pigment and is highly opaque. Bright juicy color notes can be achieved when painting over a dark underlay. Also the painter can develop extremely fine detail using small brushes and painting over dark. These are very important advantages of this medium. It is important to know that when casein paint is applied, the light colors dry darker and the dark colors will dry lighter. This can take a bit of getting used to but it's worth it. I love applying a deep ultramarine violet or blue as a base note in a composition and watch it dry and come to life! It is luminous. It is also important to note that when applying casein thickly, the artist should not use a hairdryer. This is because it can cause the surface of the paint to dry before the underlying pigment and can cause cracking.

In the past, artists were trying to create a similar look with oil paint. Edgar Dégas used the method called "distemper." He placed cotton fabric on the outside of his palette and squeezed his paint along the fabric. The material absorbed most of the excess linseed oil, leaving a lot of pigment with very little binder. Working this way, the paint had a drier, velvety look. Today, I know a very well-known oil painter who paints on a clay coated board that in a sense creates the same effect. The clay absorbs the binder leaving the raw paint itself.

Casein will bind to any non-oily surface. If the paint is used in a normal water media technique, any support including thinner watercolor papers can be used. However, if the paint is to be used heavier and more impasto, a rigid support should be used. This could include anything from 300 # watercolor paper, watercolor board, gessoed Masonite panels, basswood panels, and mounted canvas board. Depending on the way I'm applying paint I will use either a synthetic water media brush or a stiffer synthetic acrylic brush.

Backlight, Autumn Aspen
(right) 2019
casein, 34" X 26"
Private Collection

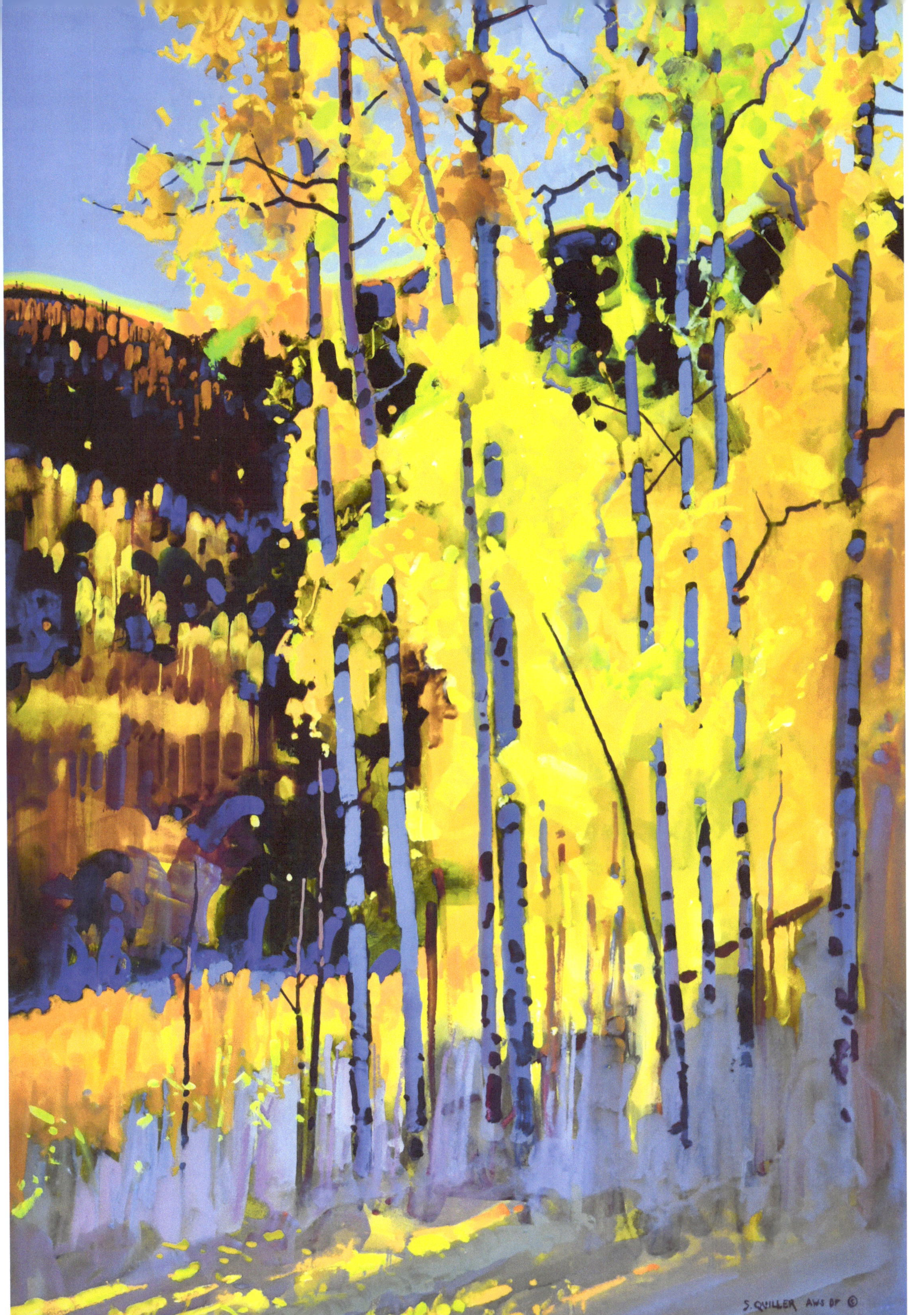
S. QUILLER AWS DF ©

Permanency of Casein

The pigment makeup of every medium - watercolor, oil, pastel, acrylic, or casein - is the same. A cerulean blue pigment in oil paint is the same as that of casein. What makes each medium different is the binder. In oil it is linseed oil; in watercolor it is gum arabic; in casein it is the curd protein from milk. As you will see in the following charts, almost all of the casein colors are rated lightfast # 1. What I find interesting, emphasizing the durability and lightfastness, are the following two stories.

My internet research found an article in the Chicago Tribune on June 18, 1933, page 42. The article was about the vivid colors of the buildings, both interior and exterior, at the Chicago World's Fair. Mr. Joseph Urbane had received a well-funded contract to select the color of the walls and paint the buildings. He asked the leading paint makers to submit their colors, and among them was Ramon Shiva. Each candidate painted vivid color panels and placed them on the south side of a building, exposed to sunshine for months. Shiva was awarded the contract, as his beautiful flat colored paint made from a skim milk product held up better than the others. The casein, lime, pigments, and a bit of oil and chemicals, were fade resistant and did not peel. These colorful and glowing structures were truly a hit at the event.

My second story is about the centuries-old covered bridges in New England. People were always interested in knowing why all the bridges were the same color of red and why they held up so well. Red oxide was the one pigment that was commercially available at that time, the pigment that was used on these covered structures. However, the binder was milk base or what we know as casein. Obviously, the paint has held up well in two harsh environments.

Late Sun on the Ridge Trail
(right) 2012
casein and transparent acrylic underwash
35" x 26"
Collection of David Benson

Louis Kaep Memorial Award,
American Watercolor Society

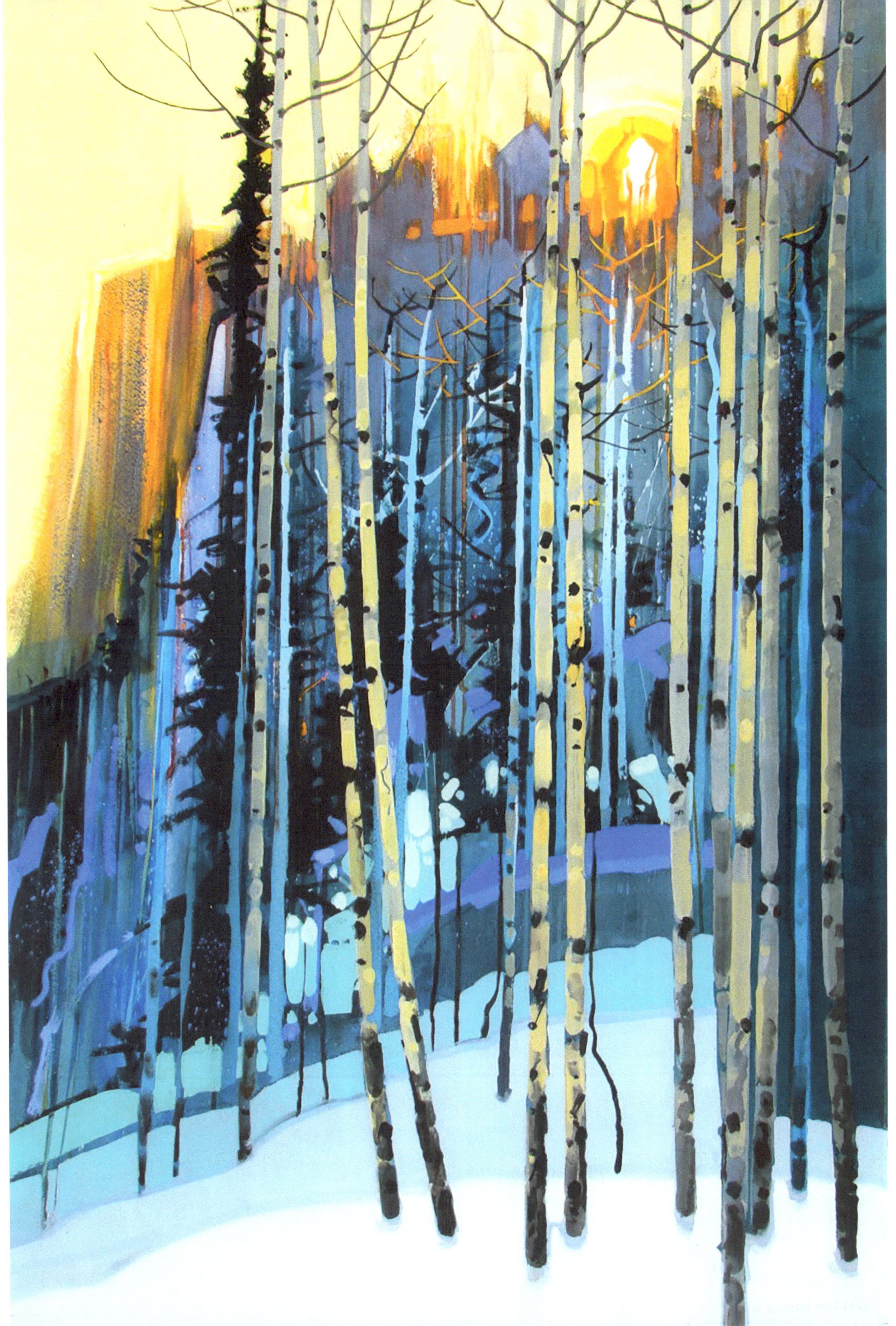

Casein Palette of Colors

Below is a display showing the complete line of casein colors. Each color provides information about the chemical pigment make-up, followed by the lightfastness rating, the complementary color that is used to mix a beautiful neutral, as well as its ability to enhance the pure view color.

Each chart from left to right starts with the color swatch that is transparent, followed by a color swatch that is opaque. The third swatch shows the true neutral "gray" when mixed with its complement. The fourth smaller note is the complementary color. This is followed by a brush mark of the color painted over black to show the pigmentation and opacity or transparency. The last swatch shows the liftability of the paint after it has set for one day. As you will see, the mineral and earth colors such as cerulean blue, ultramarine blue, and ultramarine violet along with yellow ocher, raw sienna, and raw number lift more readily than the transparent, staining synthetic organic pigments such as phthalocyanine green and blue. It's important to know that after a period of about two weeks, the paints have cured and become insoluble.

I feel it is important to note the beautiful neutral grays that each color has when mixed with the complement. All of the casein colors have a true complement. That excites me!

CADMIUM YELLOW LIGHT

PY 3- arylide yellow & PY 35:1 - cadmium yellow light

Lightfastness #1

Complementary color: ultramarine violet

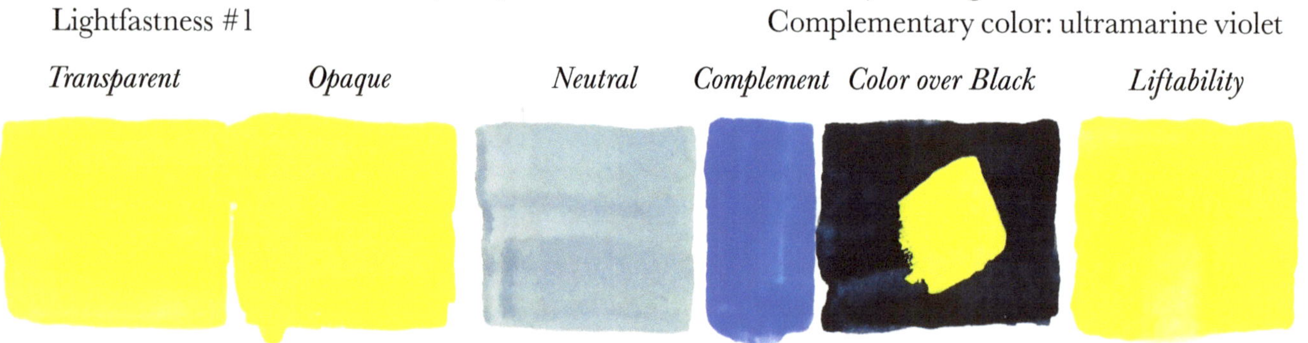

Analysis: This is the primary yellow and is the lightest value color on the palette. Painted on white paper, it seems weak, but surrounded by a darker value the color sings. It neutralizes beautifully with its complement, ultramarine violet.

CADMIUM YELLOW MEDIUM

PY35:1 and cadmium yellow light

Lightfastness #1

Complementary color: ultramarine violet

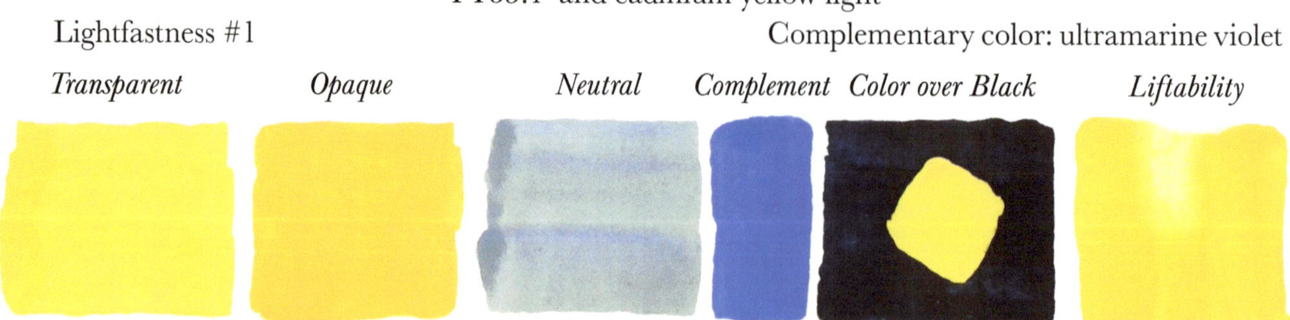

Analysis: This is a rich, powerful and juicy color. It has strong color power and can be a beautiful opaque color note placed over dark.

NAPLES YELLOW

PW4, PY35, PY42 zinc white, cadmium yellow light, arylide yellow, synthetic iron oxide

Lightfastness #1 Complementary color: ultramarine violet

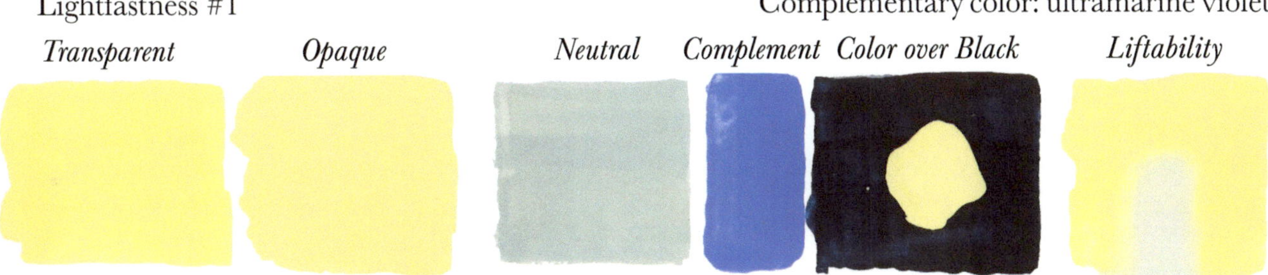

Analysis: I use this color frequently, as it has a softness and earthiness when mixed with other colors, or by itself for use in painting mountains. It has very good opacity and has a chalky feel.

CADMIUM ORANGE

PO20 and cadmium orange

Lightfastness #1 Complementary color: ultramarine blue

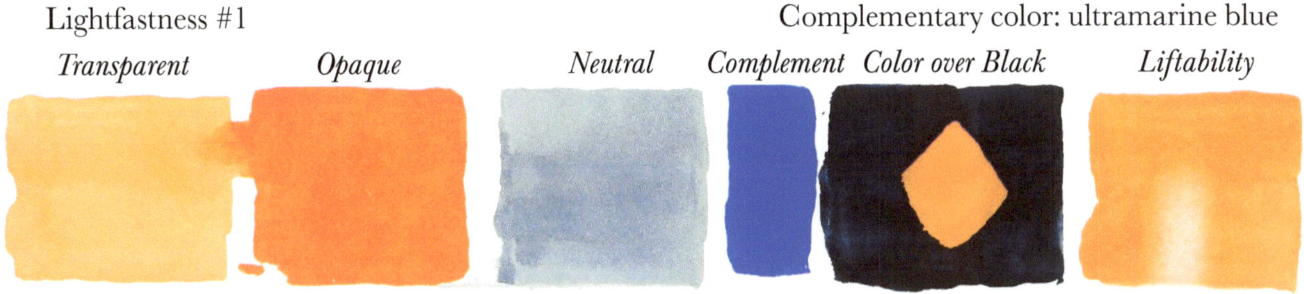

Analysis: This is my intermediate yellow orange color note. It is the perfect yellow orange to neutralize with its complement of ultramarine blue. It has good pigment opacity.

CADMIUM RED PALE

PR108:1 cadmium-barium red light

Lightfastness #1 Complementary color: permasol blue or Shiva blue deep

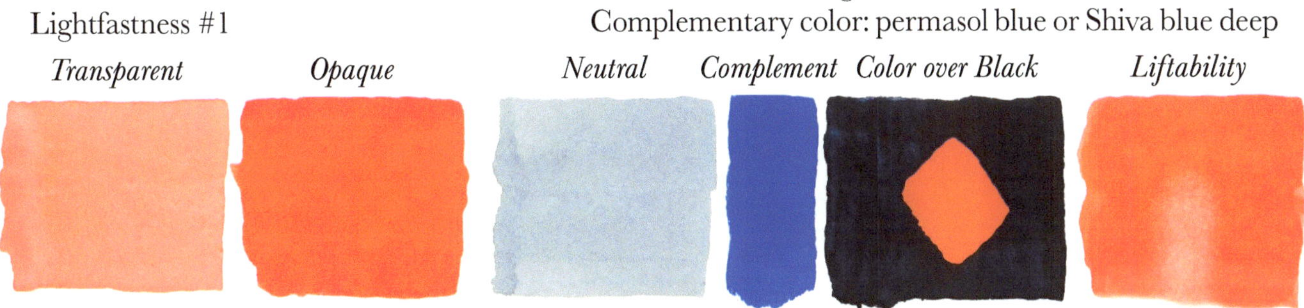

Analysis: This is the secondary orange on my palette. It has good pigmentation and strong color note as in all the cadmium colors.

CADMIUM RED SCARLET

PR 108:1 cadmium-barium red deep

Lightfastness #1 Complementary color: phthalocyanine turquoise

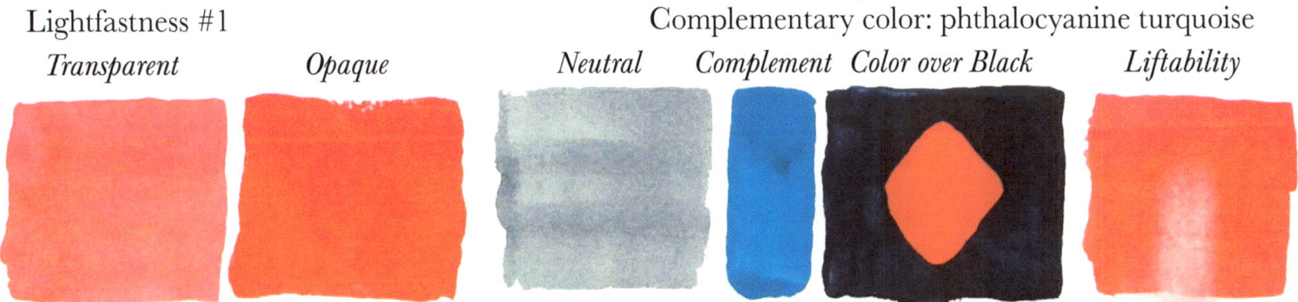

Analysis: This is my intermediate red-orange. The color is truly beautiful and a discovery. It has a very strong color note with great opacity that neutralizes perfectly with phthalocyanine turquoise.

CADMIUM RED DEEP

PR108 cadmium red deep

Lightfastness #1

Complementary color: phthalocyanine turquoise

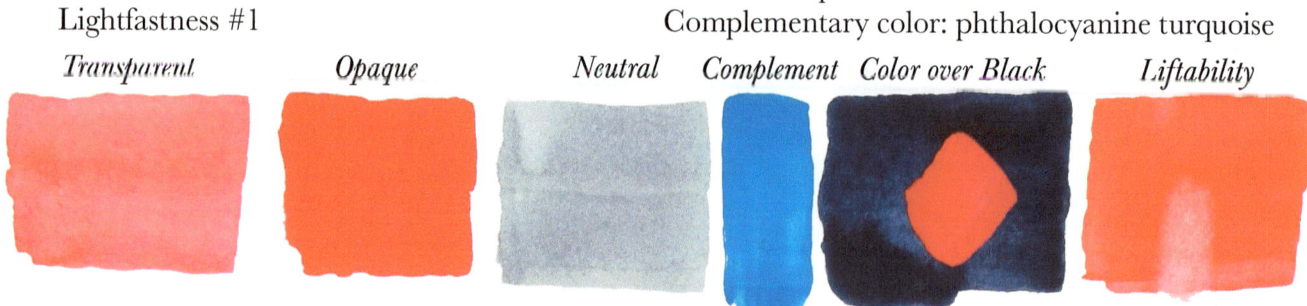

Analysis: This color is very similar to cadmium red scarlet. It's a very opaque strong color note. I find it a little darker than cadmium scarlet and is not a lively color.

ROSE RED

PR122 quinacridone magenta and PR19 quinacridone red PR122

Lightfastness #1

Complementary color: Shiva (phthalocyanine) green

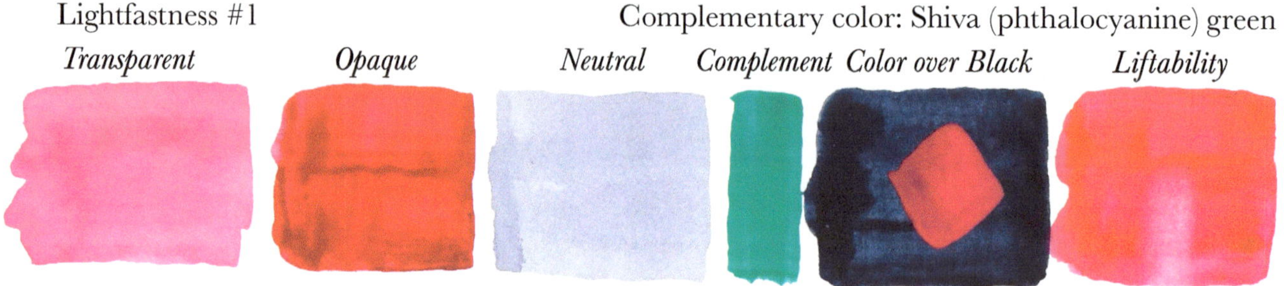

Analysis: This is the color I use for my primary red. It is a beautiful cool red that is made from quinacridone synthetic pigments and is very lightfast. It's a deep color that comes to life by adding a touch of white. It mixes beautifully with permasol blue to produce a beautiful range of violets.

SHIVA ROSE

PV19 and PR83 rose madder alizarin and quinacridone red

Lightfastness #3

Complementary color: Shiva (phthalocyanine) green

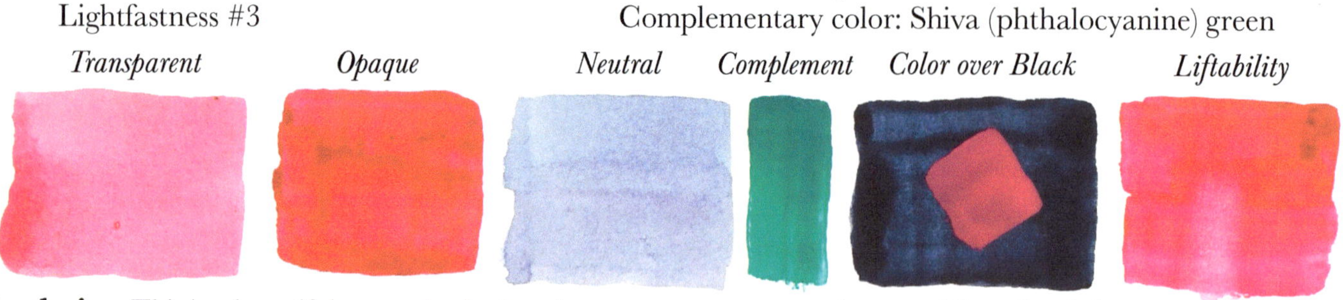

Analysis: This is a beautiful rose red color but does not use permanent pigments. Therefore I choose to use rose red for my painting.

ALIZARIN CRIMSON

PR83 rose madder alizarin

Lightfastness #3

Complementary color: Shiva (phthalocyanine) green

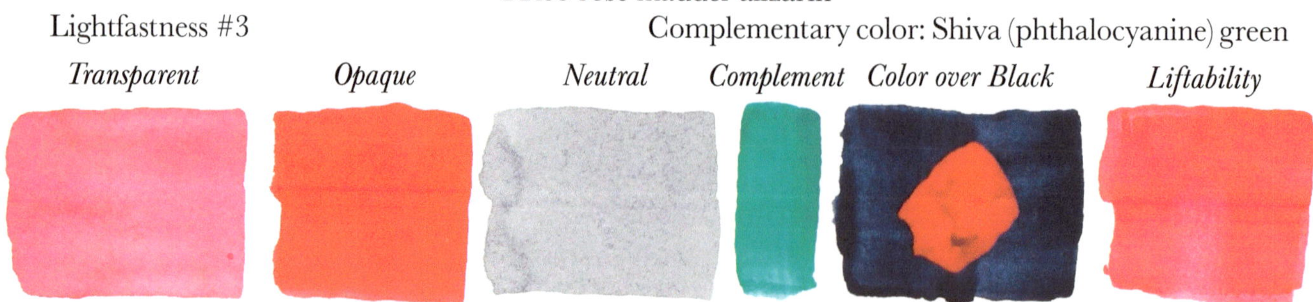

Analysis: This color is not lightfast and will tend to brown with age. However, it is a very popular color in every medium and artists choose to use it because of its beautiful color properties.

QUINACRIDONE VIOLET

PV19 quinacridone magenta

Lightfastness #1 | Complementary color: permanent green light

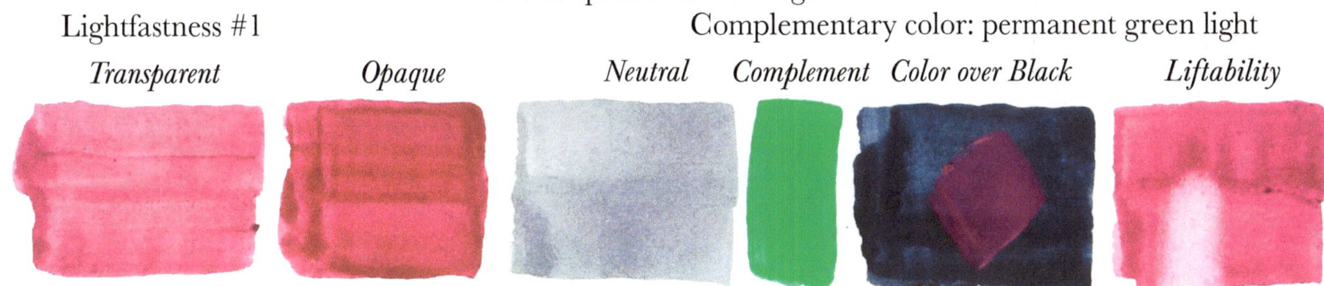

Analysis: This is the color note I use for my intermediate red-violet. It has beautiful pigment properties and grays out beautifully with its complement permanent green light.

SHIVA VIOLET

PV23 dioxazine purple red shade

Lightfastness #2 | Complementary color: permanent green light

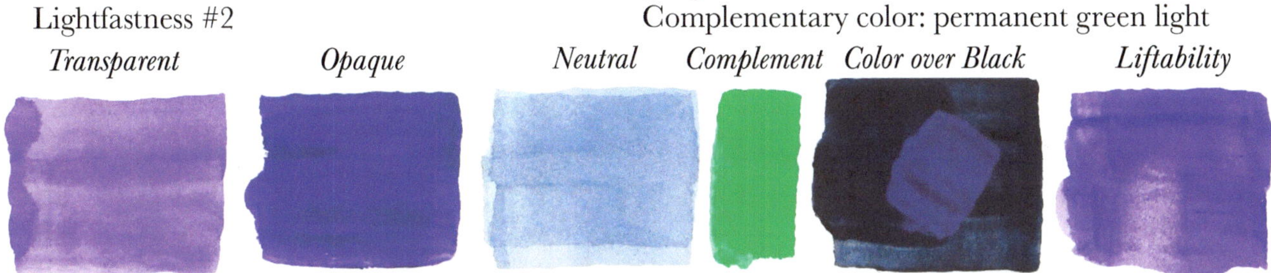

Analysis: Shiva violet is a dark pigment that neutralizes beautifully with permanent green light. It can be used in combination with other color mixes to achieve a darker value. It is not rated as permanent lightfastness so I use this color sparingly.

ULTRAMARINE VIOLET

PV15 complex silicate of sodium and aluminum with sulphur

PB 29 complex of calcine kaolin, soda ash, sulphur, silica, coal, and sodium sulfate

Lightfastness #1 | Complementary color: cadmium yellow light

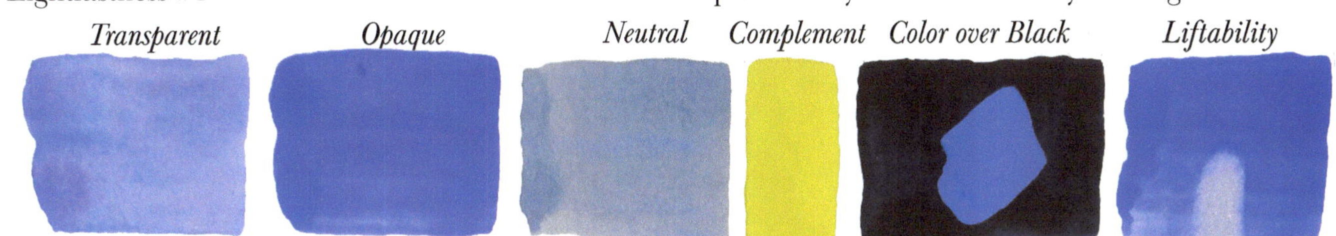

Analysis: This is the color I use for my secondary violet. This color is spectacular. It is a light value color but grays out beautifully with yellows. It has good pigmentation properties and is very opaque painted over dark values. The color will sing in a painting.

ULTRAMARINE VIOLET BLUE SHADE

PV15 complex silicate of sodium and aluminum with sulfur

PB 29 complex of calcine kaolin, soda ash, sulphur, silica, coal, and sodium sulfate

Lightfastness #1 | Complementary color: cadmium orange

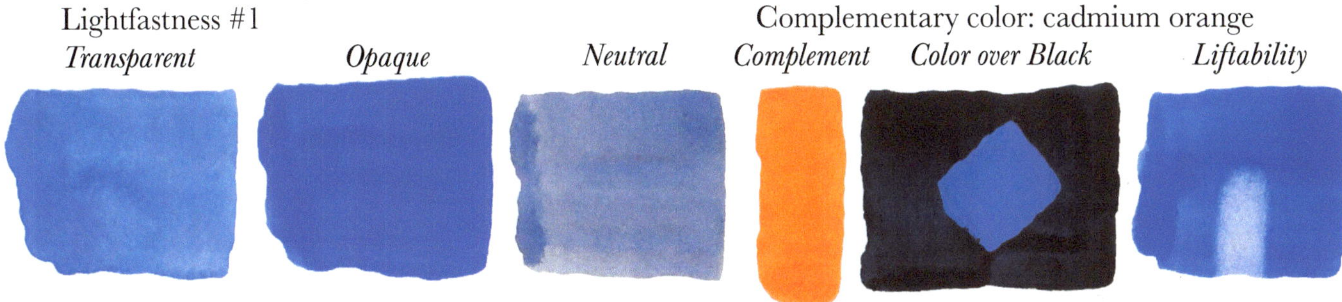

Analysis: This color has a bit deeper value and is a touch bluer than the ultramarine violet. It's very opaque and a brilliant color.

ULTRAMARINE BLUE

PB29 complex of calcine kaolin, soda ash, sulphur, silica, coal, and sodium sulfate

Lightfastness #1 Complementary color: cadmium orange

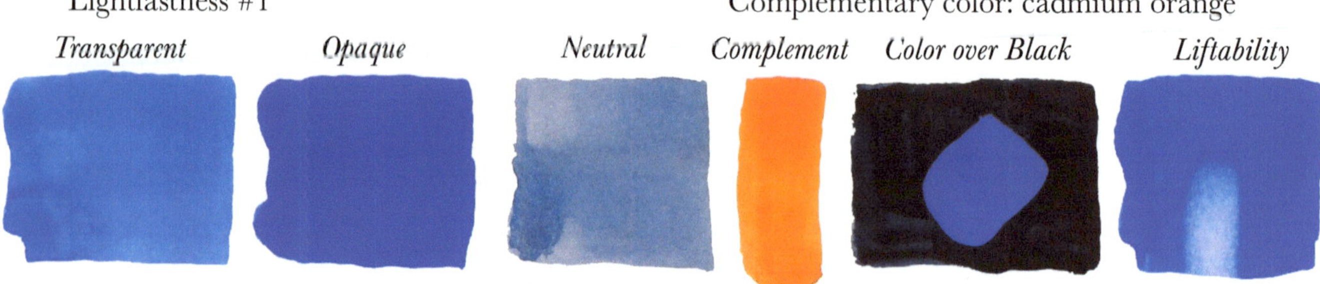

Analysis: This is one of my favorite colors. As with most of the colors, when first applied it will appeared darker but as it dries, it comes to life. The rich stunning blue violet weaves through many of my paintings.

COBALT BLUE

PB28 oxides of cobalt and aluminum

Lightfastness #1 Complementary color: permanent orange

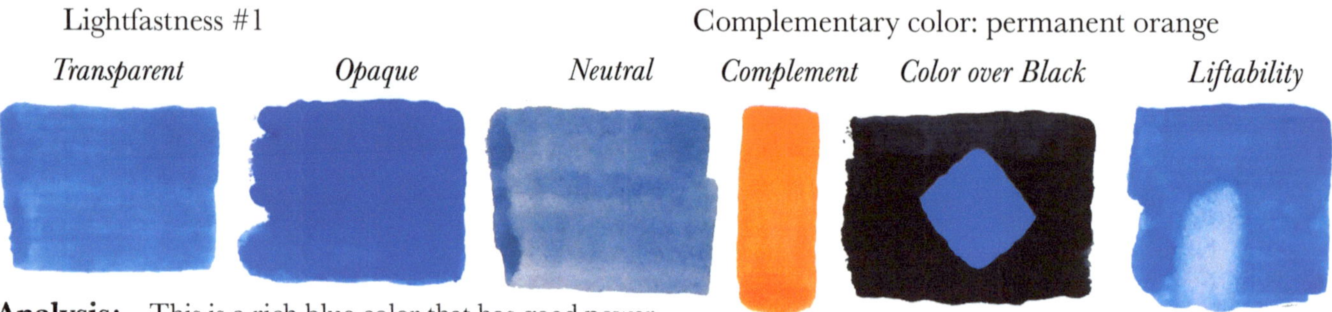

Analysis: This is a rich blue color that has good power.

PERMASOL BLUE

PB15 copper phthalocyanine and PW 6 titanium white

Lightfastness #1 Complementary color: cadmium red pale

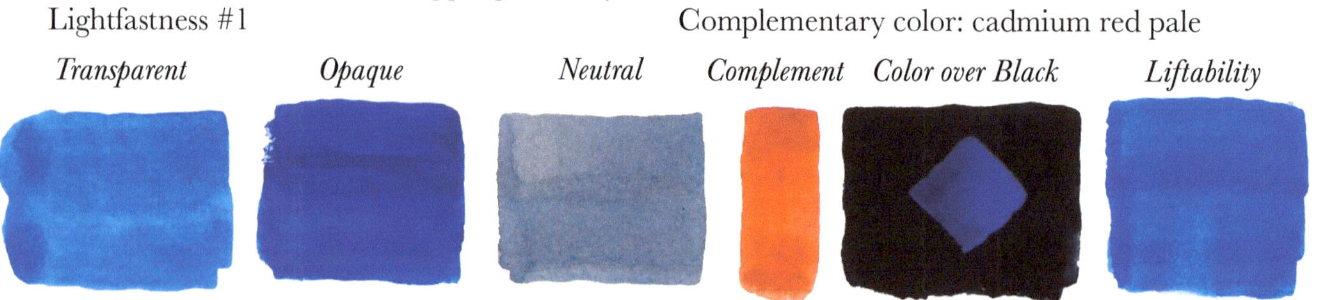

Analysis: This color was a real discovery. I now use this for my primary blue. It is simply phthalocyanine blue with a bit of titanium white added, but the little bit of white lifts the color from the darkness and gives it life. I find that when mixed with rose red, it produces a beautiful violet.

SHIVA BLUE DEEP (PHTHALOCYANINE)

PB15 copper phthalocyanine

Lightfastness #1 Complementary color: cadmium red pale

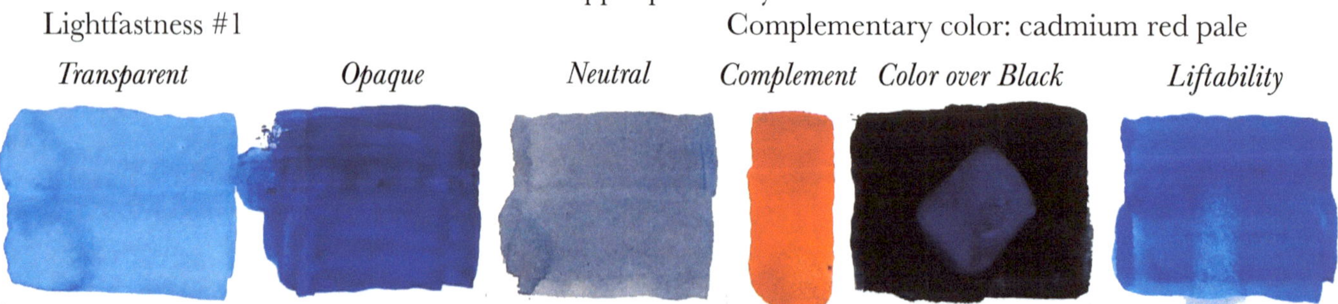

Analysis: This color can be used as a primary blue. However, I found that the permasol blue is richer and more lively. The Shiva blue seems to be a little more sticky and a bit harder to blend out.

CERULEAN BLUE

PB 36 oxides of cobalt and chromium Lightfastness #1.

Lightfastness #1 Complementary color: cadmium red scarlet

Transparent *Opaque* *Neutral* *Complement* *Color over Black* *Liftability*

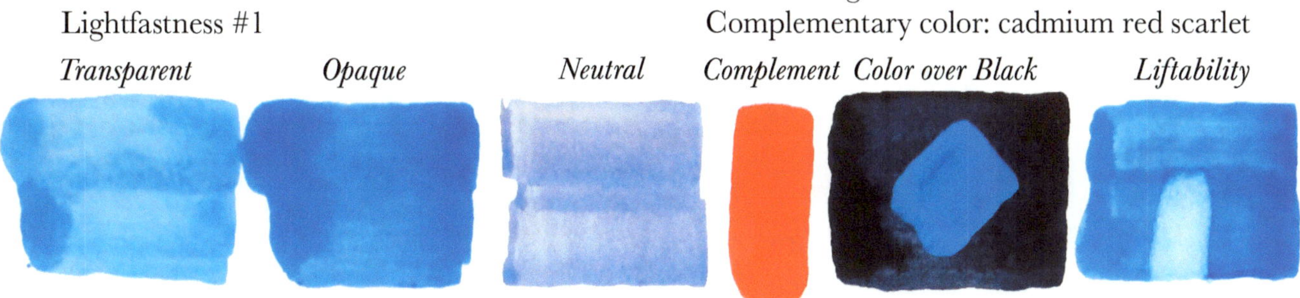

Analysis: Cerulean blue is a beautiful yet fairly weak color. More concentrated pigment is necessary to get a strong color note. It neutralizes beautifully with its complement.

PHTHALOCYANINE TURQUOISE

PB29 complex of calcine kaolin, soda ash, sulphur, silica, coal, and sodium sulfate

PG7 chlorinated & brominated phthalocyanine

Lightfastness #1 Complementary color: cadmium red scarlet

Transparent *Opaque* *Neutral* *Complement* *Color over Black* *Liftability*

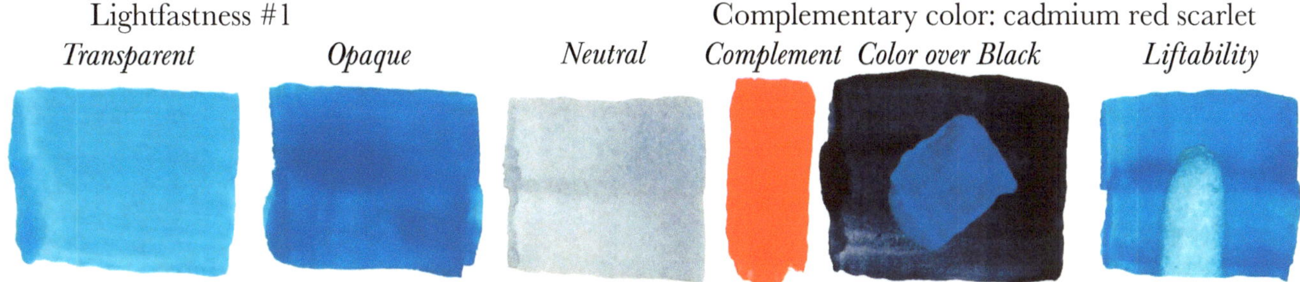

Analysis: This is a beautiful turquoise. I use it for my intermediate blue-green. It neutralizes well with its complement cadmium scarlet. The color note painted over a dark value is rich. It can also be mixed with quinacridone violet to produce interesting neutralized blues.

SHIVA GREEN (PHTHALOCYANINE)

PG7 chlorinated & brominated phthalocyanine

Lightfastness #1 Complementary color: rose red

Transparent *Opaque* *Neutral* *Complement* *Color over Black* *Liftability*

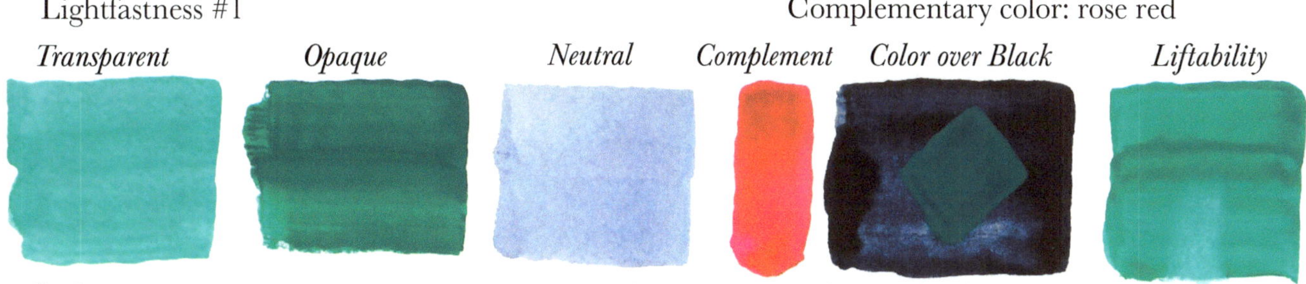

Analysis: I use this for my secondary green. This is a fluid, very deep pigment that is very rich. It can produce dark values when mixed with other colors such as rose red, Shiva violet, ultramarine blue, permasol blue, or cadmium red scarlet. It is a beautiful neutral to the cool side when mixed with its complement rose red.

PERMANENT GREEN LIGHT

PY 35:1 concentrated cadmium zinc sulfide, PG7 brominated phthalocyanine, PY3 arylide yellow

Lightfastness #1 Complementary color: quinacridone violet

Transparent *Opaque* *Neutral* *Complement* *Color over Black* *Liftability*

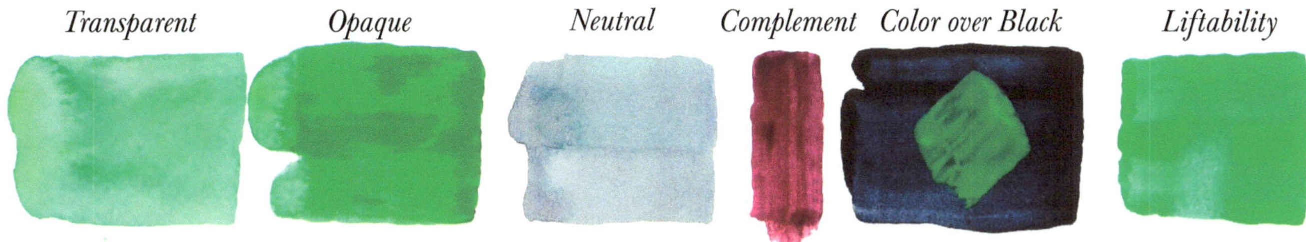

Analysis: This is a rich and beautiful color that I use for my intermediate yellow-green, a deep beautiful color that is transparent and can provide beautiful darks when mixed with Shiva violet, quinacridone violet or rose red.

CADMIUM GREEN

PY35:1 cadmium yellow light,, PG7phthalocyanine green, PY3 arylide yellow

Lightfastness #1 Complementary color: Shiva violet

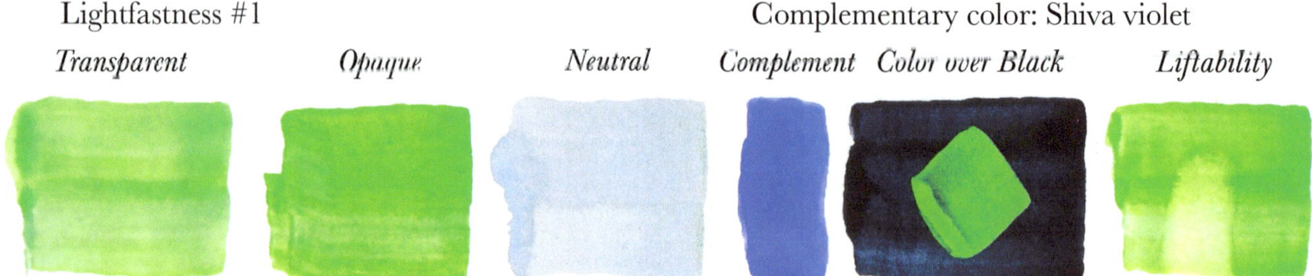

Analysis: This is another color that I omit from my palette. I find that I can mix a beautiful yellow-green color note using cadmium yellow light with a bit of permanent green light. However, this color seems to be a bit gummy and hard to clean from the brush.

HALFTONE BLACK

PBk7, PBr7 carbon black and natural iron oxide

Lightfastness #1 Complementary color: ultramarine blue

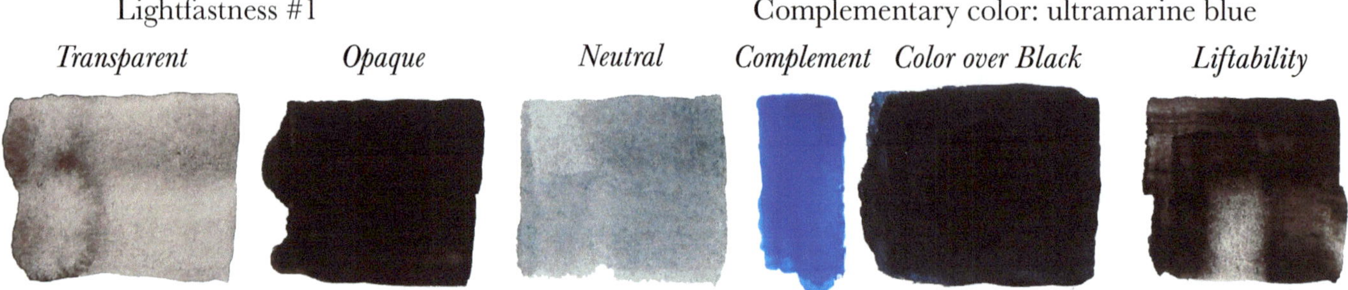

Analysis: Many people swear by this color, and is often used in illustration. It has finely ground pigment that glazes beautifully. It reminds me of the color sepia in that it is a warm brownish dark.

IVORY BLACK

PBk9 amorphous carbon produced by charring animal bones

Lightfastness #1 Complementary color: ultramarine blue

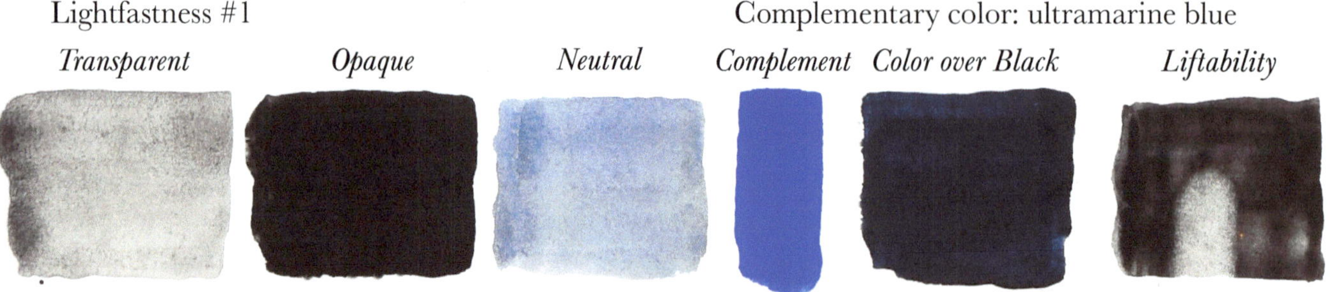

Analysis: In almost all of my paintings in every medium, I mix my blacks. However, in casein there are times that I use this black purposely. It is a velvety rich black, has a unique visual quality, and brings other colors on the palette to life. It is a warm black. To achieve a true neutral, add a touch of ultramarine blue.

PAYNE'S GREY

PB 29, PBk7 complex silicate of sodium and aluminum with sodium and carbon black

Lightfastness #1 Complementary color: cadmium red pale

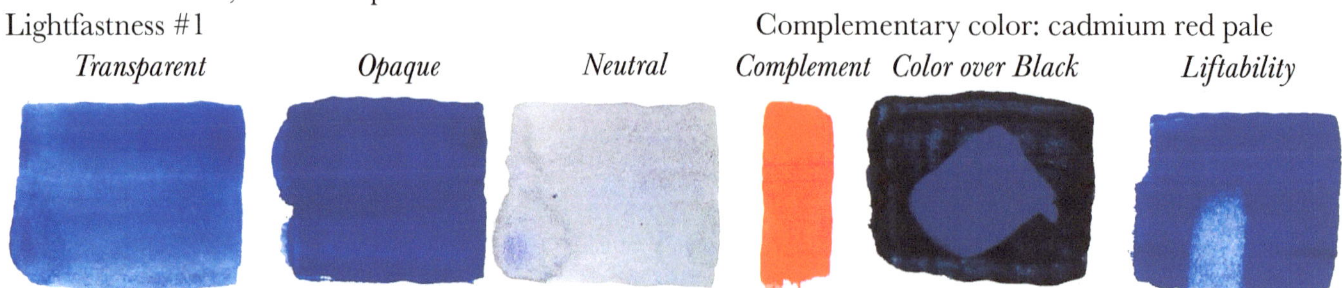

Analysis: This is a rich blue-black using the actual black carbon pigment with ultramarine blue. It's on the cool side and can be a beautiful color to work with. To achieve a pure neutral, add a touch of cadmium red pale.

YELLOW OCHER

PY43 natural hydrated iron oxide

Lightfastness #1

Complementary color: ultramarine violet

Transparent *Opaque* *Neutral* *Complement* *Color over Black* *Liftability*

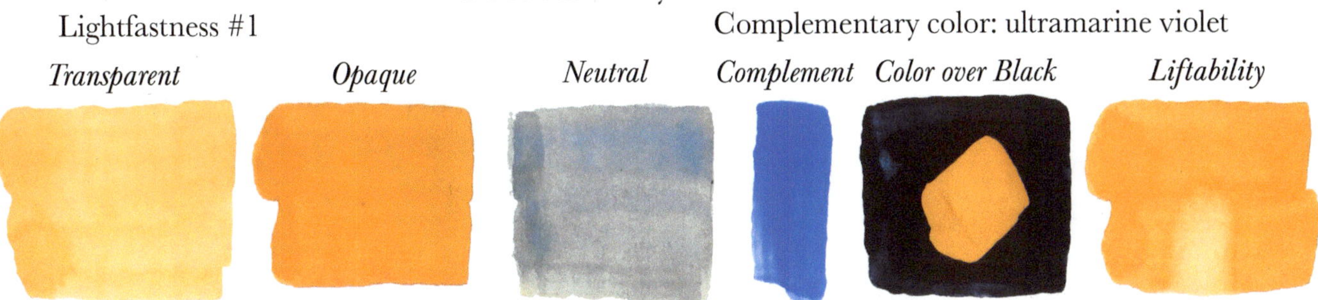

Analysis: Yellow ocher is a natural slightly earthy color that has good pigmentation and opacity. It's in the same family as golden ocher and raw sienna. It is a bit yellower than golden ocher and its complement is ultramarine violet blue shade.

GOLDEN OCHER

PY42 synthetic hydrated iron oxide

Lightfastness #1

Complementary color: ultramarine violet (blue shade)

Transparent *Opaque* *Neutral* *Complement* *Color over Black* *Liftability*

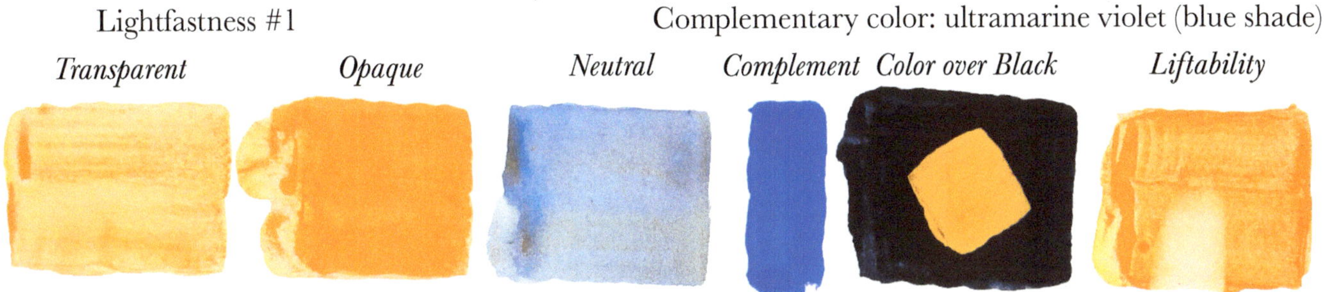

Analysis: Golden ocher is a touch warmer or oranger than yellow ocher. It has a good warm earthy quality and I prefer it to yellow ocher.

RAW SIENNA

PY42 synthetic hydrated iron oxide

Lightfastness #1

Complementary color: ultramarine blue

Transparent *Opaque* *Neutral* *Complement* *Color over Black* *Liftability*

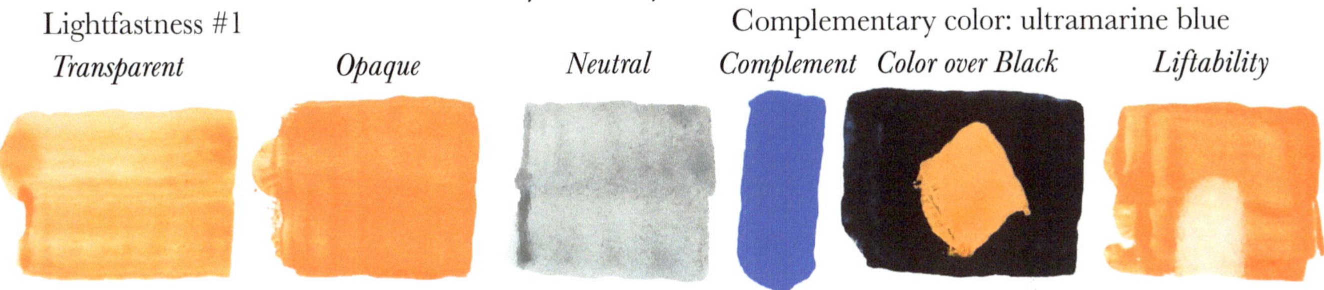

Analysis: This is a beautiful earthy color to the warm side. Using its complementary color ultramarine blue, the artist can neutralize it further to get a raw umber, a beautiful true neutral gray, or take it to the blue violet side.

RAW UMBER

PBr7 natural iron oxide containing manganese

Lightfastness #1

Complementary color: ultramarine blue

Transparent *Opaque* *Neutral* *Complement* *Color over Black* *Liftability*

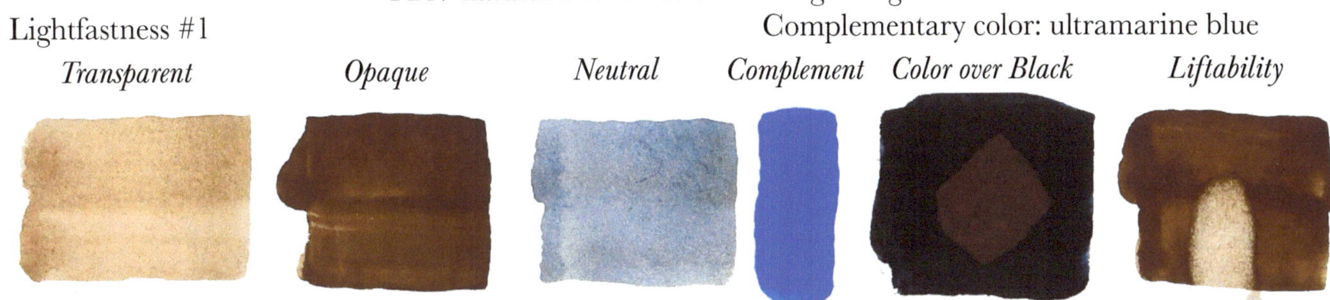

Analysis: This is a very dull earthy pigment. It has good pigmentation and opacity. I tend to mix my semi neutral browns so do not use this color often.

BURNT UMBER

PBr7 calcined natural iron oxide containing manganese

Lightfastness #1 — Complementary color: permasol blue or Shiva blue deep

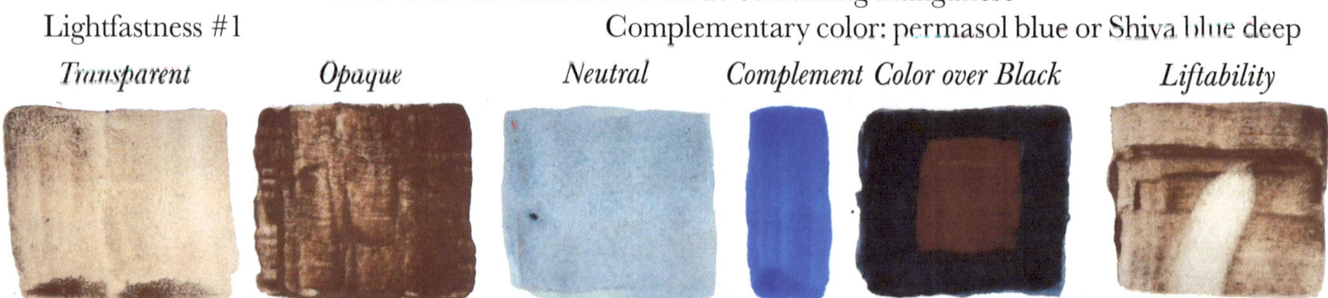

Analysis: This is a natural earthy pigment that can be used for a warm deep brown. It has good pigmentation and strong deep color.

BURNT SIENNA

PBR7 calcined natural iron oxide

Lightfastness #1 — Complementary color: ultramarine blue

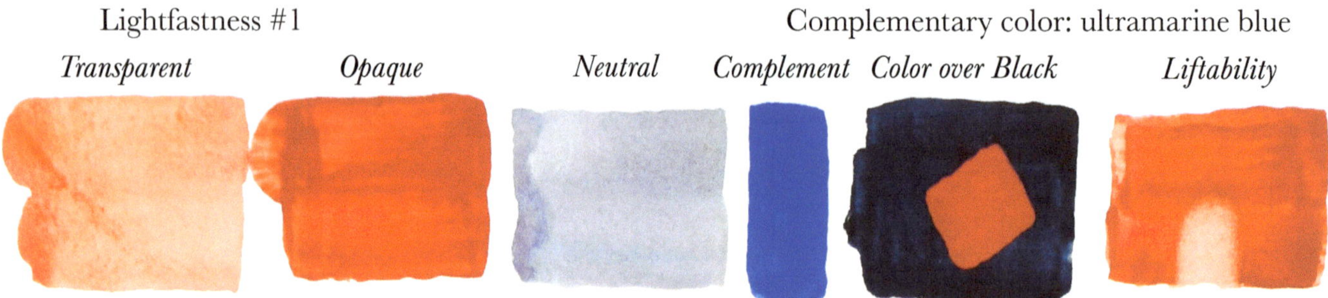

Analysis: Burnt Sienna is a natural pigment that I like a lot. It is a warm red-orange earthy pigment that can be added to a predominantly cool painting to produce color balance.

VENETIAN RED

PR101 synthetic iron oxide (yellowish hue)

Lightfastness #1 — Complementary color: permasol blue or Shiva blue deep

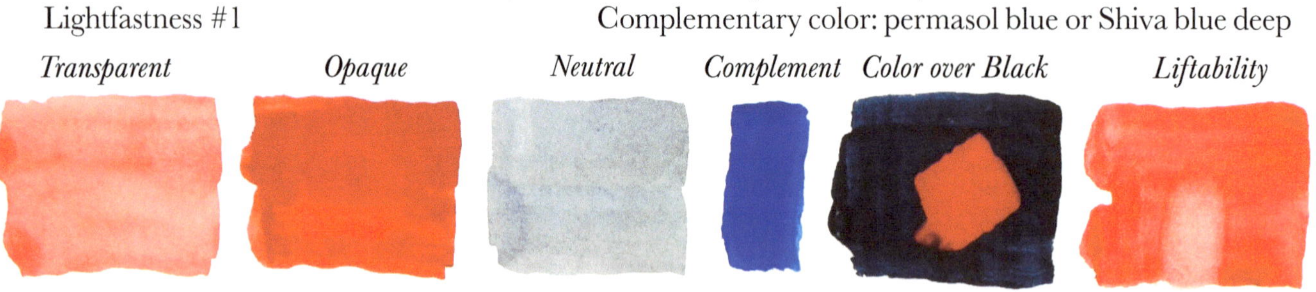

Analysis: This is a warm beautiful earthy pigment. It has great pigmentation and opacity.

LIGHT RED

PR102 calcined yellow ocher

Lightfastness #1 — Complementary color: Shiva turquoise (phthalocyanine)

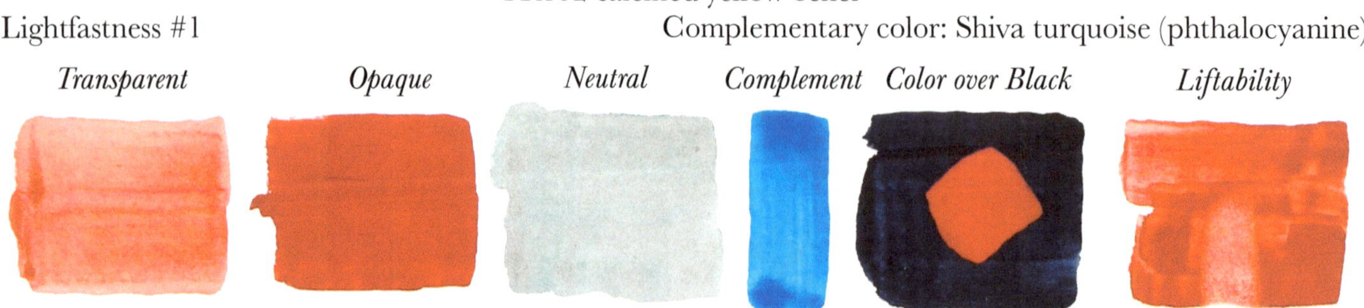

Analysis: This is a beautiful warm earthy color that is a touch redder than Venetian red. It has good pigmentation and great opacity.

CHROMIUM OXIDE GREEN DEEP

PG17 anhydrous chromium sesquioxide

Lightfastness #1

Complementary color: ultramarine violet

Transparent *Opaque* *Neutral* *Complement* *Color over Black* *Liftability*

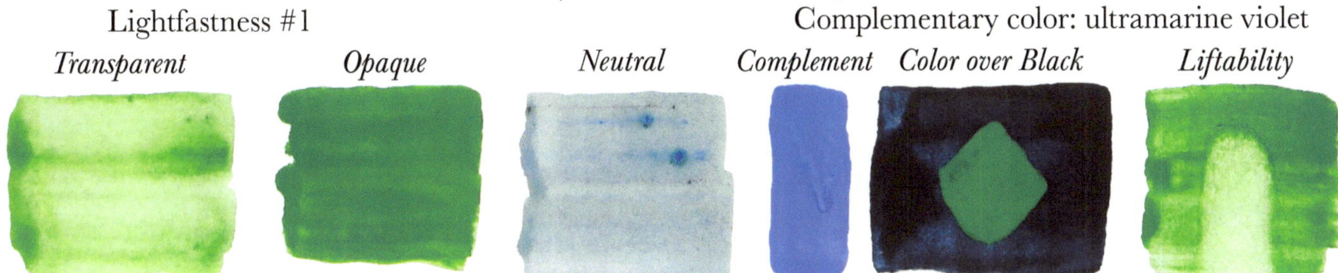

Analysis: This is an earthy green with good pigmentation.

TERRA VERTE

PG23 ferrous silicate with clay, inorganic

Lightfastness #1

Complementary color: ultramarine violet

Transparent *Opaque* *Neutral* *Complement* *Color over Black* *Liftability*

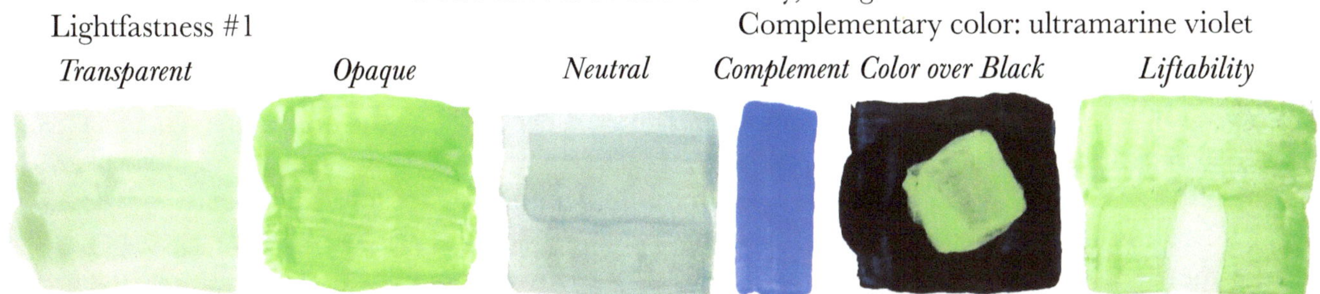

Analysis: This is a very weak pigment that I very seldom use.

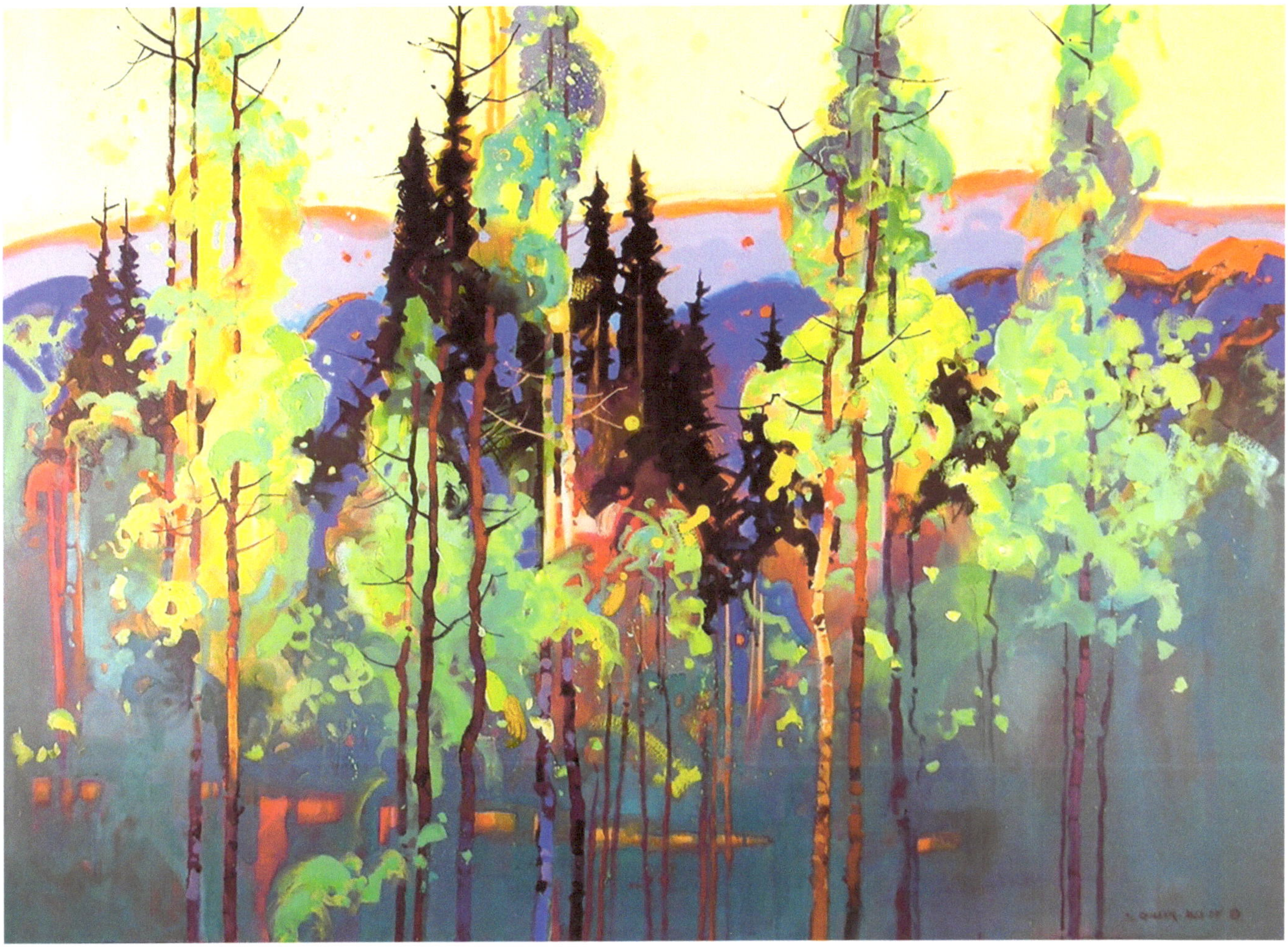

***Aspen Patterns & La Garitas, August** 2006*

casein, 19" x 26", Artist's Collection

Foundation for the Quiller Spectral Palette

HISTORY OF THE QUILLER COLOR WHEEL

There is a 150 year history for my color wheel. Its genesis is with the French scientist, Eugene Chevreul, who had been appointed the head of the wool and dye industry in France. He began to notice in production how one color influenced how he would see another color. Although he was not an artist, he was great friends with artists such as Eugene Delacroix, and he also sat on art academy boards. His observations led to authoring the book "Principles of Harmony and Contrast of Colors." This book, published in 1839, became the foundation for many artists and changed their approach to color.

In the mid-1800s the Pre-Raphaelite painters in England worked with the system of primary, secondary, and intermediate colors and painted on a white gessoed panel. They became known for their brilliant use of color. The Impressionists and Postimpressionists used a similar system. The Ashcan School in the early to mid 1900s worked with a similar approach referring to the Dudeen Color Triangle. I took this system and turned it into a circle so that complements were much easier to locate. I removed fugitive colors and replaced them with new colors that had not been invented at the time of the Dudeen Color Triangle. This color wheel is made primarily for painters. Below is the list of primary, secondary, and intermediate colors for the casein palette.

WHY THIS COLOR WHEEL?

We are all aware that red and green are complements; blue and orange are complements; yellow and violet are complements. But which red and which green are true complements? True complements are located directly opposite on the Quiller Wheel and if mixed together at a certain point will totally neutralize each other out and produce an absolute "gray." So, referring to the Quiller Wheel, a permanent green light mix with the cadmium red pale will produce a warm brown tone. Phthalo turquoise combined with quinacridone violet will make a violet gray. However, Shiva (phthalo) green mixed with rose red will create an absolute neutral "gray." This is because they're located directly across the color wheel.

This is so important to know because the neutrals and the semi-neutrals are what will bring pure hue to life.

I like the analogy of the concert pianist. If the piano keys are randomly placed on the keyboard it would be impossible to make a coherent sound. Likewise, if the artist arranges the palette logically as the keynotes on the color wheel and practices enough, he or she can let go and express! The next page displays a chart showing the primary, secondary, and intermediate colors of casein. Organizing a palette in this logical way will make all the difference in mixing color.

PRIMARY, SECONDARY and INTERMEDIATE CASEIN COLORS

PRIMARY	Yellow	cadmium yellow light
	Red	rose red
	Blue	permasol blue, Shiva (phthalo) blue
SECONDARY	Orange	cadmium red pale
	Violet	ultramarine violet
	Green	Shiva (phthalo) green
INTERMEDIATE	Yellow-Orange	cadmium orange
	Red-Orange	cadmium red scarlet
	Red-Violet	quinacridone violet
	Blue-Violet	ultramarine blue deep
	Blue-Green	phthalo turquoise
	Yellow-Green	permanent green light

MONOCHROMATIC COLOR SCHEME

One color using the opposite color to neutralize

COMPLEMENTARY COLOR SCHEME

Two opposite colors on the color wheel - one dominant and one subordinate

ANALOGOUS COLOR SCHEME

Three adjacent colors on the 12 color wheel from pure hue to the neutral of each color

DOUBLE ANALOGOUS COLOR SCHEME

To use three adjacent colors on the 12 color palette and their complementary colors as subordinates

TRIAD COLOR SCHEME

To use every fourth color on the 12 color palette such as cadmium red pale, ultramarine violet, Shiva green

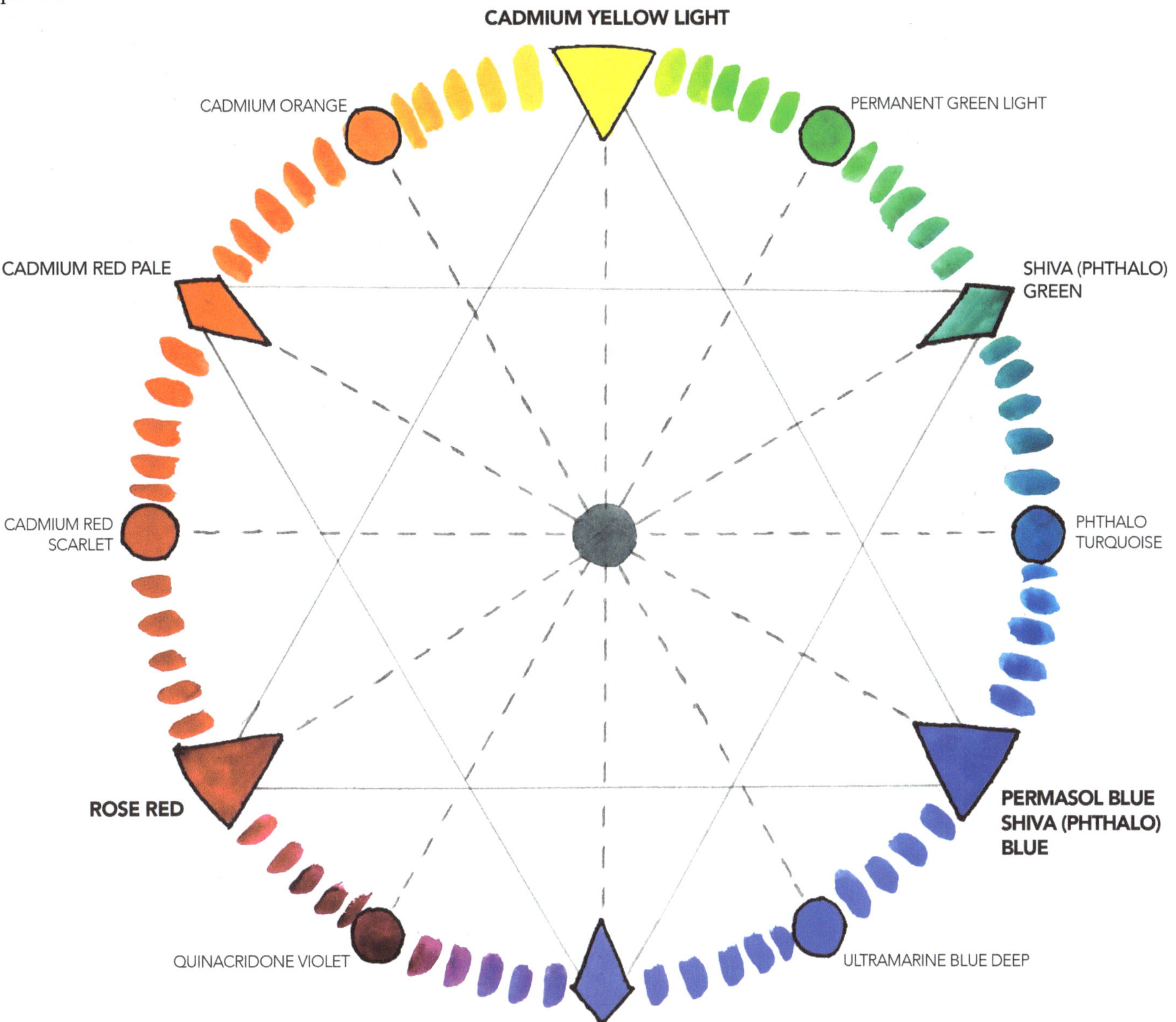

This chart shows the 12 primary, secondary, and intermediate colors on this spectral palette. This diagram can be used to locate complements directly across from each other, any three adjacent analogous colors, or major triad color schemes. Note that you can also paint between two adjacent colors to get subtle color shifts. To see the complete Quiller Casein Wheel refer to page 29.

For more extensive information of color theory:
Please refer to my books, *Painter's Guide to Color* and *Color Choices*, or my video series *Color Foundation for the Painter.*

Six Casein Complementary Color Sets

The 36 colors in the Richeson Shiva Casein line all have absolutely true complementary colors. This can be seen on the charts of the casein palette of colors. This is so important. Below are the primary, secondary and intermediate colors displaying their intensity chart. This goes from the brightest color on the outside of the color wheel, moving through the absolute neutral at the center of the color wheel, and back out to the pure hue at the other side.

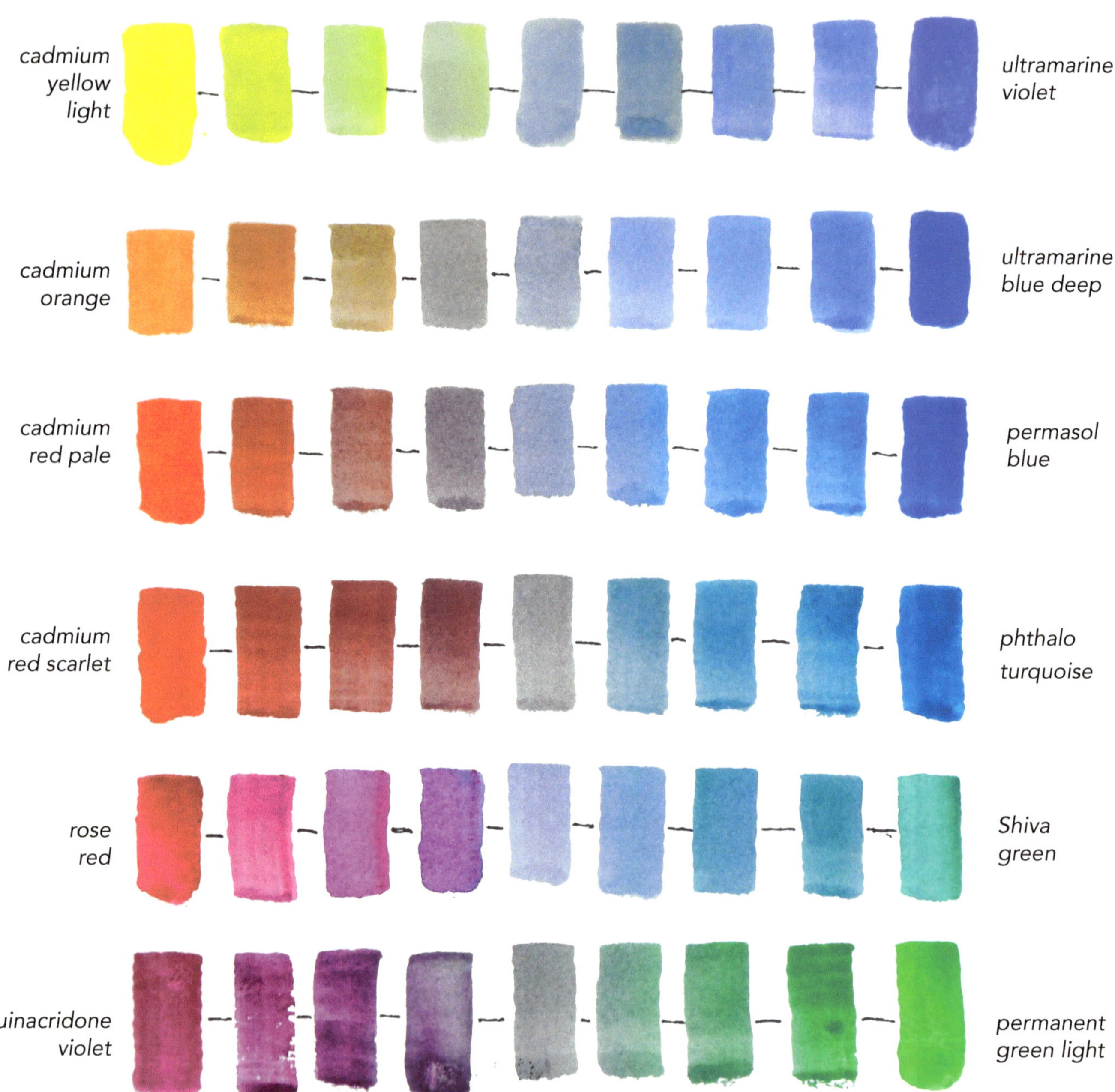

This chart displays the six major complementary sets with this universal palette. Absolute neutrals can be mixed with each set as well as beautiful, harmonious semi-neutrals.

Quiller Casein Color Wheel

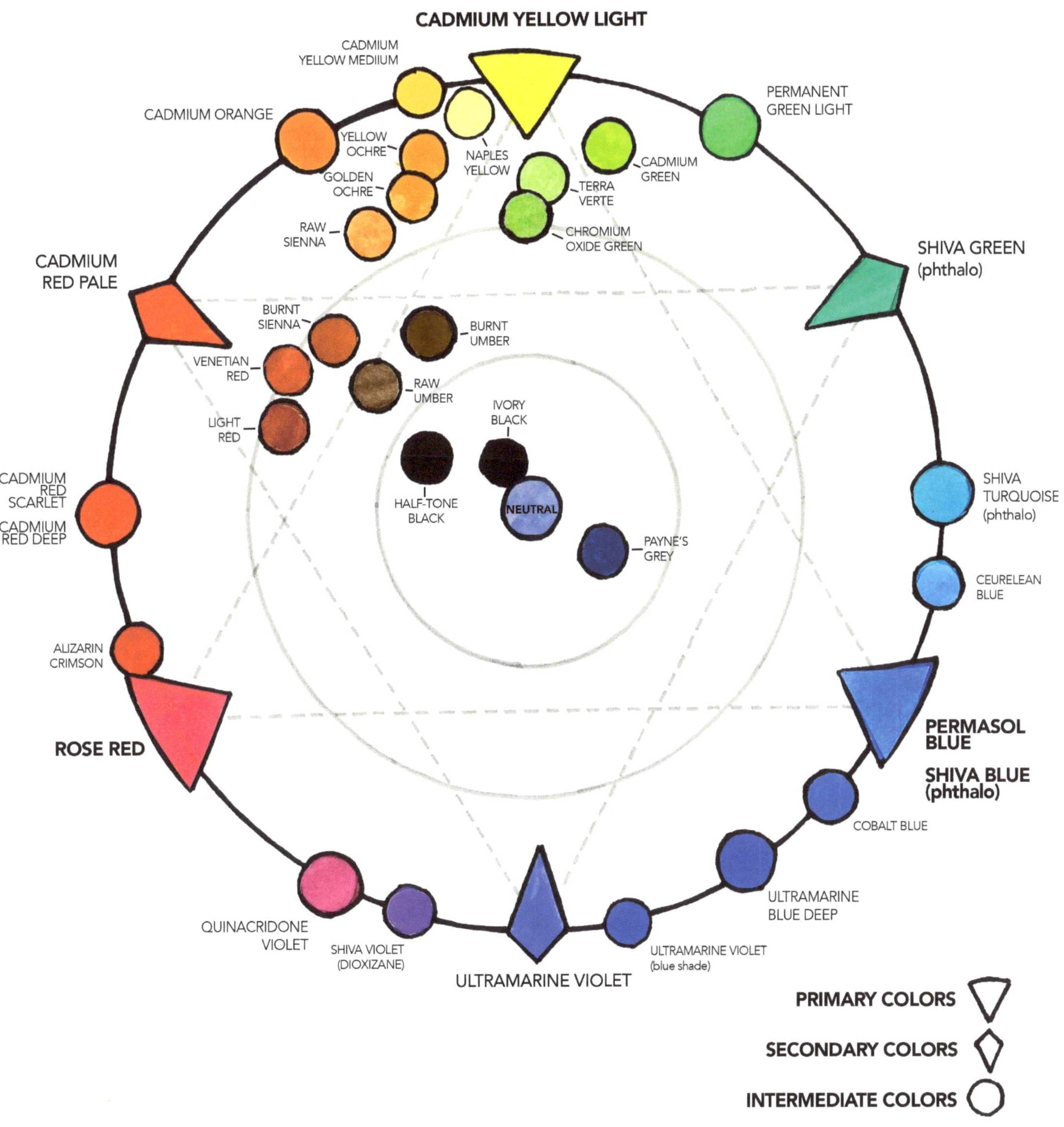

Expanding the Palette: Grays and Near Grays

So far I have discussed the importance of this color palette. Now you can mix semi neutrals and neutrals using true complementary colors. I would like to expand the palette to demonstrate how you can move freely from side to side of your direct complements. Below is a diagram using one color as the key "mother color" (ultramarine violet). Directly above is the complement (cadmium yellow light) and when it is mixed with the ultra violet it will create a true neutral.

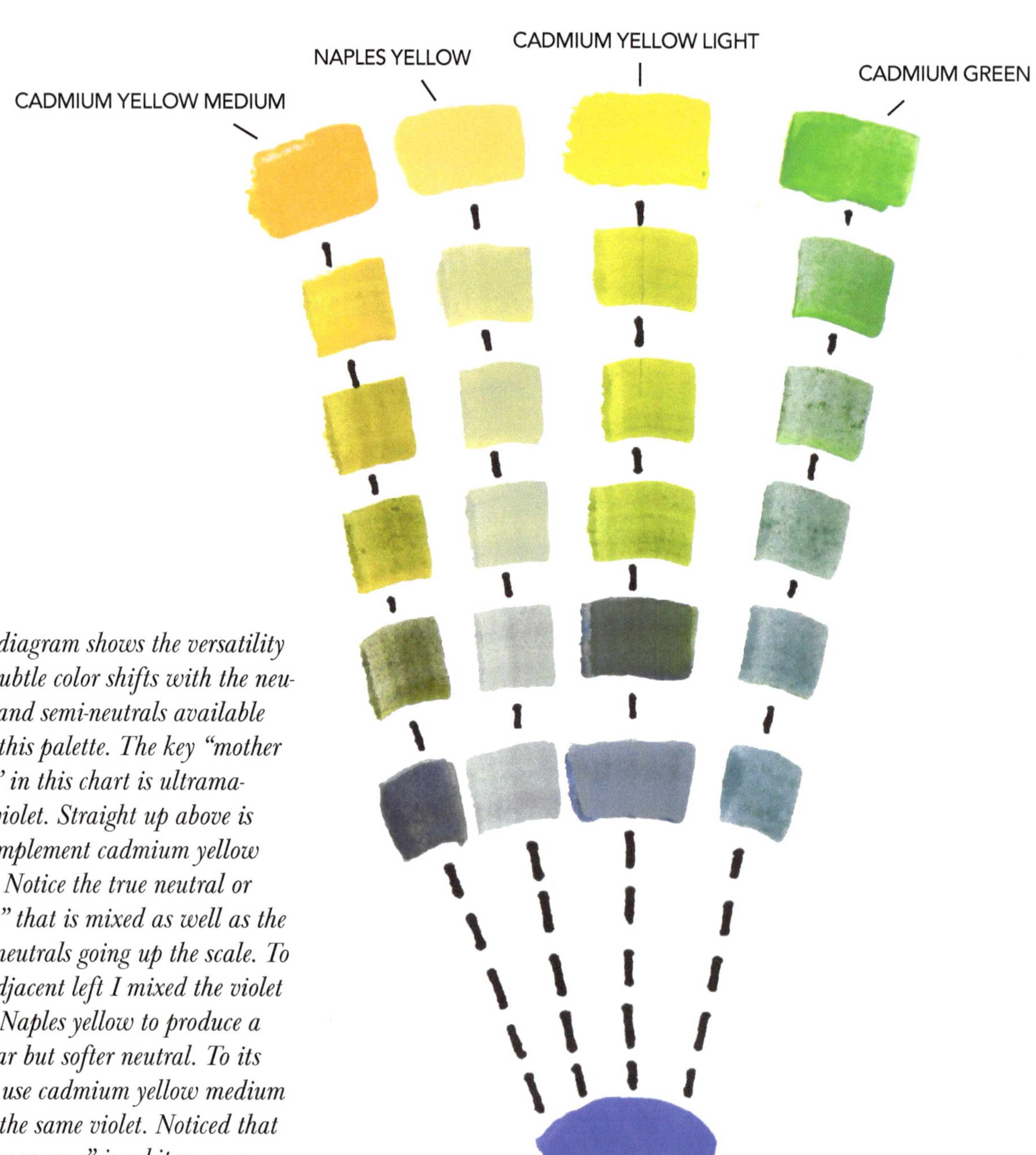

This diagram shows the versatility and subtle color shifts with the neutrals and semi-neutrals available with this palette. The key "mother color" in this chart is ultramarine violet. Straight up above is its complement cadmium yellow light. Notice the true neutral or "gray" that is mixed as well as the semi-neutrals going up the scale. To the adjacent left I mixed the violet with Naples yellow to produce a similar but softer neutral. To its left I use cadmium yellow medium with the same violet. Noticed that the "near gray" is a bit warmer. Now I mix the altering violet with cadmium green. The near gray is to the cool side.

Night Hoops
(right) 2016
casein with acrylic underwash
33" x 25"
Artist's Collection

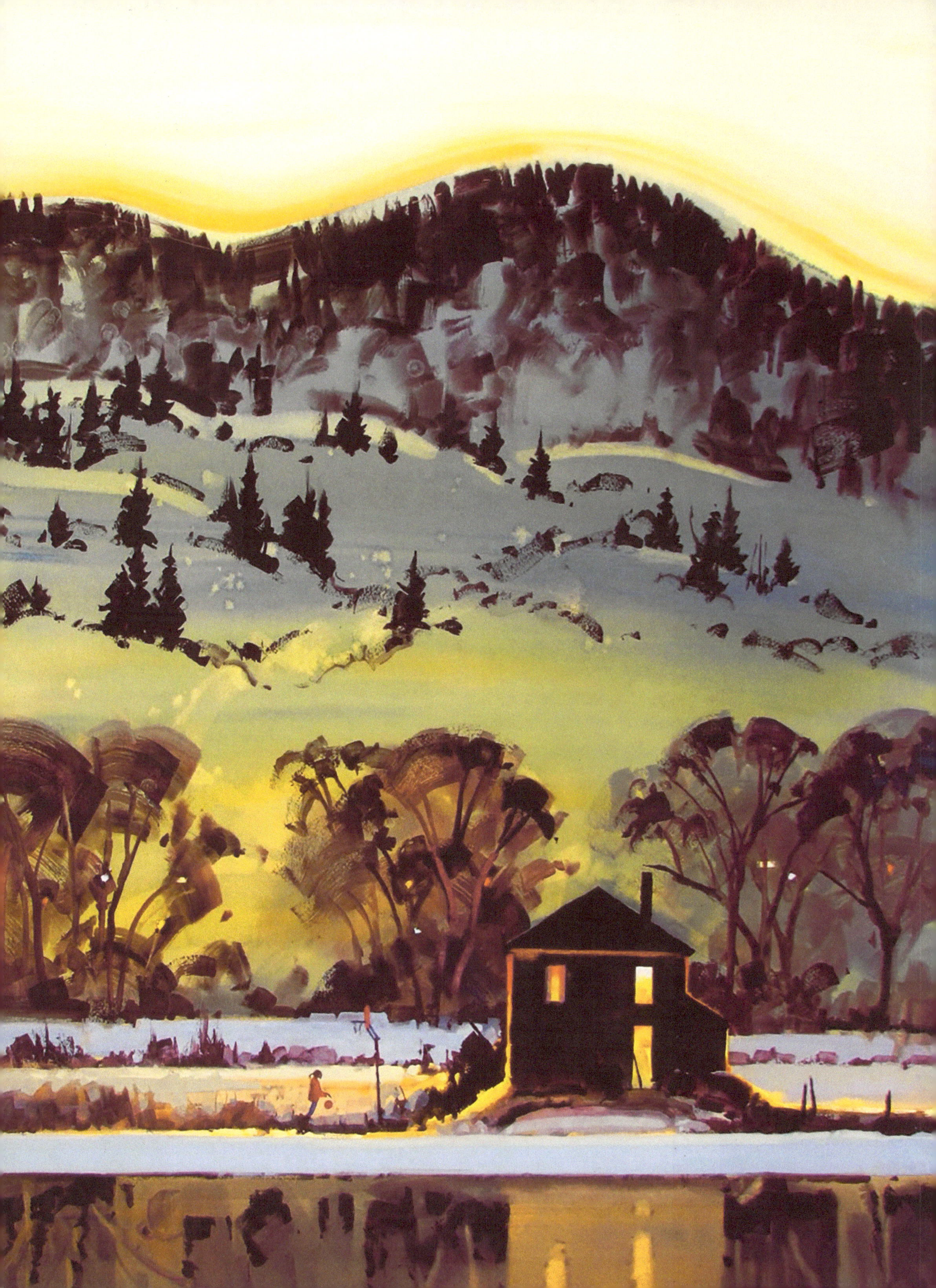

Liftability of Casein Colors

Casein paint is very unique in its properties. This milk-based paint actually cures in a short amount of time. Some of the colors cure faster than others. The mineral and earth colors as well as titanium white and ivory black cure much slower. This is because these pigments are ground more coarsely and are heavier. These pigments can take up to two weeks before they are totally impervious to water.

The other colors such as the phthalos and quinacridones are what we call synthetic organics. This simply means that they are chemically made. These newer colors are transparent and the staining pigments are ground much finer, tending to infiltrate the support such as paper or canvas. These cure much more quickly and within a few days can be resistant to moisture.

QUINACRIDONE VIOLET

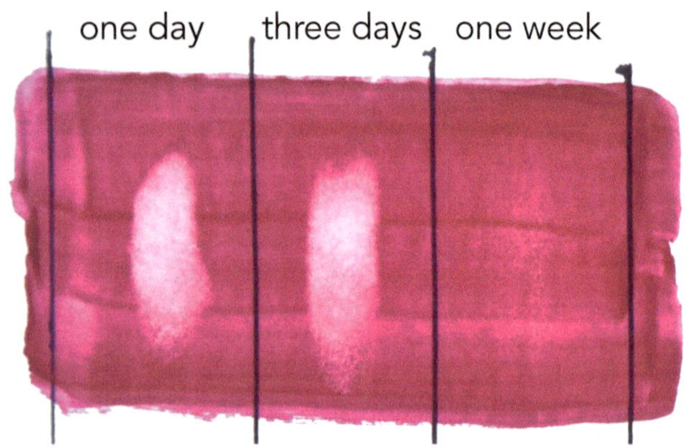

RAW SIENNA

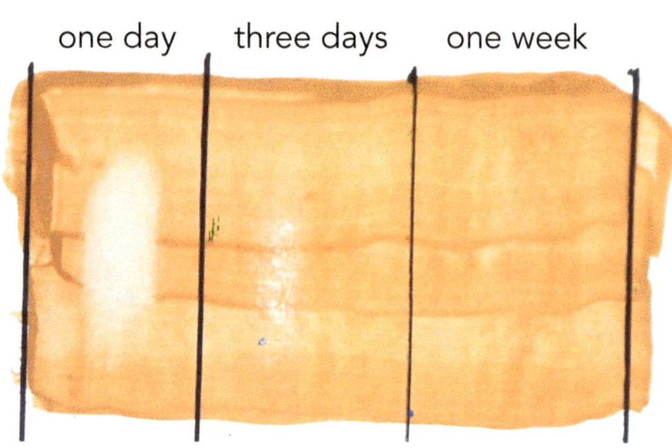

SHIVA GREEN

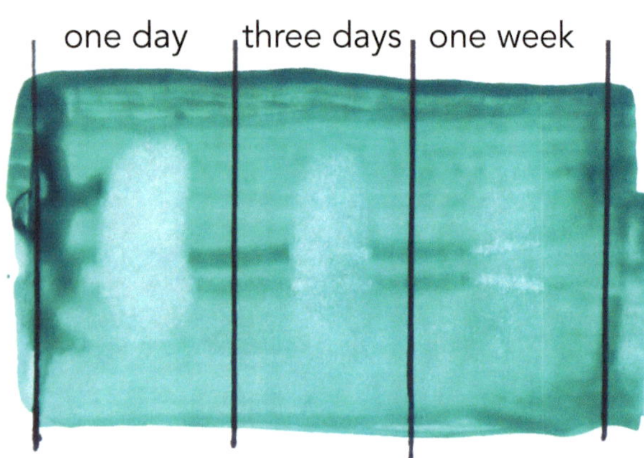

ULTRAMARINE BLUE

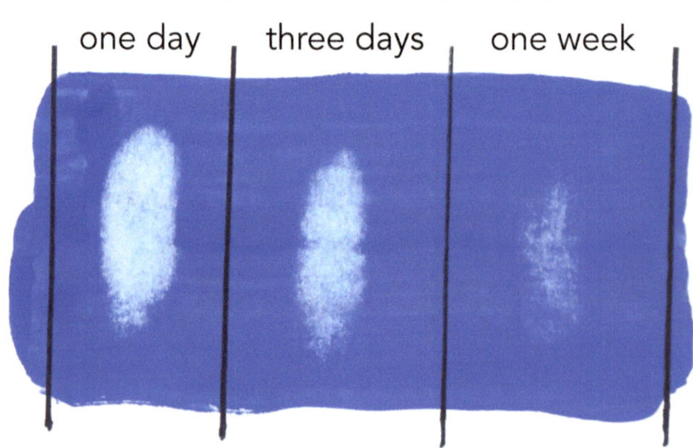

The above diagram shows the liftability of casein depending on how long it has cured and whether it's a synthetic organic color or an earth/mineral color. On the left are two colors, quinacridone violet and Shiva (phthalo) green. They are broken down into three sections, the first lifting after one hour; the second lifting after three days; the third lifting after one week. On the right side are two earth and mineral colors, raw sienna and ultramarine blue deep. They are broken down in the same way. Notice that they have a longer lifting time before they are insoluble.

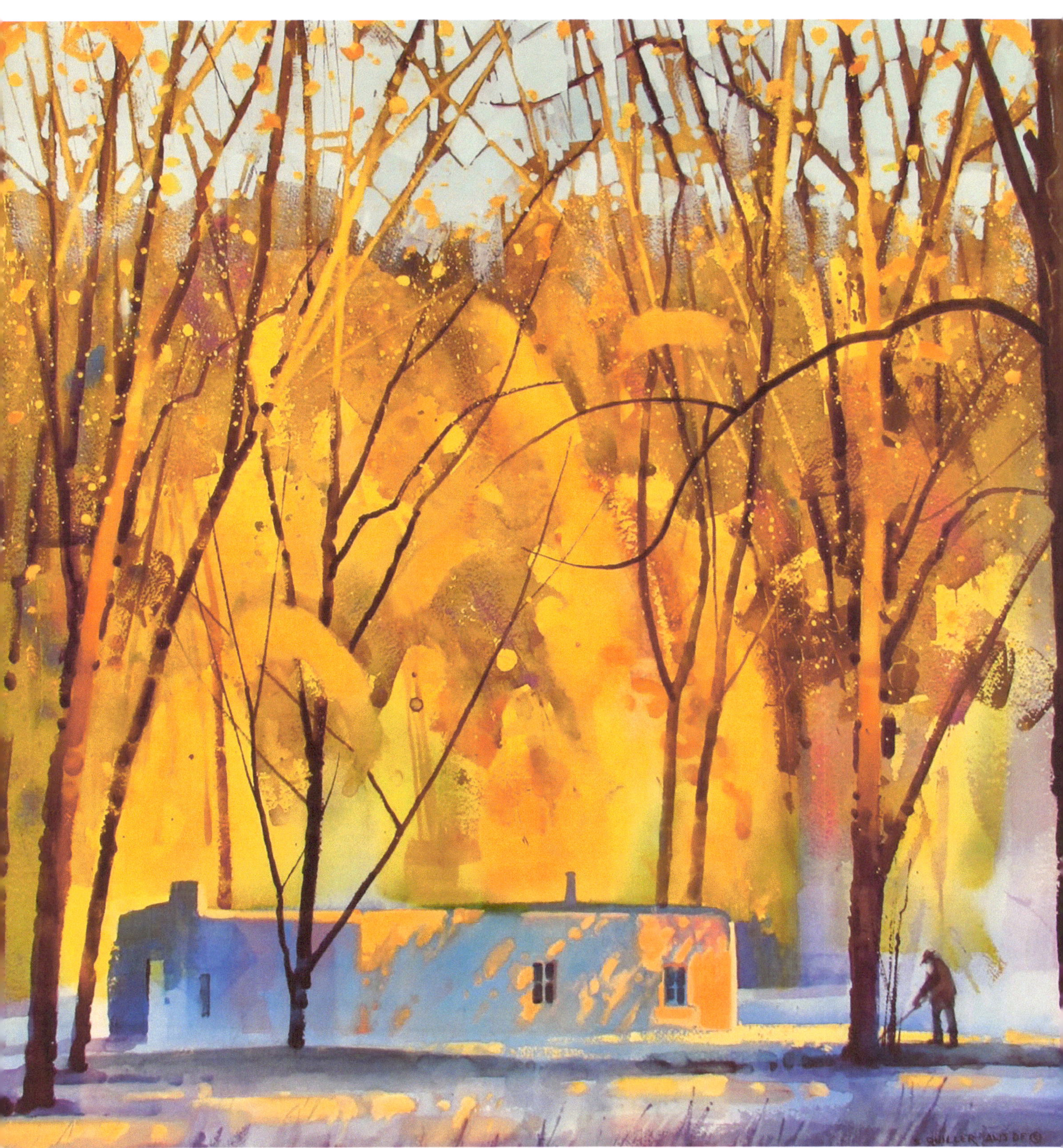

Raking Leaves 2017

casein,acrylic & watercolor 26" x 26", Collection of Deena Altman

Painting Darks

Casein is considered a "blonde" medium. This is because the paint when dry has a velvety, soft quality about it that has a look unlike any other painting medium. However, that is not to say that you cannot achieve strong darks. In fact, the darks can be made in many different ways. Any phthalocyanine color mixed with its complement or near complement can give you a good bold dark resembling black. For example, Shiva (phthalo) green combined with rose red, cadmium scarlet, quinacridone violet or Shiva violet will achieve brilliant darks. Also permasol blue combined with cadmium red pale or cadmium scarlet will give similar results. There are many other combinations, as seen in the chart below.

In most media, I normally mix my blacks; they are richer and have more "life" to them. Often an ivory black or lamp black actually absorbs light, deadening that area of the composition. However, I have found ivory black casein has a beautiful rich quality that can be incorporated very nicely into some paintings. Many well-known painters throughout recent art history have avoided black, though Renoir called it the "queen of colors" and used it to set off jewellike notes such as an earring against black hair.

I have found ivory black to be a beautiful color note that can set off pure hues in a composition. Normally when I use this color I add a bit of rose red to it to give it some richness. However, I do not use the black to "gray" down a color as it tends to deaden it. Instead I use the complement or near complement to create a semineutral with life. Furthermore, Paynes gray is actually a black made with carbon and phthalo blue pigment added. So it will produce a black to the blue side.

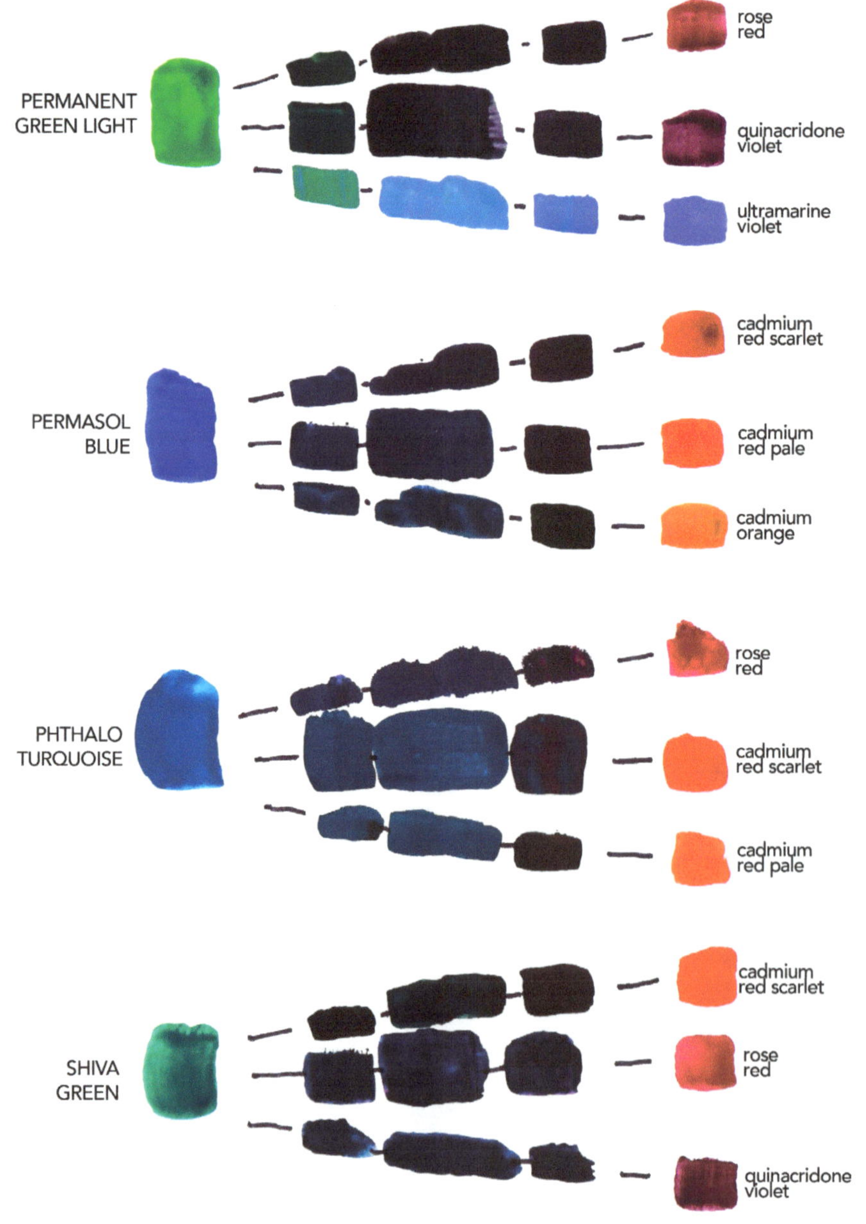

This chart shows many of the different ways to mix darks that resemble black without actually using ivory black or Payne's gray. There are many different ways to mix darks. The artist can choose which color mix works best with the color relationships in the painting.

Night Air 2008
casein, 21" x 33", Artist's Collection
Louis Kaep Memorial Award, American Watercolor Society

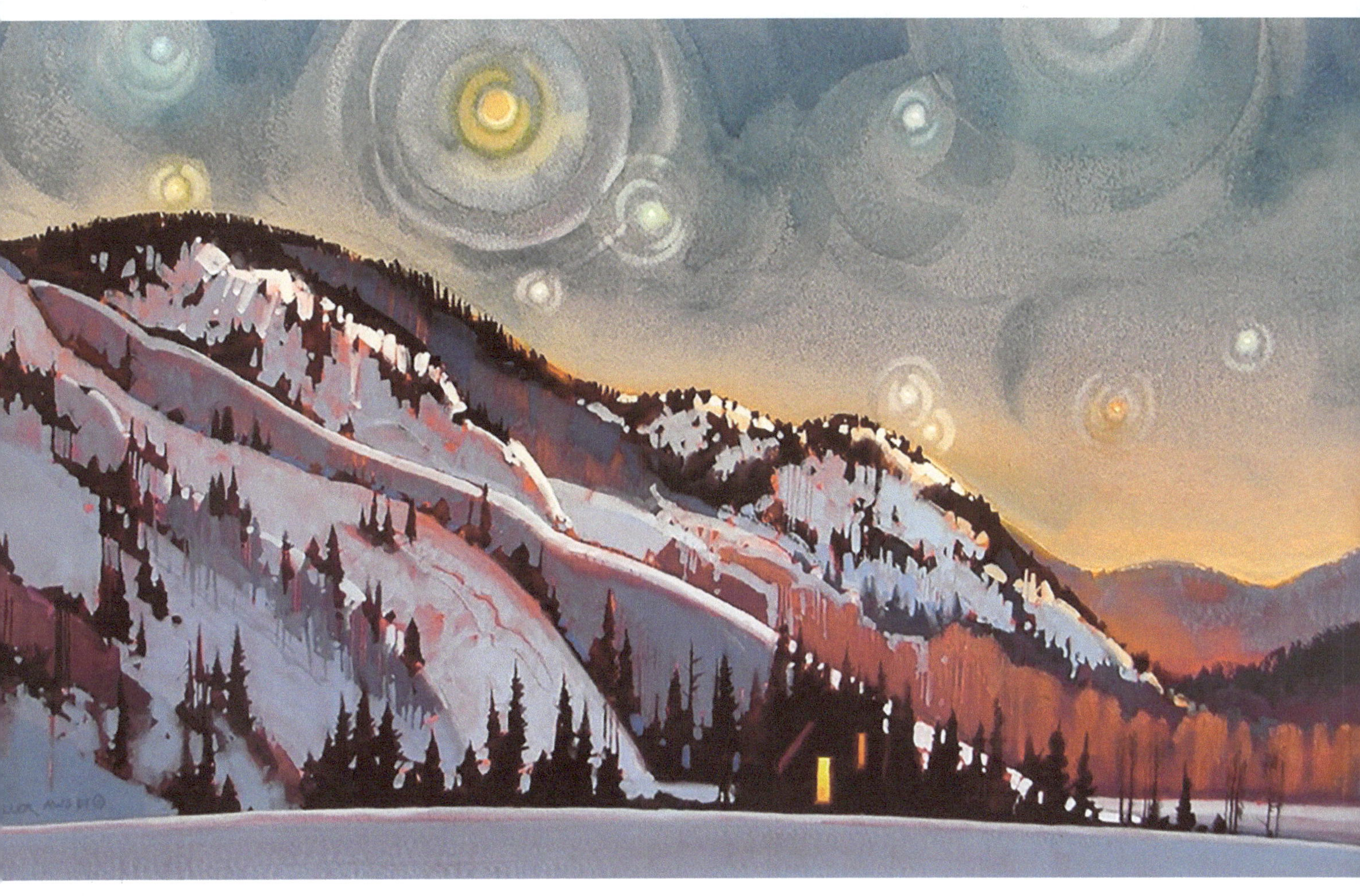

This is a view that I see late evenings in winter, leaving my studio on the way to the house. The cabin in the distance has warm lights radiating from the blackness while highlights and shadows produce a beautiful rhythmic quality to the mountain forms. This mountain is part of the Snow Shoe Mountain that is directly across the road from our house. Syncopated patterns of the dark spruce punctuate the night air. On some evenings a new moon and evening stars dance. This painting was selected for the Louis Kaep award at the American Watercolor Society's international exhibition in New York City.

The Universal Palette

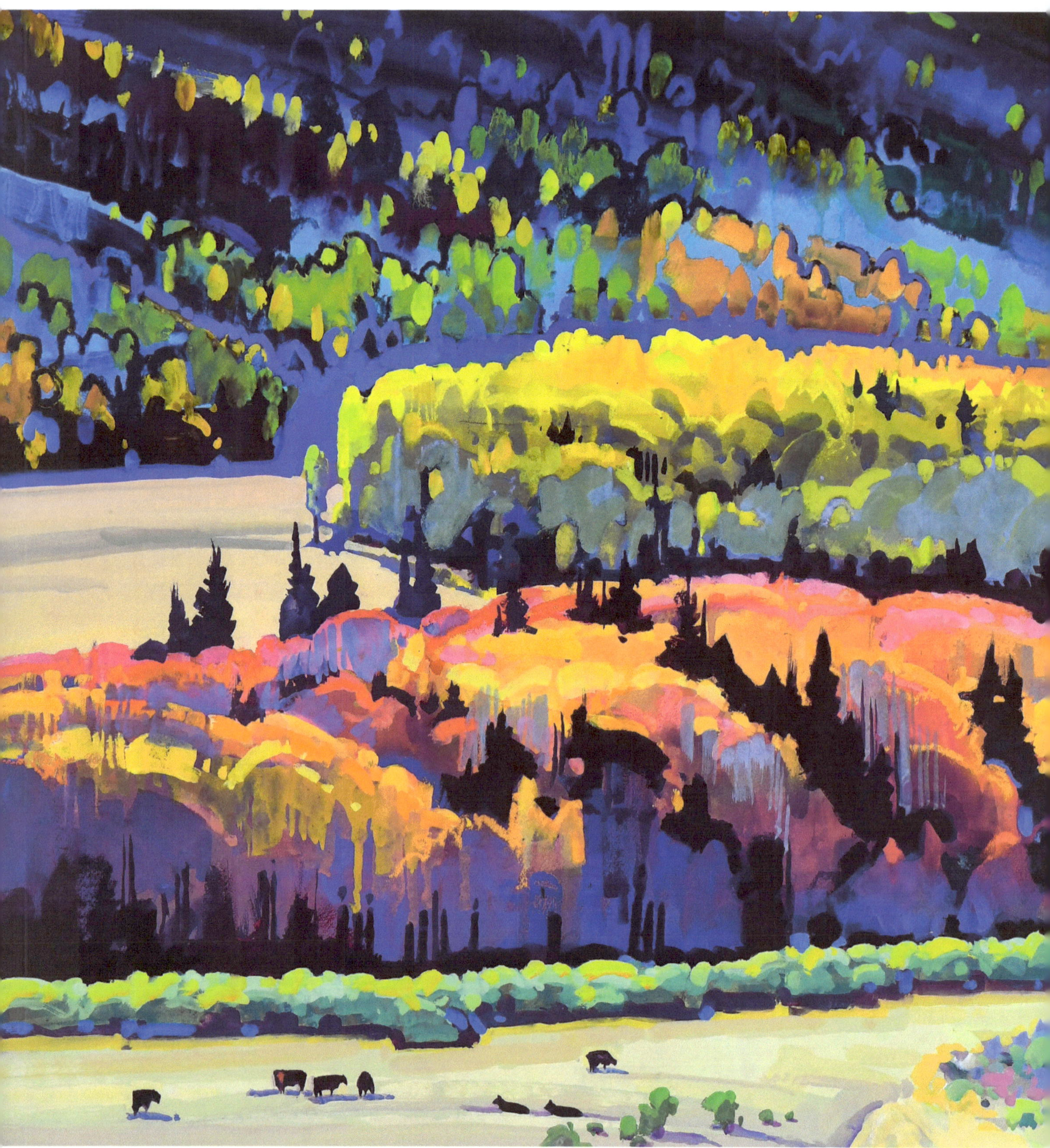

This palette of casein colors is sometimes known as the spectral palette or a universal palette. This is because you can mix any color that you see with this palette. I've taken it to Hawaii, the south of France, Italy, Scotland, Ireland, Canada, and China. You can take it anywhere and capture how you feel about what you see. The following pages show two paintings demonstrating the range of atmospheric light and mood that can be made with casein.

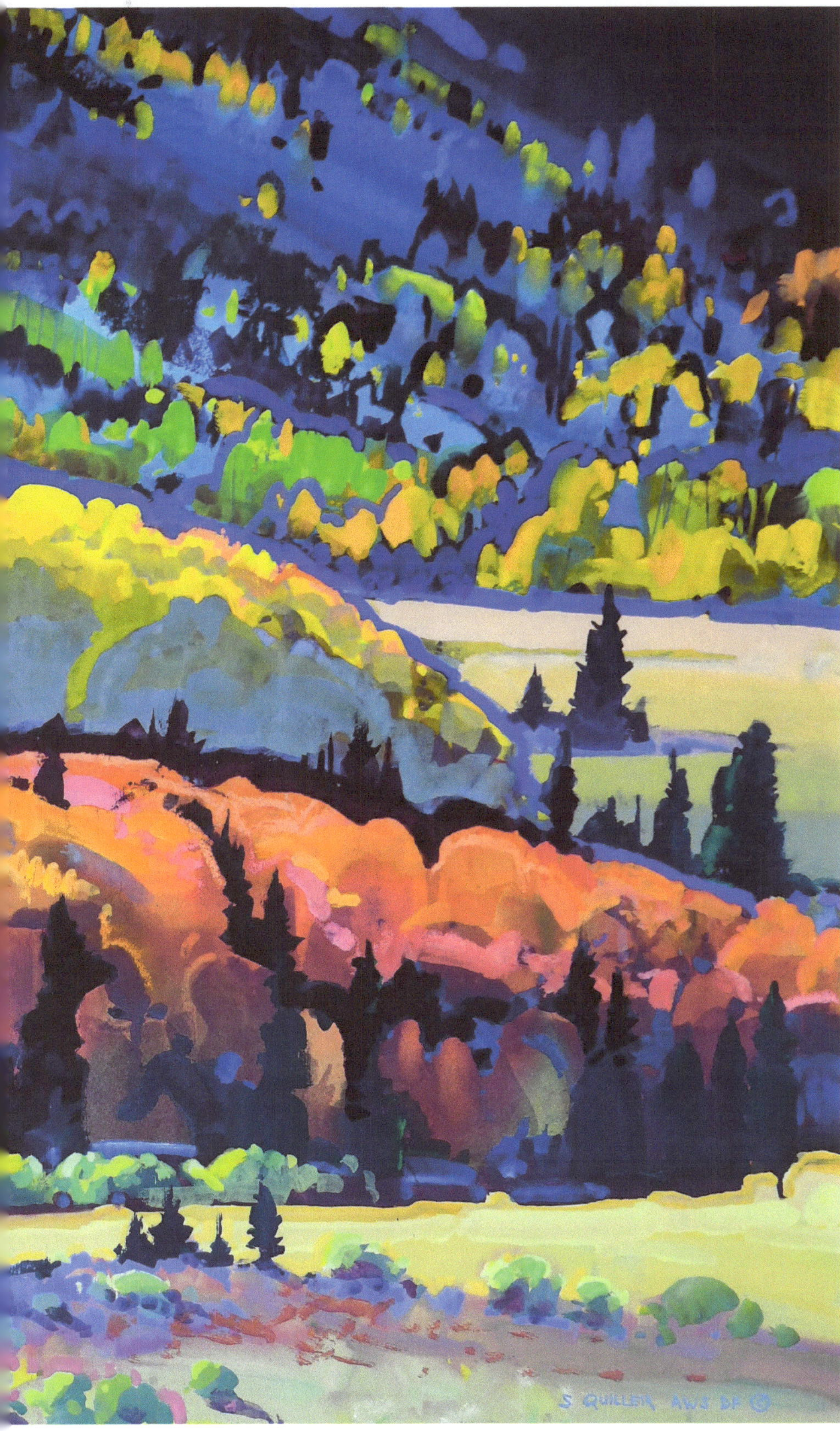

This pattern of aspen patches in deep mountain forms is a subject that I've wanted to paint for many years. The rich autumn color was almost surreal. I took a photograph on my tablet and did a color study from the photo. Then I worked directly from my study. Casein was the perfect medium to capture the dusty dry rich colors that permeate the subject. A few cows meandered in the field in the lower middle.

Autumn, Ptarmigan Meadows
2019
casein, 23" X 37"
Artist's Collection

Two Examples using the Universal Palette

Late Light, Looking East, Rena Rosequist 2015
casein & acrylic underwash , 24" x 34", Private Collection

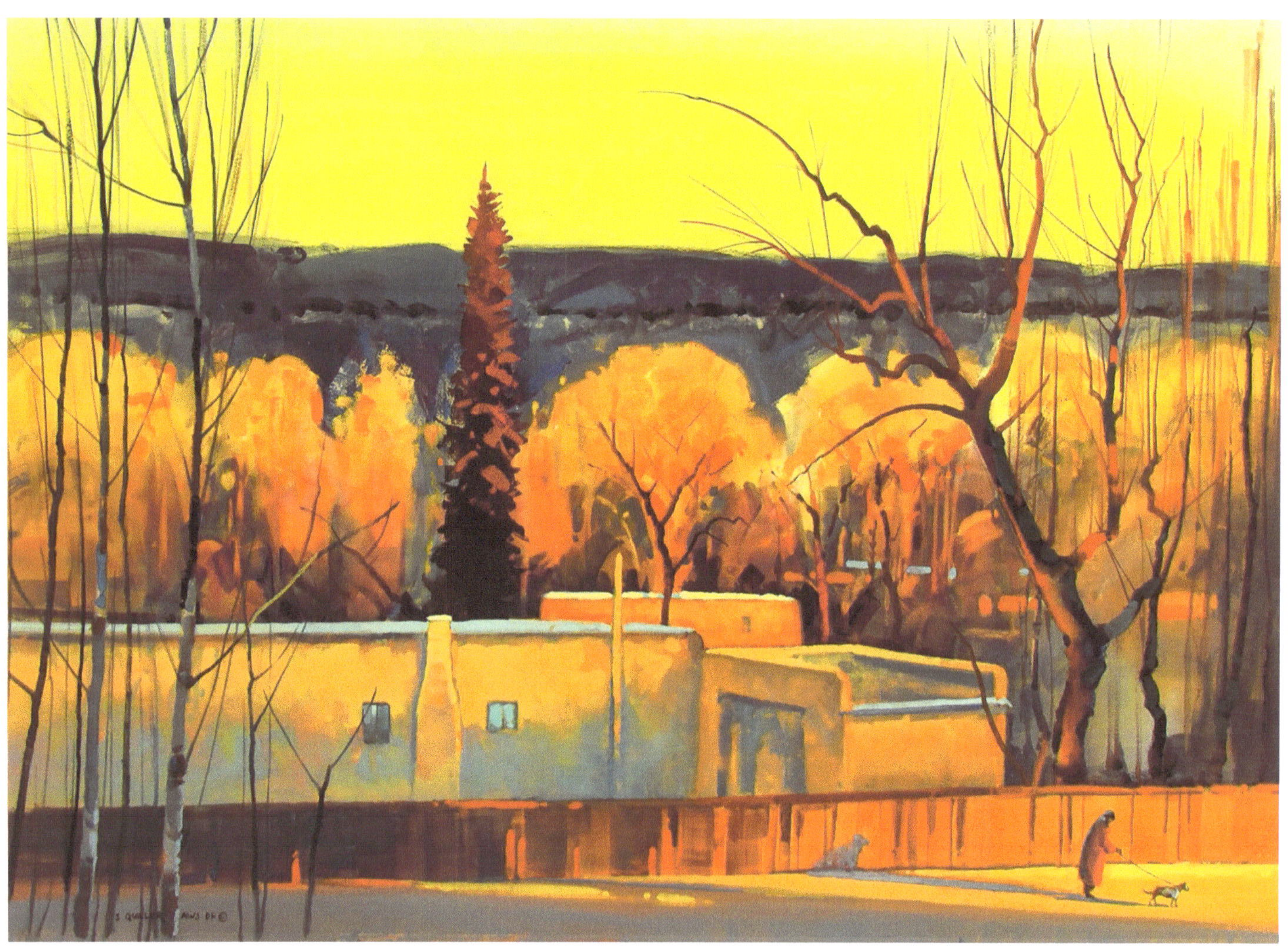

For 36 years I exhibited at the Mission Gallery in Taos, New Mexico. It was an honor and a privilege to show my work with owner Rena Rosequist at this venue. One late winter afternoon I was at the porch across the street and witnessed these glowing, warm, intense colors with the cottonwoods and adobes. Rena often took her dog walking along this path. I grabbed my sketchbook, did a contour drawing with a few notes and eventually did this painting. Casein was the perfect medium to capture the glow and earthy quality.

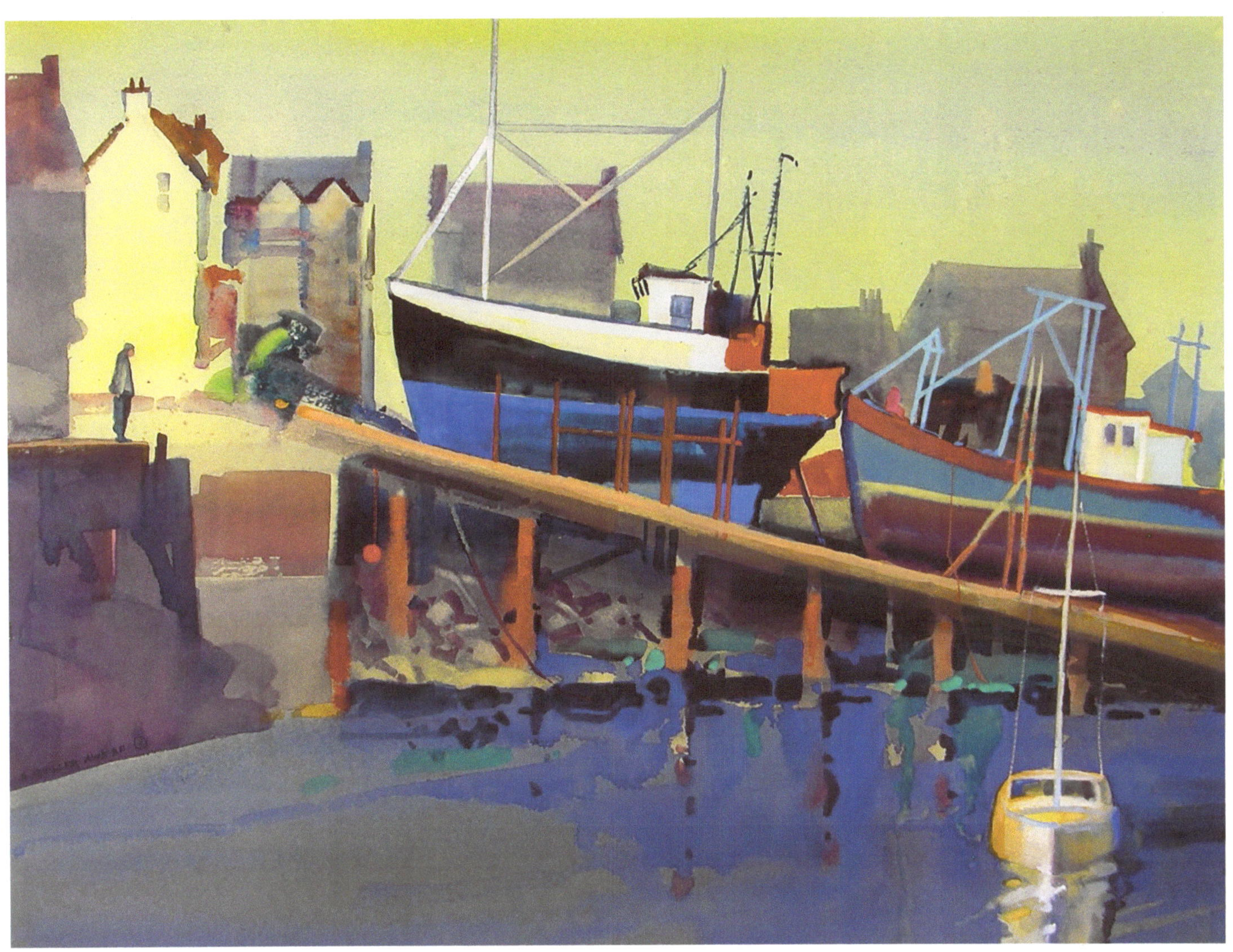

Dry Docked, Scotland 2017

casein & acryic underwash, 20" x 30", Private Collection

I did this painting in Mallaig, Scotland, during a six-week long painting trip. I set up across the harbor and decided to paint this dry docked boat. I'd been working a good while when I noticed a man on a bicycle riding around the harbor, and he stopped next to me. He asked, "How are you coming on the painting?" I replied that I was doing fine, why? He then said " We want to move the boat but we do not want to disturb your painting!" Overwhelmed with gratitude I said, "Thank you and please move your boat as I'm doing just fine!"

Exercise #1 On a glass palette squeeze out the six complementary sets on the 12 color palette. With each set mix the true neutral. Then mix the semi neutrals to either side adding more of the pure hue.

Exercise#2 Arrange your 12 color palette in a circular manner with the complements straight across from each other. Now mix two true complements to get an absolute neutral and then mix the near complement to either side get a warmer neutral. For instance, take the ultramarine violet and mix it with the cadmium yellow light to achieve a true gray. Now take the ultramarine violet and mix it with the cadmium orange to mix a warmer near gray. Then take the ultramarine violet and mix with permanent green light to achieve a cool near gray.

Exercise#3 Arrange your 12 color palette in a circular fashion having each complement directly across from each other. Now experiment with how many ways you can mix a dark with each one having its own life.

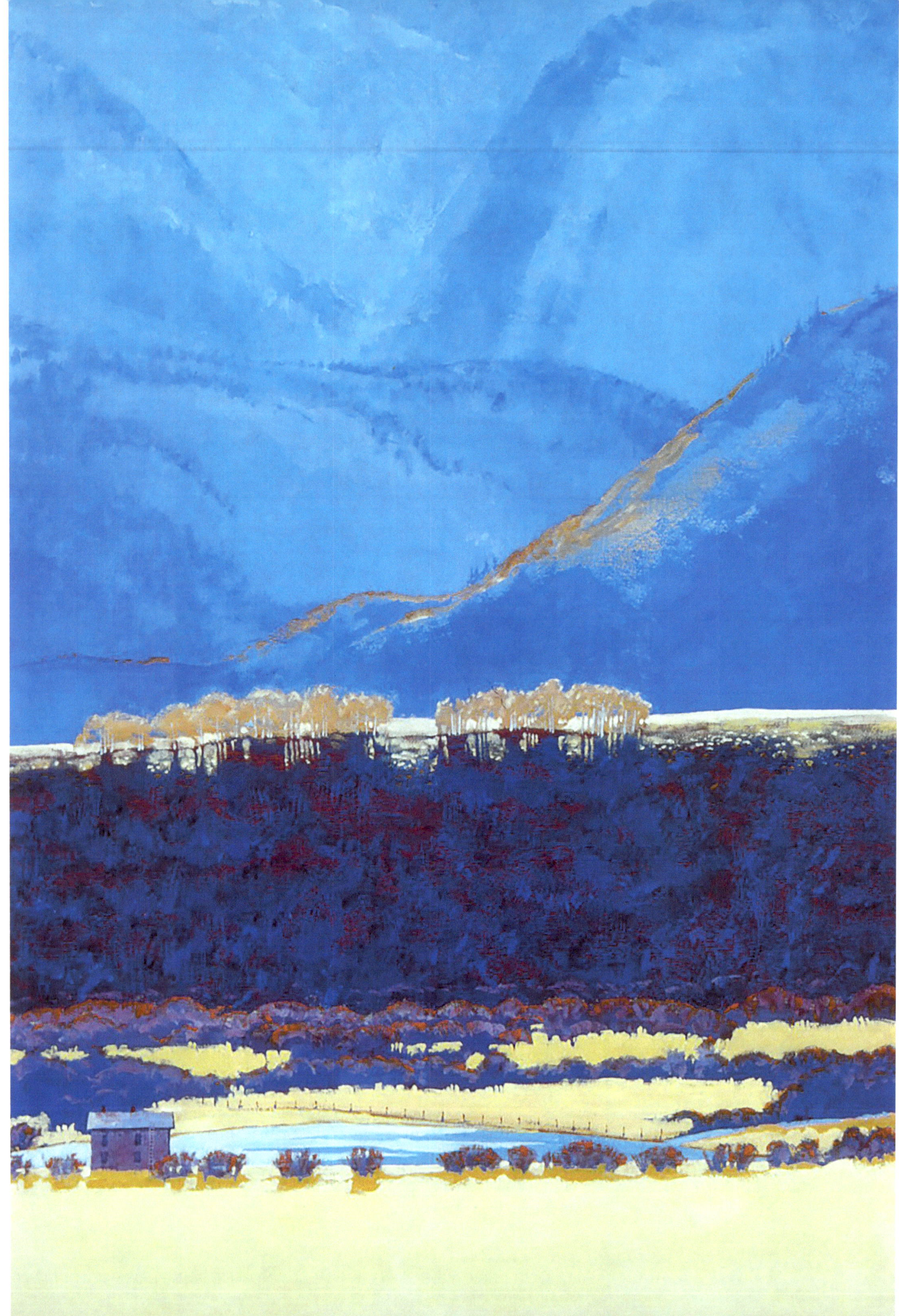

2 Materials Chapter both Studio and Plein Air

I'm reminded of an experience when my brother and his two sons and I were fishing on a very well-known river in northern New Mexico. There were many fishermen on the river and no one was having any luck, including ourselves. Then one angler appeared, casually meandering down the riverbank on the other side. It seemed he was catching a fish on almost every cast. When he was directly across the water I said to him, "It looks like you know what you're doing!" He countered by saying, "It's the fly!" Obviously that helps but there is a lot more to it than the fly.

It also brings to mind another story about the late John Pike, an internationally known watercolor painter, who at the time was teaching a plein air workshop somewhere in the Midwest. He was sitting by a tree when one of his workshop participants asked him what kind of brushes he liked best. He reached down and picked up a branch, took a knife out of his pocket, and started incising the end of the branch into brush-like fibers. He then dipped the branch into a mud puddle and began painting on his paper. Of course it helps to have the right materials but the most important thing is "mileage" on the brush!

In this chapter I want to talk about casein, its advantages and why it's a personal choice, while also discussing the arrangement of my universal palette. I will talk about how I set up in my studio as well as how I organize when I'm painting on location with casein. I will share my choice of brushes for a water media approach, as well as a standard easel painting method. I will discuss a variety of surfaces and supports and why I'd use each one. All of these supports are archival and it's important to know what each surface has to offer. I certainly have my favorites and I will explain why. In the final analysis I feel it is important to use high quality materials. The 36 color range of Richeson Shiva Casein, with two exceptions, have a number one lightfast rating so that we know the paint is archival, if displayed properly. It's also important to use brushes that have the right snap and flow, making it easier to apply the paint. In this chapter I hope to give you some positive tips that will help you develop and grow in your painting process.

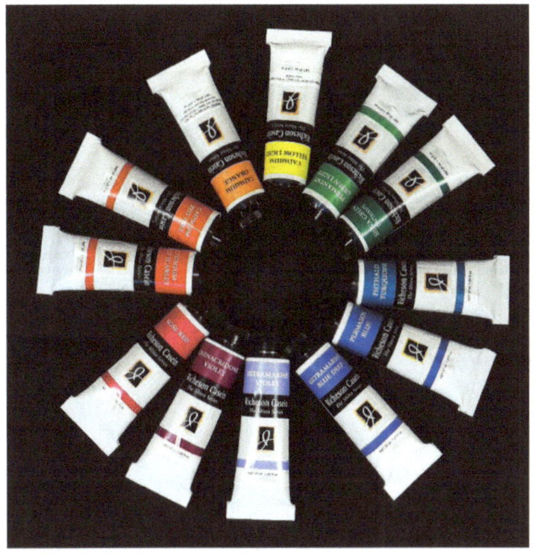

This photo shows the circular arrangement of the 12 color palette using the Richeson-Shiva line of casein. Of course white would be added to this palette as well.

October Haze, LaFont's
(left) 1980
casein, 30" x 20"
Private Collection

Studio Set-Up

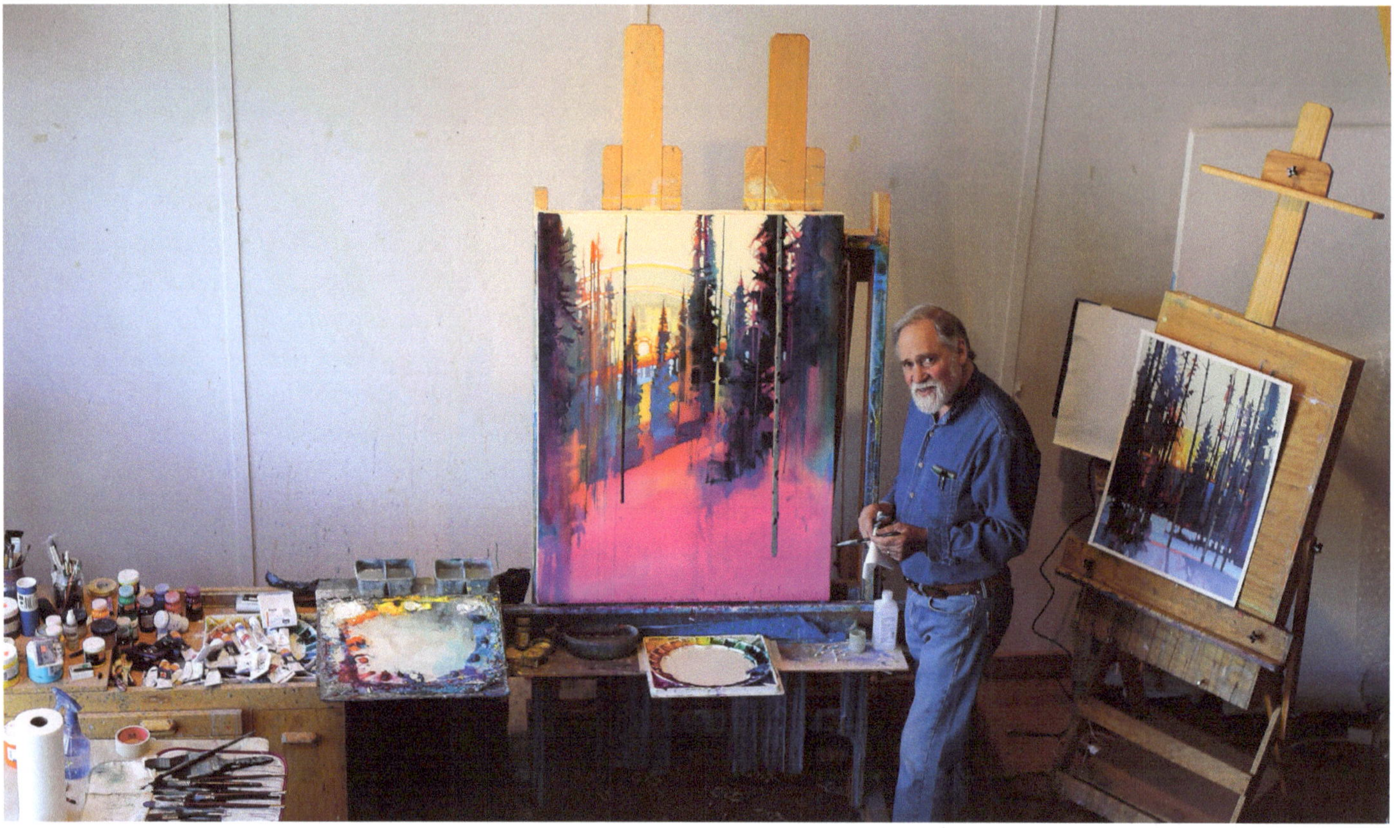

This is the setup in my studio. I've had this Richeson Abiquiu Easel for 25 years and it has held up very well. I can raise or lower the painting easily with a crank on the lower right. It will hold a very large painting. On the left is a cabinet that is called "Shawn's Watercolor Station." I find it very convenient as the side panels can be moved to the right or left, where I place my glass easel. There are drawers and sufficient storage space for paint and paper sketching supplies.

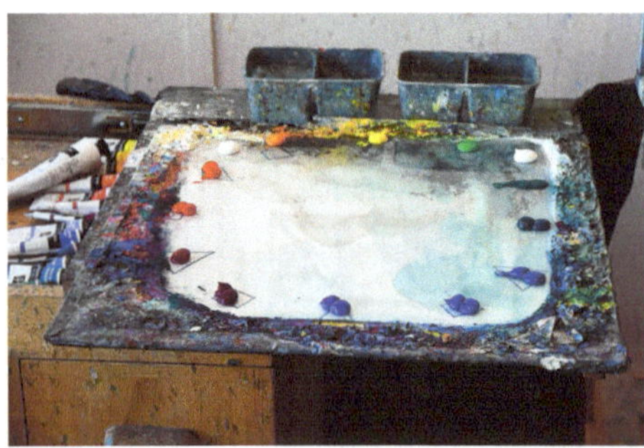

***#1** This is how I set up my studio palette. I have a double strength 24" x 24" glass taped to a white mat board on which I have drawn out my 12 major color notes. I arrange the 12 colors of casein onto the glass with white on each corner. I atomize this often to keep the paint moist.*

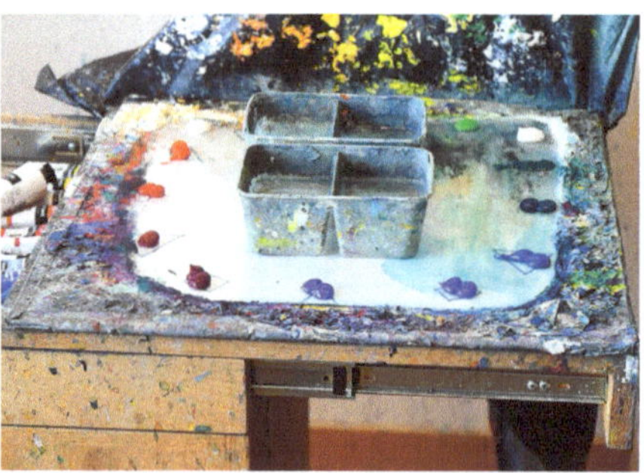

***#2** If I want to keep my paint fresh for painting the next day, I simply atomize the paint, place my water containers in the center, and fold a large black plastic sheet over the palette.*

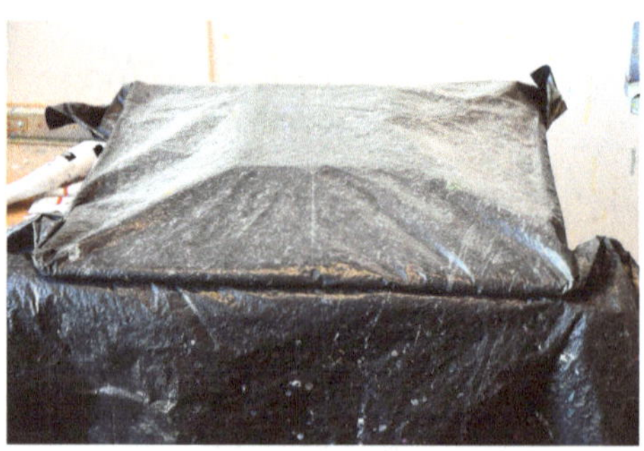

***#3** I then take this plastic sheet and wrap it tightly around the palette. This seals the palette and the interior creates its own humidity. If this is done well the paint will stay fresh for a number of days. Normally I come back the next day, unwrap the flap, and begin to paint.*

During early to mid June I enjoy seeing summer emerge and the wild iris springing up in meadows and along stream beds. Many times I do watercolor sketches on location and save those in my files. On this particular solstice, I sat on the deck by my studio in late light and observed the early evening light fade to dusk. The inspiration for this painting came to me, and thus the title.

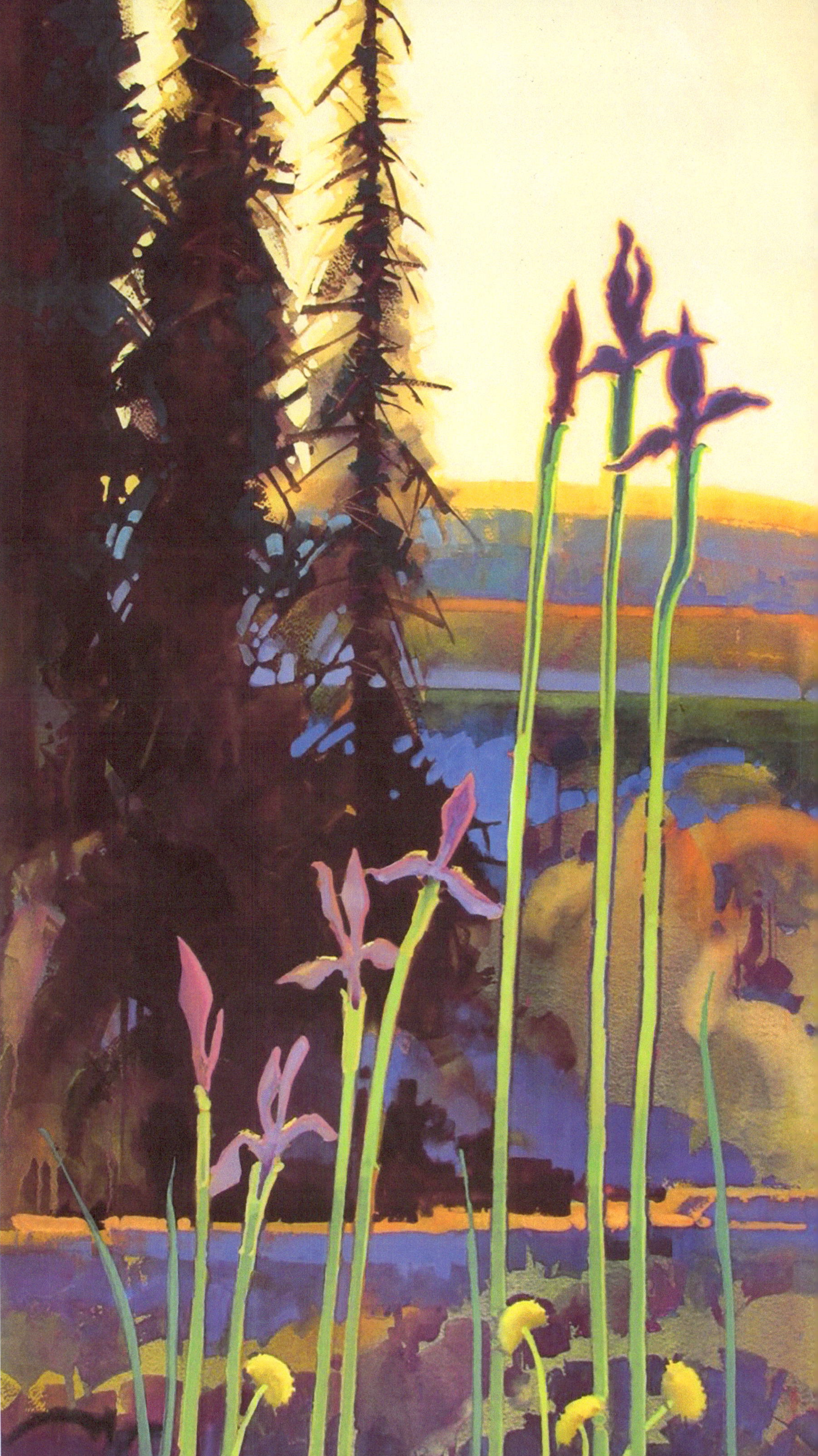

Wild Iris and the Summer Solstice
2019
casein and acrylic underwash
37" x 20"
Artist's Collection

On Location Set-Up

This is typical of what I do, working larger than most people do when working outdoors. It is important when you hike into a special spot to remember all the essentials: wide brim hat, sunscreen, bug spray, water and water container, paper towels, atomizer, and of course your palette, paint, and easel. I like to wear a long sleeve shirt and pants that tend to blend in with nature. There is nothing more exhilarating than working directly from life. The Richeson French Companion, which folds out, holds my brushes and paint.

In late spring, summer and autumn I love getting out into the high country to paint. On inclement days or when I'm working on a large project I will paint in my studio, and definitely tuck in there during the winter. I feel that the two settings are very compatible. I take all the energy, color, and spontaneity of painting outdoors into the studio, and conversely I can also bring the thoughtful arrangement of composition, studies, color relationships and mixed media interaction from my studio work, to painting on location.

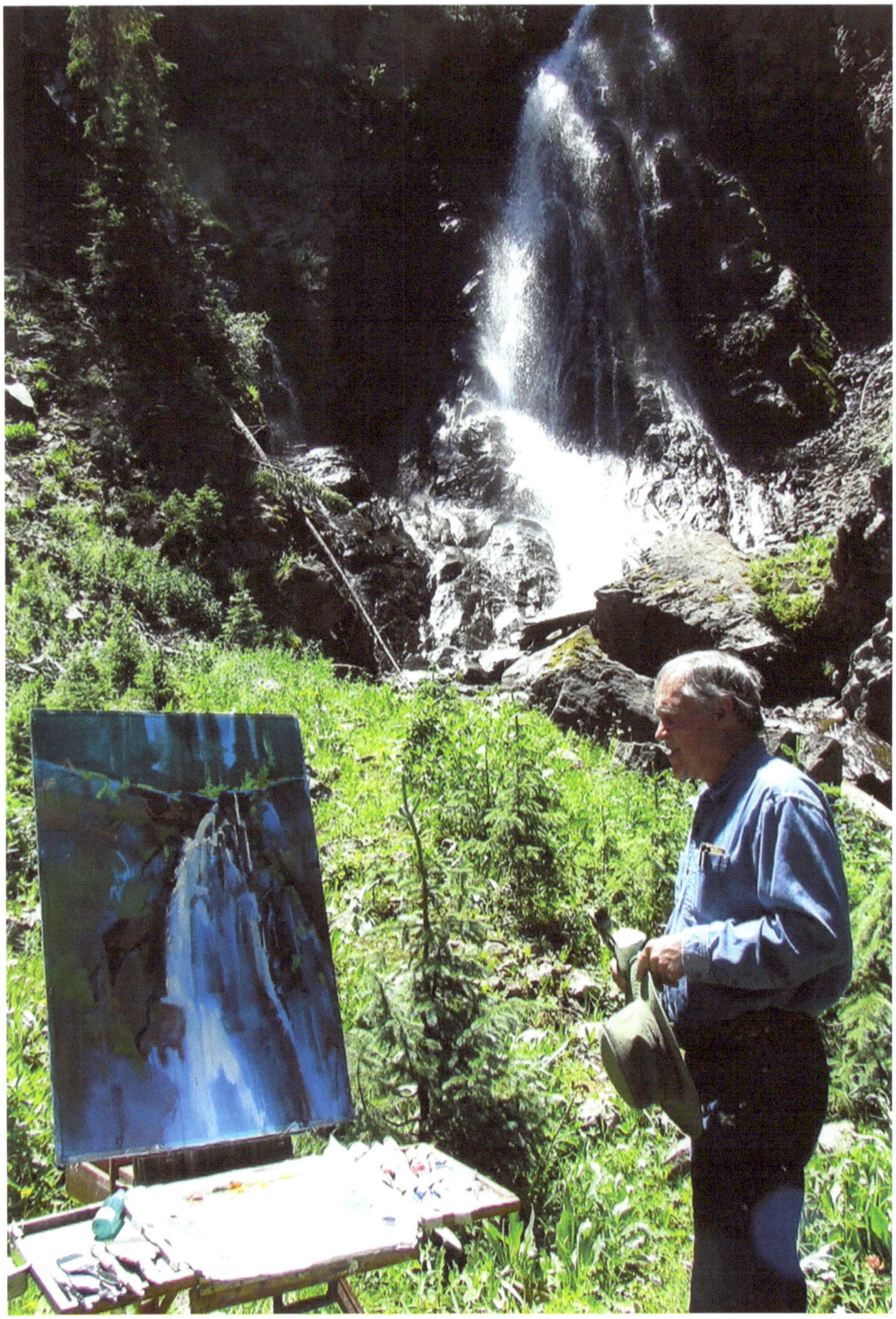

There's nothing like the experience setting up in a beautiful spot and connecting to it. This is one of my favorite haunts and I savor these moments.

I did the painting opposite on location at "Hidden Falls." I went to the painting site with an already toned watercolor board on which I had applied a transparent blue acrylic under wash. On site I did the the entire painting with casein. I love the way the opaque and translucent casein interacts with the undertone to give it a glow. The small bird at lower right is called an Ouzel, often called a "Dipper Bird."

Water Ouzel and Hidden Falls #8
(right) 2014
casein with acrylic underwash
35" x 23"
Collection of Rick Lundt

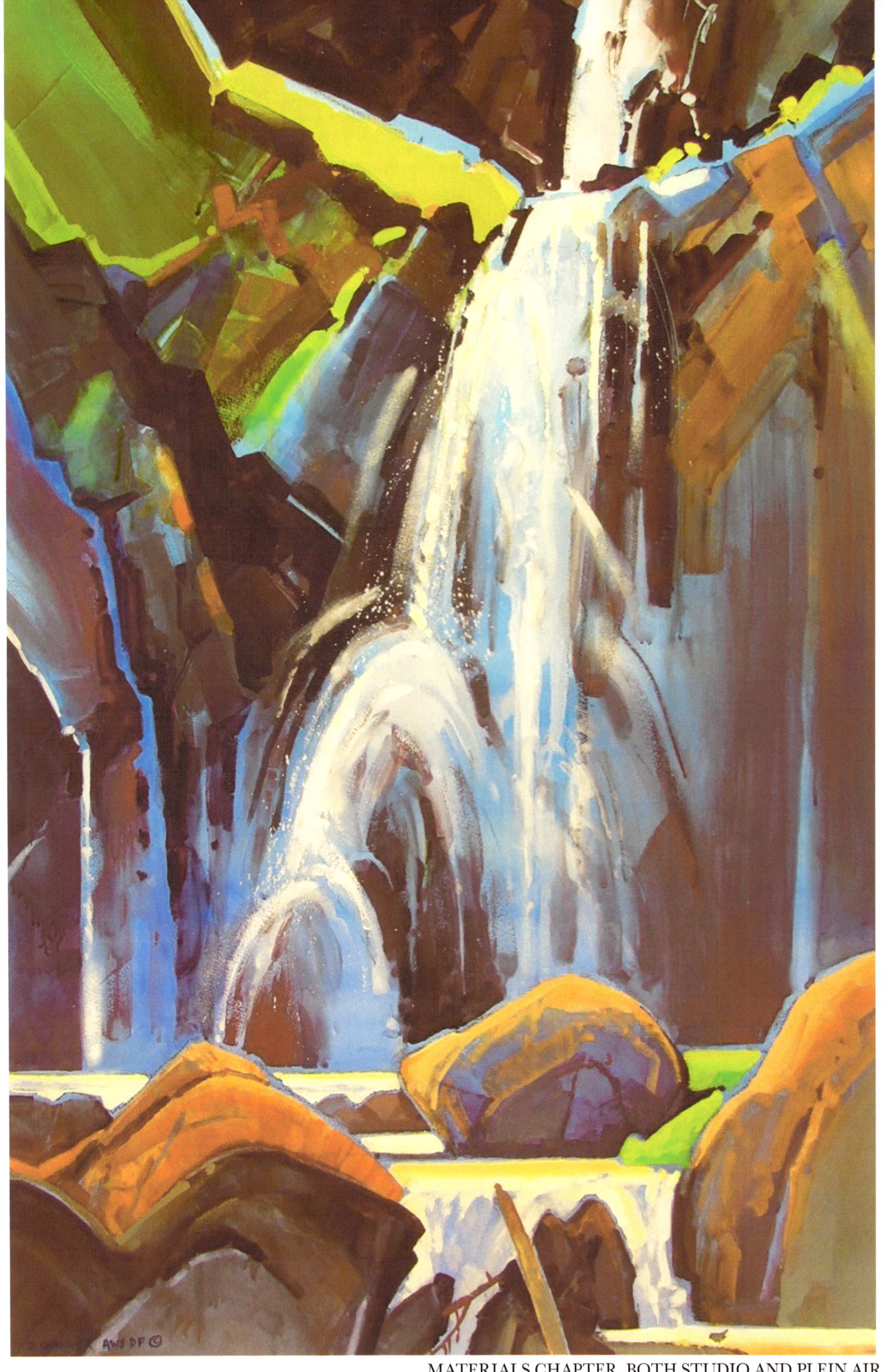
AWS DF ©

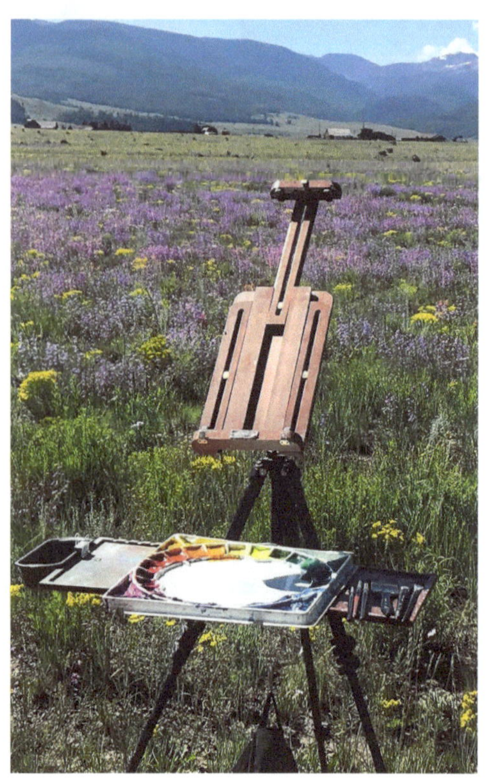

The photo to the left is that of my favorite outdoor easel of all time, the Richeson Sienna Easel. In my studio I have an easel "morgue" with every kind of easel imaginable. I'm very hard on my easels and they tend to fall apart. I've had this one for a good while; it's sturdy and designed so well that it's user-friendly.

The photo on the right shows me organized with my painting board and palette, water container and paper towels, working in a field of wildflowers. In these photos I'm using my watercolor palette that is arranged in a similar fashion to that of the casein palette.

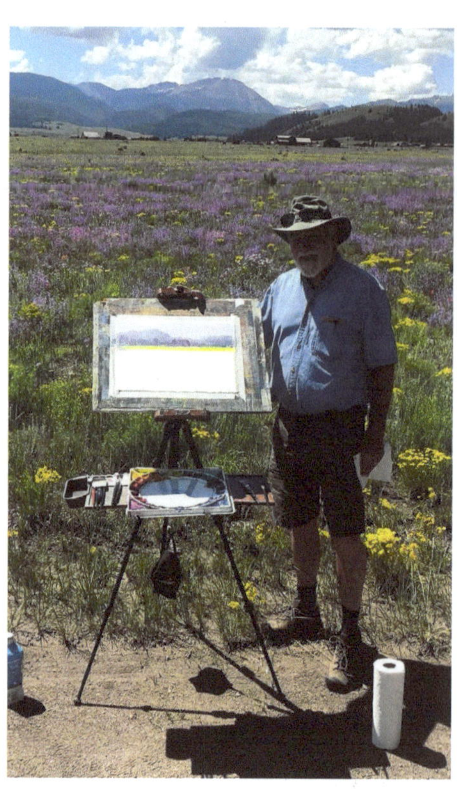

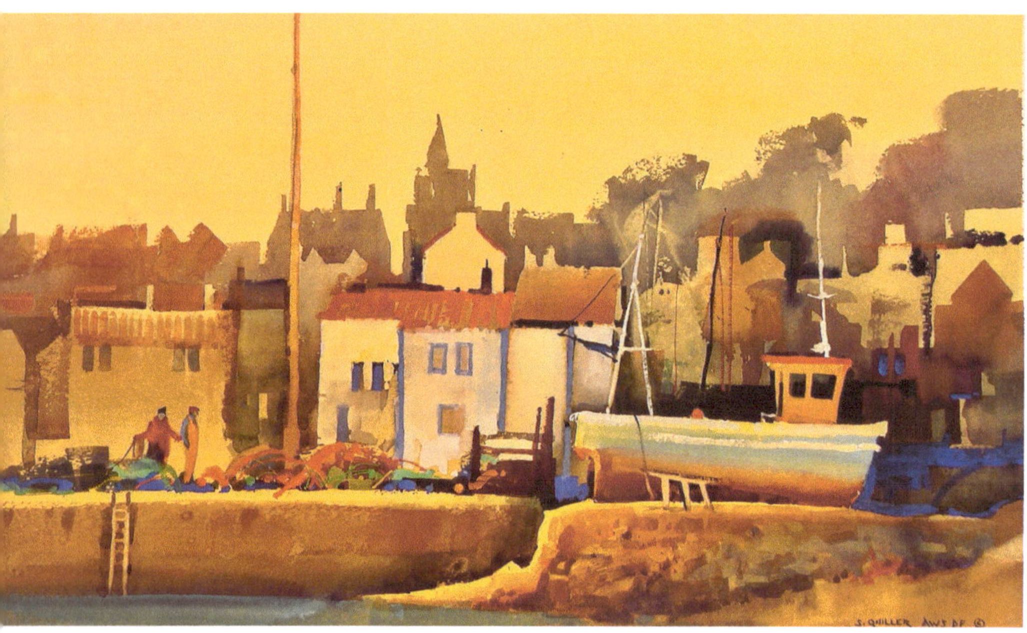

Gold Light, Pittenweem Harbour, Scotland
2011
casein, 16" x 26"
Artist's Collection

Above is the finished painting that I did at the harbor in Pittenweem, Scotland. It is a working harbor and fishermen were mending nets and bringing in their catch. They were also very kind about my presence there. Here I'm working with a small half French style easel. In Scotland as in most of Great Britain, one must be ready for all kinds of weather. That is a challenge but also an opportunity.

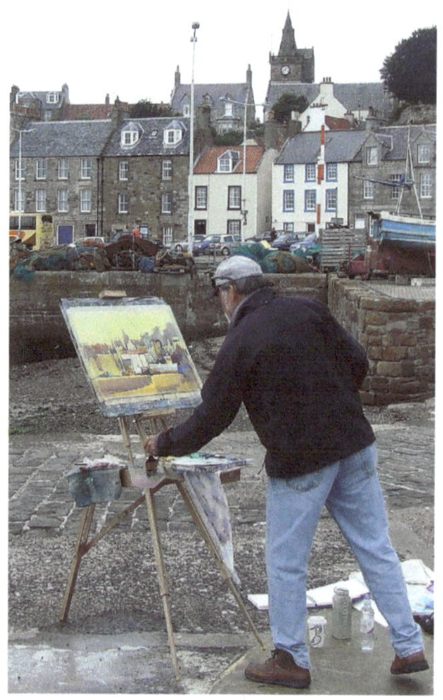

International Plein Air

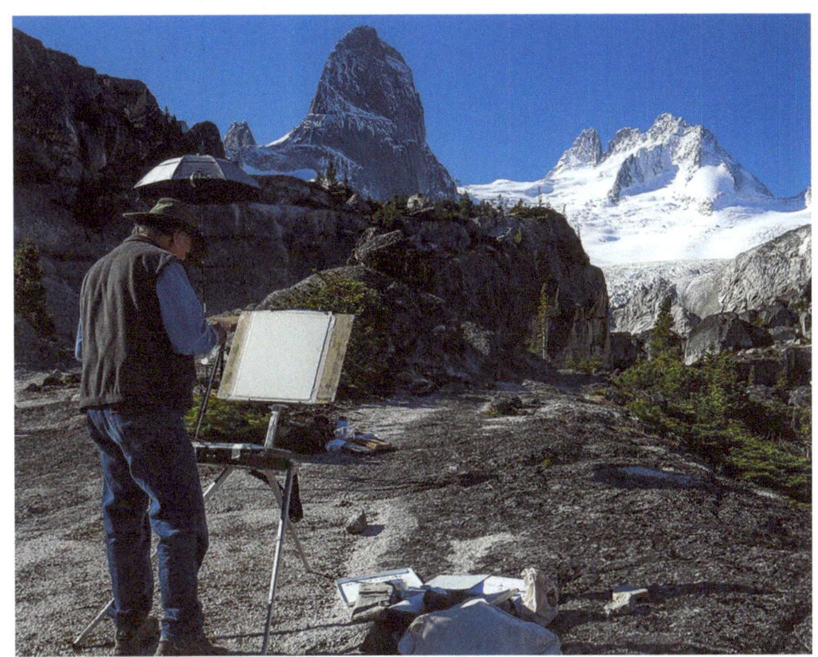

Painting in the Bugaboos of British Columbia, Canada

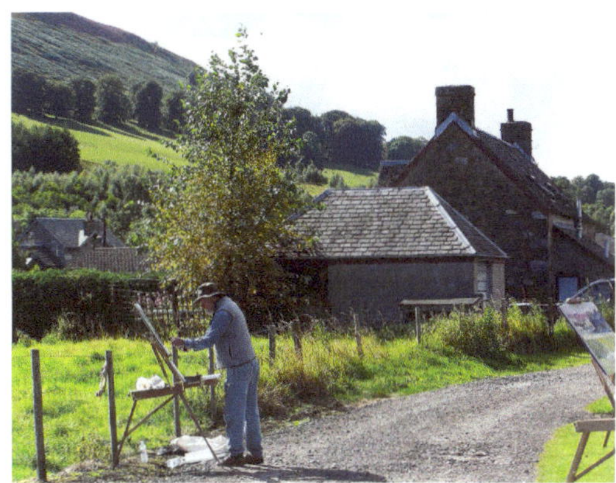

Painting in the Highlands of Scotland

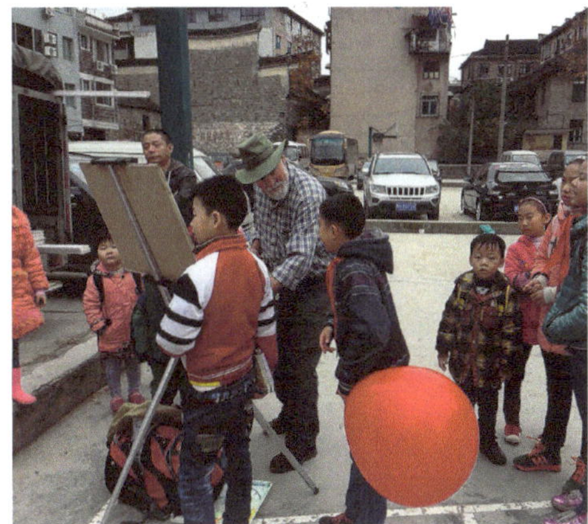

Painting at a Chinese village

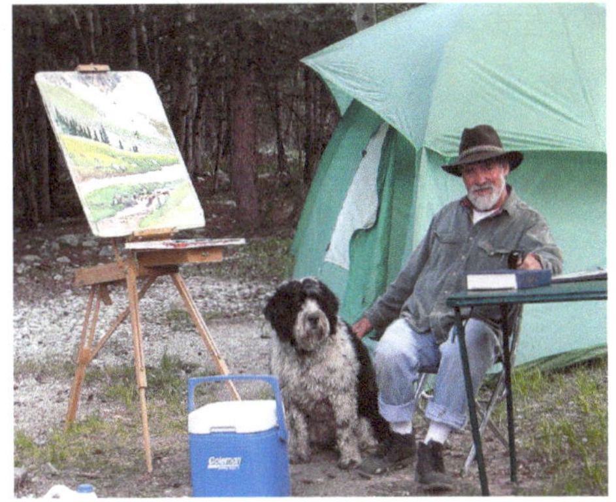

High country painting and camping in Colorado

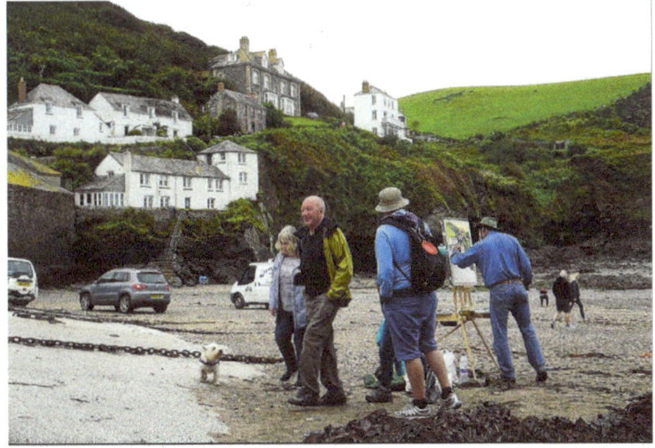

Port Isaac harbor, the filming location for "Doc Martin"

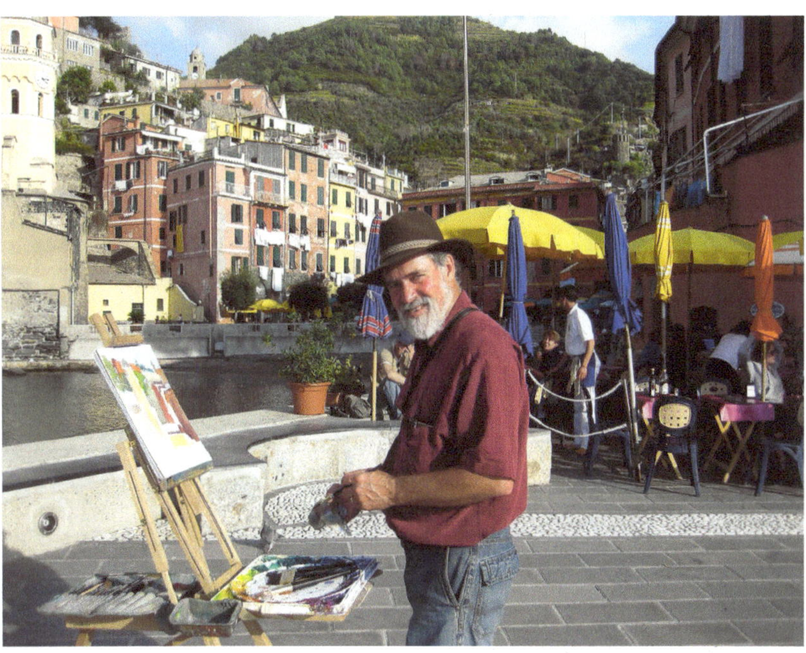

Painting at a harbor in the Cinque Terra, Italy

Water Media and Studio Painting Brushes

I have used these water media brushes since the early 1990s. They are simply the best. They are used by many major artists and rated number one by a top art magazine. These are the 7000 series Jack Richeson Company brushes with my "signature" on them. They hold a lot of paint, have a great flow, snap, and hold a beautiful edge!

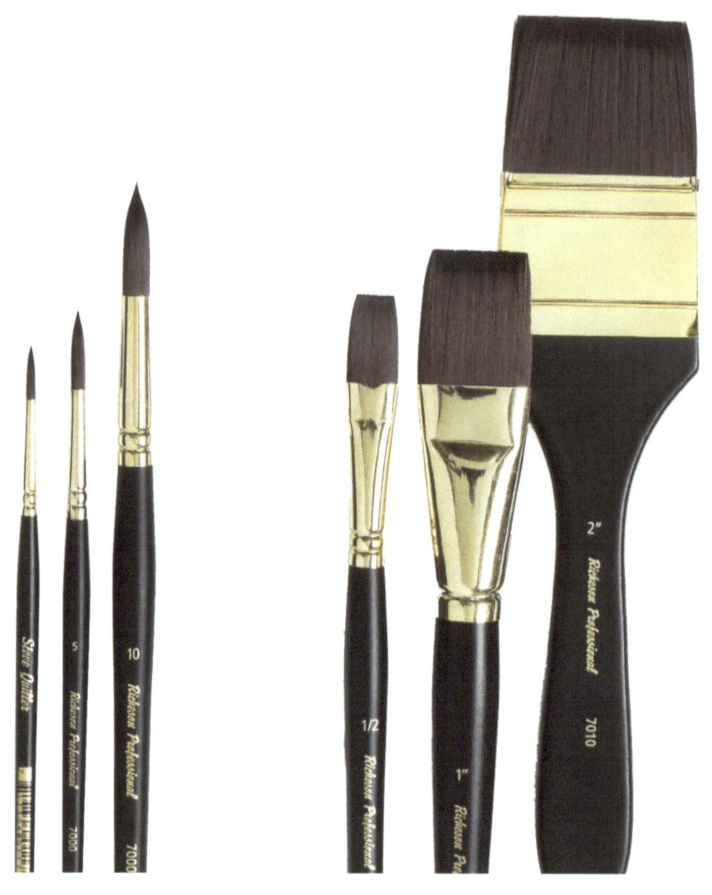

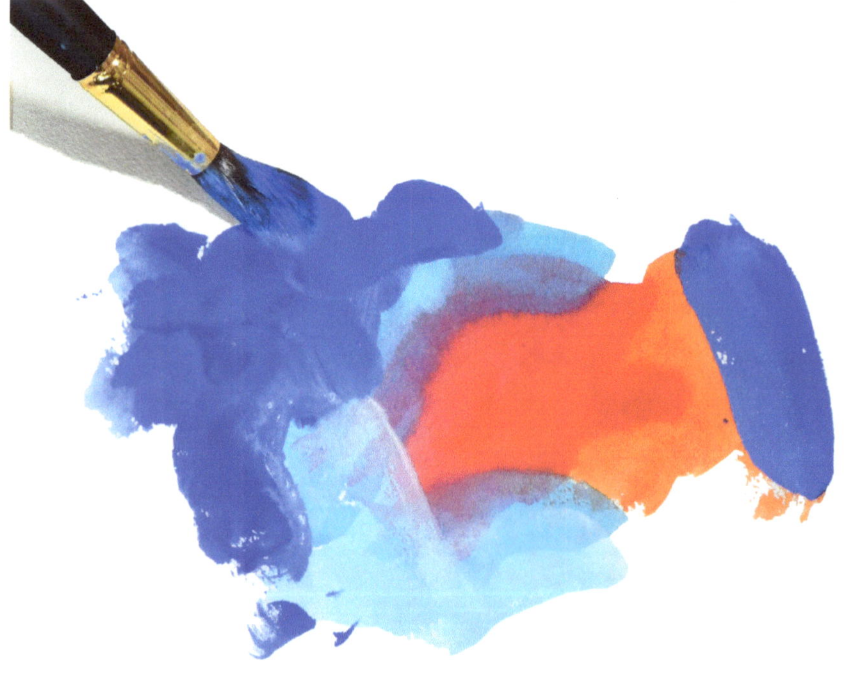

This study depicts some of the versatility of casein. I worked on a piece of 300 pound watercolor paper. First I applied a transparent wash with cadmium orange and rose red. While wet, I mixed a cloudy, translucent layer using phthalo turquoise and titanium white. This is thin enough that you can see through its veil to the rose undertone. Next I mixed ultramarine blue deep and titanium white in a juicy opaque manner. This application is heavy enough that you cannot see anything under this layer. I love the visual qualities that interact with the transparent, translucent and opaque. I used a Richeson 7000 series number 24 round brush.

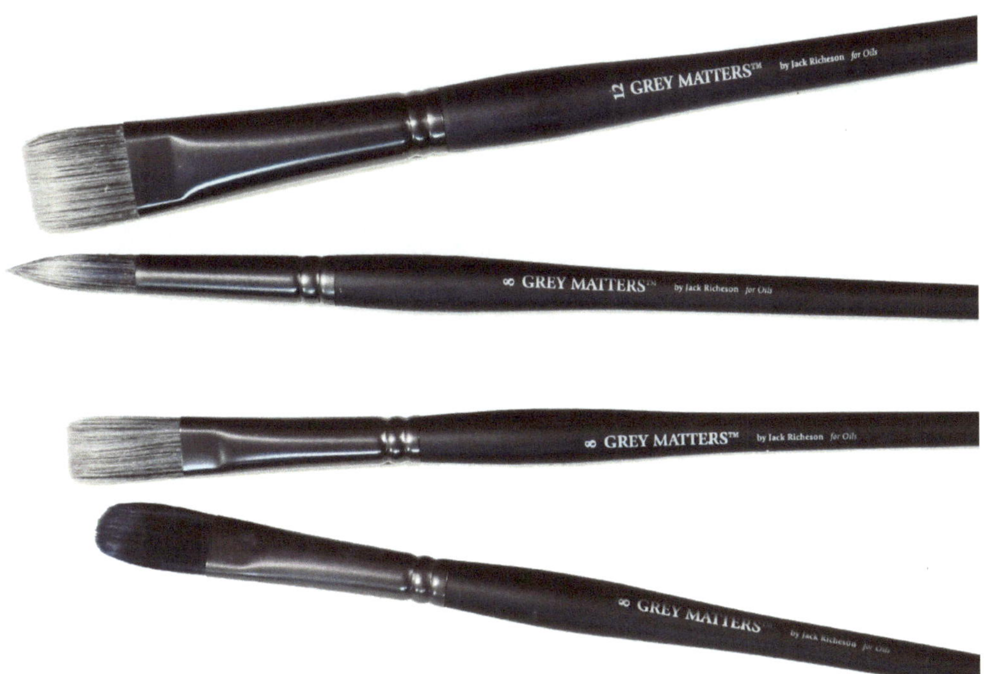

I found these brushes to be ideal for painting in casein. They certainly can be also used for acrylic and oil painting. They are the "Grey Matters" brushes by the Jack Richeson Company. The long handles, the ferrule, and the hair are non reflective, and thus there is no distracting shine. It should be noted that working in a thicker manner, the painter should use a rigid support such as 300 pound watercolor paper, watercolor board, Aquabord®, or linen or cotton canvas mounted on board.

Here I'm playing with the transparent orange wash against juicy opaque sky and foreground forms. I'm working very thickly in some areas, using a piece of Aquabord®.

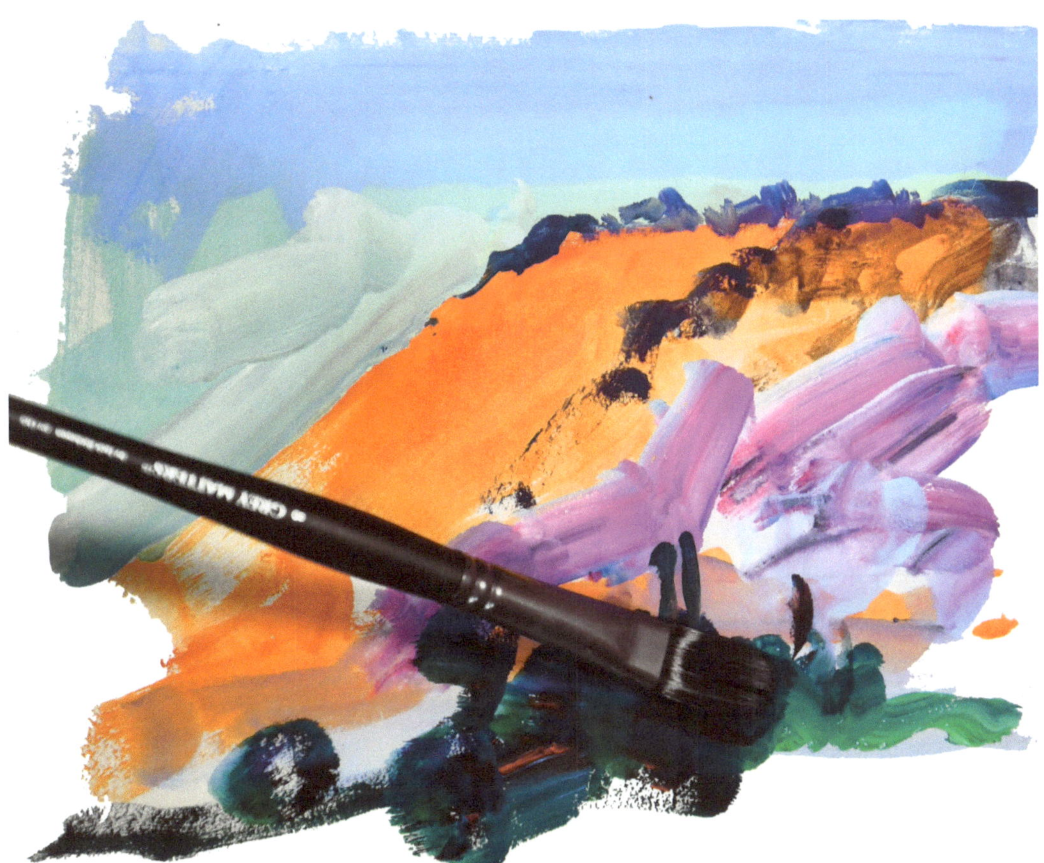

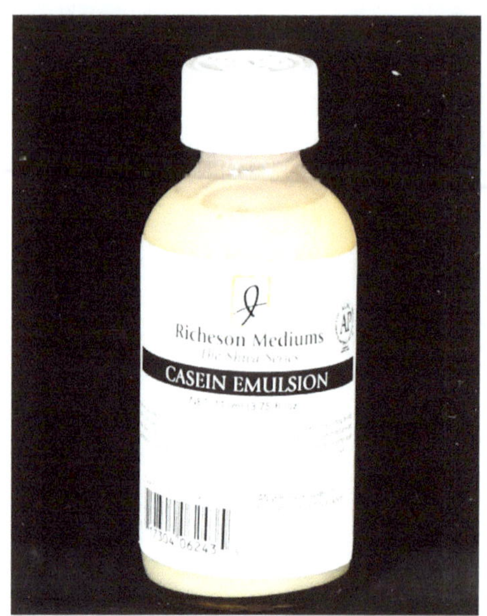

CASEIN EMULSION

This painting medium can be used much like copal painting medium for oil paint. The painter can glaze or thin the paint while keeping the binding power, the velvety matte visual quality, and the integrity of the mark. This is a wonderful tool when working in an easel painting direction.

BRUSH CLEANERS

From time to time brushes can stain from the pigments or a buildup of pigment particles. Although I do not find this to be much of a problem when working in water media, it can happen when I use staining colors. It's always recommended when finished to clean the heel of the brush in the palm of your hand with liquid soap and a little warm water. Then rinse and reshape the brush, and position it so that the bristles are not disturbed.

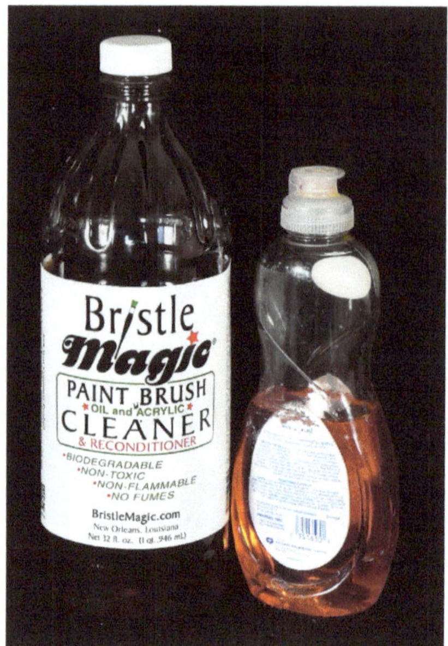

However, if the pigment builds or stain appears, I found this product to be superb for cleaning. "Bristle Magic Paint Brush Cleaner" does a great job and is also non-toxic, biodegradable and non-flammable. Simply just put a small amount of the liquid in a small jar and rinse the brush.

Autumn, South Fork Hill *1991*
casein with acrylic underwash, 15" x 30", Private Collection

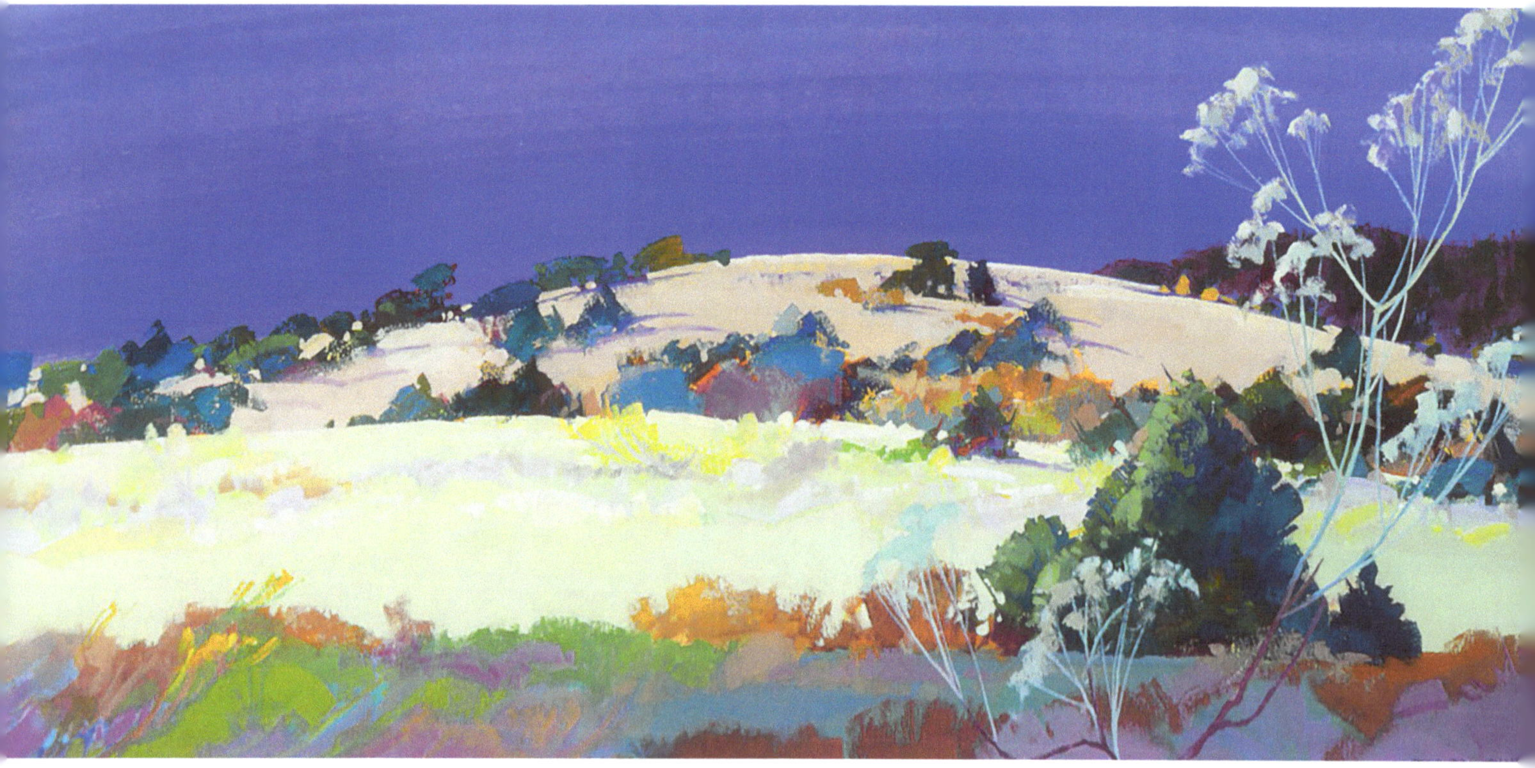

Head Waters, Rio Grande
(right) 1994
casein with acrylic underwash,
Private Collection

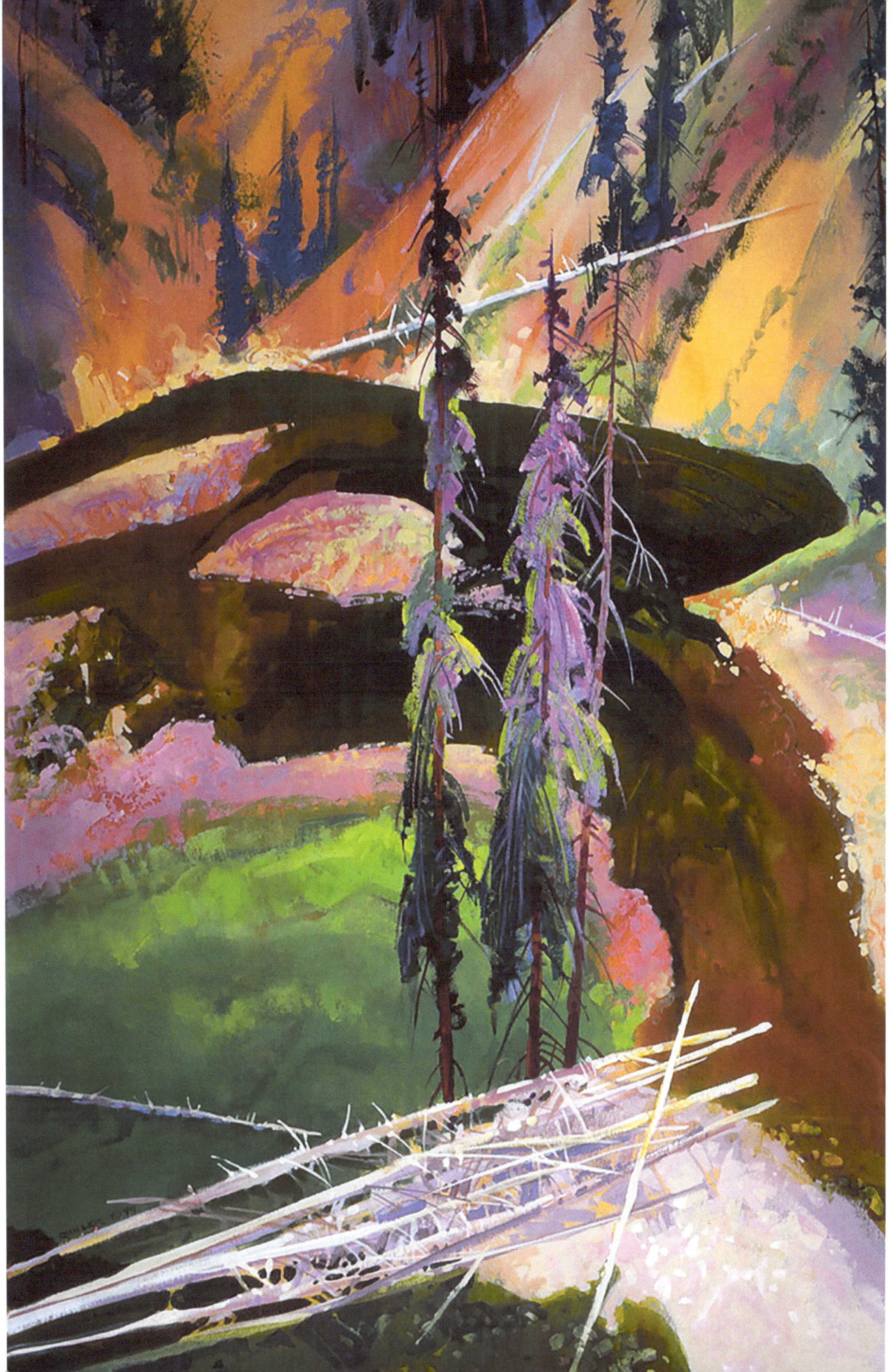

Casein Painting on Different Supports

Cold Press Watercolor Paper - 300#

Casein applied on watercolor paper in the water media fashion is simply beautiful! If the paint application is to be rather thick the paper should be 300#. The weight of the paper is determined when there are 500 sheets of 22" x 30" stacked in a bundle. Thus, 500 sheets of this watercolor paper weighs 300 pounds. There are several major brands of watercolor paper. Among these are Fabriano, Waterford, Arches, and Lanaquarelle. Recently I've been using Hahnemuhle from Germany. It is a 280# paper that works wonderfully.

Watercolor papers are made in three different surfaces: cold press, rough, and hot press. I use the first two. Cold press paper is made with tightly woven cotton fibers and it is made for applications of controlled wet on wet washes, uniform and controlled shapes, and for fine detail. Below is a study of casein on the surface.

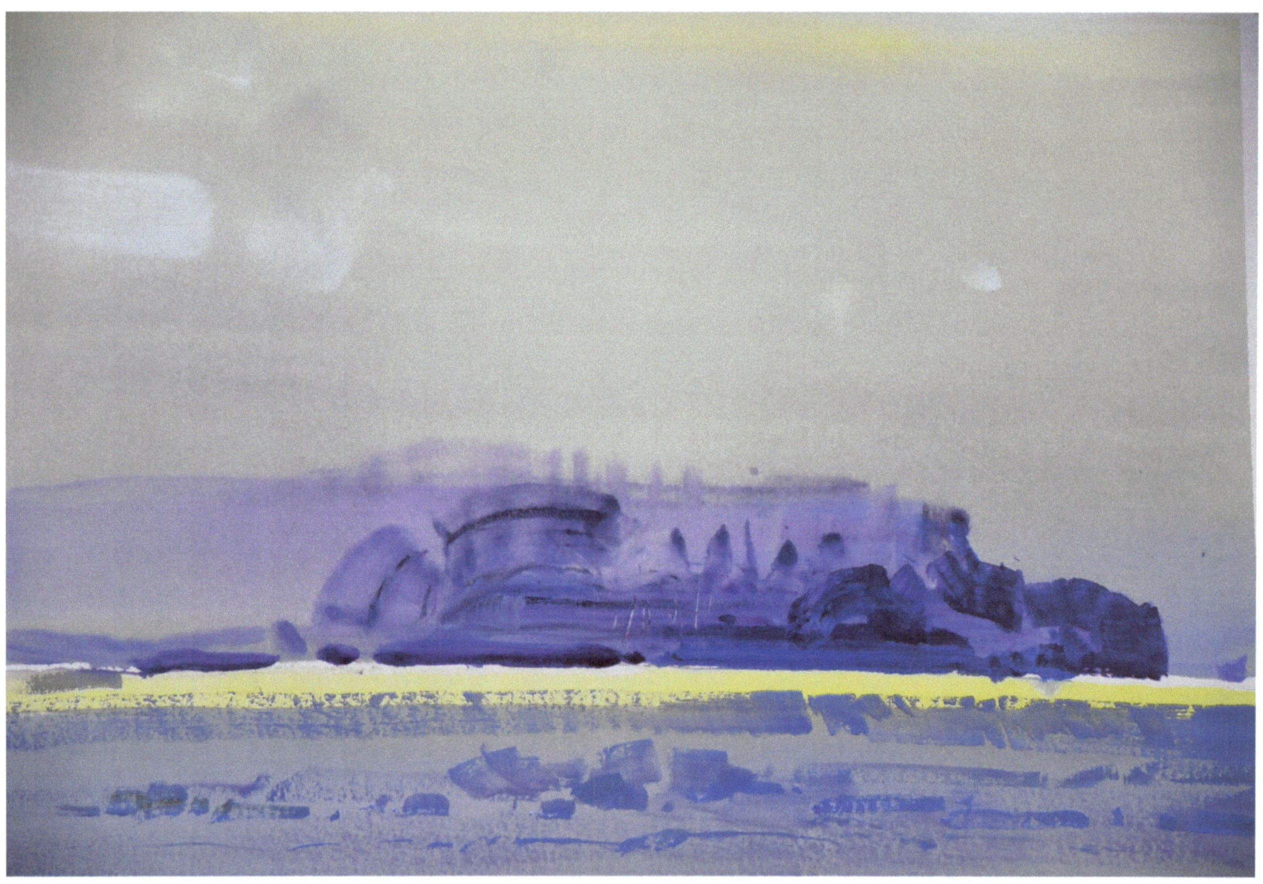

I wet the 300# cold press paper and applied white casein to produce a nice undercoat. Then with a 2 inch watercolor brush I washed in cadmium yellow light and ultramarine violet to achieve a soft gray background. I added a few white marks with casein to the sky area. I then mixed ultramarine violet and quinacridone violet to paint the soft landform, and as it dried I applied darker applications with the same colors along with permasol blue. When it was almost dry, I washed the yellow violet gray mix in the foreground, and then dragged a loaded brush to scumble over the soft textures of the paper.

September Snow 2003

casein with transparent acrylic under wash on cold press 300 lb. watercolor paper, 26" x 33" Private Collection

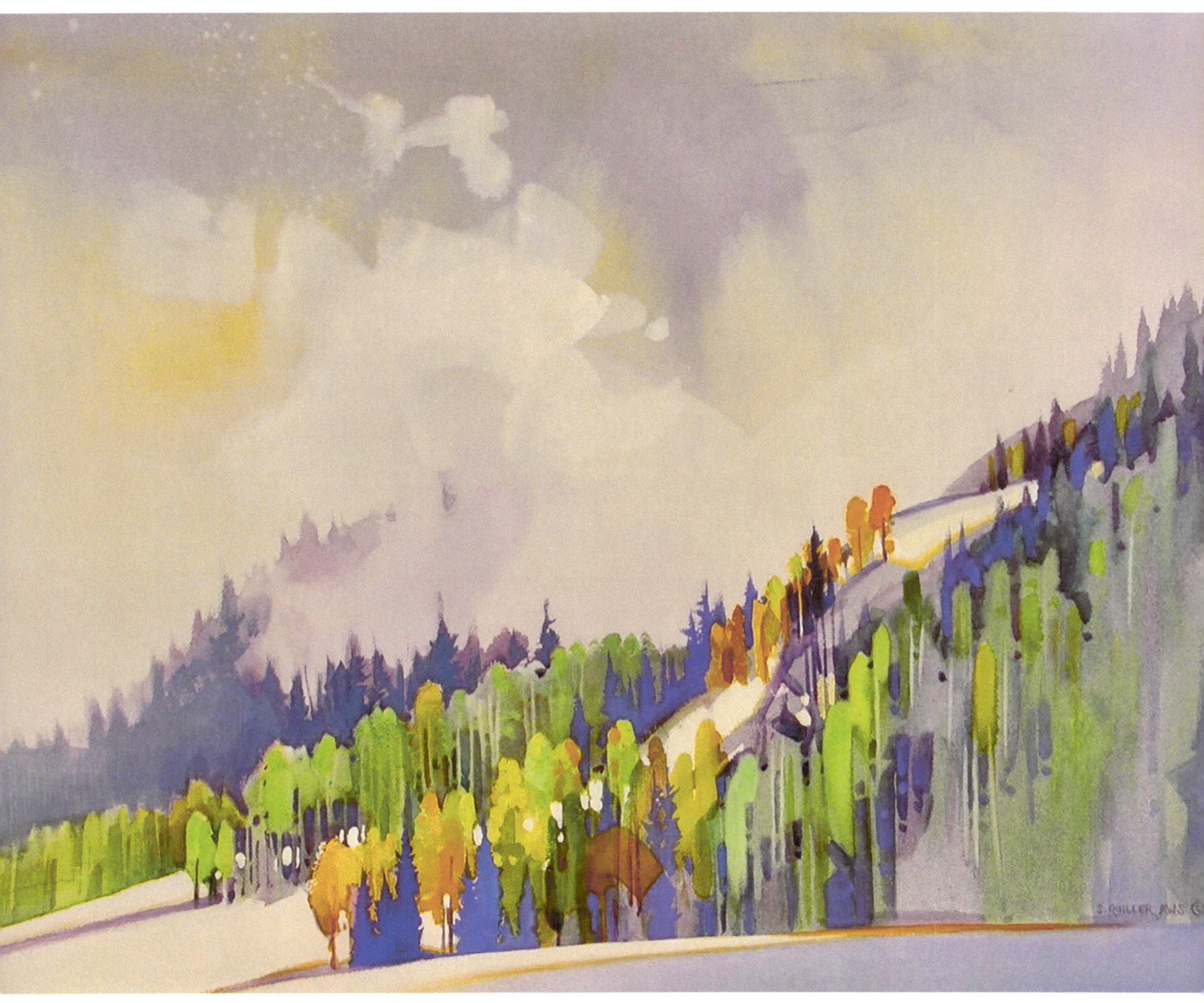

I did this painting September 23, 2003. The mountain across from my home was turning into beautiful autumn color. That night we had an early four inch snow. I looked out of my studio as the sunlight emerged from the clouds and saw this syncopated pattern between the aspen and spruce in the sunlit snow pockets. A soft diffused snow cloud was rising from the earth. It was the ideal subject for working on cold press watercolor paper.

Rough Watercolor Paper - 300#

I live in the high country mountains of Colorado. Often my choice when working with casein is rough watercolor paper. It helps me achieve the texture I want when working with the spruce and aspen in winter, the cascading waterfalls, and the rocky cliff patterns. In other words, I select the surface that's going to best achieve the power and effect that I want. I look for a paper with an organic rough texture. Some papers are a more uniform machine rough. The paper that I often use is 280# rough from Hahnemuhle of Germany. Other papers from companies mentioned earlier also work well. Again, it's important to use a heavier weight paper if the applications are thicker. Below is a study demonstrating the texture of a rough paper.

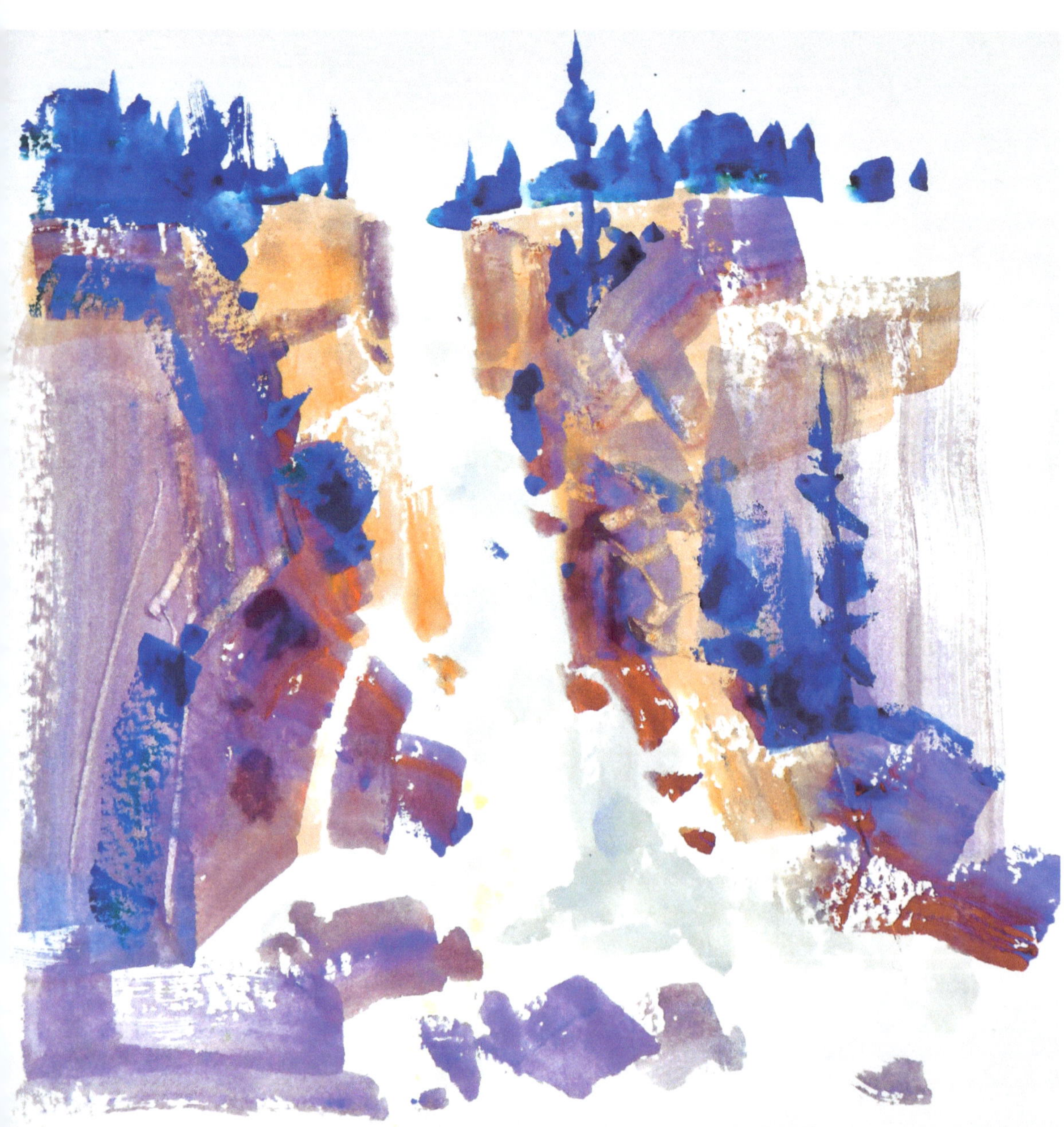

This study demonstrates the texture that can be achieved with rough watercolor paper. I used flat water media brushes and dragged the flat edge against the rough surface of the paper to expose the texture. I started with the lightest tones and built to the dark blue violets. The white of the moving waterfall is the paper itself.

April Morning, Sangre de Cristos *1991*

casein, 21 ¾" x 30", Private Collection

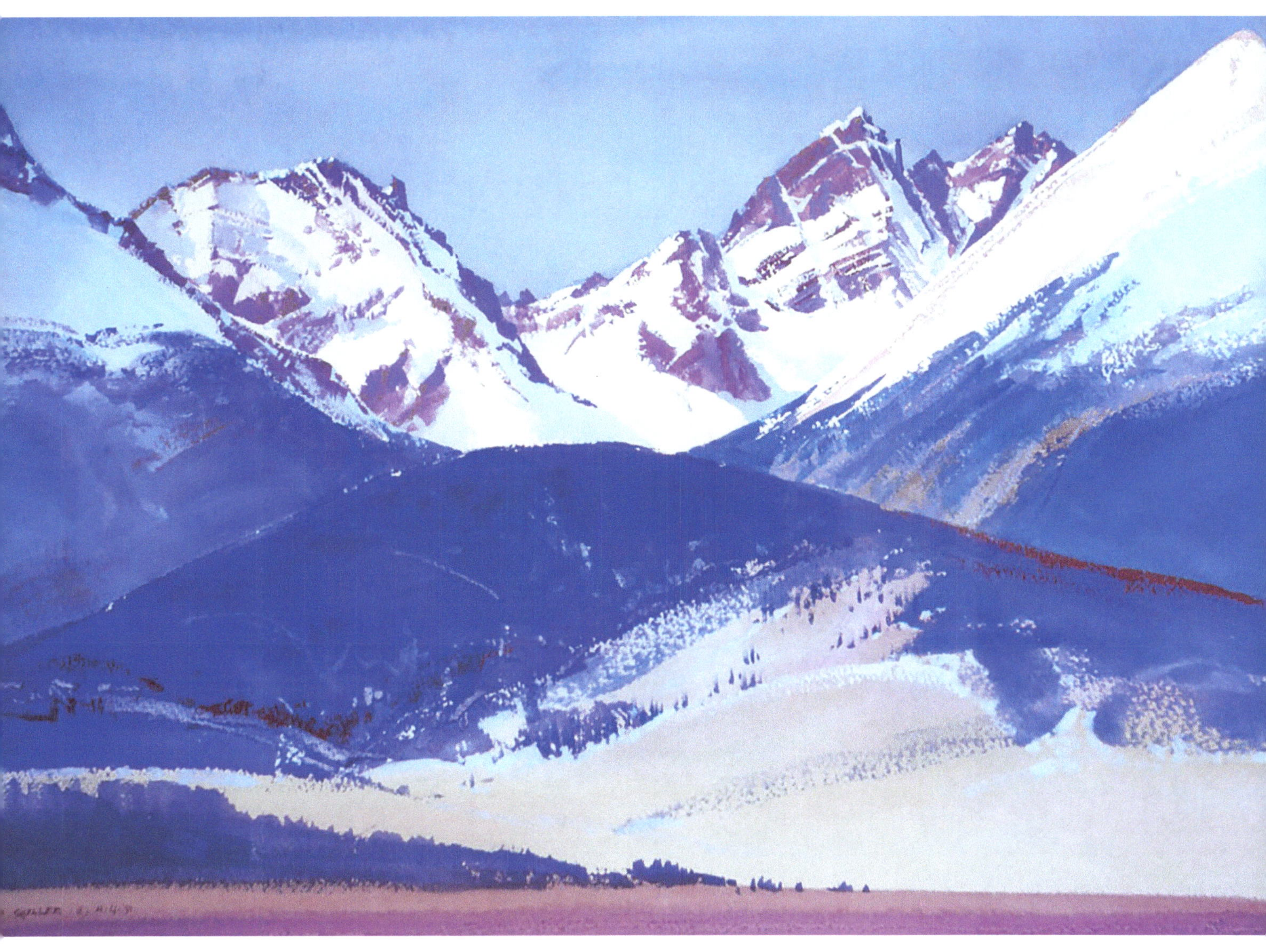

I love the early spring in the high country of Colorado. It can be challenging because there can be heavy winds, snow and even rain, but on good days you can sense the seasons change as the sun moves higher in the sky and creates a raking light. The rivers are opening and the snow is melting, creating sunlit snow pockets and open land forms. I did this painting on location in the Wet Mountain Valley on the east side of the Sangre de Cristo range. I chose a 300# rough watercolor paper to help me achieve the texture of the mountains and the distant tree forms. It's easy to see where I have turned my brush on the flat edge and dragged it against the dry under color to show the roughness of the paper. It was a windy day and there was a time when I stood back from the painting, and my painting board acted like a sail while it was taped onto the arm of the easel. The whole easel flew 10 yards, spilling water and paint. This is part of the challenge and opportunity that happens during this time year.

Crescent Cold Press Watercolor Board

There are many different kinds of watercolor boards. This is the one I have used for many years and have had excellent luck. About two thirds of my paintings are done with this support. Crescent makes two boards with the same cold press watercolor paper mounted on the surface. The first, #411, handles the same as the second board but is a regular board surface with the paper mounted, and is not acid-free. The second is #5114, and the under board is acid-free as well, which is what I like to use. When I'm working with casein or acrylic I like a more rigid hardboard support on which the mark holds more easily. It is also beautiful for layering color one over the other. Below is a detail of the painting on the opposite page.

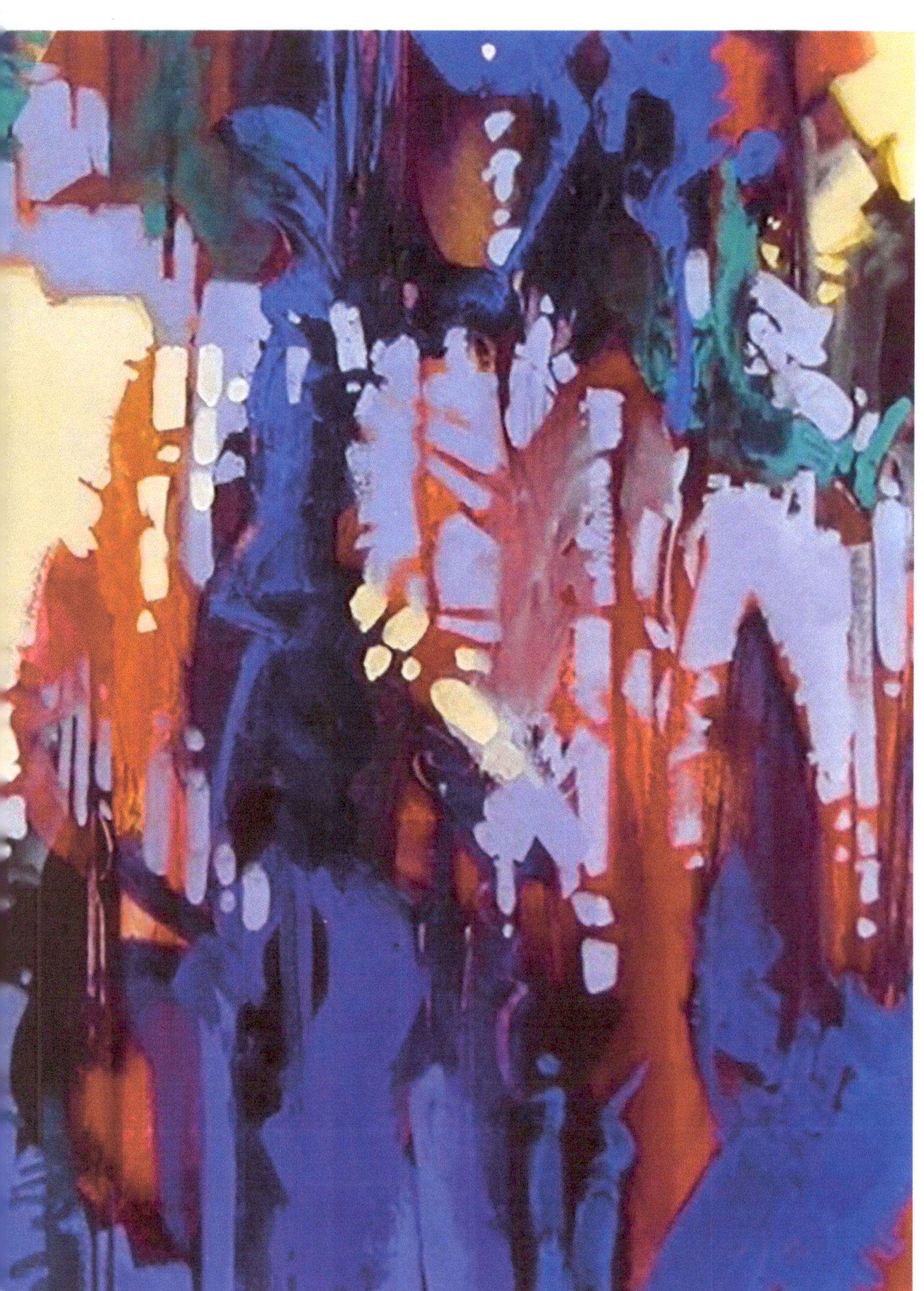

This detail shows the rich color and layering process that works so well with casein on this cold press watercolor board. I started with an under wash of transparent acrylic in yellow oranges to reds. When dry I began layering the cool blues and warm yellow white, painting negatively around the under color. In some areas I glazed translucent white to see a cloudy veil of the under color, while painting very opaquely in other areas around the bright warm undertone.

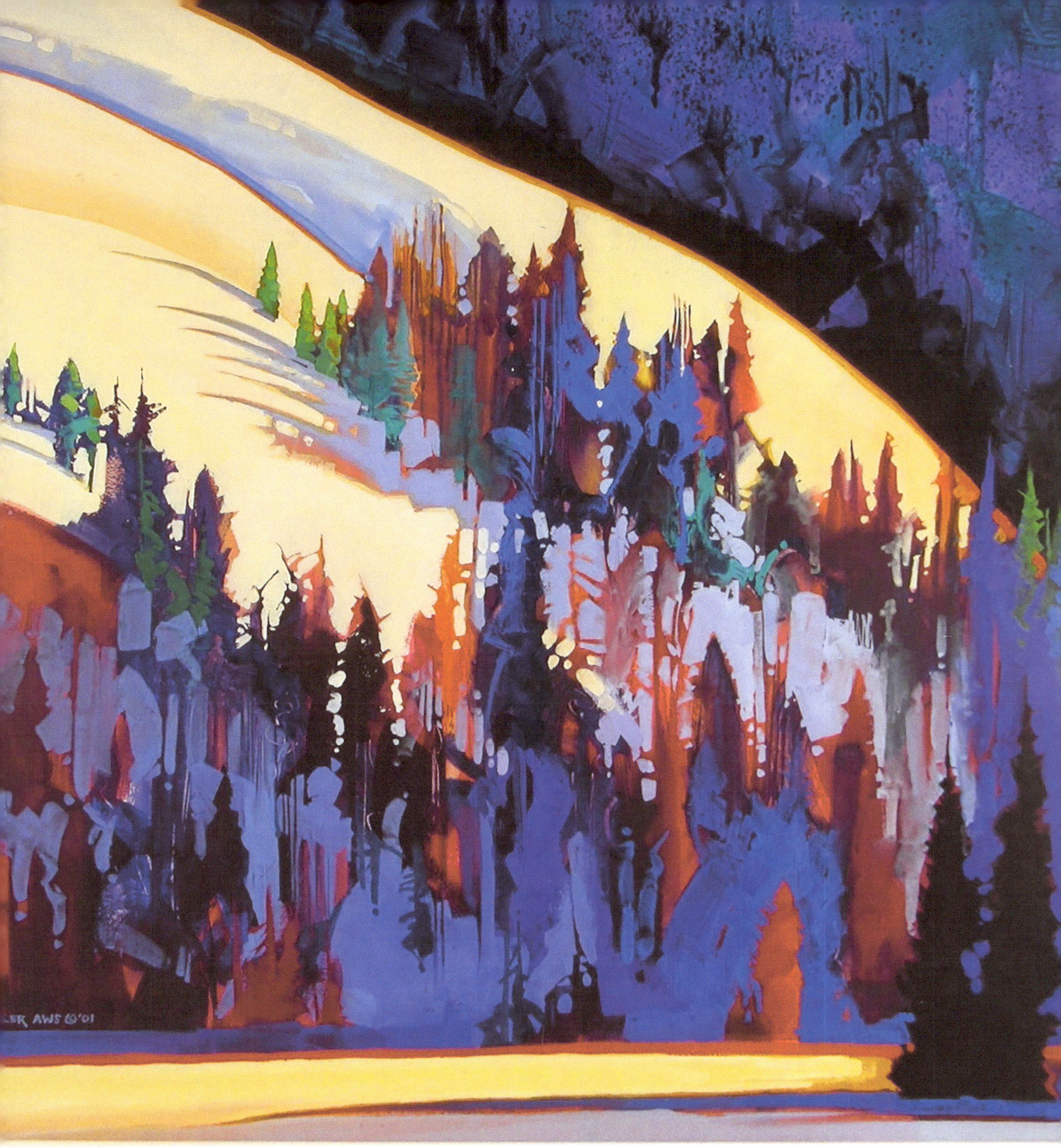

When we moved to our home and studio in the mid-1990s I embraced the views up and down river, and to the meadow and mountain vistas to the west and north. However, I originally discounted the mountain view to the east. To this date I have probably painted the views of the mountaintops to the east as much as any other. The changing shadows and light, the different atmospheric conditions, and the different times of day and year provide a constant feast for painting. I see this view every morning framed from a window in our bedroom. It inspires me and gives me the excuse to put paint on paper!

February Light
2001
casein, 28 ½" x 28 ½"
Artist's Collection
Award, National Watercolor Society

Aquaboard ®

Casein is ideally suited for Aquabord® (Ampersand), a product I have used for the past 25 years. A good painter friend of mine, Charlie Ewing, developed the product and helped start Ampersand. This support is a hard board archival surface covered with a layer of kaline clay. Working with casein on this support would be like painting on a fresh limestone fresco. The paint seems to melt into the surface and layers can gradually build one on top of the other in a beautiful fashion. Below is a small detail of the painting on the opposite page. There is also a painting I did on location in France that I used as a study for this larger painting.

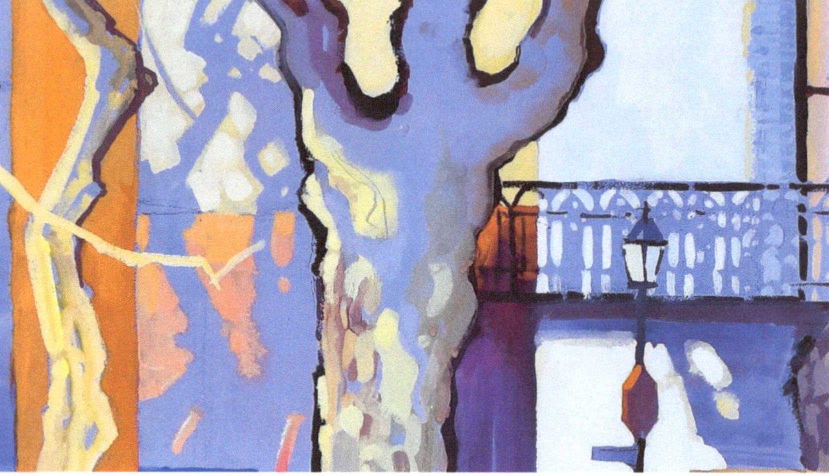

This is a detail from the painting on the opposite page. I began by toning the entire clay coated surface with a deep neutralized blue violet casein wash. Then I built negatively around that color, allowing it to create the patterns on the shadowed side of the tree, while building to the lights. The paint melts into the surface in a way unlike any other support I have used.

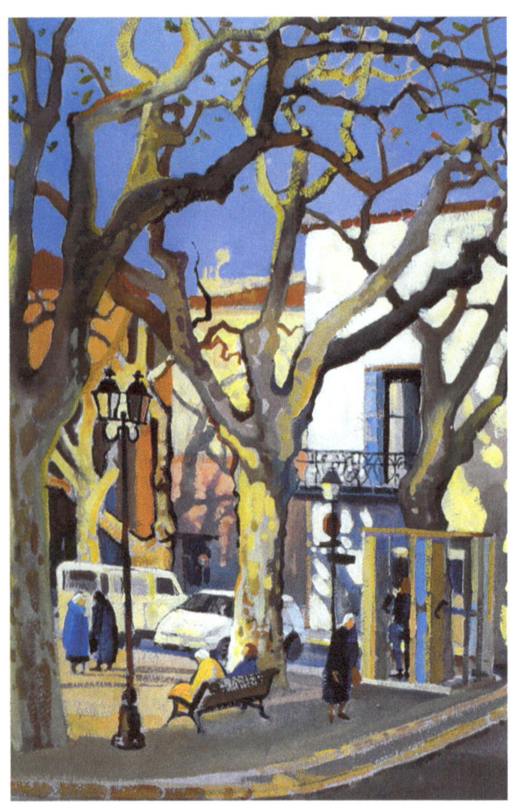

I did the above painting on location in mid-November at a town square in the south of France. It was a great time to work because it was market day, and local people meandered about without many tourists. Also the plane trees had lost their leaves and created nice negative patterns with the sky. I did this whole painting on-site with casein on a watercolor board. I've come to enjoy painting while people mill around, observing my work and commenting!

I did this painting (pg. 59) on a 36" x 24" Aquabord ® panel when I returned home from a four month stay in the south of France. I had done 70 paintings on location while there and shipped them home. I then took a few weeks to finish those paintings. I liked the painting that I did on site (left) and decided to do a larger version. Aquabord ® is a very rigid support, accepting casein beautifully, and can also be shown framed without glass. I also added a few personal images in this painting, our daughter Allie in the phone booth as well as our dog Mickey.

Cassis Town Square, November
(right) 2002
casein, 36"x 24"
Artist's Collection

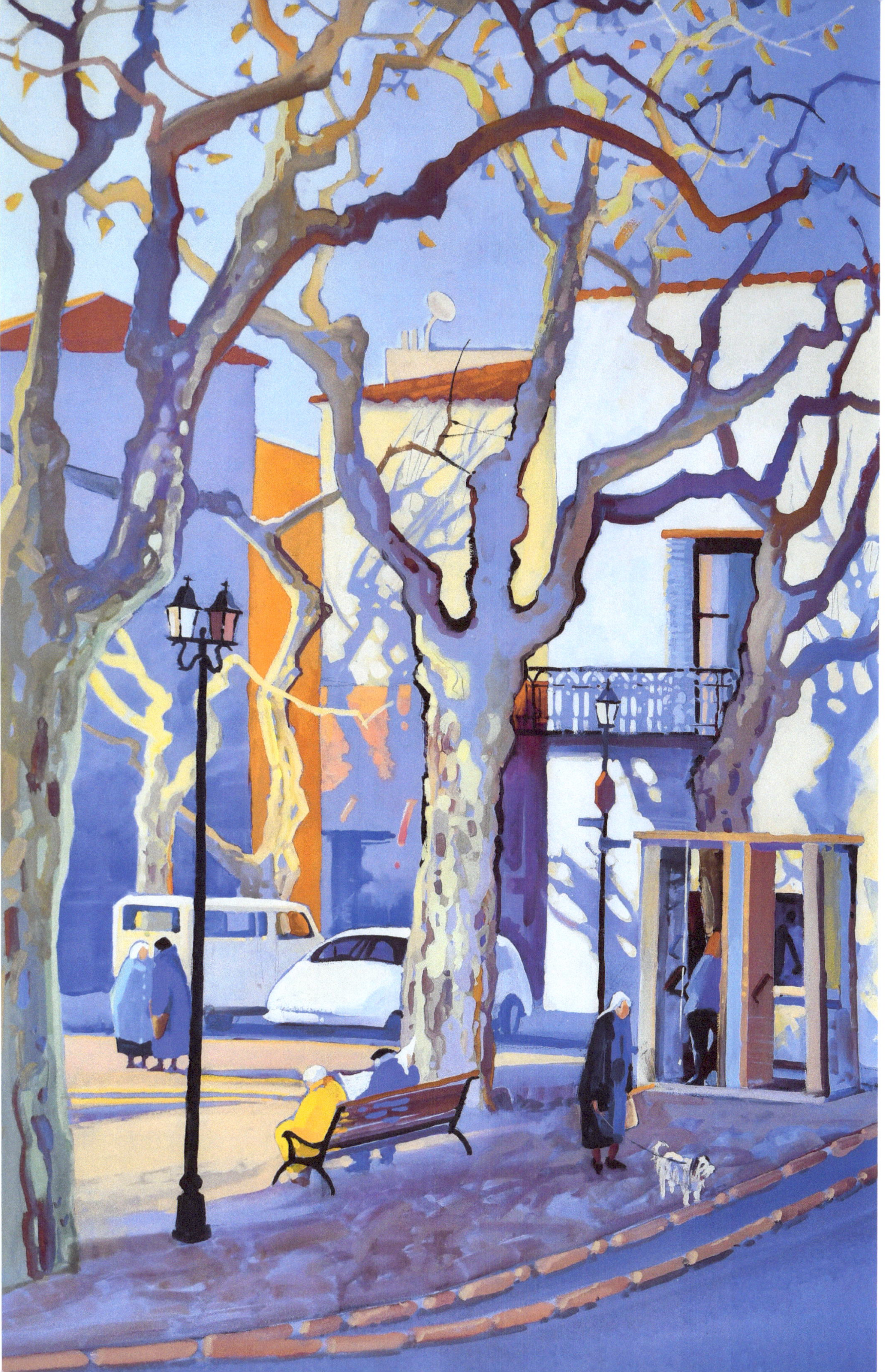

Casein on Wood Panel

Wood panels can be purchased or ordered through your local art stores. They come in basswood and maple, and you can also purchase them cradled, a wood support that can act like a frame and be hung just as it is. In this case I used a 10" x 10" basswood unprimed panel by Ampersand. This is a marvelous surface to work with! I first primed the surface with Golden's GAC 100 paint medium, a clear liquid. When the primer is dry the surface can be stained with any transparent color of casein to tone the wood. It's also advisable to prime the back side of the wood.

Working in this way reminded me that some artists in the late 1890s to mid 1900s, when on location, painted small studies on the wooden lids of cigar boxes. The Group of Seven, artists from Canada, painted on location doing small studies in oil on wood panels. Working in this manner, it's important to leave some of the wood exposed. Below is a detail of the painting on the opposite page.

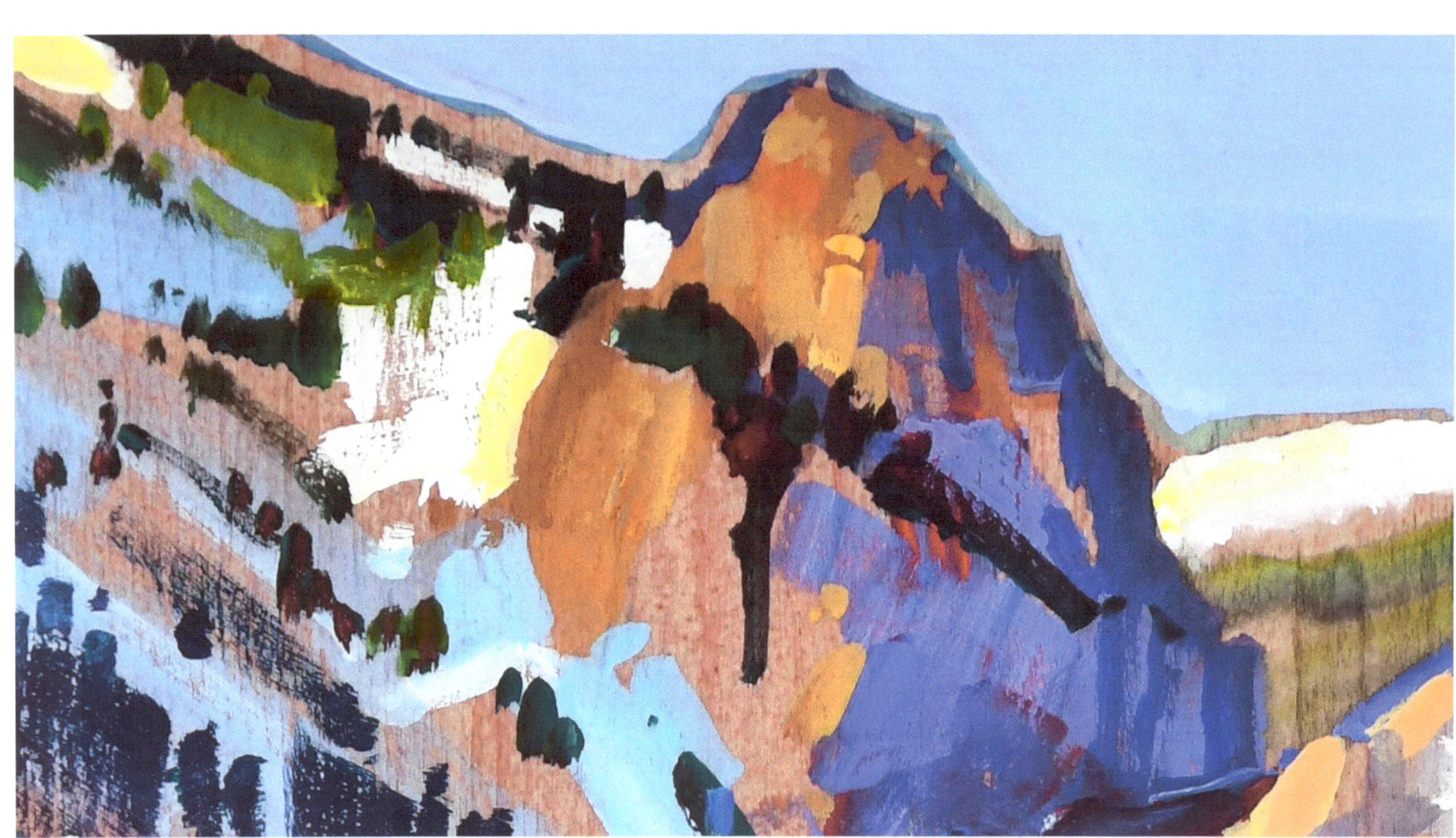

This is a detail of the painting on page 61. As you can see, I've left some of the toned wood exposed. That is the beauty of working in this way. The exposed wood is a unifying thread with the common color and ties the painting together. I found that casein is absolutely ideal for working on these panels. The paint dries quickly, and juicy opaque marks hold well on this very rigid support.

View Of Creede, January 7, 2020
(pg. 61) **2020**
casein on basswood panel, 10"x 10"
Private Collection

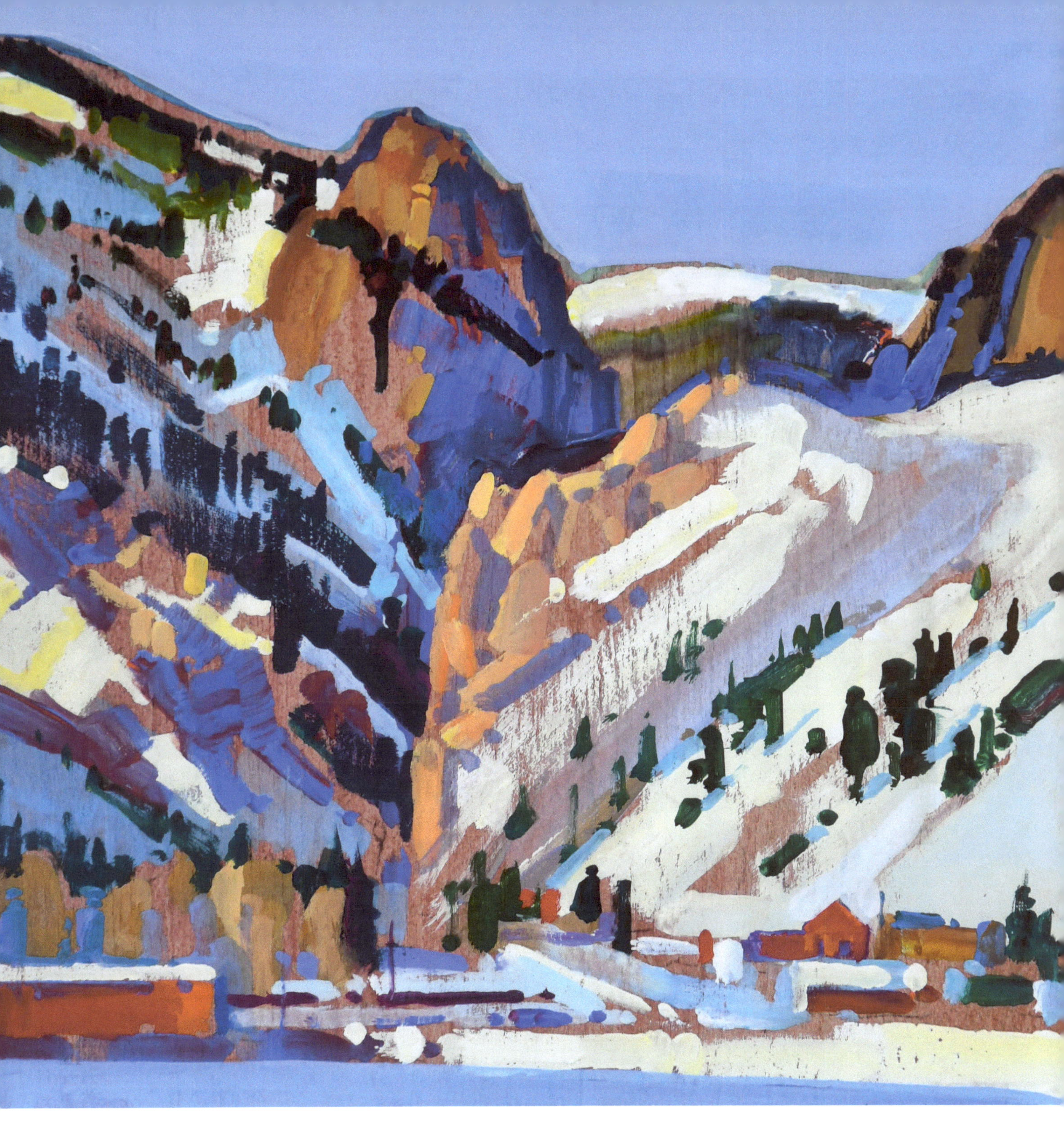

The subject for this painting is a view that I see almost daily when I drive to the town near where I live. It's a spectacular view with dramatic cliffs as a backdrop to the main street. In the 1890s it was a booming mining town with over 10,000 people. Today, the year-round population is around 400. I had the best time working with this small painting, leaving some of the stained wood exposed to tie the piece together. Casein bonded nicely with this panel and created a beautiful velvety matte look. The paint dried quickly and allowed me to be very spontaneous with my paint applications, yet the paint was still workable, as I could come back and soften edges and work in layers to build the casein. I highly recommend giving this method a try with the subject of your choice!

Casein on Linen Canvas Art Panel

Casein is ideal for working on a linen canvas panel. It's important to remember that casein should not be used on a stretched linen canvas with stretcher bars, as the material expands and contracts, and it is hard for thicker casein paint to adhere. However, on the board it bonds very well and you can build the surface to impasto textures. As opposed to oil, the paint dries quickly and you can build layers and desired effects much more readily. Compared to acrylic, casein dries to a velvety matte visual quality and does not have a plastic sheen. For this study I used the linen art panel made by the Jack Richeson Company. It is archival, triple primed with an acrylic gesso, and warp resistant on a 1/8 inch tempered hardwood panel. I've had great success with this product. When the painting is finished, it can be gently buffed with a cotton ball to bring out a beautiful luminosity. This is a detail of the painting on the next page (left). You can see the texture of the linen and how the paint responds to the support.

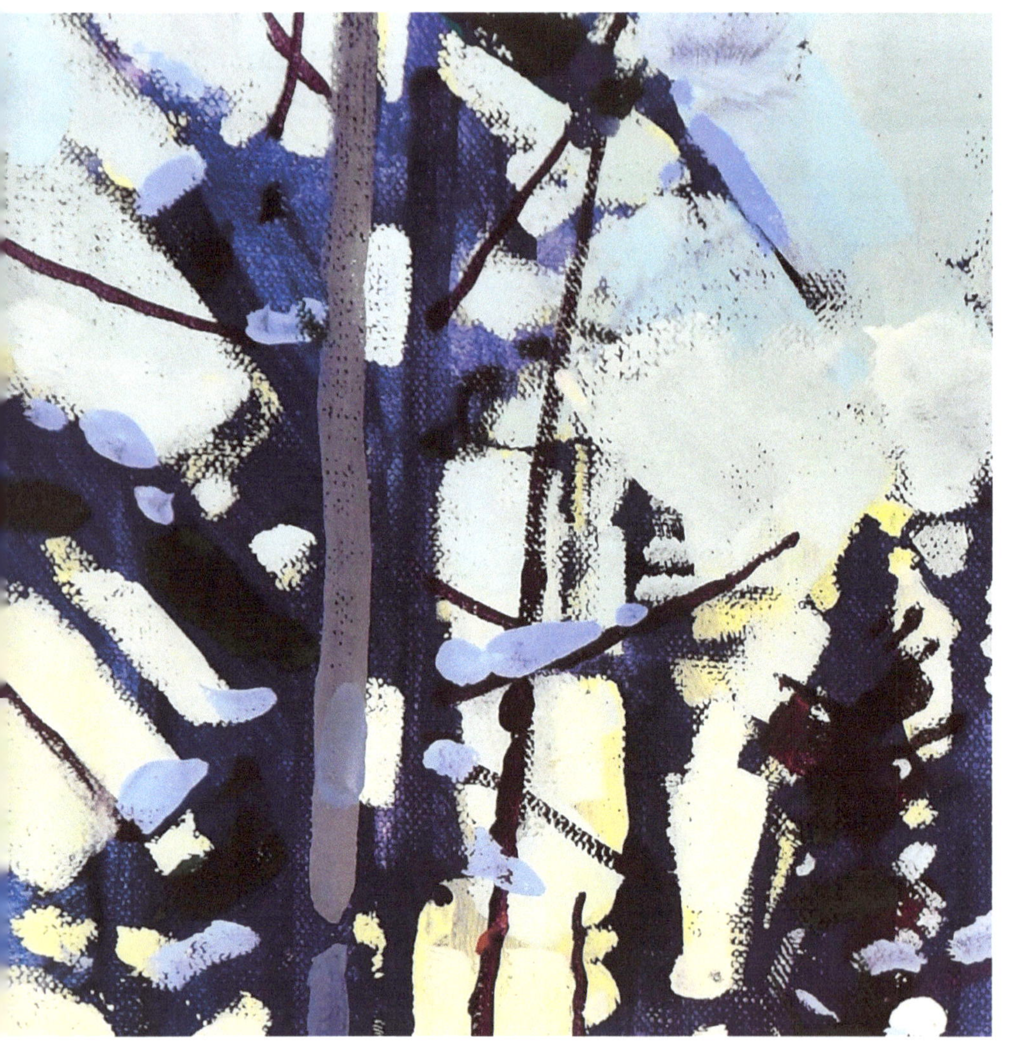

This is a detail of the finished painting (page 63). It shows the fine texture of the linen canvas. I found it a beautiful support for casein. Allowing each layer to dry, it was easy to build layer upon layer, dark to light.

Working on this linen canvas I started by washing in dark shapes that would eventually be the trunks and evergreen foliage. Once it was dry, I started painting negatively around these shapes with light casein: pale yellows, yellow greens, ceruleans in the sky, and the yellow orange and rose in the alpine glow on the mountain. I wanted this painting to be about pattern, by focusing on painting the clumps of snow and negative shapes.

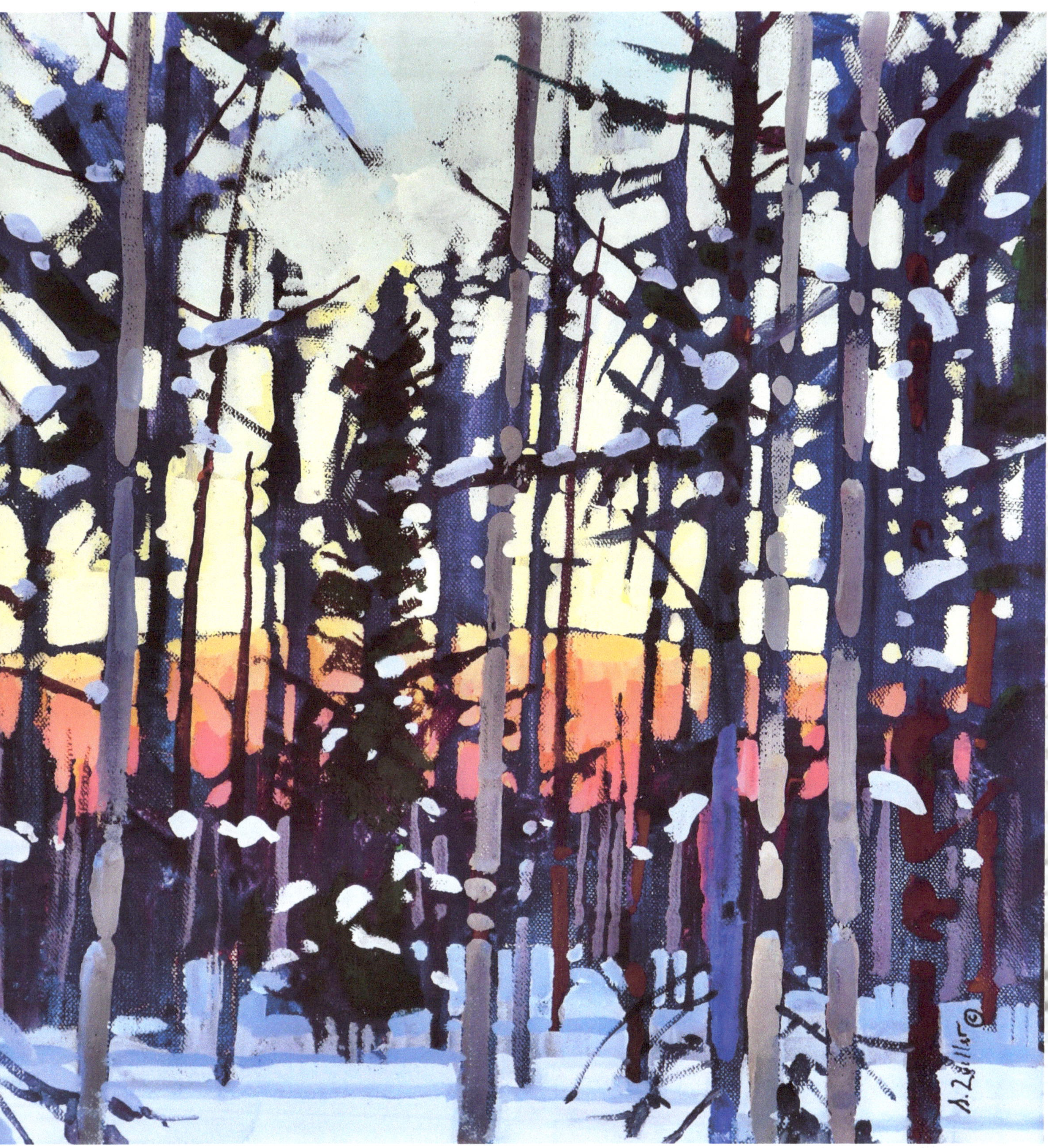

Alpenglow, La Garitas
2020
casein on linen canvas, 12"x 12"
Private Collection

I did this painting "Alpenglow, La Garitas" on a 12" x 12" triple primed acrylic, warp resistant, ⅛" gessoed cardboard panel made by the Jack Richeson Company. It is a very fine weave and a beautiful painting surface with casein. This is an area where I ski in the evenings, and I did it with inspiration after the fresh snow and late light.

Toned Gessoed Hardboard

This hardboard support is coated with an even, high quality gesso to isolate the paint from the board. The gesso is primed smoothly and thus every mark and brushstroke is not interrupted by texture. The most common gesso board is white. Painting on the white panel is fairly straightforward.

A toned surface has a long history. Painters of the Dutch school, including Rembrandt and Vermeer, worked on the mid gray toned canvas. This was called the "en grisaille" method of painting. They drew on gray paper, going darker with charcoal or ink, and then added white with chalk. Artists in the English school, including JMW Turner and Peter de Wint, worked on gray, tans, blues, and earthy red papers when painting with watercolor.

Working on a toned support allows the artist to really think about value, the darks and lights in the composition. The artist must build to the lights and work down to the darks. When I am working on a toned panel, I feel is important to leave some of the color showing. On this page are two small 8" x 10" studies, one on a mid gray tone and one on the mid-umber tone as examples for this approach.

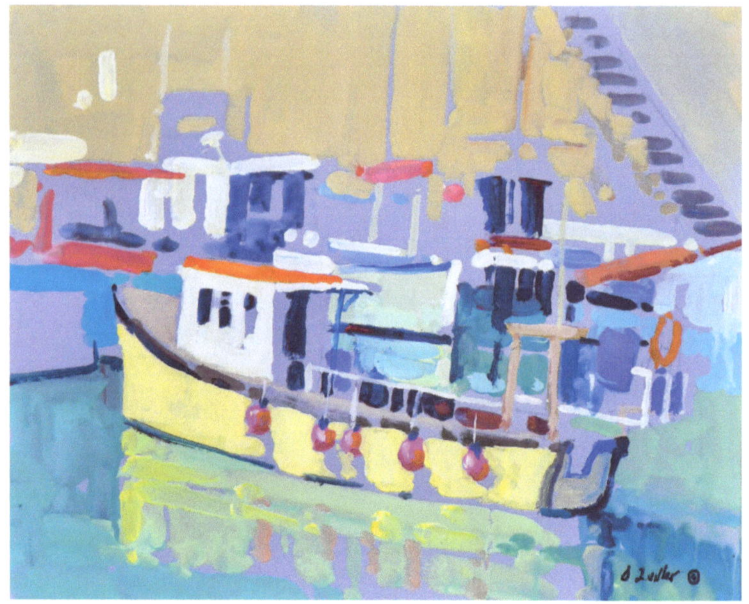

I had the best time painting this small panel with casein. The paint was almost like butter melting on this panel. The panel is actually a mid-gray tone coated gesso, manufactured by the Jack Richeson Company. All the gray that you see in this painting is the unpainted area! What's interesting to me is that in the neutral area, which is surrounded by warm yellow to yellow orange, the neutral appears as a violet-gray. However, on the far left central area, where the neutral is surrounded by a blue-green, the gray appears to the red violet side.

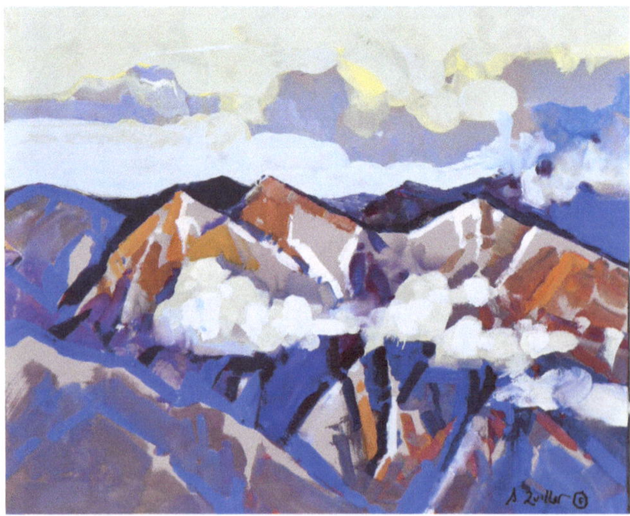

This small panel has a light beige tone. All the areas you see that are a light tan are the unpainted areas. I picked a color palette of yellow, yellow orange and orange against the blue and blue violet. This will maintain the same color theme as the beige under coating.

Exercise #1 Take your casein palette outside to a favorite spot. With the 300# watercolor paper do three small studies, one in early morning, one in mid-afternoon, and one in early evening. Notice how the palette of color changes.

Exercise#2 Select a small basswood or maplewood cradle board panel. First size it with an acrylic matte medium. Find a favorite sketch or photograph and paint the subject, leaving the exposed wood to be part of the composition.

Exercise#3 Obtain a small 9" x 12" piece of Aquabord®. Find a small sketch of a landscape that can be built in layers such as sky, distant landforms and shapes nearer the viewers eye. Play with the casein and layer one over another. Notice how the casein seems to melt into the clay coated surface.

Presentation of Finished Paintings

A while ago I visited the Fitzwilliam Art Museum in Cambridge, England. There was a painting at this venue by Pierre-August Renoir that had kind of an ordinary and somewhat dull grayish blue-green frame around it. As it turns out, Renoir had made the frame himself and selected color that would set off his painting. His gallery agent told him that this painting would never sell with this frame. Collectors at that time were often buying for the frame and were not that concerned with the actual painting. These beautiful ornate Victorian frames were placed on walls inside the homes of the aristocracy. Ironically, today this painting is worth much more because Renoir created the frame as well.

The presentation of the finished work of art is of utmost importance. I have seen incredible paintings that have been very poorly framed and viewers walk right by. On the other hand, I seen average paintings that have been framed beautifully and the viewer will take time to look more closely.

Most important, the frame should allow you to see the painting and not distract from it. I've seen very ornate or brightly colored frames and two and three colored mats that show off the framing but don't allow you to see the work of art.

Casein paintings can be framed different ways. The general rule to follow if the painting has been done on paper or a paper support, the work should be framed with a mat, cap molding and glass. I like to use a museum quality AR reflective free acrylic glass. This is rather expensive but it certainly makes a difference. Often I use a double warm white inner and outer mat that is 3 1/2 inches around the artwork. Sometimes I use a single warm white linen mat with a classic gold or silver fillet on the interior edge.

If the casein painting is done on a linen panel, wood panel, Aquabord® panel or gessoed panel, the work will not need glass. It can be framed with a single molding that sets off the work. For large paintings that are 24" x 36" or larger, I like to use a 3 inch linen wrapped wood liner with a cap molding. If this is done right, the linen completely wraps the molding and does not show the miter.

If the casein panel is not covered with glass, the artist has two choices. The painting can be gently buffed with cotton balls to bring the painting to a dull luster that is quite beautiful. The second choice it is to use a spray varnish. I would allow the casein painting to dry for 10 days or so before applying the varnish. I use the UV archival acrylic varnish that has a satin finish. With this varnish the casein retains its beautiful visual quality.

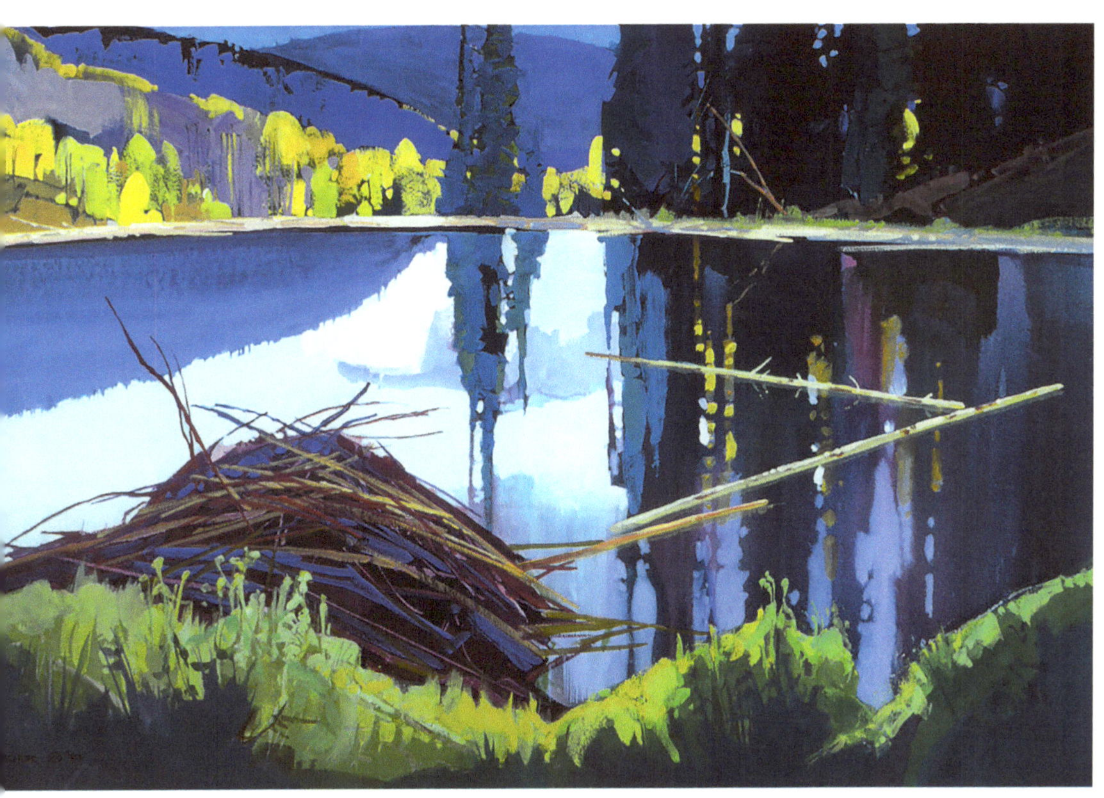

Beaver Lodge, Deer Horn Park
1995
casein, 26" x 34"
Collection of Tedd & Christine Benson

Walter Greathouse Award and Medal American Watercolor Society

3 From Inspiration to Finished Work

I feel we paint to touch our souls. To do this we need to take risks, to find our own "voice" and discover what we uniquely want to express. I talk to painters frequently who say that they lose track of time when in the process of painting. Suddenly four hours have passed without notice. For this reason I encourage sketching and taking notes when there is an inspiration. I call these "working sketches." They're not sketches that we are going to sell, but are used as reference for a particular expression. These can be used as notes on color, value, and approach to composition.

I have found the hard way that when that inspiration hits I must take note of the sensations and record them quickly. I have, for instance, been driving down a quiet road and out the corner of my eye noticed an interesting pattern of light and shadow moving across ice and open water, and snow against a bank of sunlit spruce. Because I don't have time to stop, I take note of the time and exact place, knowing that I'll come back the next day to do the sketch. When I return the next day I am not inspired! What happened? The sunlight is the same and the subject is the same. The inspiration that impacted me is not the same. I must record it immediately or it is gone. As you'll see in the next few pages, the initial line drawing can just be a few scratches and a few notes, but it is enough information. I will then come back to do a more complex drawing with some color notes to work out my composition. It's important for me not get too much detail in my working drawings. I want enough to retain my inspiration but I want enough leeway for discovery when I start the painting. Discovery is the key to the magic that happens in the painting process.

Recently with the availability of the cell phone and tablet there are times when I'm out hiking or skiing, that I take some notes and a quick photograph or two. This is especially useful when I am with friends and don't have time to sketch. However, when I'm back at the studio I put the photograph on my monitor for sketching and take more notes. When finished I put the photograph away and work from my sketches.

I have drawers filled with these working drawings. This is my library and my "brain." I can look at these drawings and remember where I was, what the day was like, and who I was with. If somehow I lost my paintings that would be huge. But if I lost my containers of drawings over the years I would be devastated. On these next few pages I will demonstrate working sketches to finished paintings.

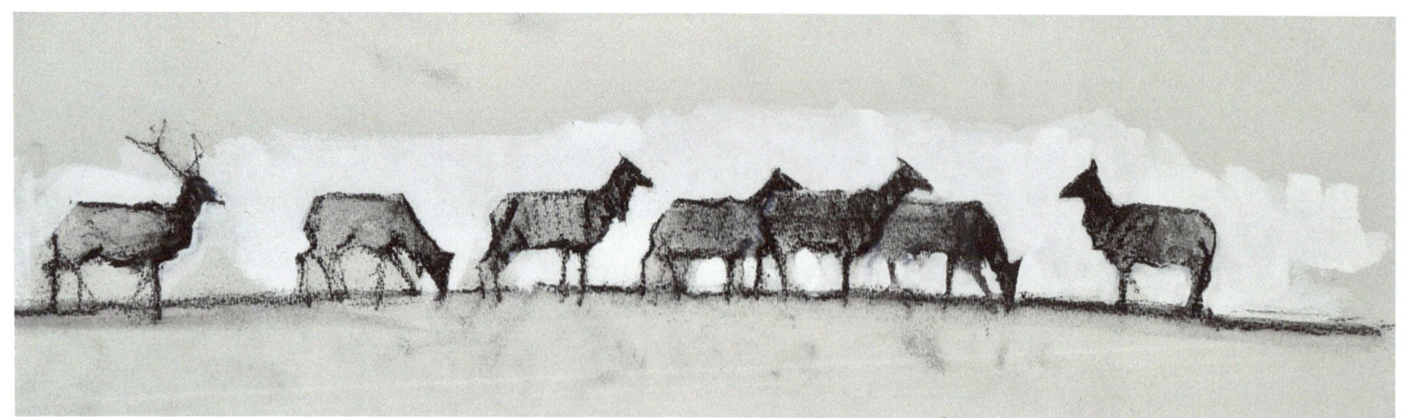

In this country there is an abundance of wildlife and many times they are close to my studio. I grab my pen or pencil and jot a few lines to capture the essence of the animal.

Sketch of Elk
6" x 20"
Charcoal with white highlights on toned paper

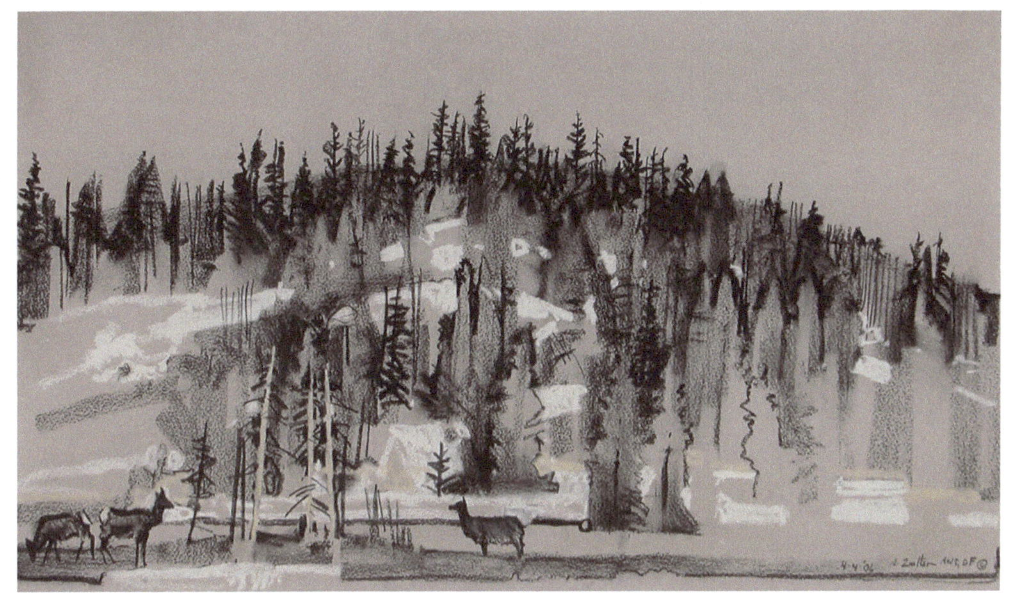

Charcoal drawing for Ghost Trees

18" x 29" Pressed charcoal with white charcoal highlights on gray toned paper

I drove by this spot one evening on the way to visit friends. I took note of the time and the mood of the subject. The mountain patterns and ghost trees were in cool shadow against the afterglow of the sunset. I went back the next day and did this charcoal sketch on a green toned paper and used white pastel to put in the snow pocket highlights.

The aura of the red orange gradated upwards to the neutral top of the sky against the cool shadow of the mountain and "ghost trees", resonated with me. I decided to keep the color scheme very simple to accentuate the mood. The red orange note of the sky was the complement of the neutral blue and blue-green. It was the perfect choice to create the mood I wanted to convey.

Ghost Trees 2006

watercolor & casein, 21" x 29"

Private Collection

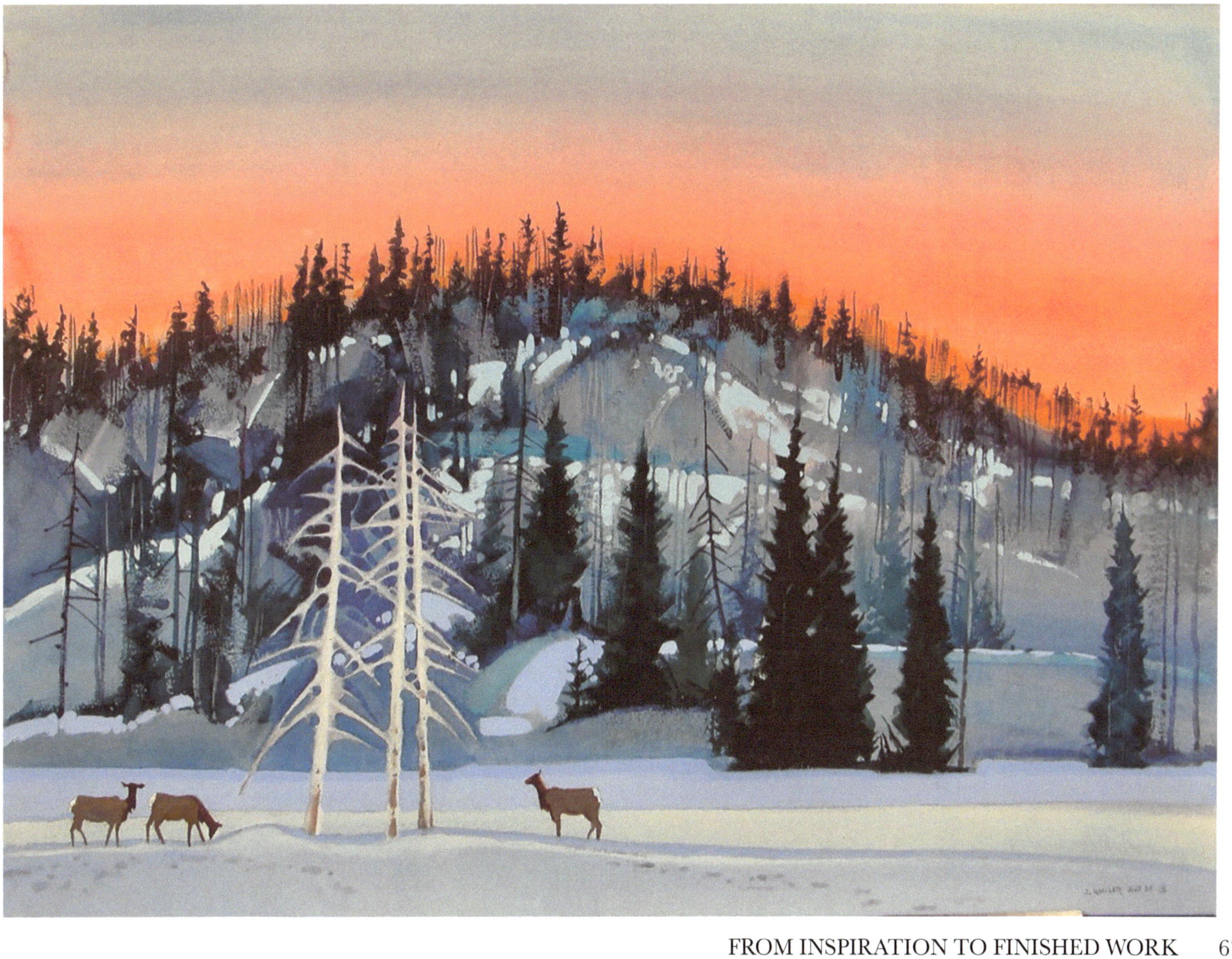

Raking Light

This subject is a good example demonstrating the process from start to finish in my studio paintings. I begin by sketching on site. This page shows a photo of me sketching at the site, and the rough line of the drawing. I then took it to the studio and developed a horizontal composition with a litho crayon and casein on toned paper. These were all used for information to do the final painting.

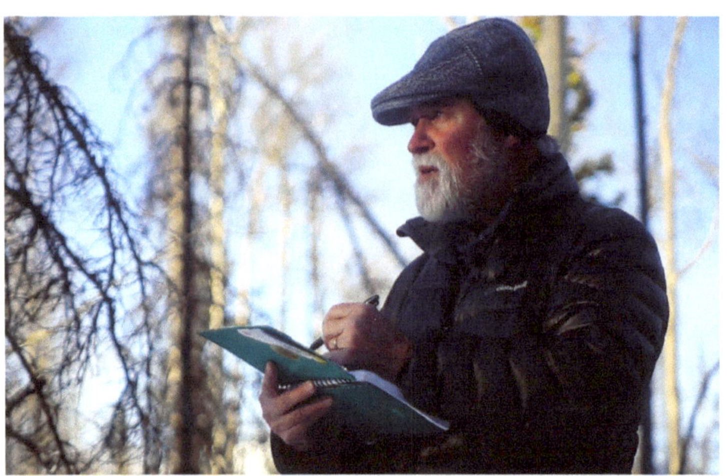

This is a photo of me sketching on location, the inspiration for the painting "Raking Light." I was doing the sketch as the sun was sinking behind the distant mountain. I wanted to retain the edge of the sun burning through with the light and shadows radiating in a symmetrical way.

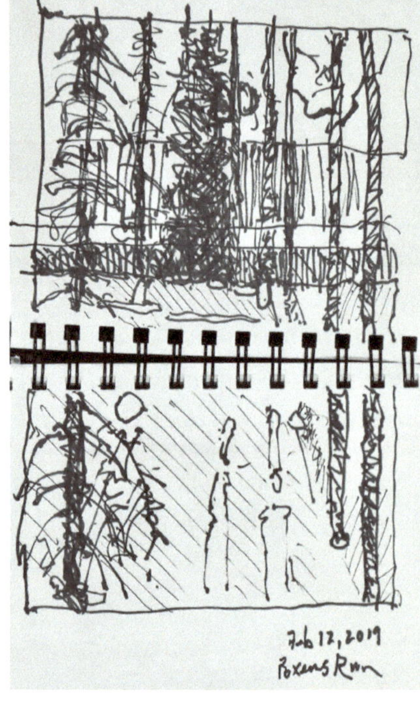

Sketch for Raking Light

permanent marker on sketch paper, 12"x 8"

I did this sketch while on a late light cross-country ski. It was probably less than 20°F. I needed to use my hand out of the glove so I was moving quickly. Normally when I go skiing I'm not looking for subject matter but I always carry a sketchbook. Then when I have that moment, I'm ready.

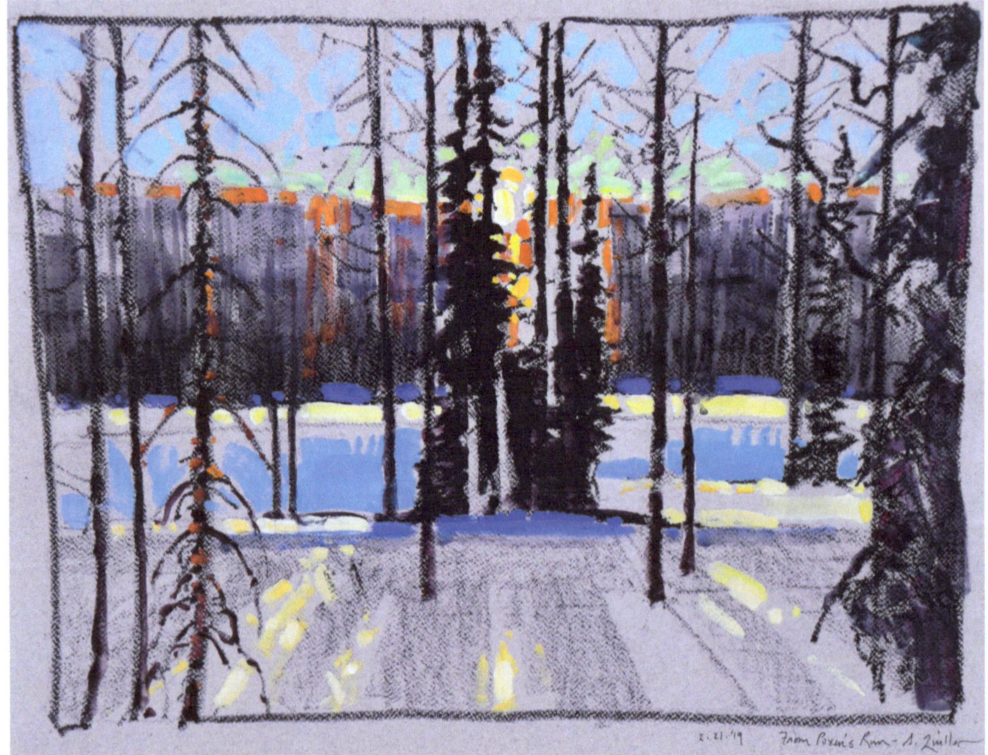

Back in the studio I took this initial sketch and decided I wanted to paint a horizontal composition with radiating light and shadow, basically a symmetrical composition that connotes a universal majestic quality. I did this drawing on toned paper with a litho crayon, and did the color highlights with casein.

Study for Raking Light

litho crayon & casein on toned paper, 19 ½" x 25 ½"

Raking Light *2019*

Watercolor and casein with transparent acrylic under wash, 21 3/4" x 30",
Private Collection, AWS exhibition 2020

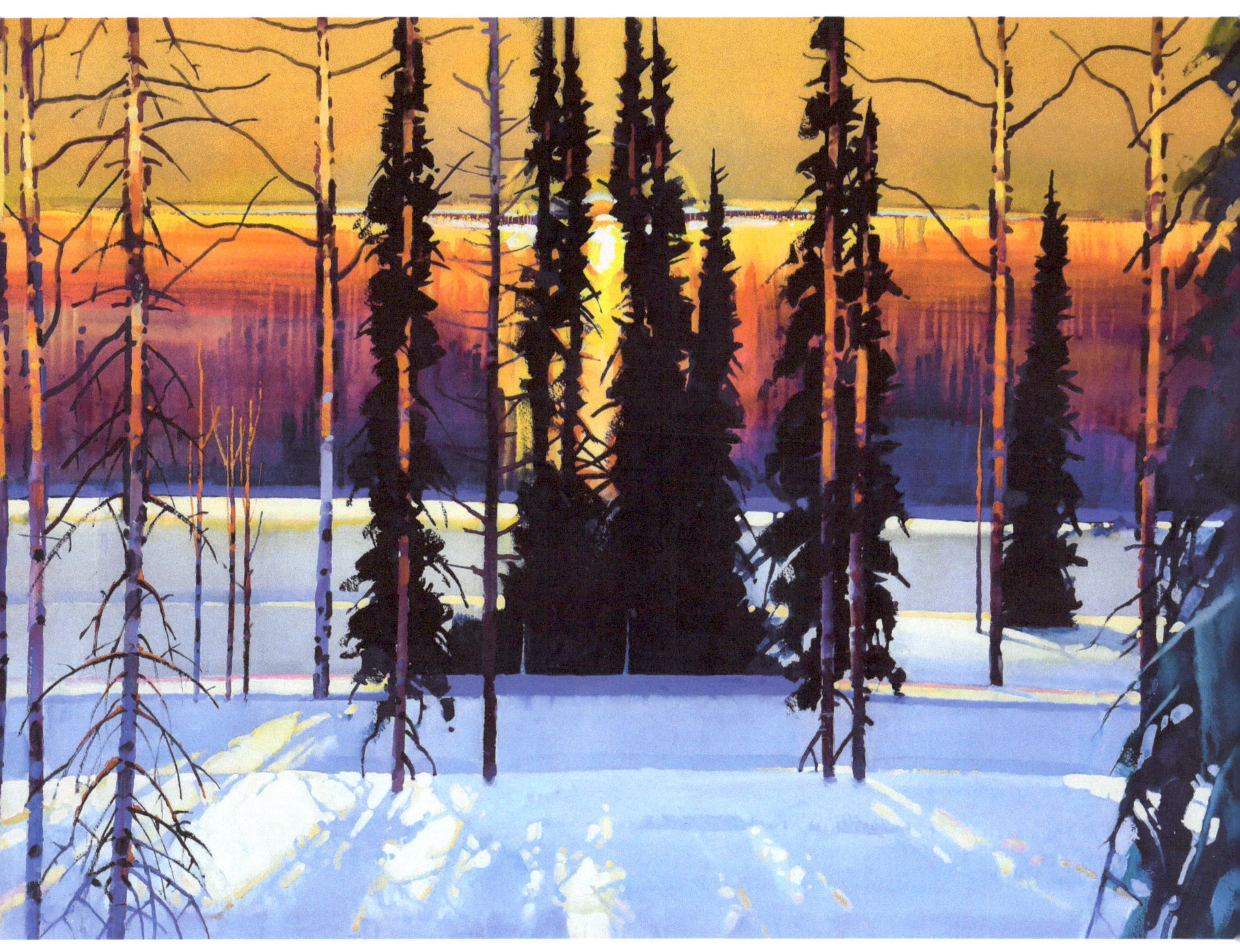

While working on this painting, I thought about the importance of the division of space in the composition as seen in the long, parallel horizontal rectangles.

Soft Day, Sheep Drive

I love a damp, soft day in the summer. We have so much sun here that it's a welcome contrast. Each late June a sheep drive passes by my studio. The sheep herders are taking them to the high country for summer pastures. I welcome this time and take a couple of days to follow the flock, sketching and photographing. This is always inspiration for painting material.

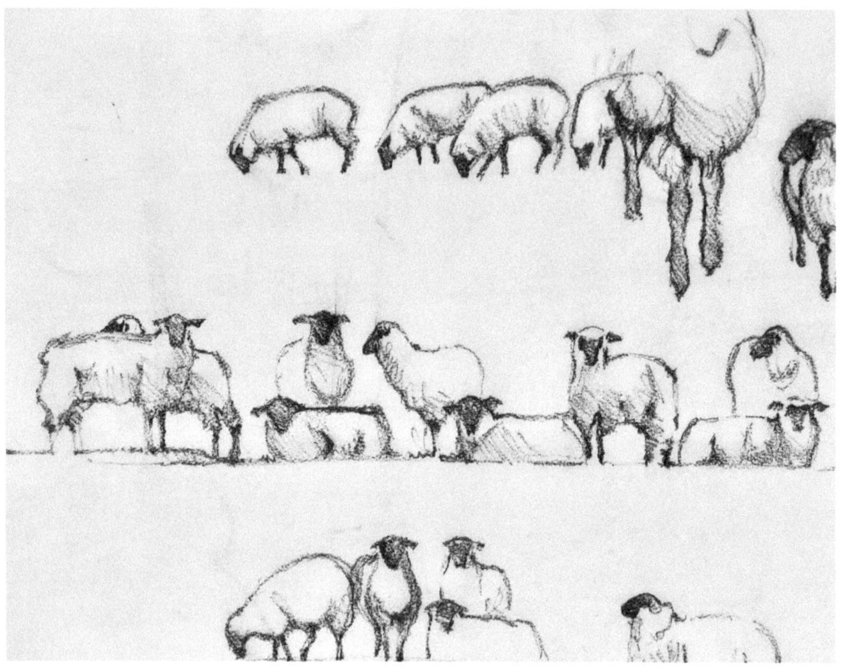

Sheep Sketch
Charcoal on white printmaking paper
16" x 18"

Many times I take a digital photograph of the sheep, and project them up on my monitor to do a series of studies. I can use these drawings for many paintings.

This is a quick study I did with a #2 litho crayon on gray toned paper, of the mountain across the road from my studio with the sheep passing. I've captured the soft day and emphasize the tree patterns with the rhythm of the sheep moving by.

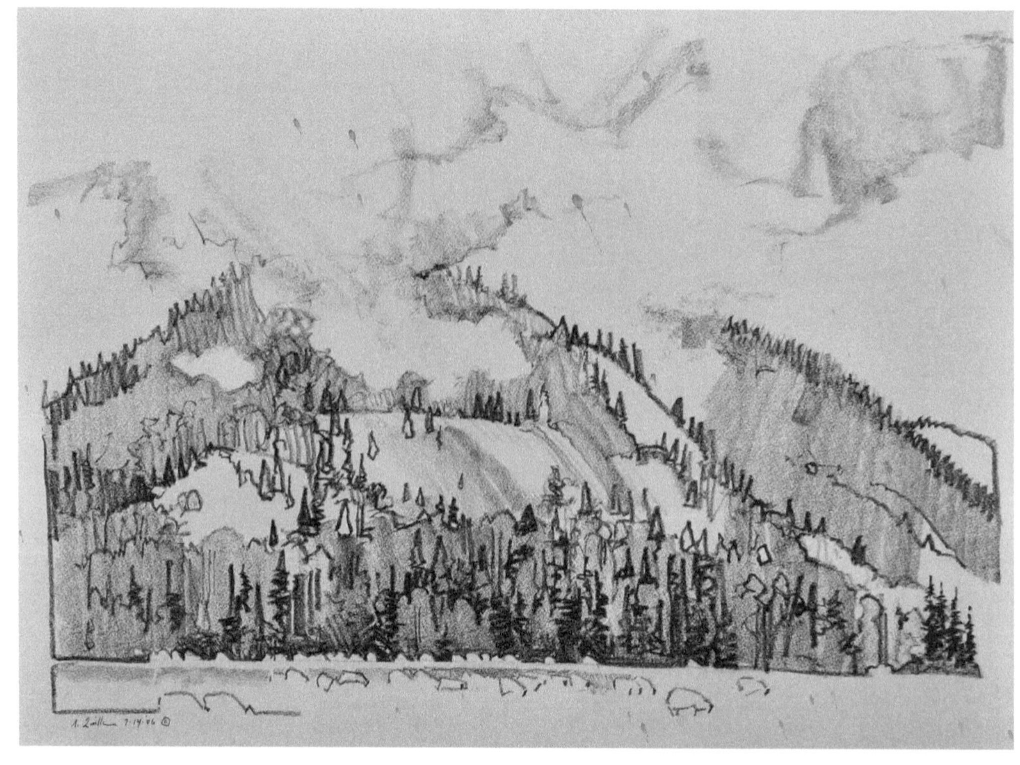

Study for Soft Day, Sheep Drive
litho crayon on toned pastel paper
22" x 30"

Soft Day, Sheep Drive 2009
casein, 28" x 34", Private Collection

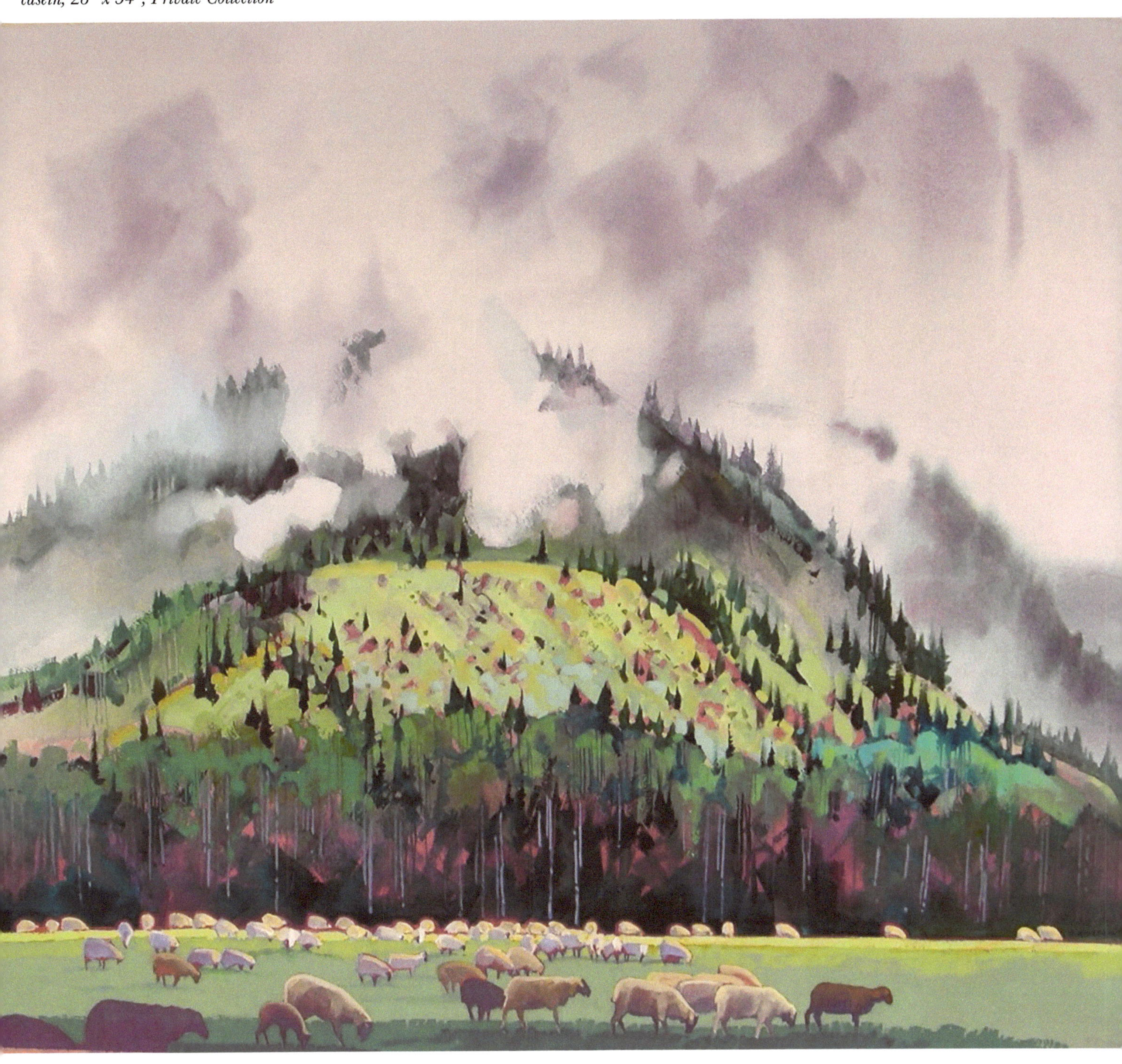

I chose a heavy cold press watercolor paper for this painting to capture the damp quality of the day. I started very wet with the casein, as seen in the softness in the distant mountain. There is a deep magenta as an under color in the earth and trees. This is also the complement of the yellow greens and greens that are predominant in the composition.

Deer Crossing

Deer Crossing
(right) 2018
casein on transparent acrylic, 35" x 25"
Private Collection

We live in a place overlooking the Rio Grande River. When the water is low we often see a small herd of deer crossing the river. Sometimes there are ten or more deer crossing one behind the other in single file. In the finished painting I actually incorporated two different mountain forms and put them together. The bottom half the composition is what I see from my studio. However, the upper snow patterns and mountain forms come from an area a few miles east of my studio. I love the snow patterns in the diagonal draw of the canyon.

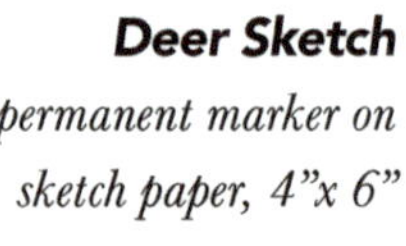

Deer Sketch
permanent marker on sketch paper, 4"x 6"

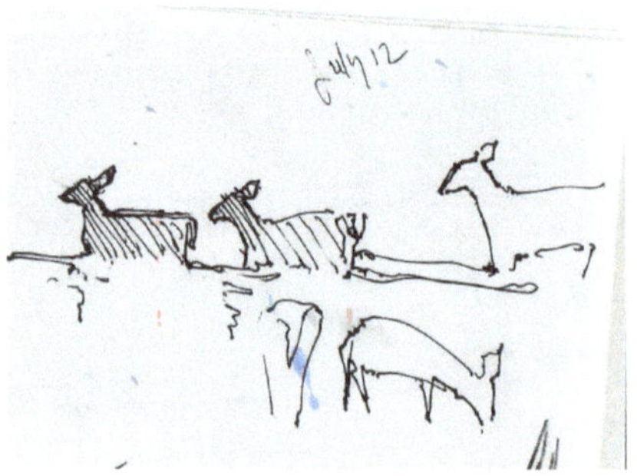

This is what I call an information sketch. It is a simple line drawing capturing the movement of the deer entering and swimming in the water. As I use this for reference, there is paint spattered on the paper as well as a note-July 12. That must be the day when I did the sketch.

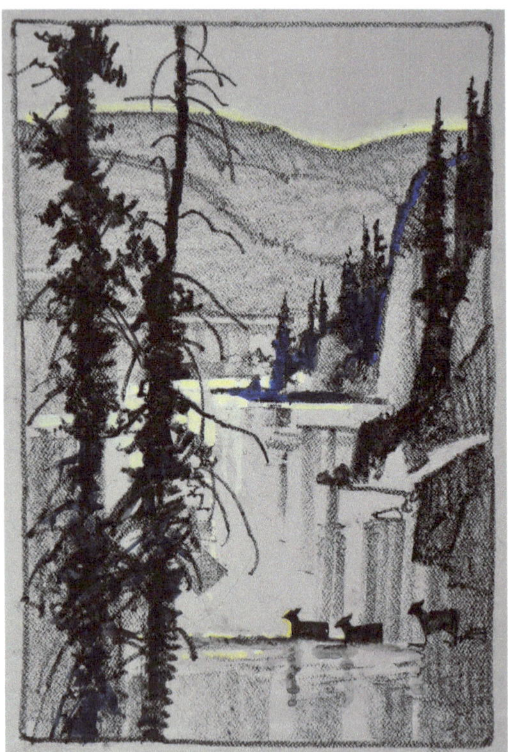

Study for Deer Crossing #1
Litho crayon with gouache highlights 25 ½" x 19 ½"

I did this litho drawing with casein highlights on the deck looking down river from my studio. This is a view that I paint often. Here I sketched a few deer crossing the stream.

Study for Deer Crossing #2 *(below)*
Litho crayon with casein highlights on toned pastel paper 25 ½" x 19 ½"

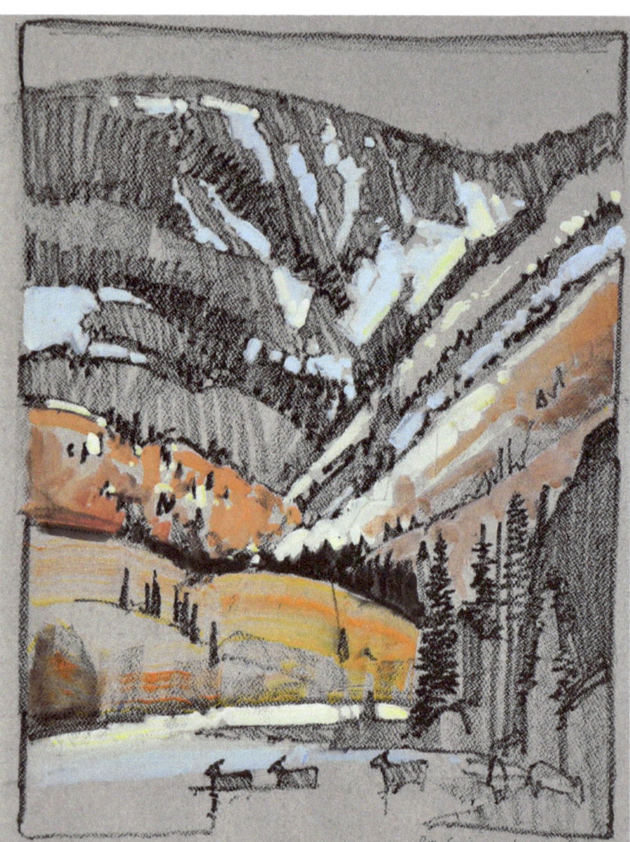

In this drawing I incorporated the view from my studio in the lower portion and added a second view of a place that is called "Dry Gulch." I incorporated the two together because I love the snow patterns from the sketch of "Dry Gulch." I did this on a gray pastel paper with black litho crayon and casein for the colored highlights.

I set up my studies close to my easel when I did this finished painting. I was aware of the repetition of diagonals in the curvilinear rhythm and movement in the painting. I also focused on the spacing of the negative patterns around the deer.

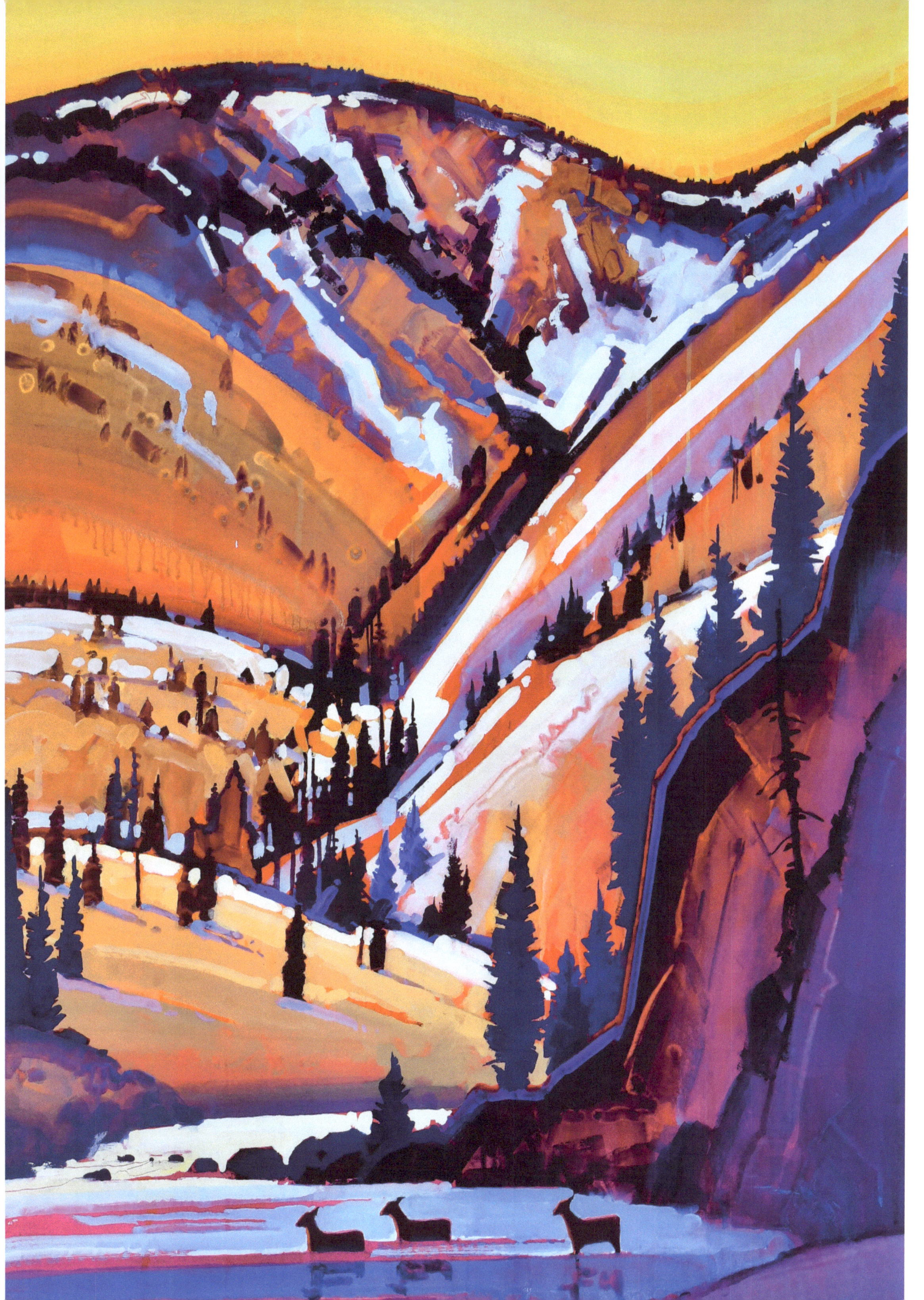

Storm on Shallow Creek

I feel it is important, if possible, to place yourself in a situation for your inspiration. For instance, if you love painting flowers, develop a beautiful flower garden. If you love painting people, place yourself in a situation where you're surrounded with figures of interest. Or, if you are in the city and are inspired by the shapes and light there, take advantage of the range of subject matter at hand. I love nature and live surrounded by it. I was in our house looking out the window when I saw an incoming storm. I grabbed a small piece of paper, did a quick line drawing, and took some notes.

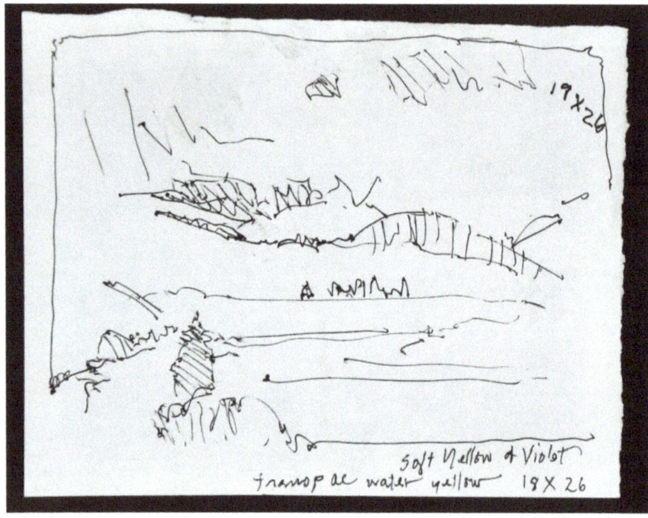

Storm on Shallow Creek Sketch
permanent marker on sketch paper
4" x 6"

As you can see, this is a very quick line sketch. If you had not seen the final painting I'm sure you would have trouble figuring out what this is. These few lines along with the notes below are enough. They say "Soft yellow and violet-transparent acrylic water-yellow"

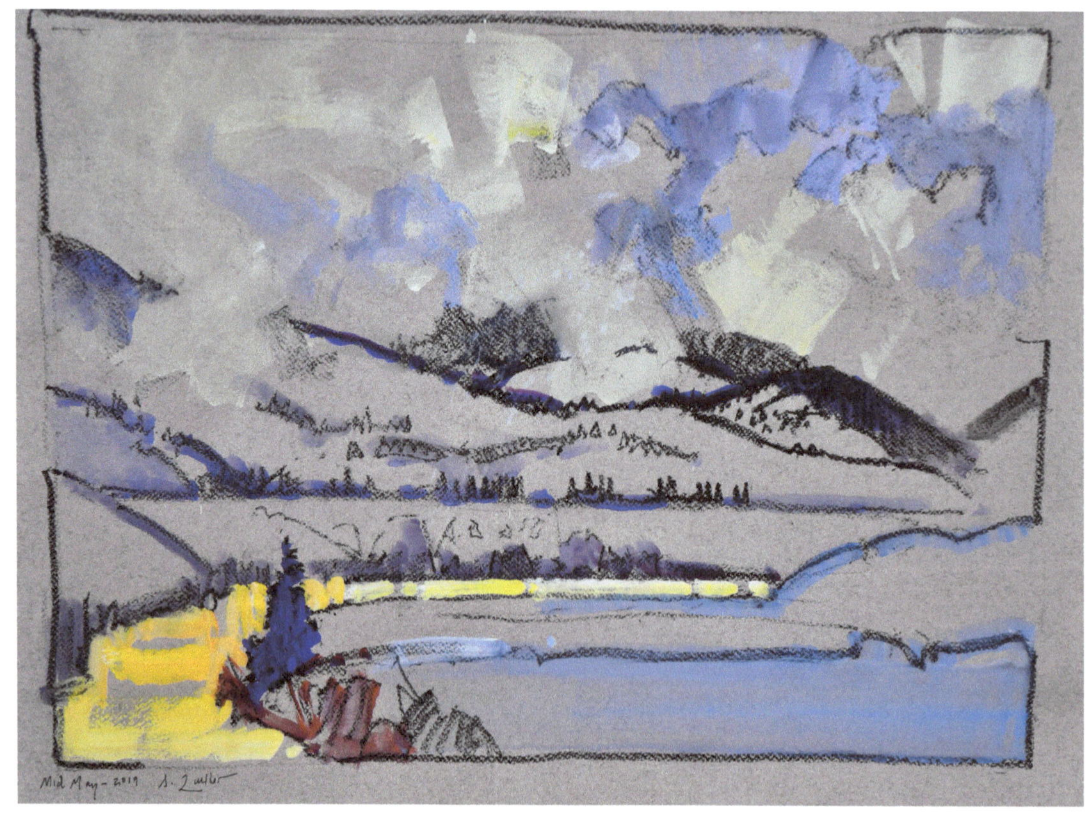

I took that initial sketch much further. Now I'm looking at the mountain, sketching with a #2 litho crayon and adding yellow and violet highlights with casein. I did this on toned paper. The key was that strong yellow white of the water against that dark blue violet spruce.

Study for Storm on Shallow Creek
litho crayon & casein on toned paper
16" x 18"

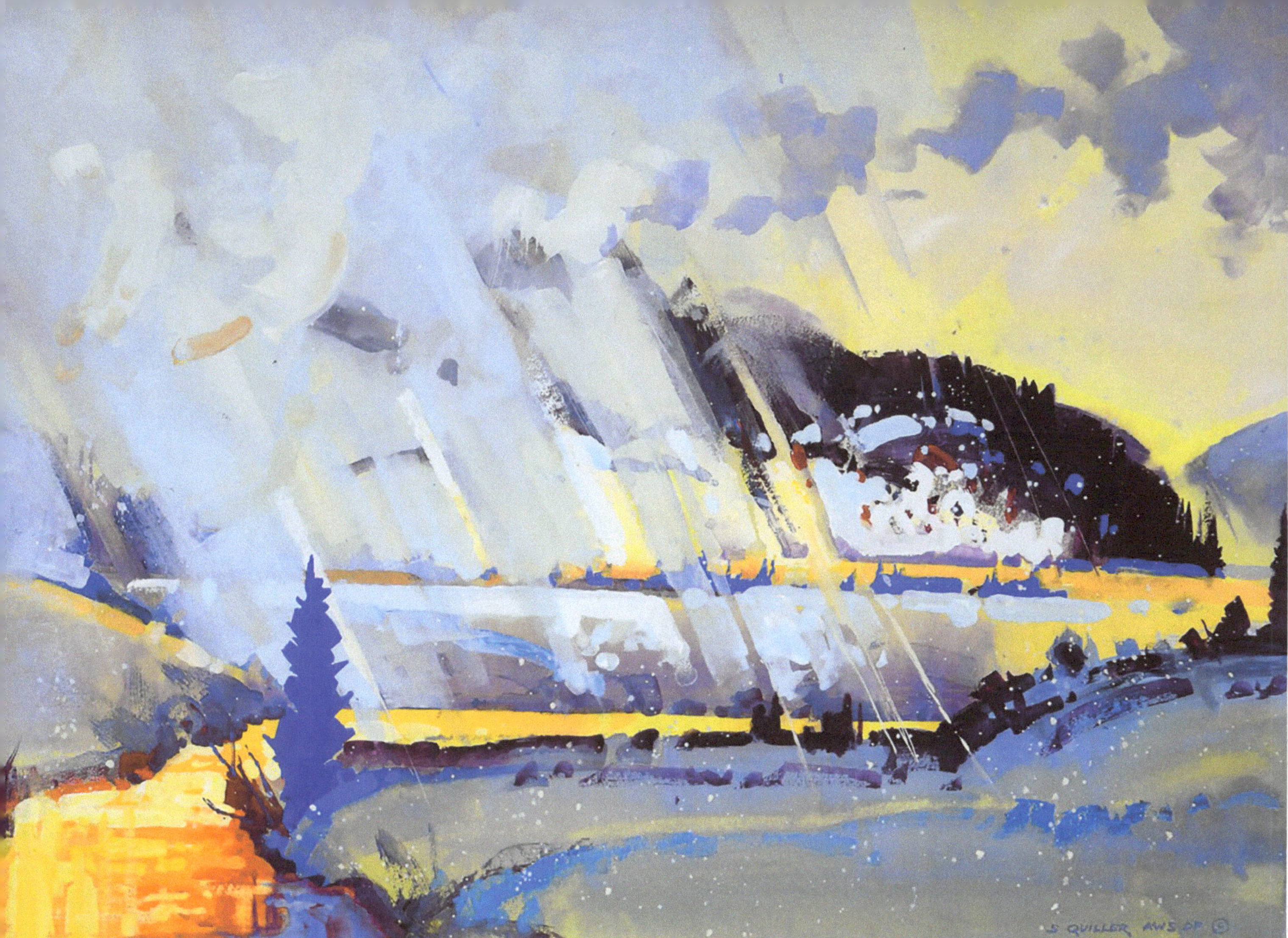

Storm on Shallow Creek 2019
Casein with transparent acrylic underwash., 16" x 24"
Collection of Stephen Dyer

In the final composition I wanted to keep the paint moving free and feel like a storm. First I put a thin transparent yellow to yellow orange acrylic wash on the cold press watercolor board. Then I re-wet the paper and charged in cloudy white-violet translucent casein as well as the opaque blacks and ultramarine blues. I intentionally let the paint spatter to have a feeling of immediacy and freedom.

Exercise #1 Pick a simple subject, landscape, still life or figure and do a simple line drawing with the intention of turning the sketch into a finished painting. Write a few notes at the edge in terms of composition and color relationships that are important. On the surface of your choice, set up your casein palette and do a small finished work.

Exercise#2 Pick the simple subject of your choice and do a line drawing. Take some notes as to the mood, color and composition. Now on a sheet of gray toned pastel paper do a more detailed litho drawing working out the value. With the casein palette build to the lights and add some important color notes. Do the finished casein painting referring to these studies.

Exercise#3 On your tablet or phone, locate a subject you would like to paint. On a sheet of pastel paper do a litho crayon drawing, and follow it up with casein for highlights and important color notes. Using this study do a finished casein painting with the support of your choice.

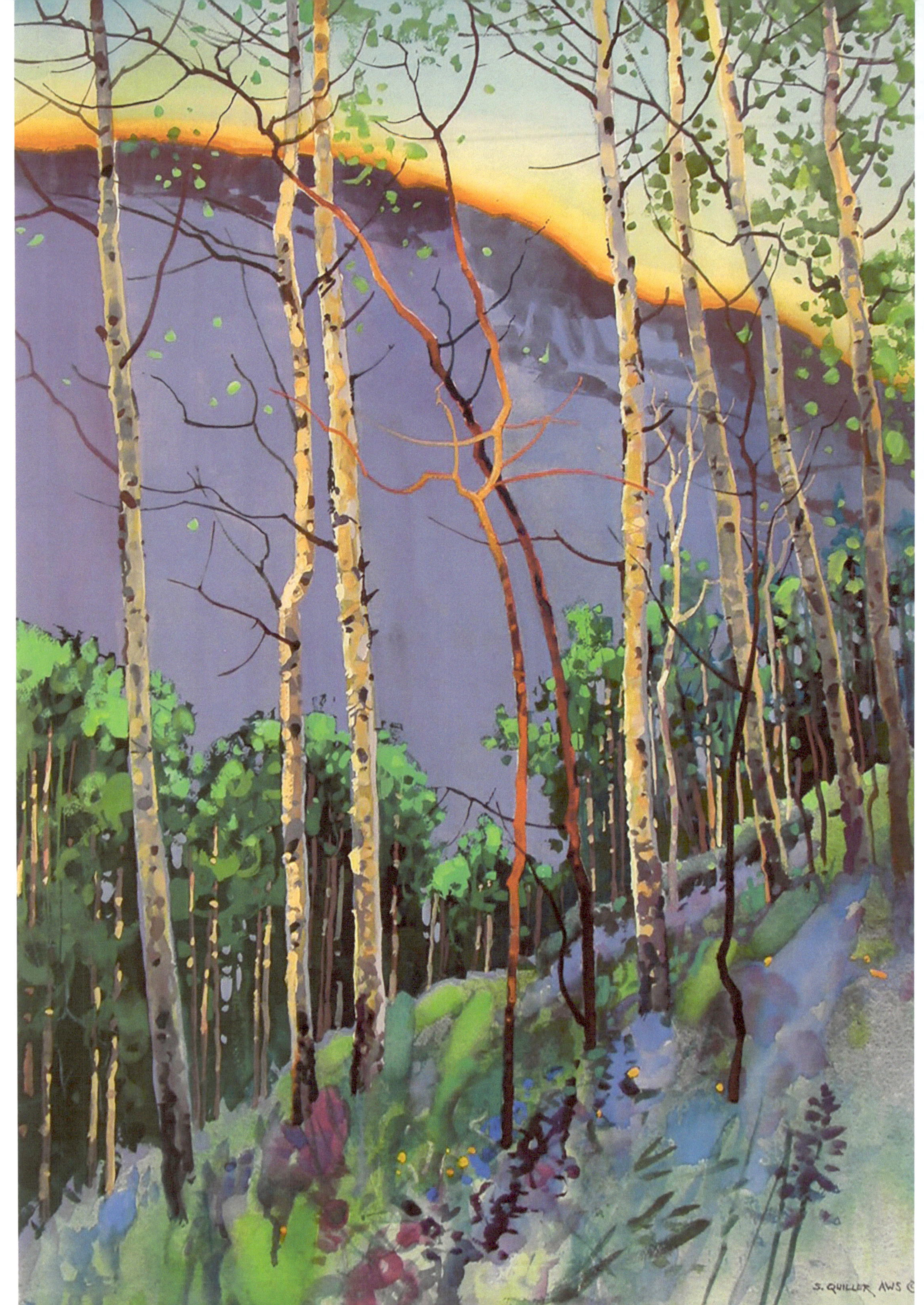
S. QUILLER AWS ©

Blue Mountain Lupin, Shallow Creek
(left) 2005
casein & watercolor
34" x 26"
Private Collection

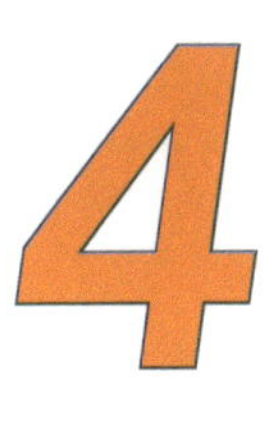

Casein and its Many Moods

Back in the early 60s when I was beginning my teenage years, I took some lessons in watercolor painting. Darrell "Skip" Elliott was my first teacher and he provided a strong foundation on technique in the handling of the medium. A few years later I studied with Thomas Curry, also a watercolor painter, who emphasized color theory. These two people were most important in my training. Later in college I worked with oil painting and then printmaking, an art form that I do to this very day.

However, I kept coming back to watercolor. I loved the spiritual quality of the medium and the way the paint moved on paper. It forced me to be in the moment when the paint was interacting with water. However, I then took the watercolor foundation and began expanding to the other water media: acrylic, casein, and gouache. I found that each medium had its own handling characteristics and visual qualities, qualities that I couldn't achieve in transparent watercolor. I started working with casein in the early 70s and have found that it is a very unique and beautiful medium! It has a velvety-matte visual quality unlike any other. In fact, looking back, it has taken me over 50 years to be able to do justice to writing a book about this medium. In this five decade process I have learned the intricacies of the medium and what it can truly do. The visual quality of this paint can capture the atmosphere, and the solidity of form, like no other. This chapter will demonstrate how I've used this medium for all types of subject matter. Here I will demonstrate some of those subjects that I think best can be best expressed with casein.

I did this painting (left) primarily on location, and applied the finishing touches in my studio. It is almost a two mile hike to get to this location, so carrying the painting board and paper, along with plein air easel, paint, lunch, and all the accessories was not easy. I did most of the foreground in watercolor with touches of casein. But as I moved into the aspen tree forms and the distant hazy blue violet mountain sky, casein was the medium to capture the dryness, the density, and the smells of nature.

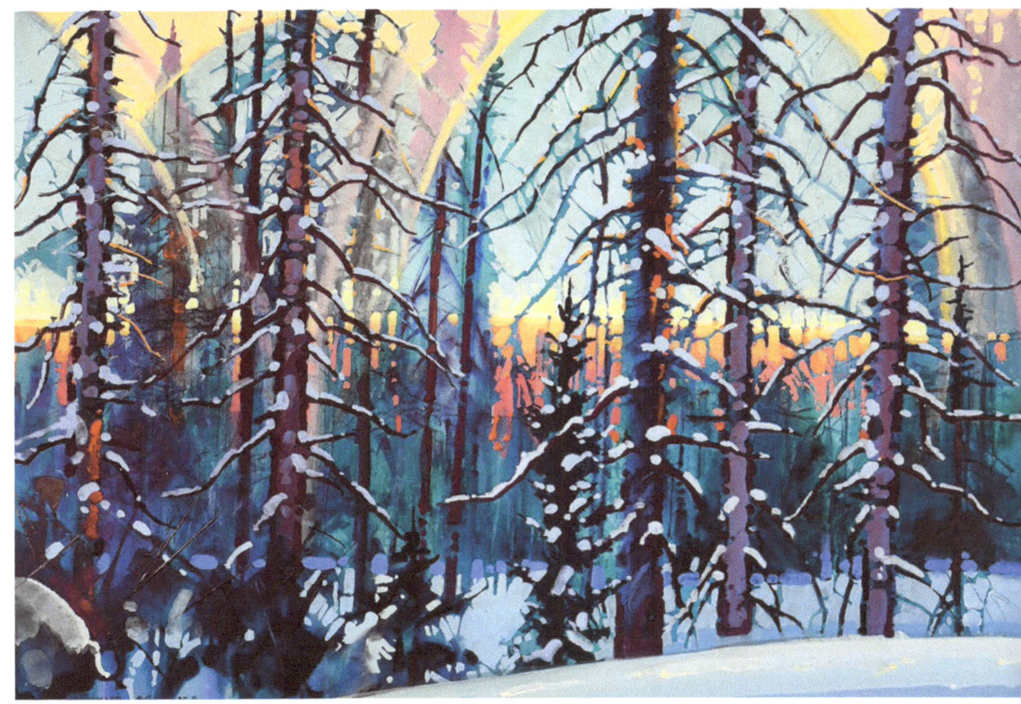

Sanctuary Shelter *2019*
casein, 22" x 34"
Collection of Bill and Teri Smith

When I ski through the woods, more and more I sense the interconnectedness of all living forms. The tree trunks and shrubs in overlapping branch forms, the snow patterns in the distant hills, and the late shimmering light are all part of this experience. I have used casein here to capture the density of snow, the solidity of the mountain forms, and atmospheric late light.

Casein and Adobe

Casein is the perfect medium to capture the texture, the dryness and the earthiness of adobe. Here are two of the many paintings that demonstrate the medium with this subject.

This was a beautiful spring morning in Alamos, Mexico. I spent a week there painting with a couple of close artist friends. I worked directly onsite, painting the façade of this church. I was particularly interested in the figures that came and went while I was painting. In my small sketchbook I did some line drawings of the figures, some sitting on the steps and some lost in conversation. I then incorporated them into the painting.

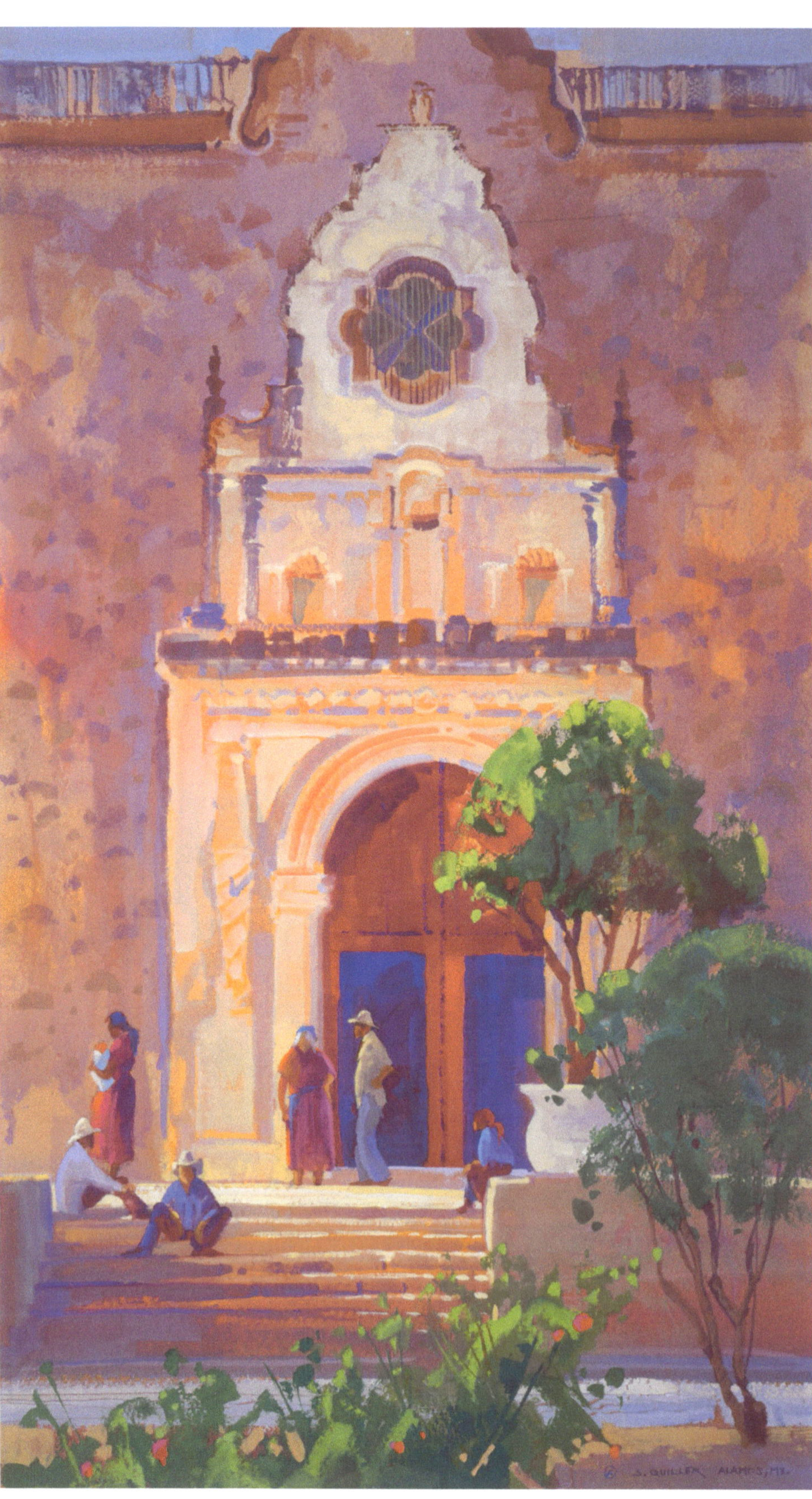

Colonial Church, Alamos, Mexico
1997
casein, 29" x 19"
Private Collection

Downtown Plaza, Alamos, Mexico *1997*

casein, 20" x 28", Artist's Collection

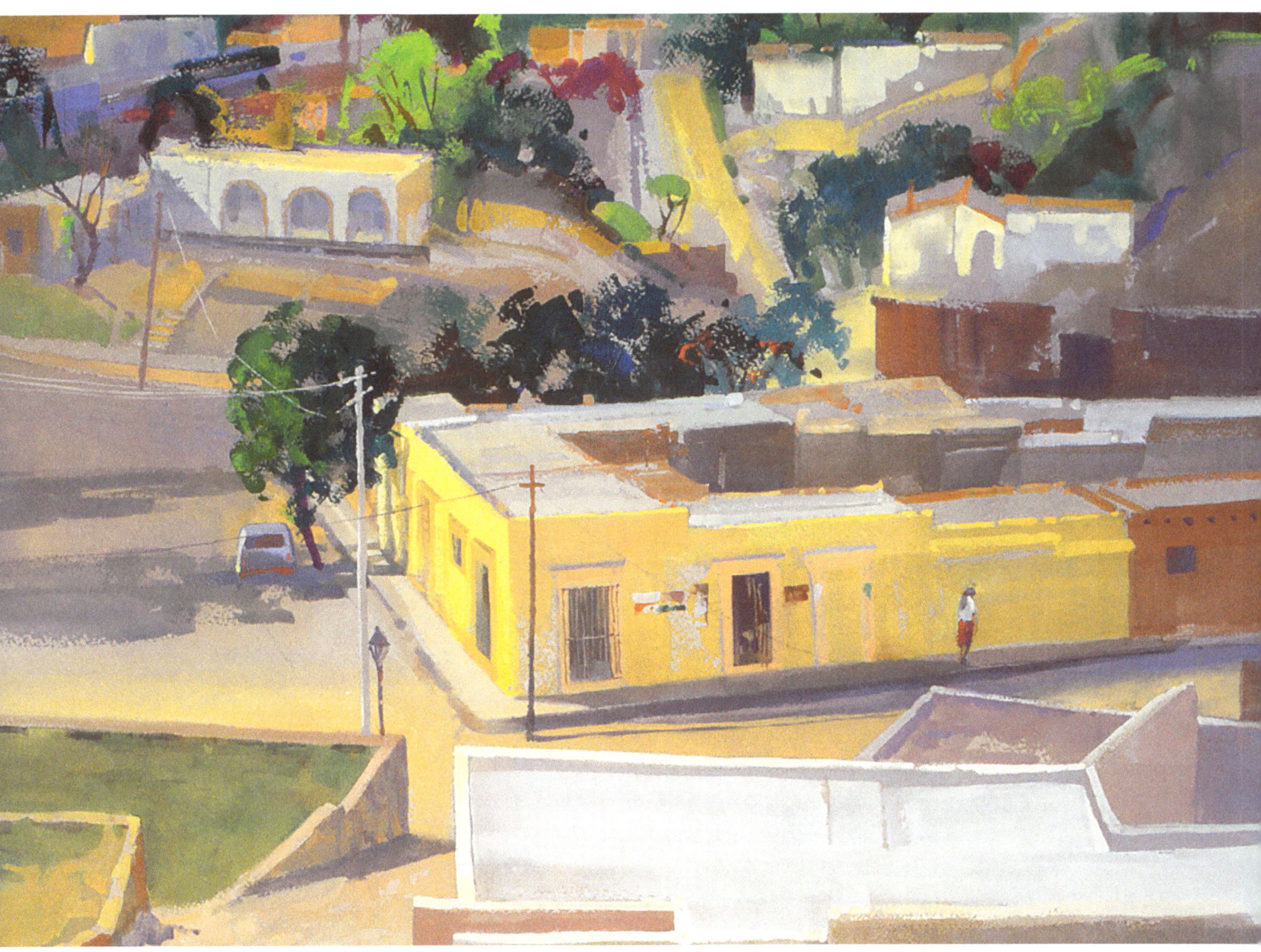

I remember this painting well. It was a very, very hot day and I was on a hill above some buildings with a bird's eye view of this composition. The abstract shapes were very interesting to me as well as the shadows and soft diagonal lines. The dusty dryness was best captured with casein. However, I had to constantly atomize my palette, as the paint was drying almost as fast as I could squeeze it out of the tube.

Atmospheric Storms and Casein

Casein is a water medium and thus can be handled much in the same way as watercolor, but with very different visual effects. Wet on wet applications can be achieved with casein similar to watercolor but with very different results. This juicy milk based paint charged into transparent, translucent or opaque areas can create beautiful organic textures and a creamy, velvety quality. Here are two examples working in this manner.

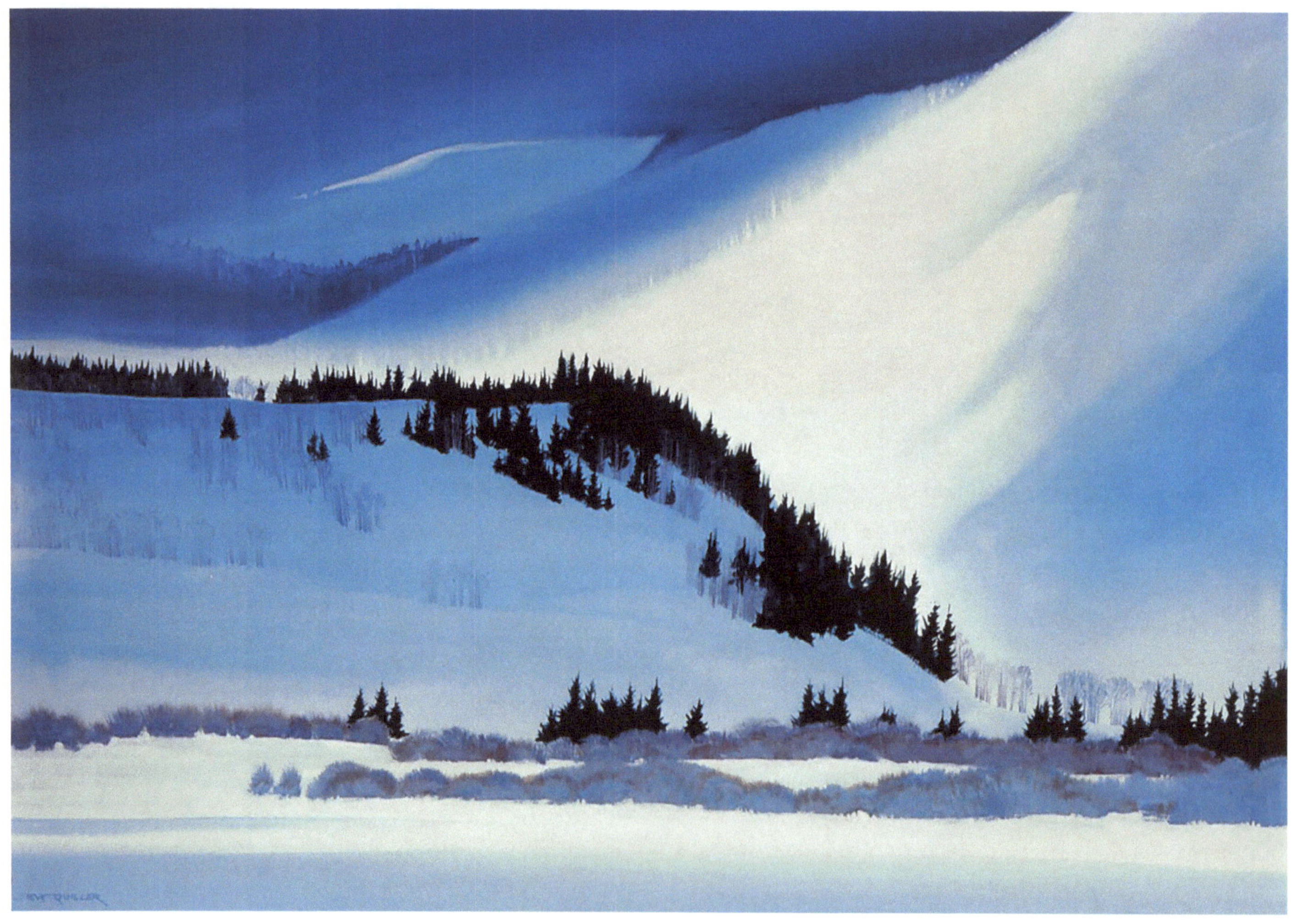

Snow Storm, McKenzie Stock Drive 1977
casein, 21" x 29" Private Collection

Back in the 1970s and early 80s this was the view from my studio. Miner's Creek runs along the valley floor and in the winter, elk feed along the willows. It is a beautiful view at all times of the year, but I especially enjoy watching winter storms. For this painting I chose an analogous cool palette, first wetting the cold press watercolor board, and then charging in the whites, blues, and violets. When the paint was dry I simply painted the foreground mountain, keeping the spruce, aspen, and willow forms very simple for the spareness of an Asian-like composition.

I love painting on cold press watercolor board with casein. There is something about the rigid support below the thin, mounted watercolor paper that moves the paint easily and helps when building layer on top of layer. This is a view of a prominent mountain in my area, the center of an ancient volcano called the Creede Caldera. I decided to use a predominantly yellow and violet color family palette. Beginning with a wet board I charged in the snow clouds. While the paint is wet there is a creamy quality to the medium as the 2 inch flat brush applies and lifts paint. Once dry I gradually built the mountain forms, dark against light, and warm against cool, while keeping a nice rhythm to the organic forms.

Storm on Snowshoe Mountain in Yellow and Violet *1992*
casein, 21" x 29", Collection of Rob Deacon

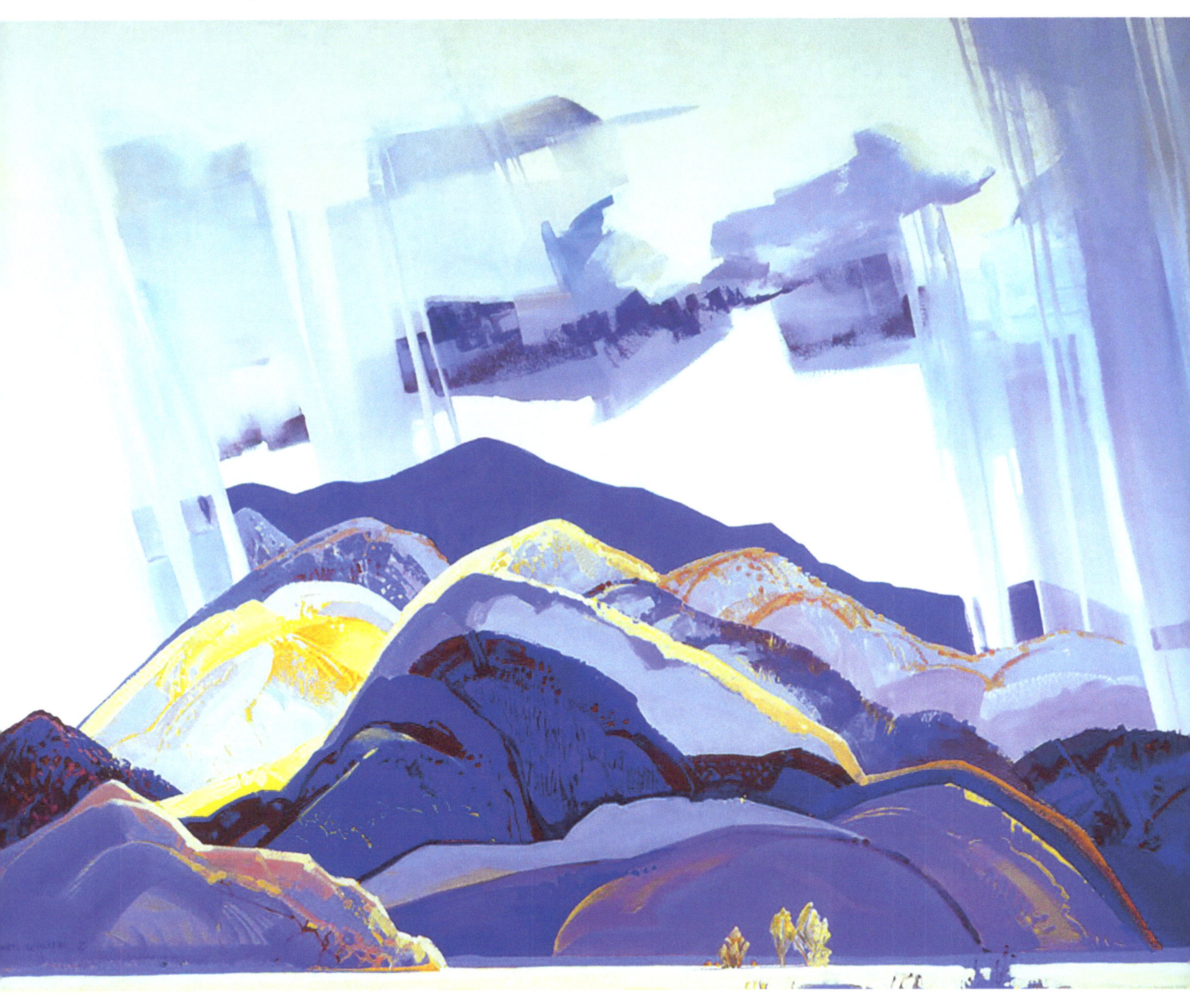

Moonlight and October Haze with Casein

Casein is the perfect medium for so many atmospheric effects. I can almost smell the atmosphere when I use this medium. In the high country of Colorado, on a still winter night with crystalline humidity in the air and a full moon, we can sometimes see what is called a "Moon Halo." It is much like a rainbow in the summer except that it's a halo circumference around the moon with iridescent colors.

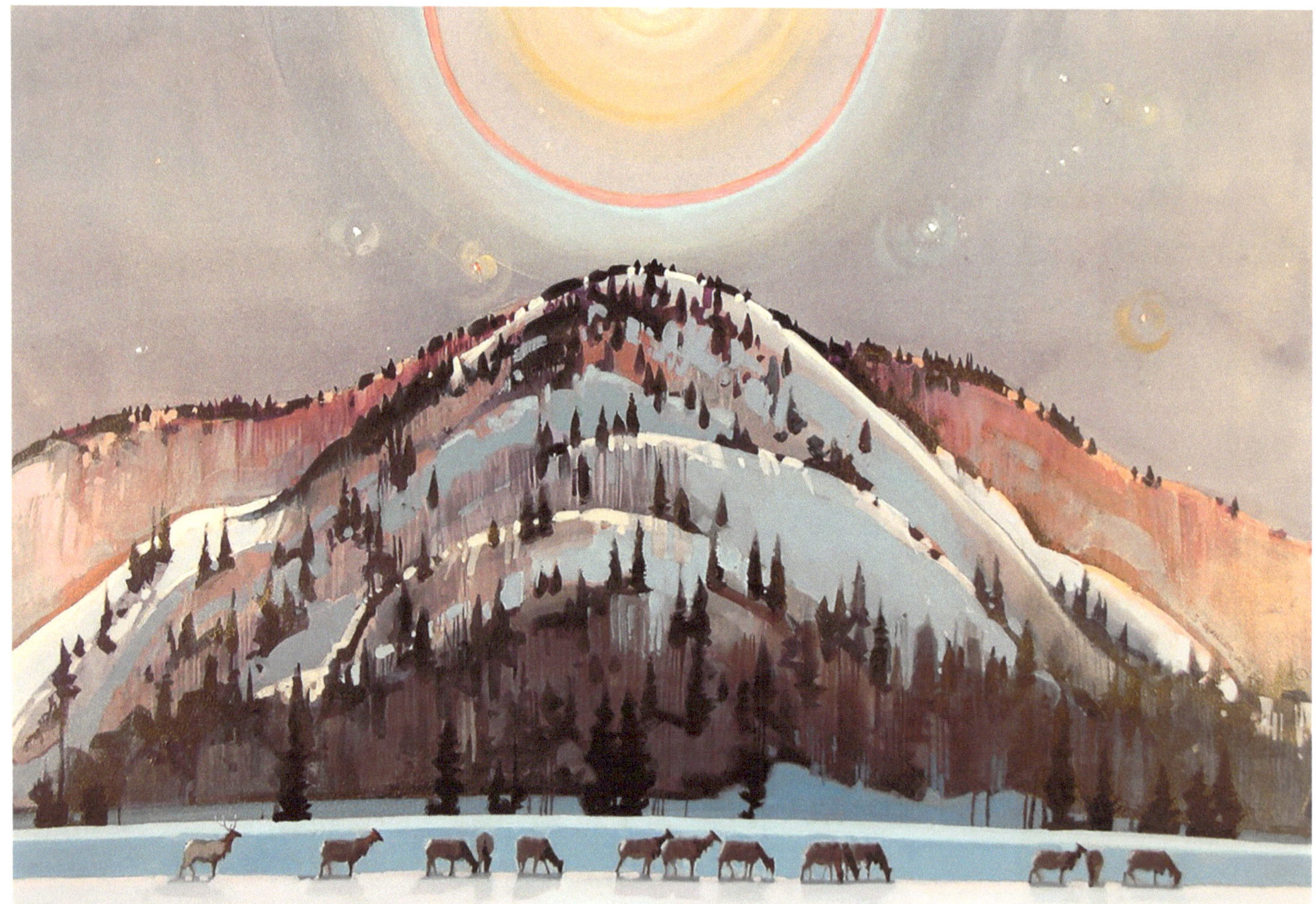

Moon Halo, Snow Shoe Mountain 2010
Casein with transparent acrylic under wash, 21" x 29"
Private Collection

Very seldom but occasionally when we have a full moon we see this atmospheric effect. There are crystalline particles permeating the air and the lighted full moon radiates a "moon halo." Its scientific name is "paraselene," meaning beside the moon. Casein captures this quality better than any medium I can imagine. On a full moon a herd of elk may also appear in the meadow. It is bright enough that you can actually see their shadows. In this painting I limit my palette to best capture this cold, crisp, radiant feeling.

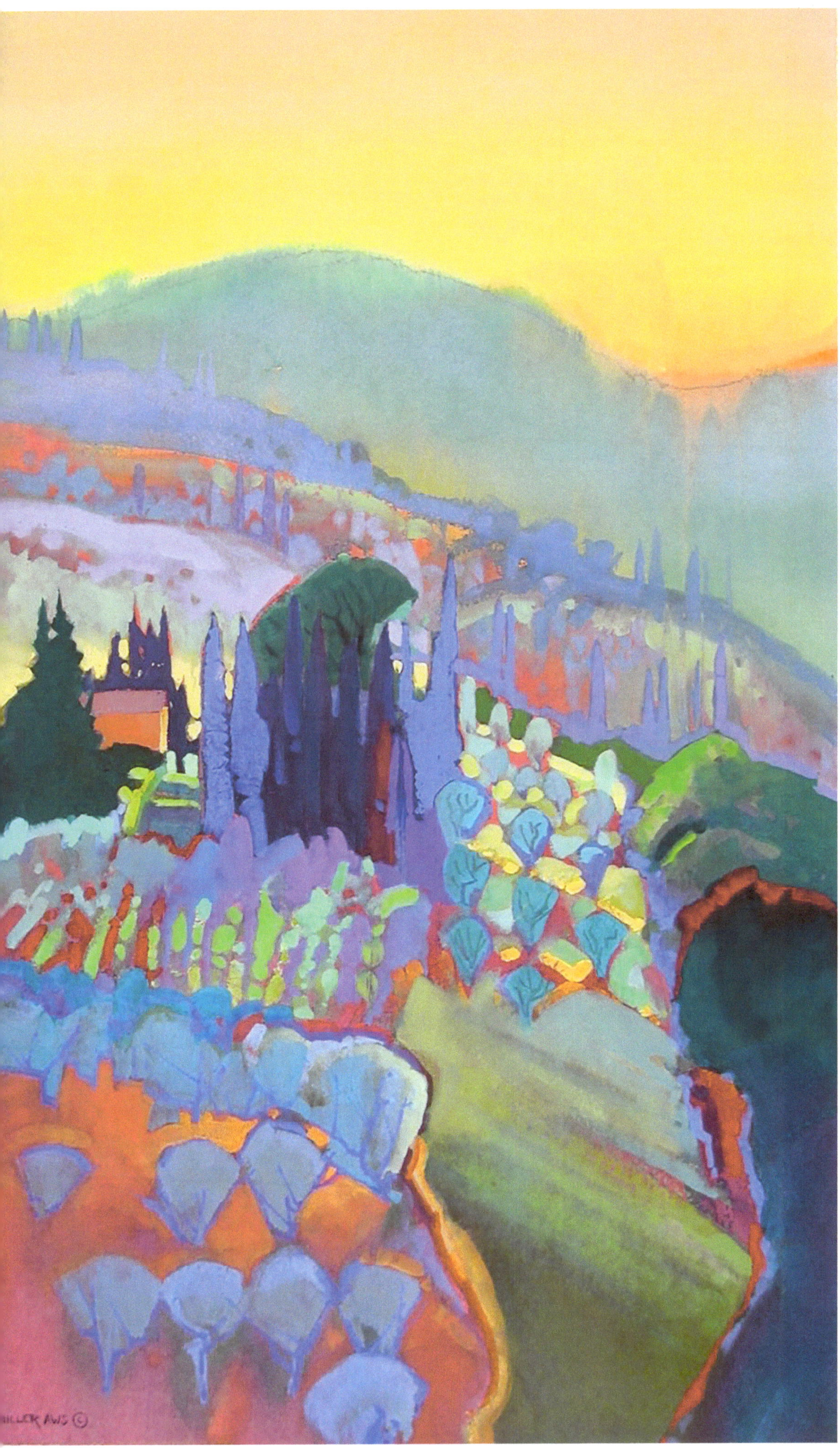

Early October, a Tuscan Hillside
2004
casein, 29" x 20"
Collection of David & Amanda Basler

I have had many occasions to spend autumn months in Tuscany. This particular time my family and I spent four months from late August through December. In October a soft blue haze fills the air. Locals are harvesting grapes and olives, and burning slash. Smoke fills the air and a density of light occurs. I did this painting on site simplifying and abstracting some of the shapes. There is nothing better than spending a day open-air, eating a few grapes, cheese and bread, and a dark chocolate bar while putting paint on paper.

Casein and Life

Although I do not consider myself a wildlife painter I have on occasion painted moose, elk, deer, dogs and cats and various birds. I believe that casein can emulate fur and feathers absolutely beautifully. I feel that cats are very interesting creatures and can also conform their bodies to any contour. On these next two pages are paintings I have done of cats, one exterior painted in 2018 and one interior painted in 1996. You'll see that I'm working with a sensuous curvilinear line throughout both paintings.

Wendy and Her Garden *2018*
casein, 24" x 34" Artist's Collection

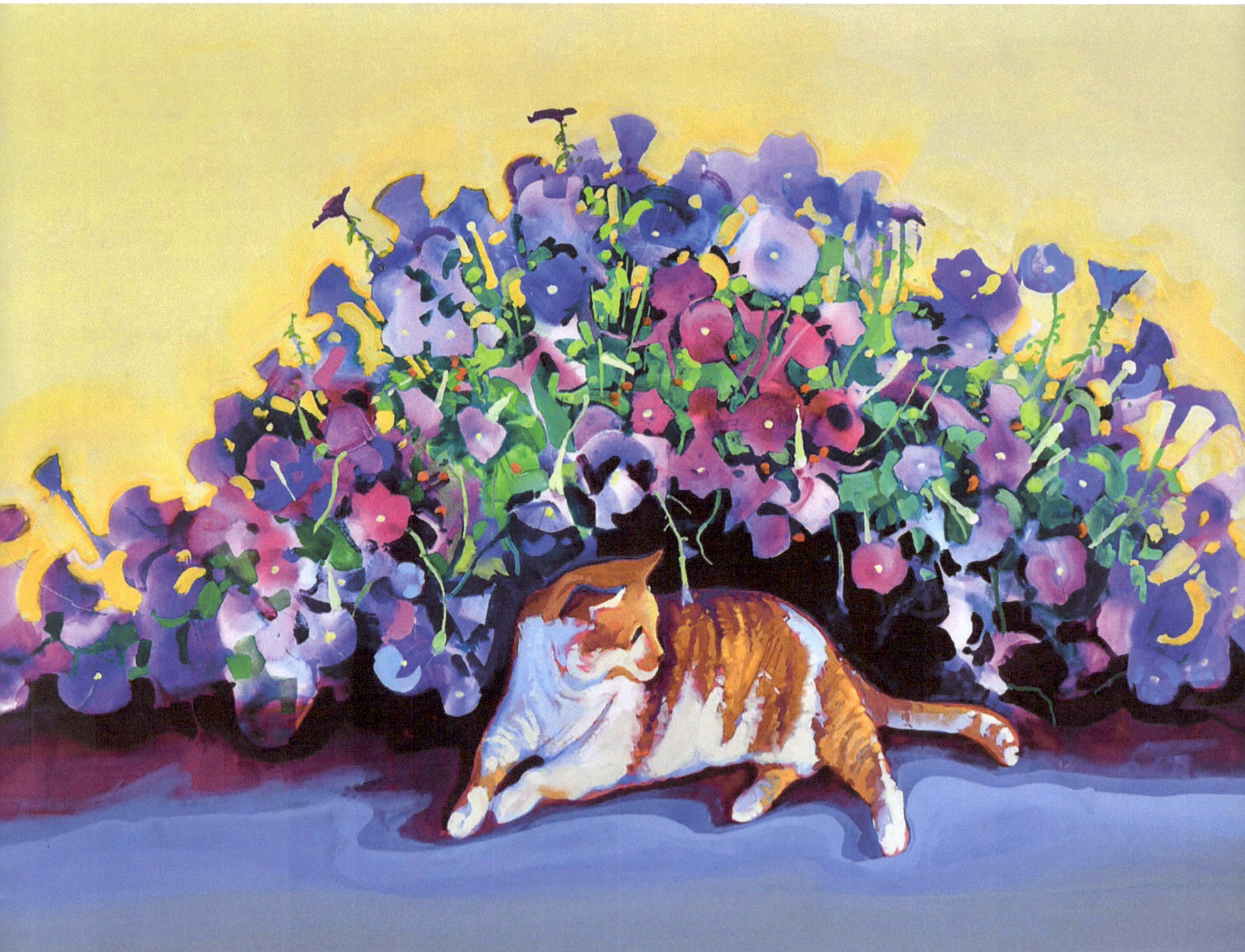

I painted a big basket of flowers, mainly in the violet, blue violet, to rose range. I had these flowers on the deck of my studio just to add to my joy during the summer. My cat posed when I sketched her in many positions. I combined one sketch with the flower arrangement for this painting. Notice the rhythmic, juicy gray casein paint flowing underneath my cat's body. This is the creamy quality that can be had with casein applied while it is wet.

Katrina in the Sun Room *1996*

casein, 20" x 30" Artist's Collection

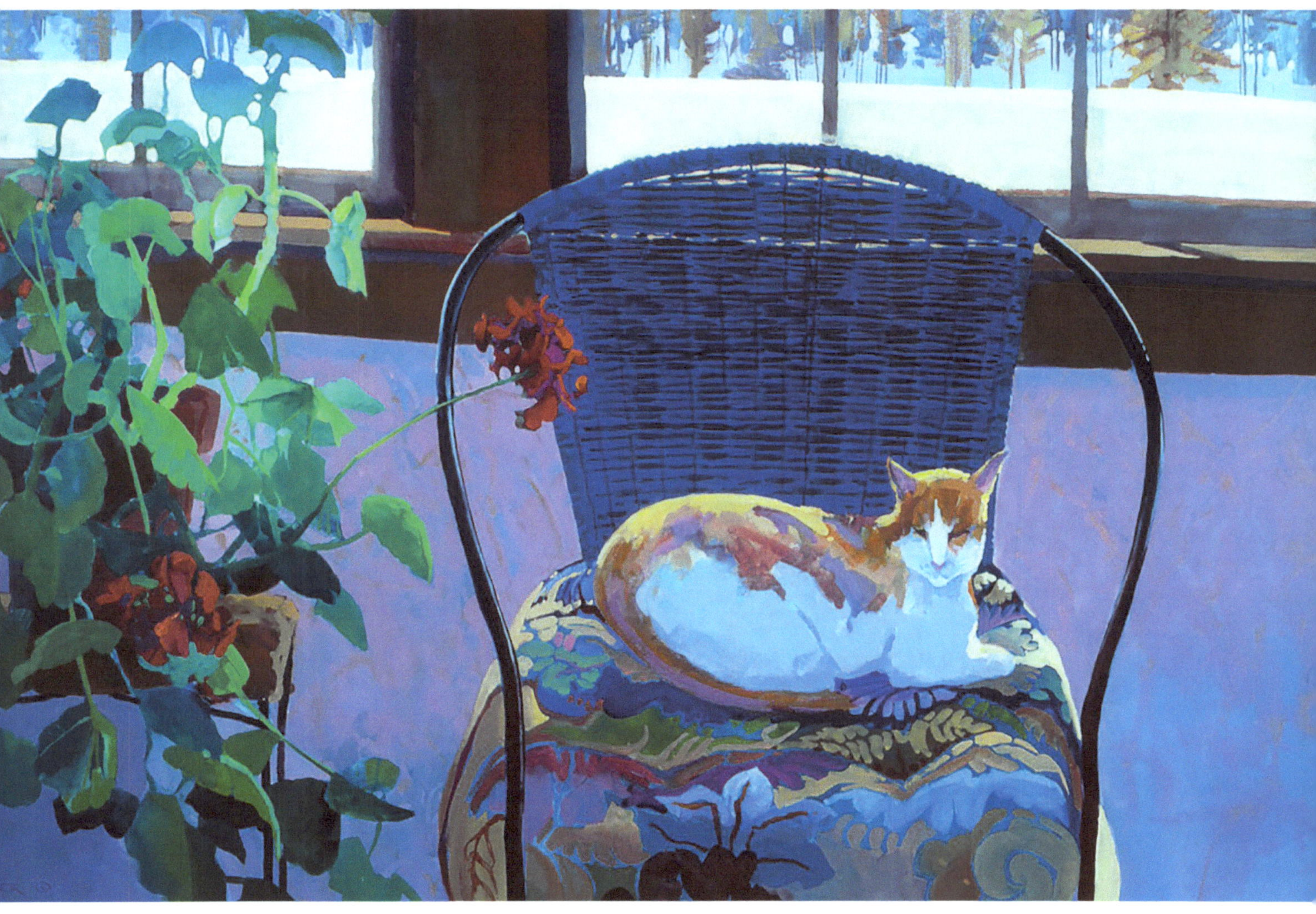

I found Katrina in the sun room reclining on the padded chair. I liked the composition, the geranium plant and the curvilinear rim of the chair along with the shape of the cat, and the pattern on the seat cover. I set my easel up and painted for a couple of days. The visual quality of casein captures the fur of the cat and also the pattern of the fabric. I feel this medium would be ideal for interior wallpaper patterns, much like Bonnard and Vuillard used for their subject matter of the Nabis School.

Casein and Snow Shadows

I live in snow country. We have good snow at least six months of the year and I love it. But we also have on average 320 days of sunshine. Naturally when I ski I am very aware of the sunlight and shadows as they move on the contour of the landscape. The fact of living in this country has made me see differently. The brilliant sunlight on the snow pops through snow pockets in the dark spruce, and forms the light surrounding the tree shapes. I see the thin cool shadow tone being formed by the warm light opaque snow that surrounds it. On these two pages there are two paintings featuring snow shadows. I did the the first one in 1983 and the second in 2013.

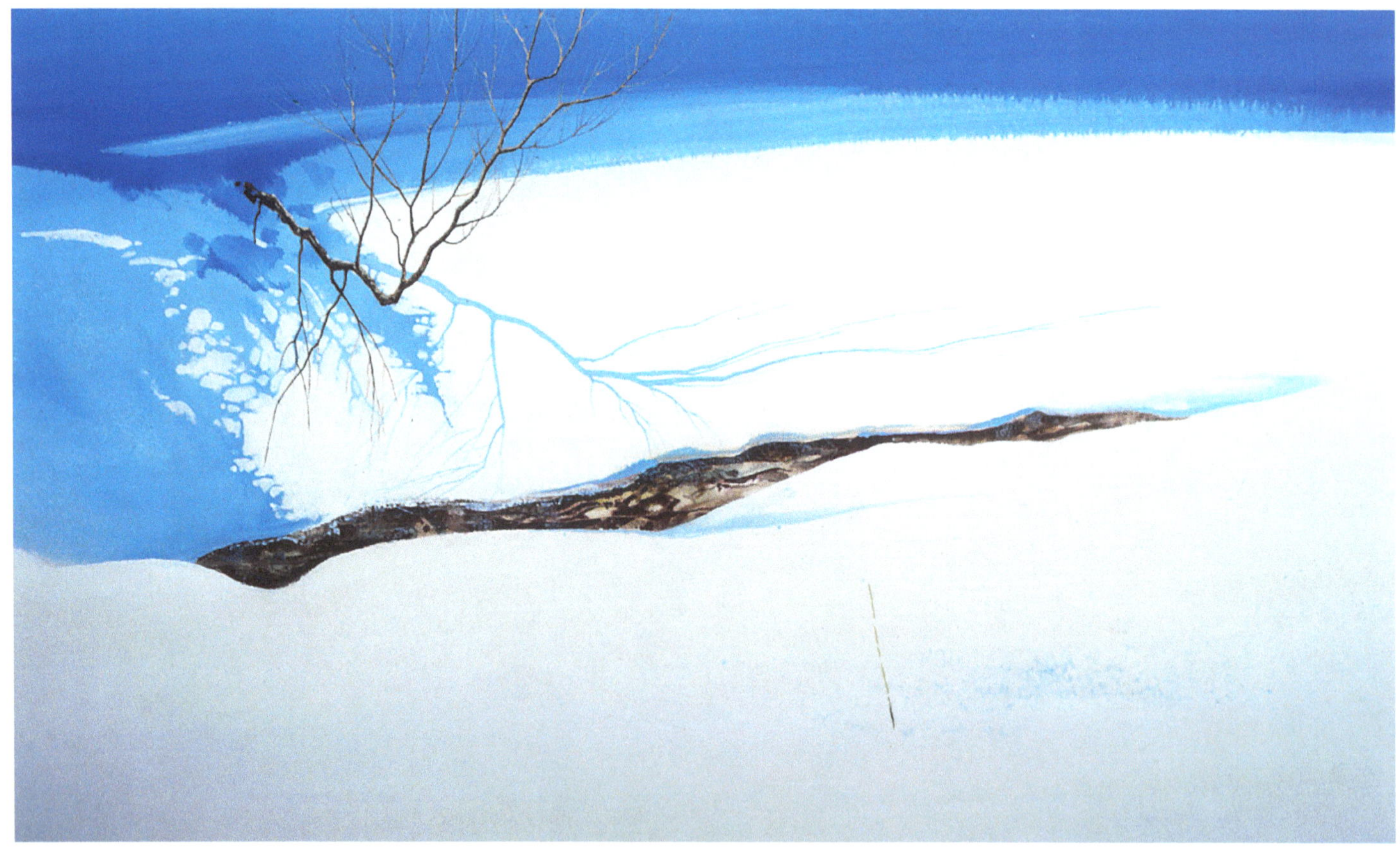

Snow Pocket on Shallow Creek *1983*
casein, 18" x 29" Private Collection

I noticed this open pocket of water while I was skiing by Shallow Creek, a canyon near where I live. I thought the simplicity was so beautiful. There was an open pocket of transparent water with rock forms visible, surrounded by a blanket of snow, and one willow branch, and with background trees not seen in the composition creating the snow shadows. I placed in the thin translucent cerulean blue shadow shape and then painted in a juicy warm white casein to form the shadow shape.

Inspiration can come when you least expect it. I had been teaching a seminar for the Utah Watercolor Society and after class a friend took me on a drive in the mountains. As we were driving back toward the city I caught this scene out of the corner of my eye. I thought about it for a while and then in an almost apologetic manner asked if we could turn around to go back to the spot. I have found that when inspiration occurs I must grab it. If not it's gone forever! We did go back and I did a few studies, and thought about it all that night. I was intrigued by the shadows and the reflections in the water, with an unusual composition. I worked it out and decided to do a demonstration the next day from my inspiration. I then went back to my studio in Colorado and developed it more before doing this final painting.

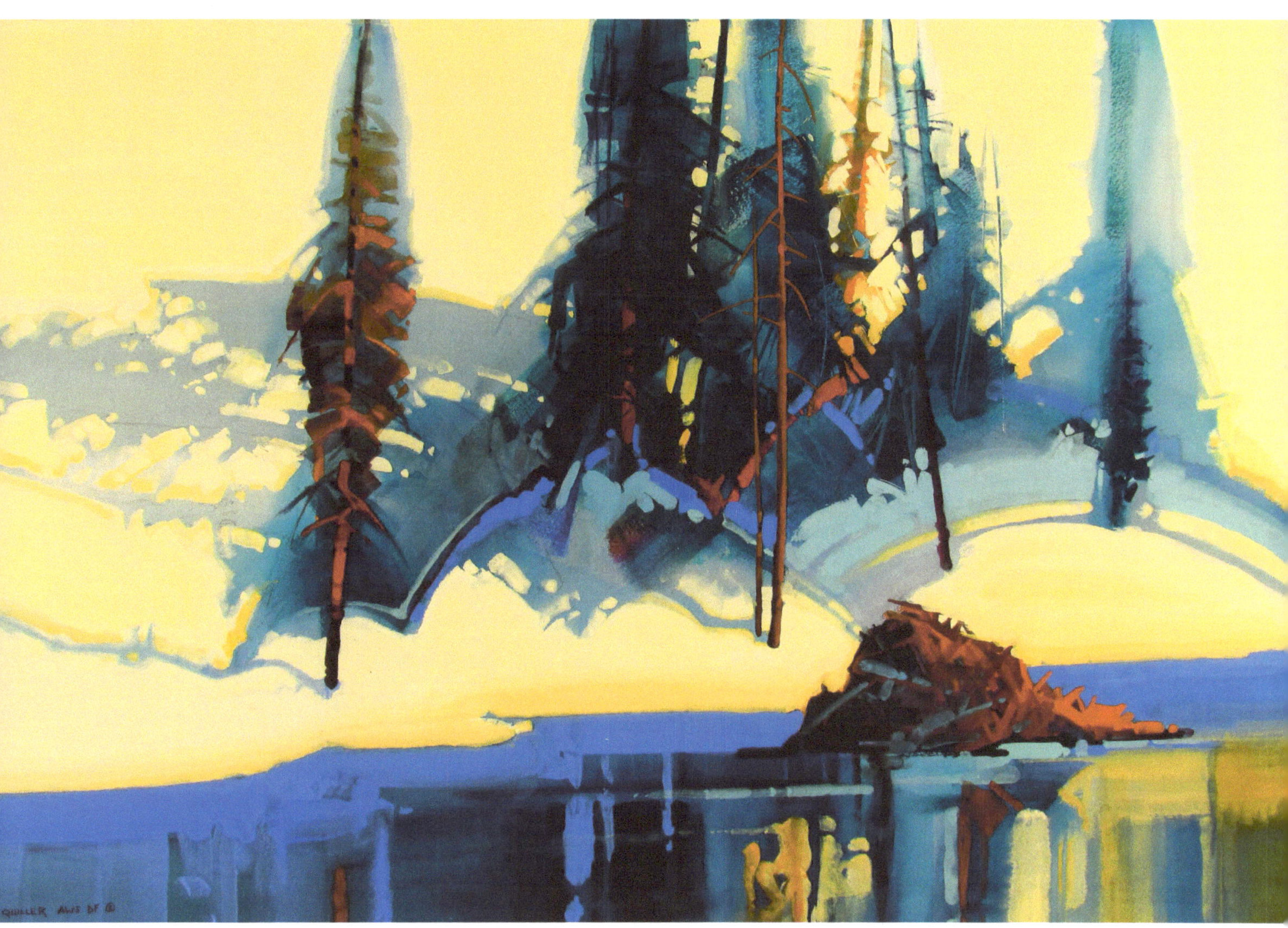

Transparency of Shadows 2014

casein, 23½" x 33" Artist's Collection

Gold Medal of Honor, American Watercolor Society

Stucco, Stone Walls and Old Boats with Casein

When I paint, I want to capture the light, the smells, the solidity or transparency, and the texture and sounds. Each subject that I paint tells me how best that can be done. Casein is the ideal medium for subjects such as old barns and wood texture, stucco and adobe buildings, and stone walls. For these various subjects, casein is my medium of choice.

Chioggia is a sea village just south Venice. It is filled with canals and hidden alleys, clothes lines draping from building to building. In fact, it is called the "Working Man's Venice." I did this painting standing on a bridge. I was attracted to the old brick, stucco walls, and the blue boat. Casein was the ideal choice to capture this subject. I can almost smell the aged walls. I was also very interested in the larger patterns and their movement.

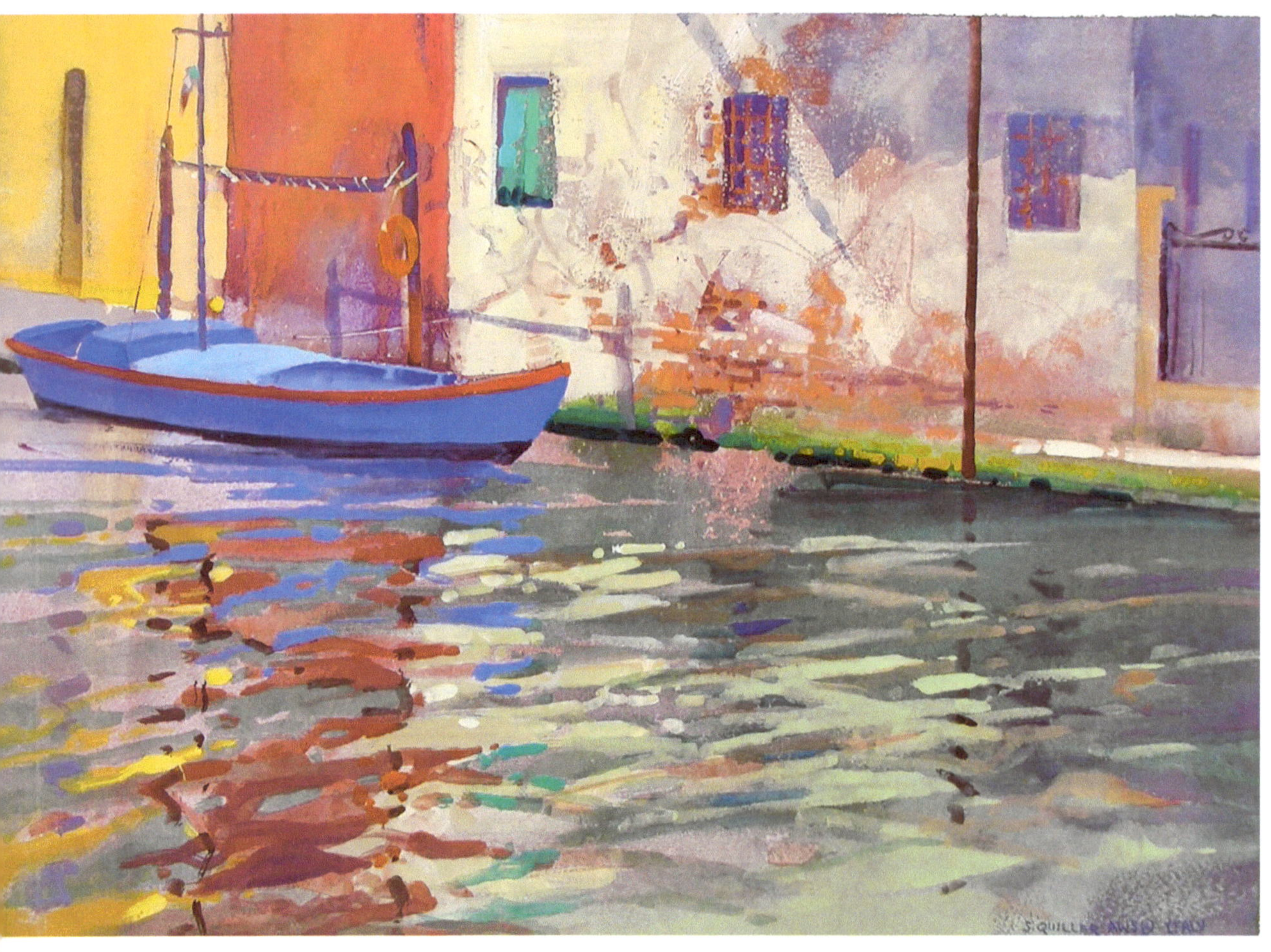

Blue Boat, Old Walls, Chioggia *2004*
casein, 22" x 30" Collection of Jackie and Charles Railsback

Dominican Monastery, Prouihle
(right) 2002
casein, 29" x 21"
Private Collection

I did this painting (right) at a monastery in the Languedoc-Roussillon region in the south of France. The villages there are walled to the south by the Pyrenees Mountains. It was a warm and sunny early October day, warm enough that I worked under the shade of a tree. There was enough humidity in the air that I did not worry about the casein drying out. Nuns strolled contemplatively and occasionally meandered over to see my work in progress. They were kind and very appreciative. I wanted to capture that feeling of the nuns and their habits, and the bark and foliage in the plein trees with the monastery in the background.

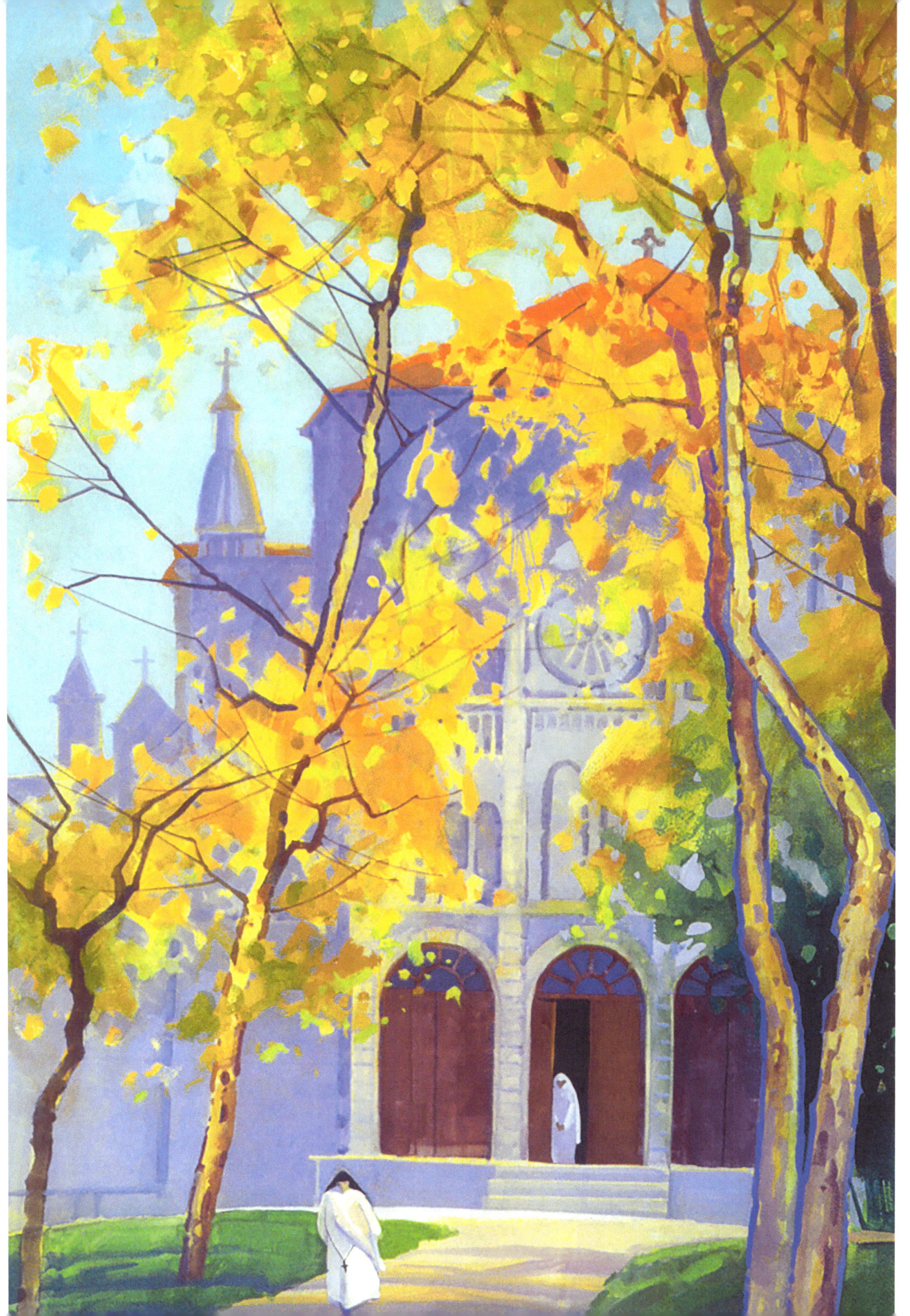

Solidity, Rocks and Mountains with Casein

There is something about the medium of casein, possibly the lime and milk base, that can give the appearance of solidity. I live in country that is monumental and has a feeling of strength, power and bold form. Thus I have come to see sky and water as transparent while the organic landforms including meadows, trees, mountains and rocks as opaque.

Below is a painting from my "Hidden Falls" series that was exhibited at the American Watercolor Society in New York in 2015. I did the painting on site in a very remote area that not many people see. I started with the toned watercolor board in blue transparent acrylic. At the site I only worked with casein. I treated the background rocks by the waterfall more translucently. I wanted them to appear in the distance. Moving into the foreground the rocks were a solid opaque casein. Very important to the painting is a small bird that you can see at lower left by the whitewater. It is an Ouzel Bird, commonly known as the "Dipper Bird." They are the most interesting bird I've ever watched.

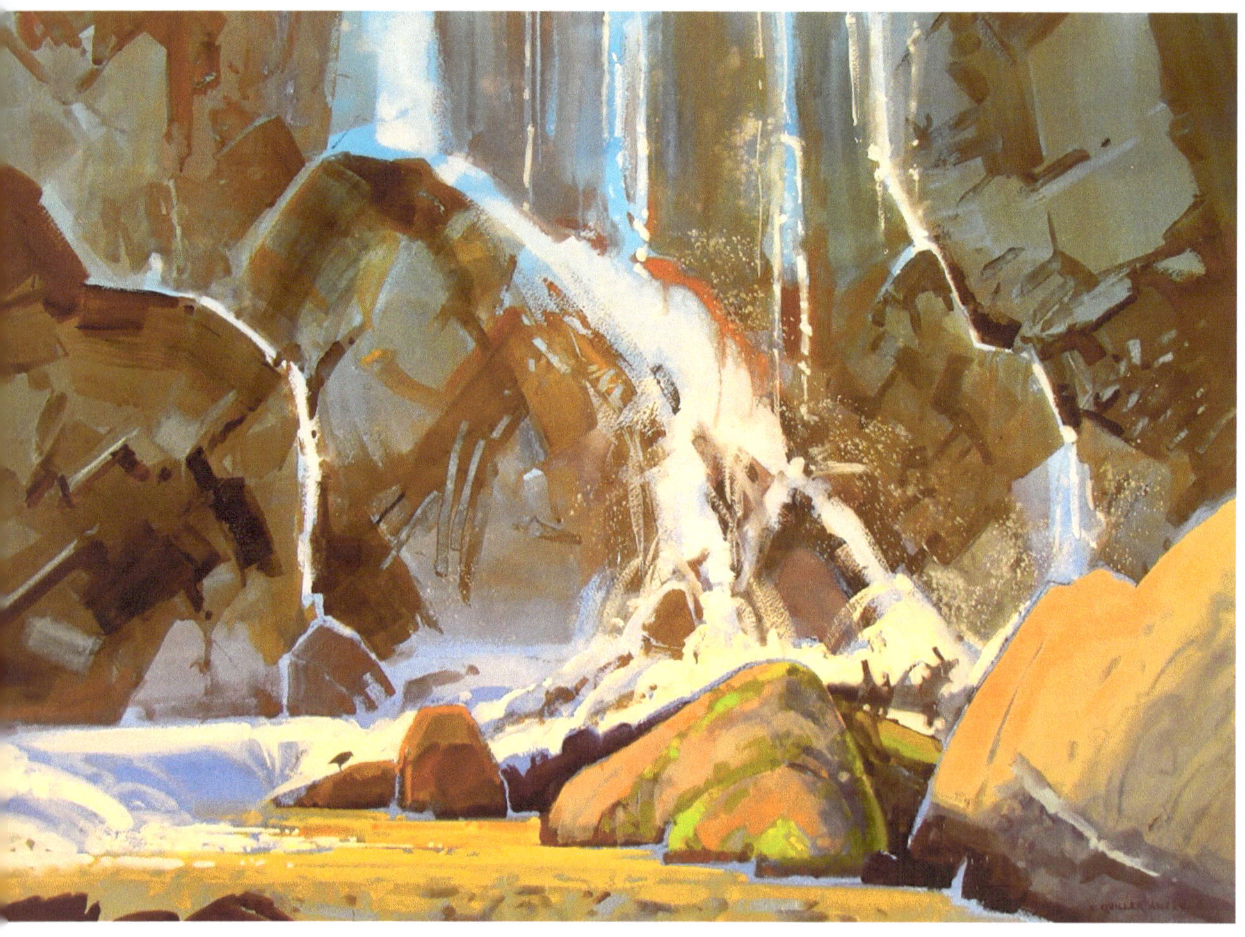

Ouzel Bird, Hidden Falls 2004
casein with transparent acrylic underwash,
23.5" x 33" Private Collection

Afternoon Light, Sentinel Peak, Yosemite
(right) 2002
casein, 32" x 23"
Collection of Jackie & Charles Railsback

(Right) I spent a lot of time painting in Yosemite. It is one of the most magnificent National Parks in America. Beginning in 1992, every other year in late October or November, I would do a painting workshop in Yosemite. Of all the rock formations there, Sentinel Peak is my favorite. I especially like it in the afternoon and evening light. I did the painting entirely in casein on a yellow toned transparent acrylic watercolor board. I wanted to capture the strength, power and density of this mountain form, and I feel casein captured it incredibly well.

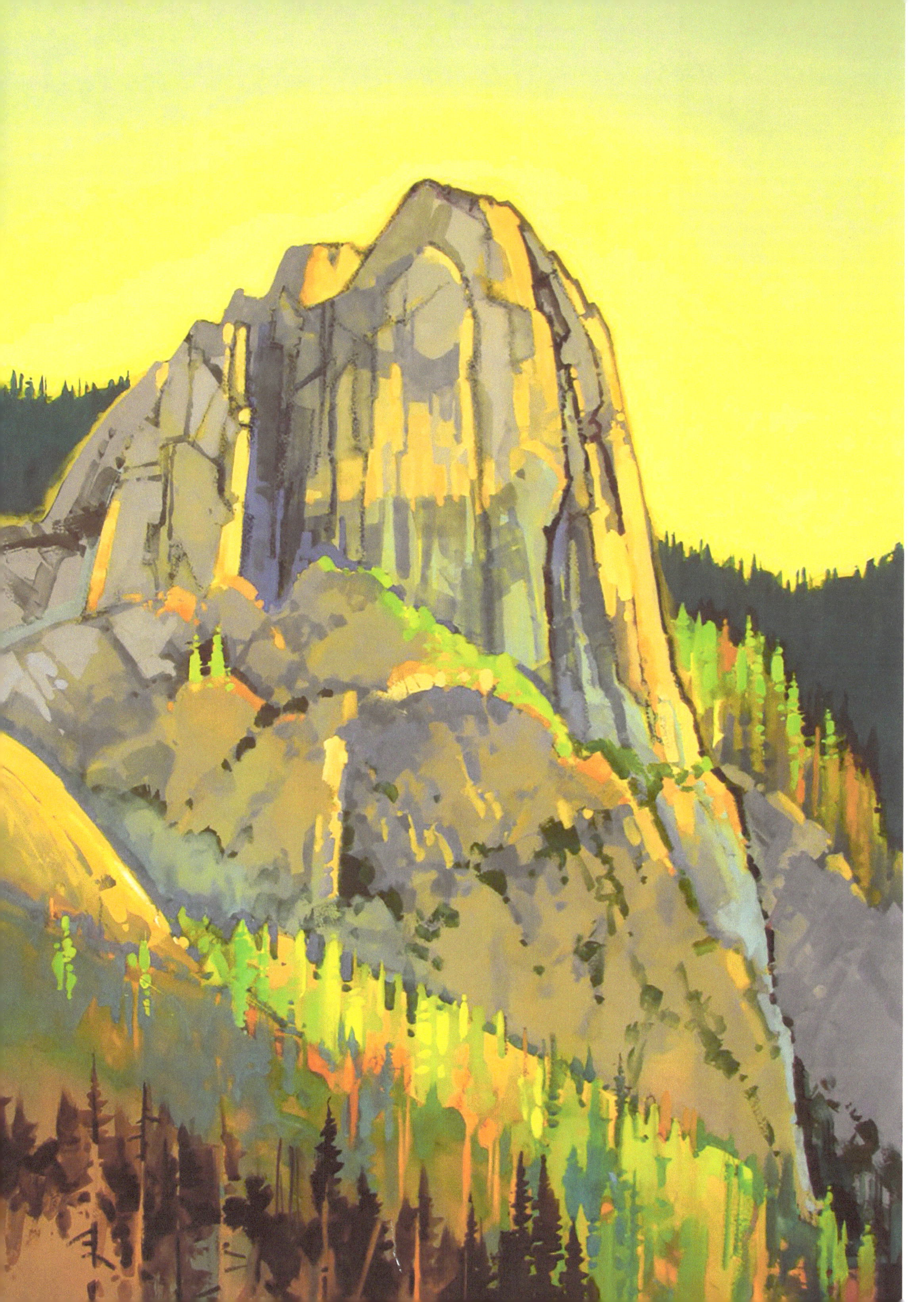

Clouds & View from the Air with Casein

I spend a lot of time flying and looking out the plane window. I study clouds, mountains and snow, field patterns and river patterns far below. Many times I'll take notes and do a few studies and some photos. I love the bird's eye view that was first implemented by the Chinese. Later it was seen in the form of woodcuts by the Japanese. They displayed these prints at the Paris World's Fair in 1878. This made a huge impression on European artists, especially the Impressionists and Postimpressionists.

Casein captures atmospheric depth as well as the softness of clouds. It is a gentle medium, one of purity and of a spiritual nature.

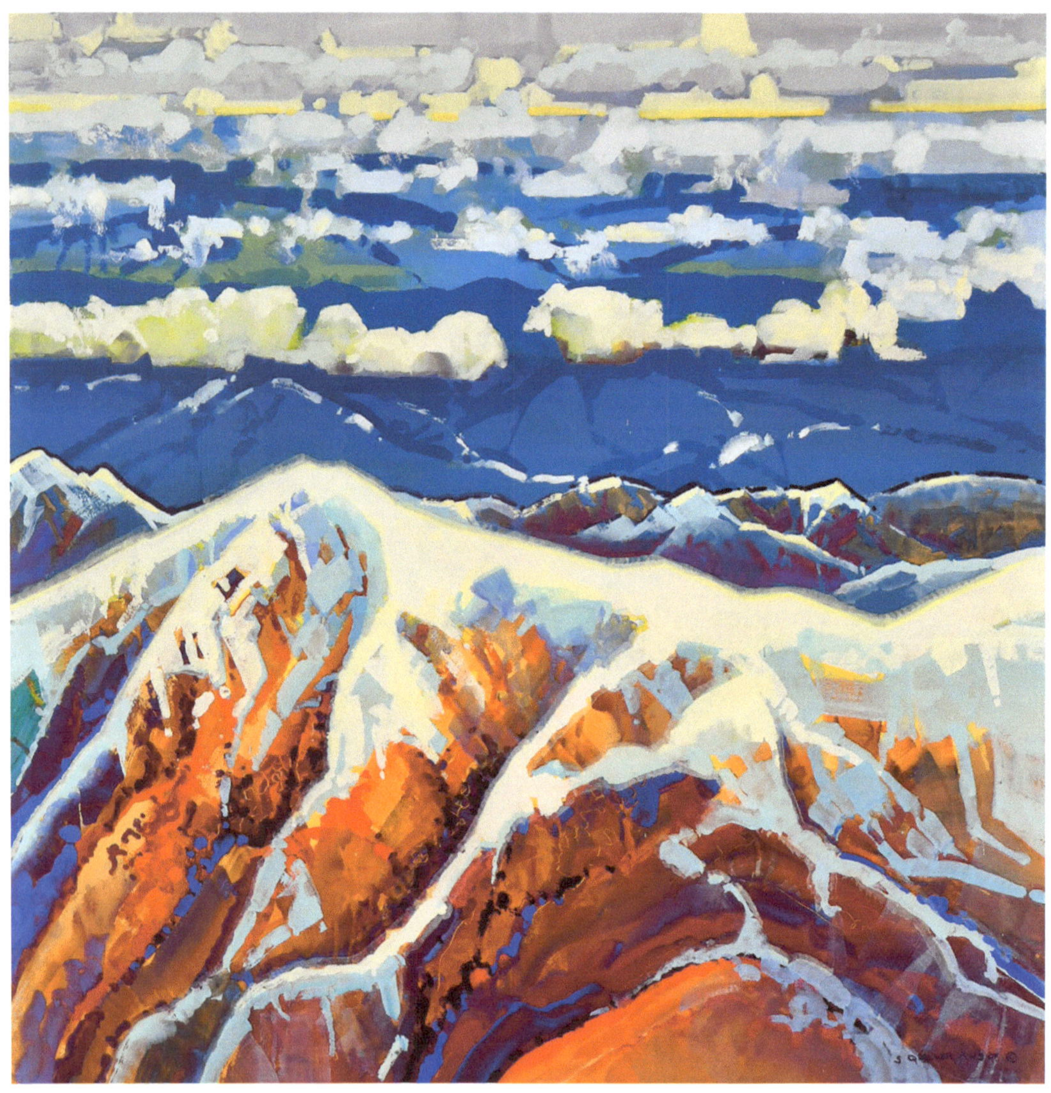

View From the Air *2019*
casein,, 29" x 29" Collection of Lori Heinrich

I took a photo as I was flying over the Sangre de Cristo Mountain Range on the way to Denver. These are very jagged peaks with beautiful snow patterns in the spring. On this day there was the added condition of cloud patterns. I love it when I can see through some of these patterns to the distant landscape. Later I put the photo on a monitor and did a drawing from those similar to the studies I've done in chapter 3. Then I just work, referring to the drawing and my memory.

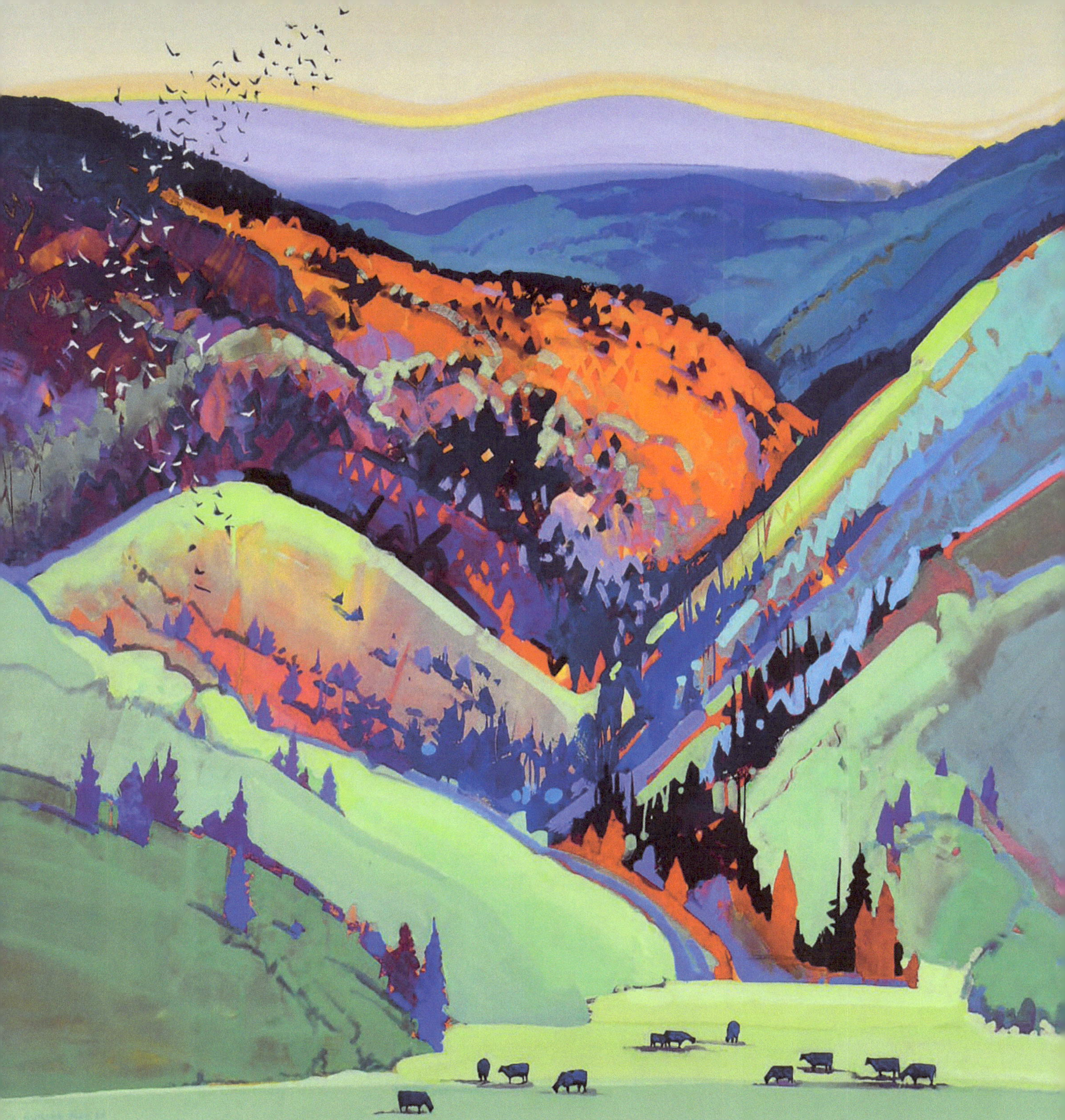

Flight, From the Air Series
2019
casein, 29" x 29"
Collection of
Bert & Jane Lucas

This work was based on mountain forms in our upper San Juan Mountain terrain. I see this drainage from a hilltop near my home. I did this from a series of sketches, color studies, and drawings of meandering cows. I love the soft sense of the high key yellows and violets in the distant range. Casein has an atmospheric depth. As I moved forward with the rhythmic mountain patterns, there was stronger color and sharper contrast for the advancing shapes. I placed in the curvilinear pattern of the blackbirds in the upper left corner to add to the movement and to overlap the shapes and create more depth. In the central foreground I was playing with the color of ultramarine violet-blue shade. It just sings!

The Coast & Casein

During the 1970s and early 80s I frequented the Oregon coast. I love the rugged coastline and unpredictable weather. This was early in my painting career. I would hole up in a small room with a north window and spend a week or two painting. This was long before the digital age and I would walk along the coast with my sketchbook taking notes and doing studies of what I call working sketches. Ambling along the shore, I would experience the distinct smells of the sea, damp atmosphere and salt, the barnacles and kelp and driftwood. Because of this, casein was my choice for many paintings.

Old Bandon Village On a Gray Day *1975*
casein ,21" x 29", Private Collection

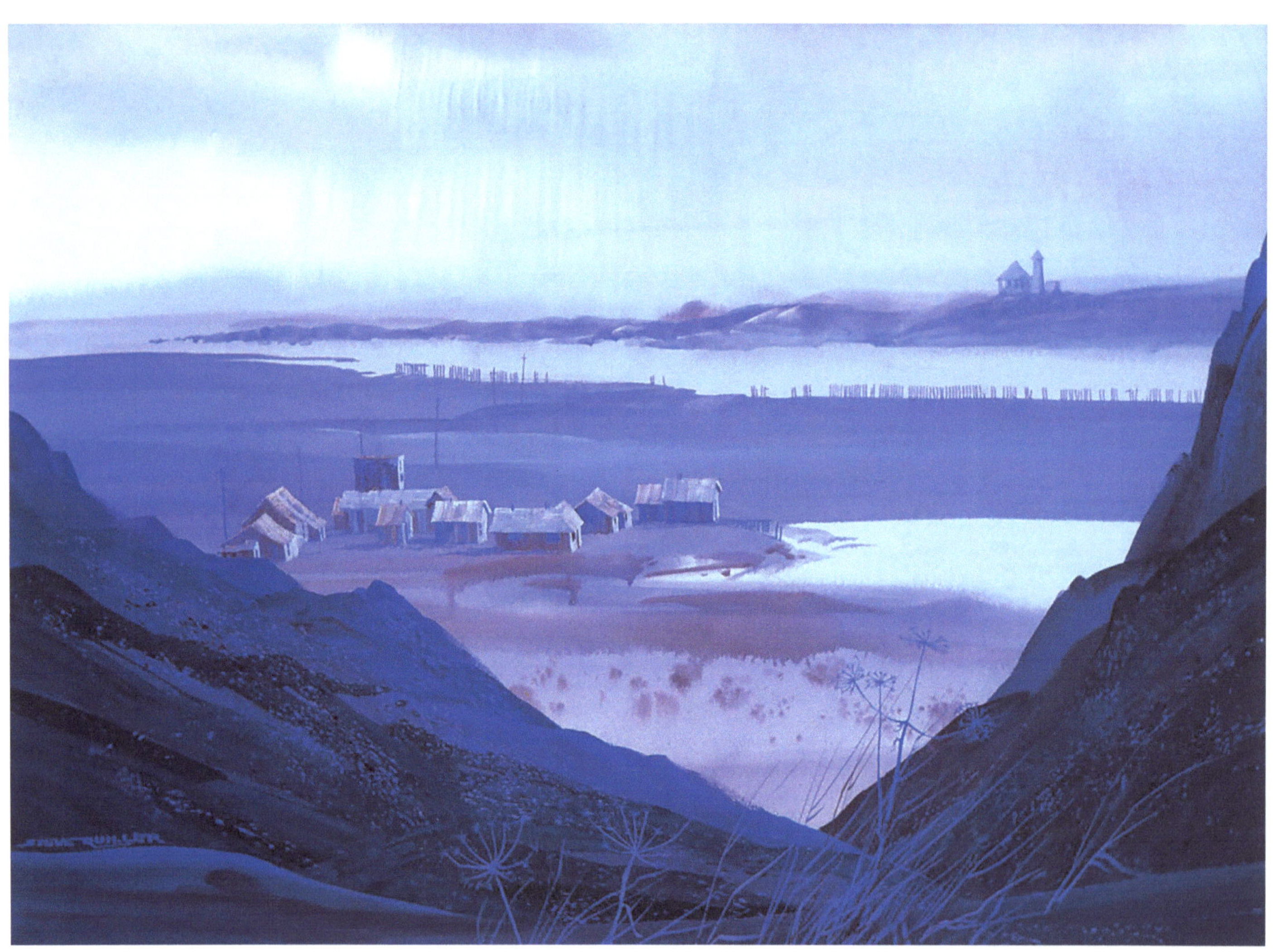

From a coastal hill I did sketches for this painting. The Coquille River empties to the sea by the jetty and in the distance a lighthouse. I could see the old village, very paintable, on the land framed by the dark of the of the foreground hill shapes. I used a limited palette of mainly neutrals and earth tones to capture this gray day, and of course this was all executed in casein.

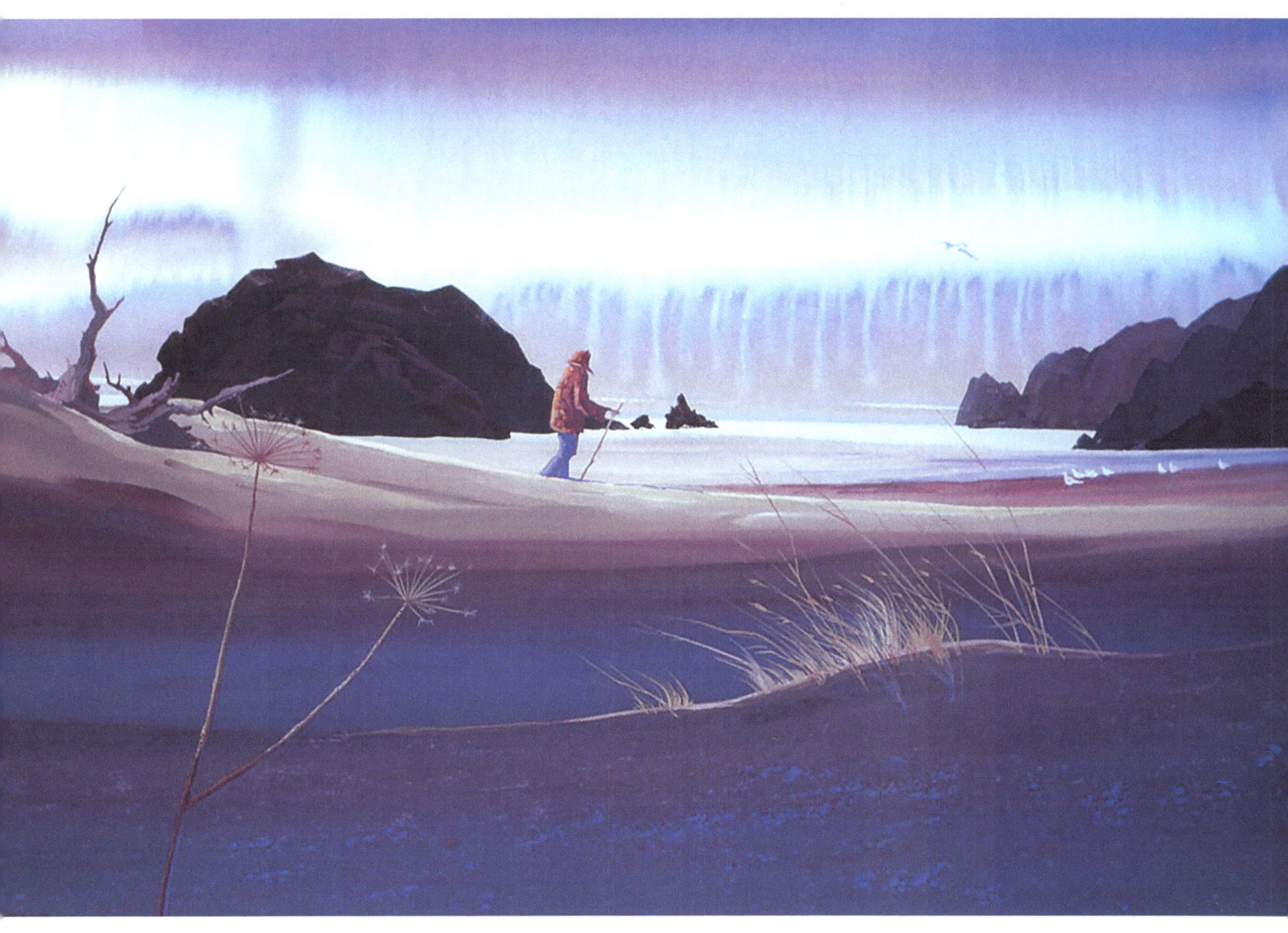

Coastal Walk *1975*
casein, 20" x 29", Private Collection

The Oregon coast during certain times of the year can be suitable for solitude and reflection. I see individuals strolling along, sometimes with a stick, lost in thought, or beachcombers digging for clams or looking for seashells or Japanese floats, or a man playing fetch with his dog. I would go out intentionally to do line drawings of these souls in the field, filling two or three pages. Then, occasionally I combined the figure and the seascape. Cold press watercolor paper is an ideal surface to capture the softness, the sand, and atmosphere on the coast. Notice the distant movement in the sky, the solidity of the rocks and figure, and the density of the sand dunes. Of course casein is the medium of choice.

Snow Patterns and Casein

Living in the high country of Colorado we have snow at least six months out of the year. I love it. I live for winter and its solitude. I cross country ski most days and make my own trails. There is nothing better then skiing after a fresh, heavy mountain snow when the next day has strong sunlight. The branches are embraced with globular patterns of snow. I try to ski through without touching the branches. If I do I get a shower of snow down my body. Casein is a wonderful medium to capture this moment of sunlight and shadow, with cool and warm pockets of heavy snow.

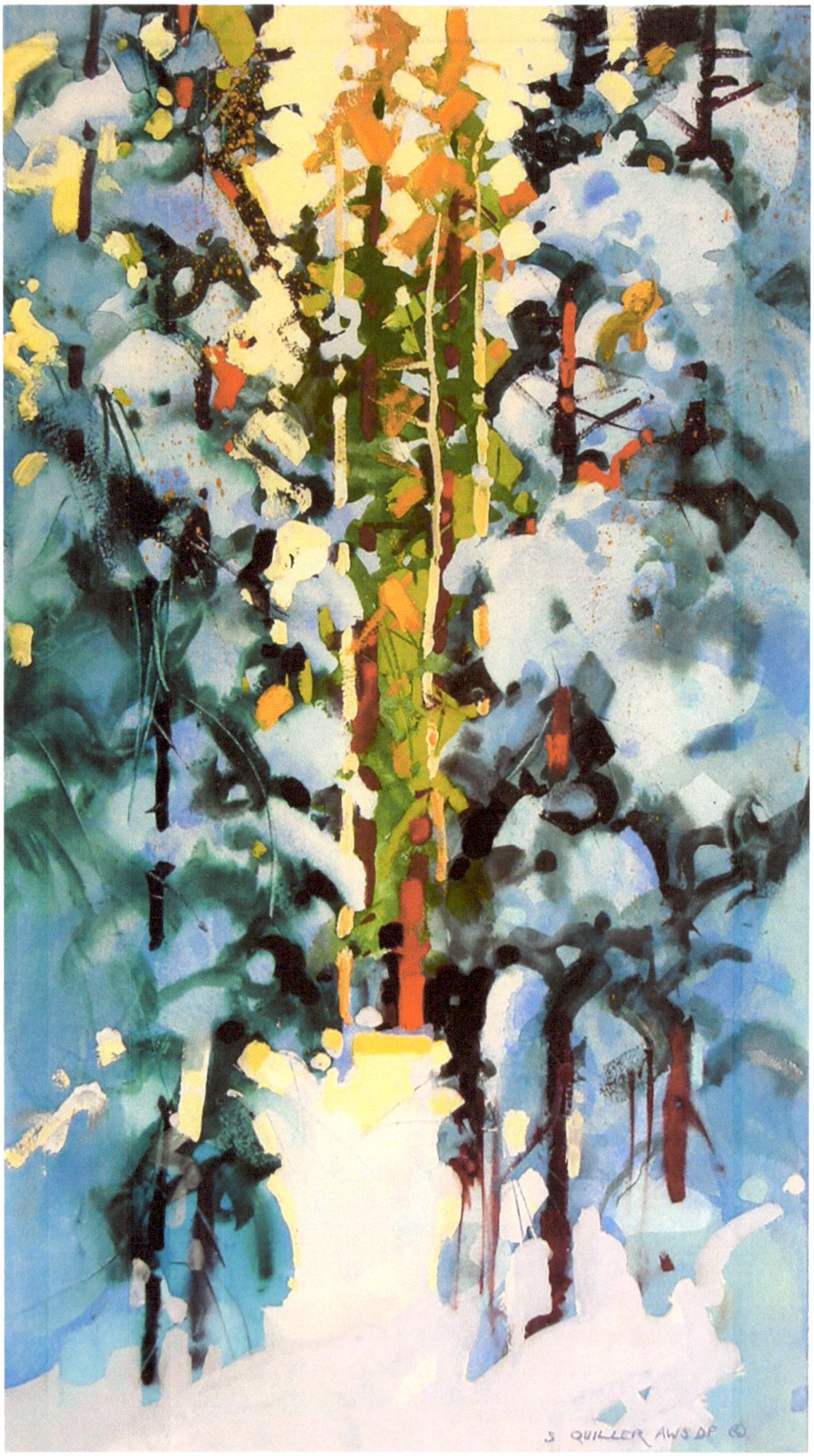

(Left) On a late sunlit afternoon ski after a heavy snow the day before, I was sliding along the "Blue Spruce Trail." As I was kicking and gliding, lost in thought, I looked up to see sunlit spruce patterns weighted on both sides by cool shadowed trees cloaked in snow. It seemed as if I were entering a cathedral. So I decided to honor this view by stopping, taking notes and sketching. I selected casein to help me with this expression. I used yellows, oranges and greens to capture the cathedral statement, while applying the bright cadmium reds on the inner side of the cool spruce to announce my entry.

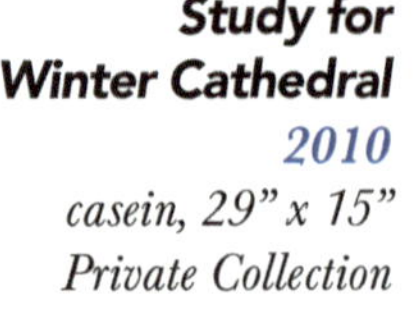

Study for Winter Cathedral
2010
casein, 29" x 15"
Private Collection

Snow Trees
(right) 2013
casein,
21 ¾" x 9 ⅜"
Private Collection

(Right) I saw this scene of the view from the north light window in my studio. It was late afternoon and the sun backlit the spruce trees. There was a fresh snow, and the weighted clumps in the branches with sunlight showing through some of the tree pockets was amazing. This was a very small study that I probably completed in less than an hour. I began by washing thin transparent cool tones across the whole paper. Then I began painting negatively around the tree branches and into the snow pockets with juicy, yellow-white opaque casein. Later I put in the dark trunks and branches, threading in and out of the snow pockets.

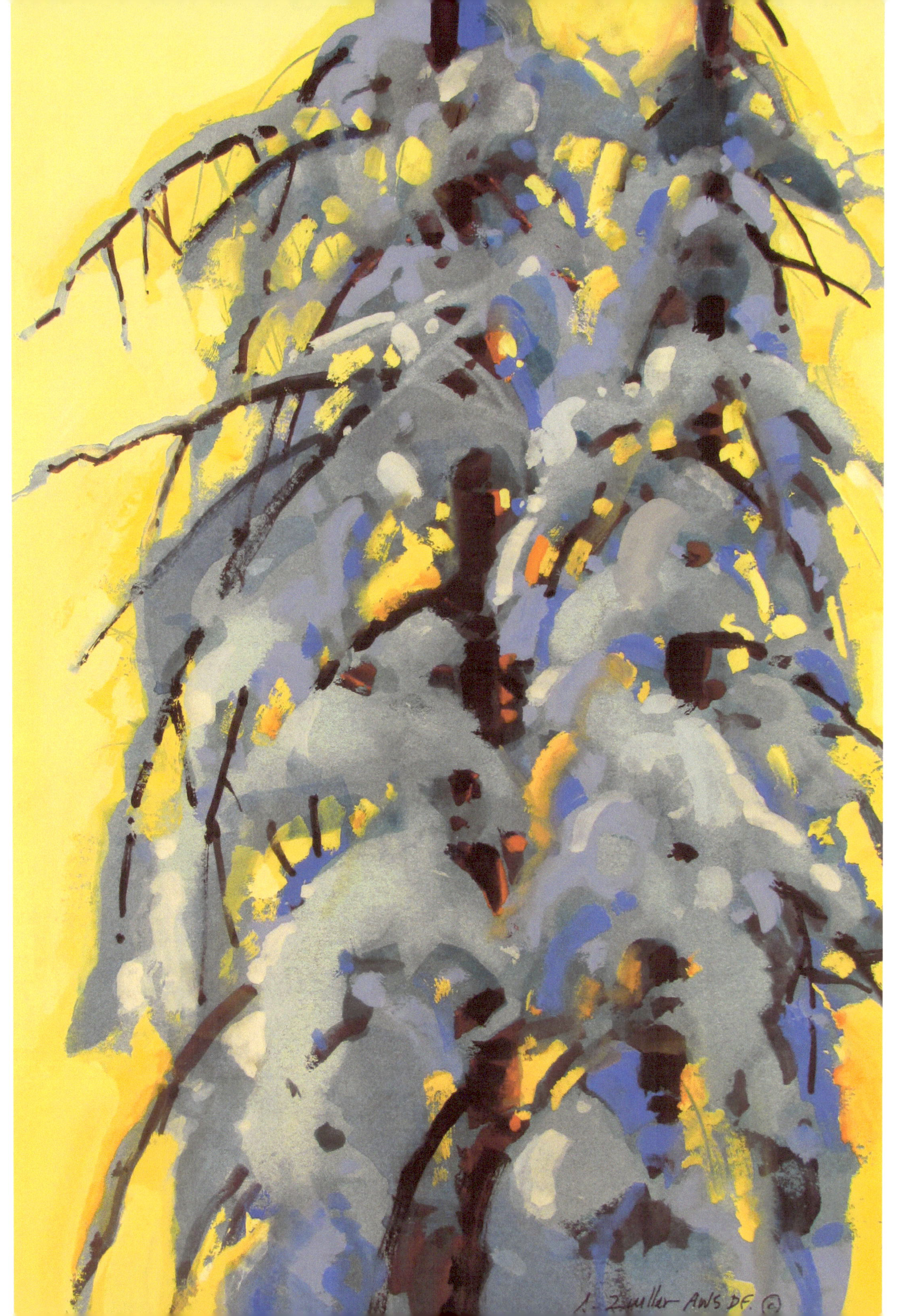
AWS DF. ©

Extreme Detail with Casein

Another huge advantage when working with casein is how fine detail can be. A very small round brush can carry a lot of fluid pigment and paint very intricate passages. Although today I'm not one who uses a lot of detail in my work, in the late 70s and early 80s I did. I painted a lot of dried thistles, milkweed pods, and sunflowers, as well as yarrow, fox tail and rose hips, projecting them up into the landscape, making important what we normally just walk past and not notice. Not only could I paint fine opaque detail over dark passages but the paint has a dry matte look emulating the weeds. Where fine detail is needed, casein is ideal.

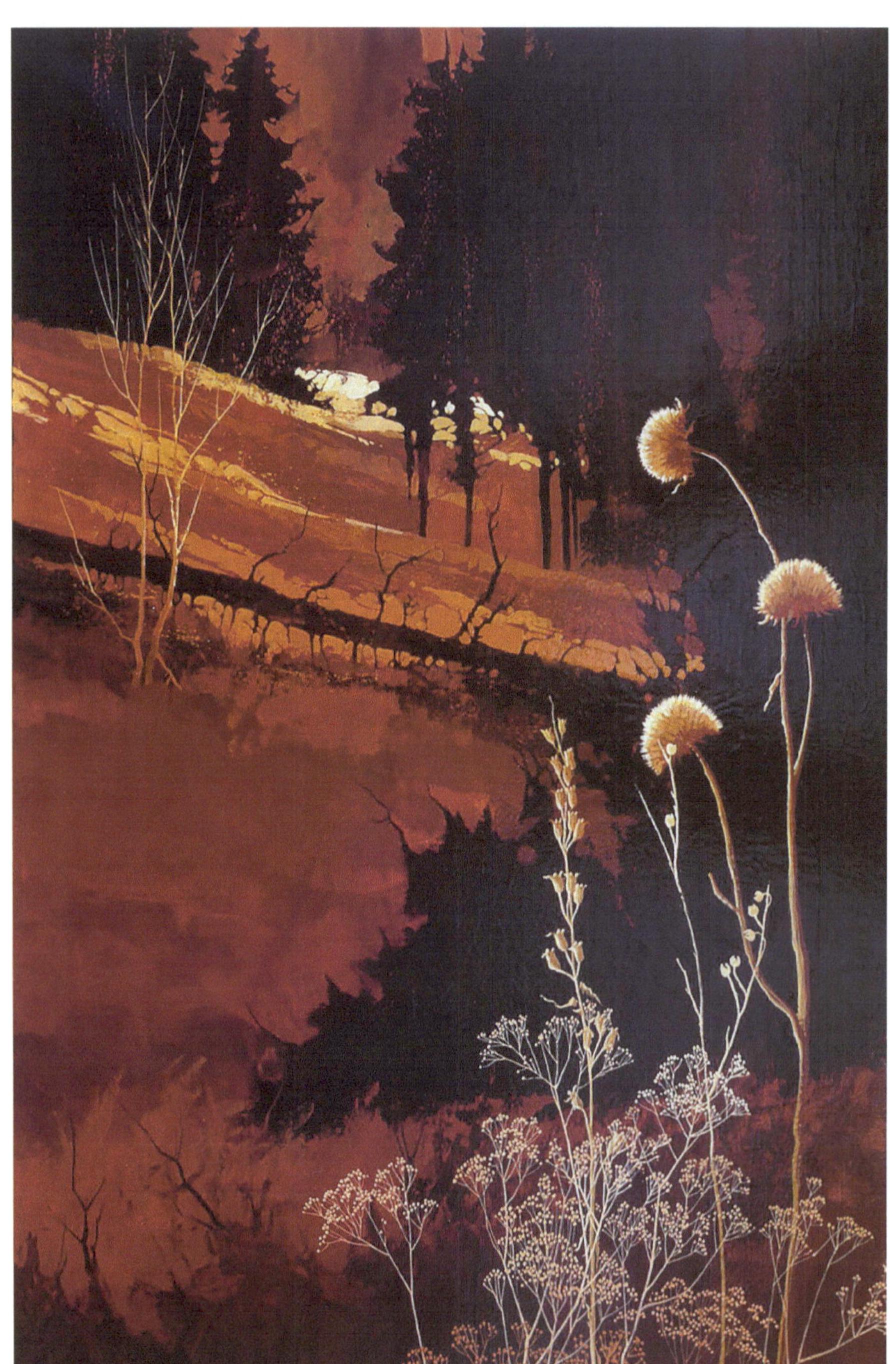

In the 70s and early 80s I became obsessed with painting late autumn leaves and vegetation. I thought the structure and texture of these subjects so beautiful. I found especially when I worked on a cold press, nontextured support I could paint very, very fine detail. This is an example of one such painting using analogous warm earthy pigments. I painted the whole background first and then with a fine brush painted in the foreground elements. It was amazing for me to see how I could build a middle value to a very high light on the dried sunflower over that dark brown background.

Late Autumn Sunflowers
(left) ***1976***
casein
Private Collection

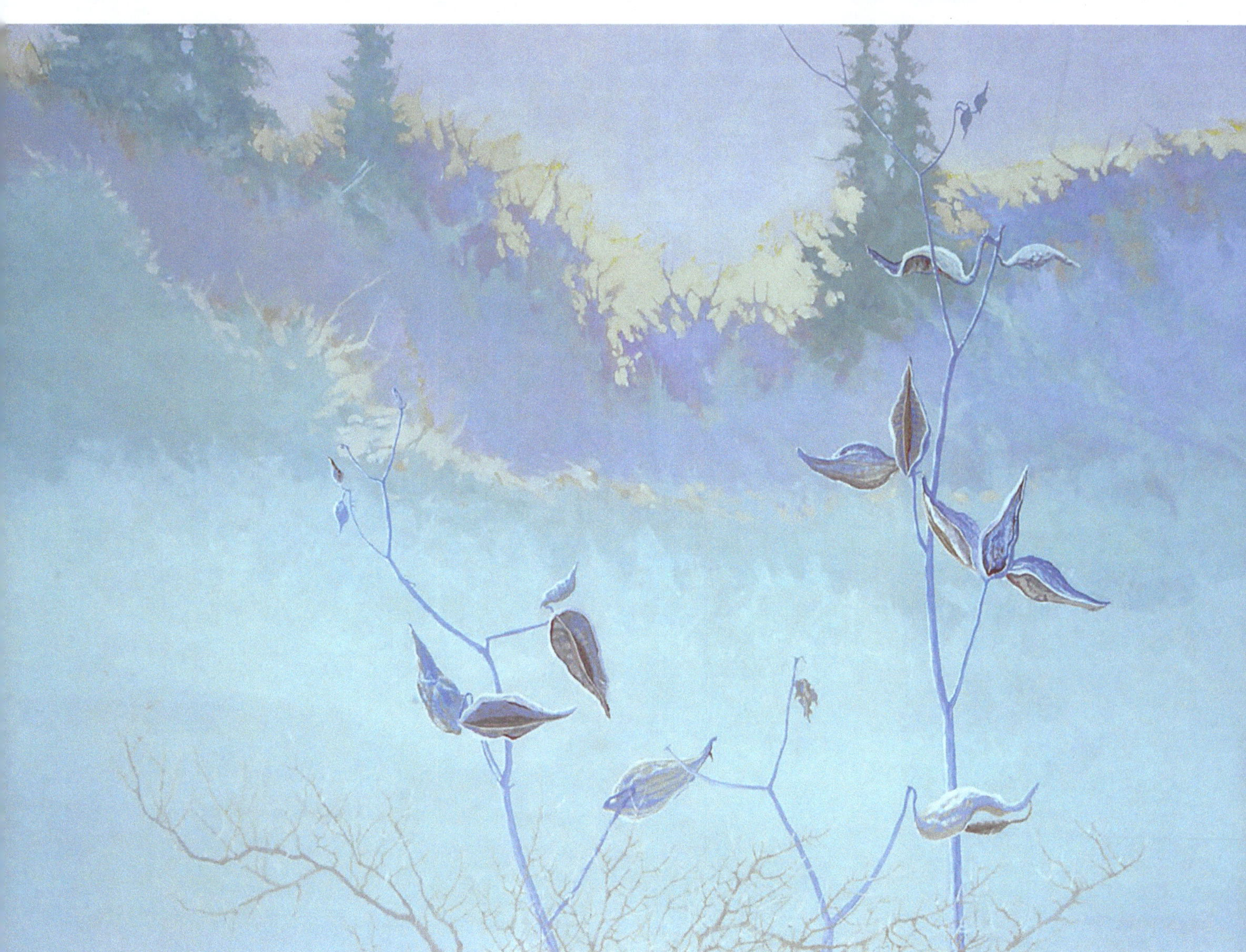

***Milk Weed Pods, November Morning* 1980**
casein, Private Collection

I did this painting in a relatively high key value, meaning that most of the composition has light pastel. I used a triad color scheme of orange, green, and violet. This is what creates the very soft mood of an early November morning. Along a road not far from where I live are these beautiful dried milkweed pods. I simply picked a few, brought them back to my studio and arranged them for the subject.

Exercise #1 On a gesso panel, cold press watercolor board, or Aquabord® support, with reference material, paint an adobe or stuccoed structure or an old boat, and try to get the character of the age and dryness and worn quality.

Exercise#2 On a dark, smooth support that could be toned or gessoed with black, take a small round brush and paint light detail over the dark. Find some dried weeds from gardens and meadows and see how much beautiful detail can be created.

Exercise#3 Paint some shadows by negatively painting around them. First tone the support, whether it be gesso panel, Aquabord®, or cold press watercolor paper, with the transparent shadow color. This could be painted in permasol blue mixed with cadmium red pale. When the paint is dry, paint negatively around the shadow to form the light. This can be the shadow of the tree on snow or sand, or a human shadow.

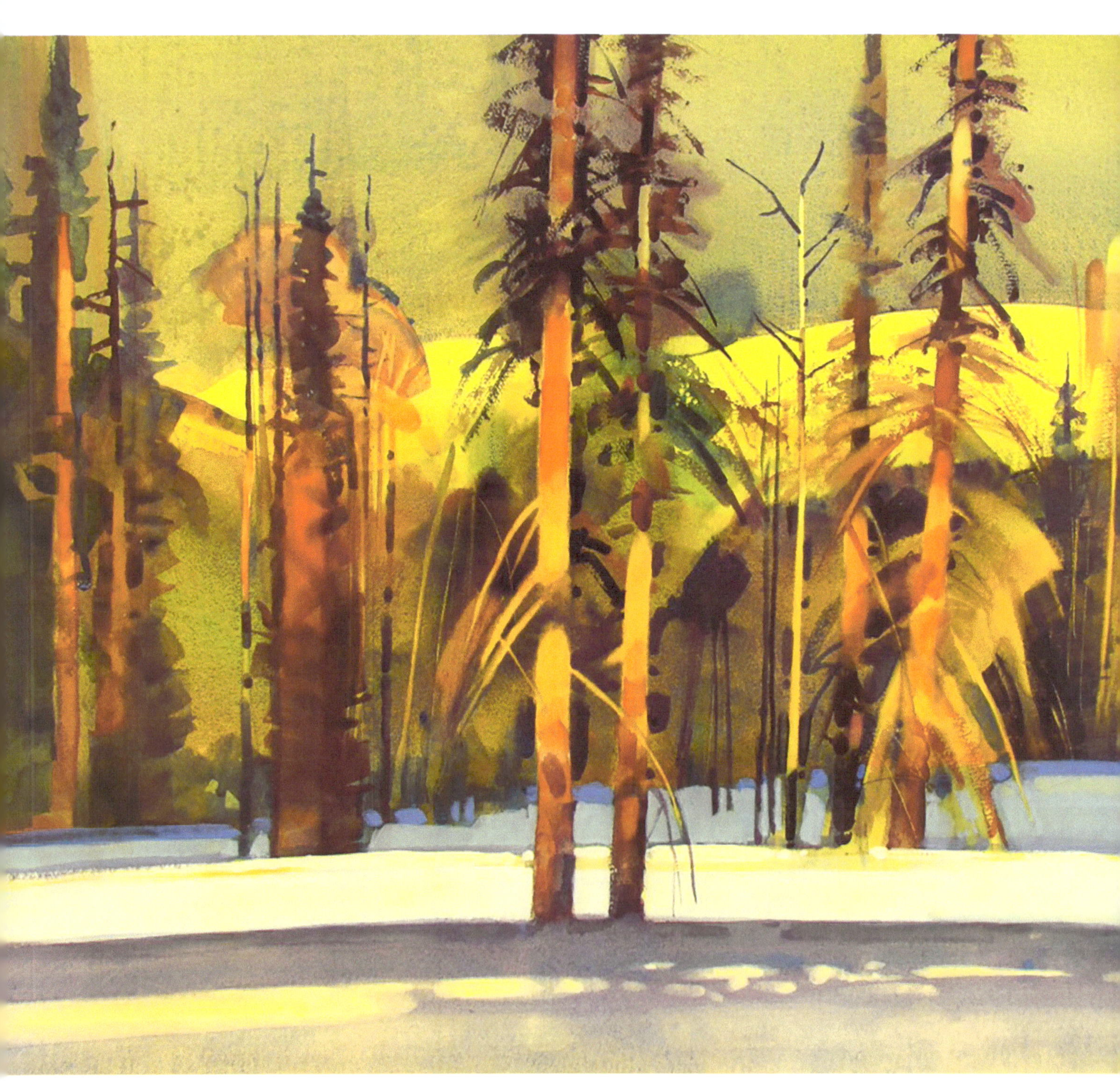

5 Casein Combined with Other Media

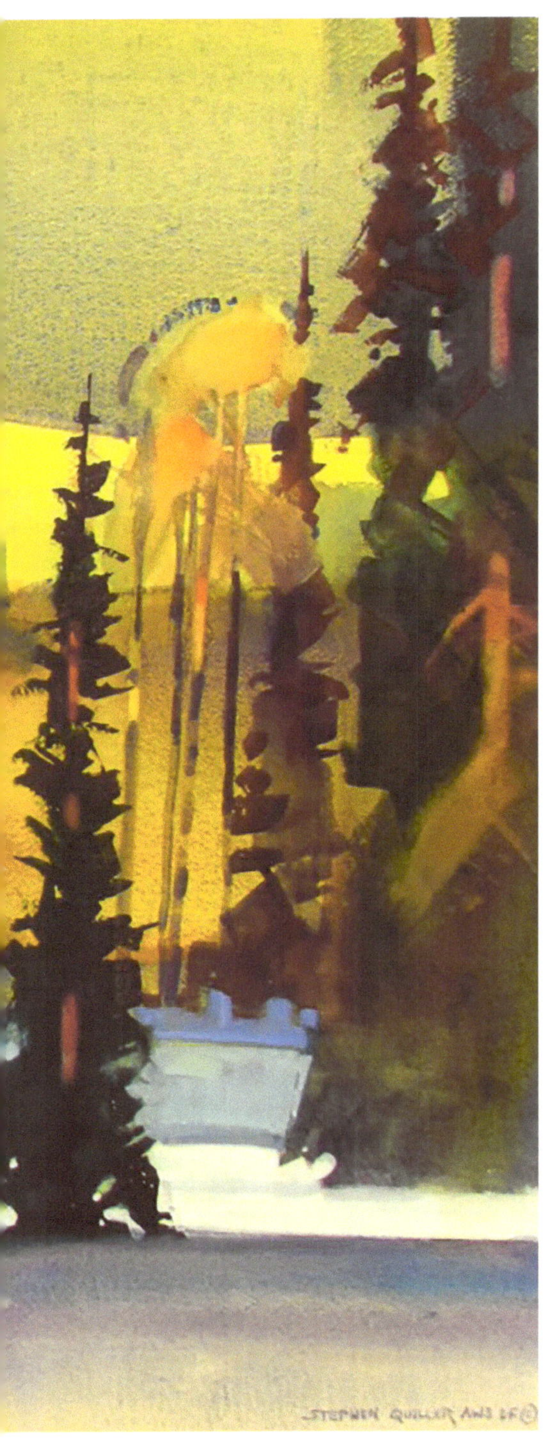

Casein is extremely versatile. It can be combined with any non-oily medium including watercolor, acrylic, pastel and drawing media. In this chapter I will demonstrate some of the ways that I've incorporated these various media with casein. It is important to know that the combination of media needs to be compatible for both expression and lightfastness. I've met many painters who, when introduced to casein, think that they can add casein to an unfinished watercolor piece and bring it back to life. Occasionally that can be true. However, most of the time the combination of media needs to be an integral part of the painting process and not an afterthought.

The idea of underpainting and overpainting is not new. The Baroque school of Rembrandt, Frans Hals, Rubens, Vermeer, Caravaggio, Velazquez and van Ruisdael toned their canvas with a neutral gray. They then painted in black and white to build the structure of the painting around the neutral, followed by glazing color over the value structure. This method was called en grisaille. Later, the British watercolor painters of the 18th and 19th centuries would work on toned papers such as soft blues, beige, burnt reddish and yellows. They painted with watercolor and developed opaque highlights with gouache for what they called "body color." Today we can take a sheet of white watercolor paper, canvas, or Aquabord®, and tone it with transparent acrylic washes to any color, or multicolor, that we want.

Late Light by Poxen's Run
2013
Transparent acrylic under wash, granulating watercolor, translucent and opaque casein
23 ½" x 37 ½"
Collection of Kelly Hoglund

Casein with Acrylic

This is the combination of water media that I personally use the most. I always begin with transparent acrylic. This in essence tones my support to the underpainting color that is needed. Why acrylic? I use acrylic mainly for two reasons. First, it is by far the most luminous, intense, rich medium that is available where color is involved. I can put down intense tones of transparent acrylic color and it will dry close to the same value in luminosity as when it was first applied. Second, once the transparent color dries, it will not lift. This ensures that the overpainting, whether it be transparent, translucent or opaque casein, will not lift and intermix with the under color. It also means that if the under color stain is rich but completely dry, the over painting with casein (while damp) can lift back to the under color. The underpainting will tie the painting together if the tone is exposed in a few places, translucently radiating the color through in some areas. This color tone is repeated throughout the painting in different ways and unifies the work!

Many artists have the misconception that when the transparent acrylic wash is dry, since it is a poly-resin binder, it will resist the overlay of casein. However, as long as the acrylic is transparent, and not applied too heavily, the medium will simply stain the fibers of the paper or the clay of the Aquabord®, and the overpainting can be applied as if there was nothing underneath. The under color, if used correctly, will influence and complement the colors in the overpainting. In other words, the underpainting should be left open in some areas, seen and felt through a veil in other areas, and completely painted over opaquely in others. Here are a few considerations when selecting the under color and overpainting.

ANALOGOUS UNDER COLOR

If the predominant color family of the painting is to be in a certain analogous range, the under color can be of the same family. For instance, if you are painting old windmills or desert scenes in neutralized warm colors such as raw siennas, burnt siennas, and burnt umbers, the under color could be a warm transparent pure hue yellow orange to orange acrylic.

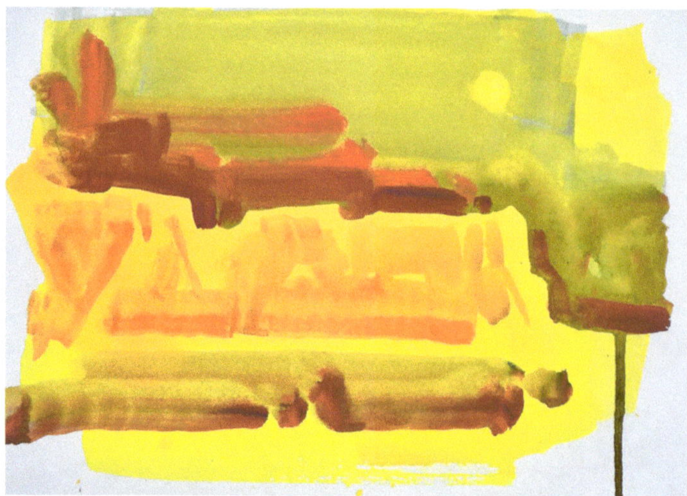

In this study I washed a cadmium yellow light transparent undertone on the surface. When it was dry I glazed over a number of colors in the yellow, yellow orange, and orange analogous families. I've neutralized with the complement to gray it down.

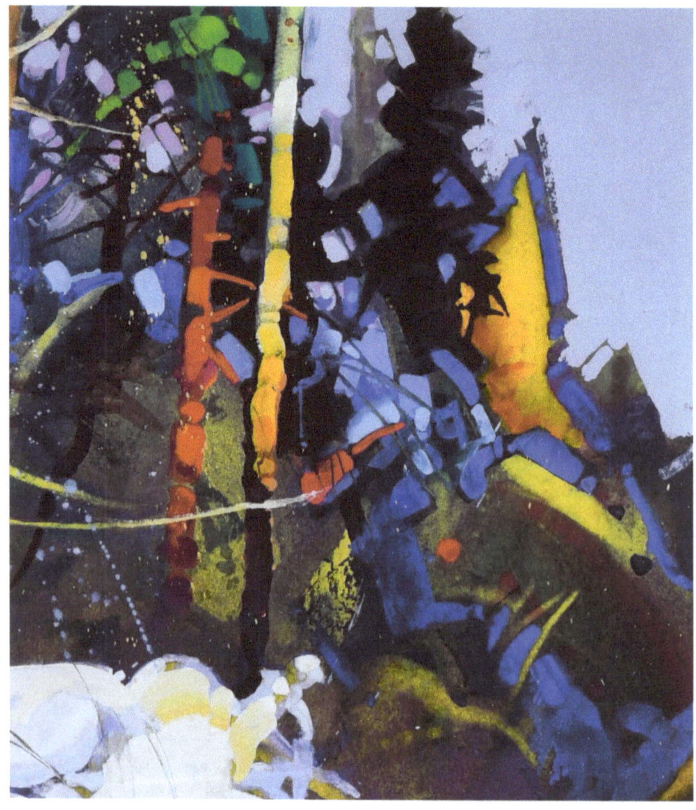

This is a detail of the painting on the opposite page. You can see the yellow and yellow-orange transparent underlay exposed and radiating through the casein washes. I have then come in with opaque casein to paint around the yellow-orange tree shape and its complementary color, ultramarine blue deep, to set off the yellow orange.

Flickering Light and Shadows, Ridge Trail 2010

casein and transparent acrylic underlay, 21 ¾" x 30"
American Watercolor Society, Ralph Smith Memorial Award 2011

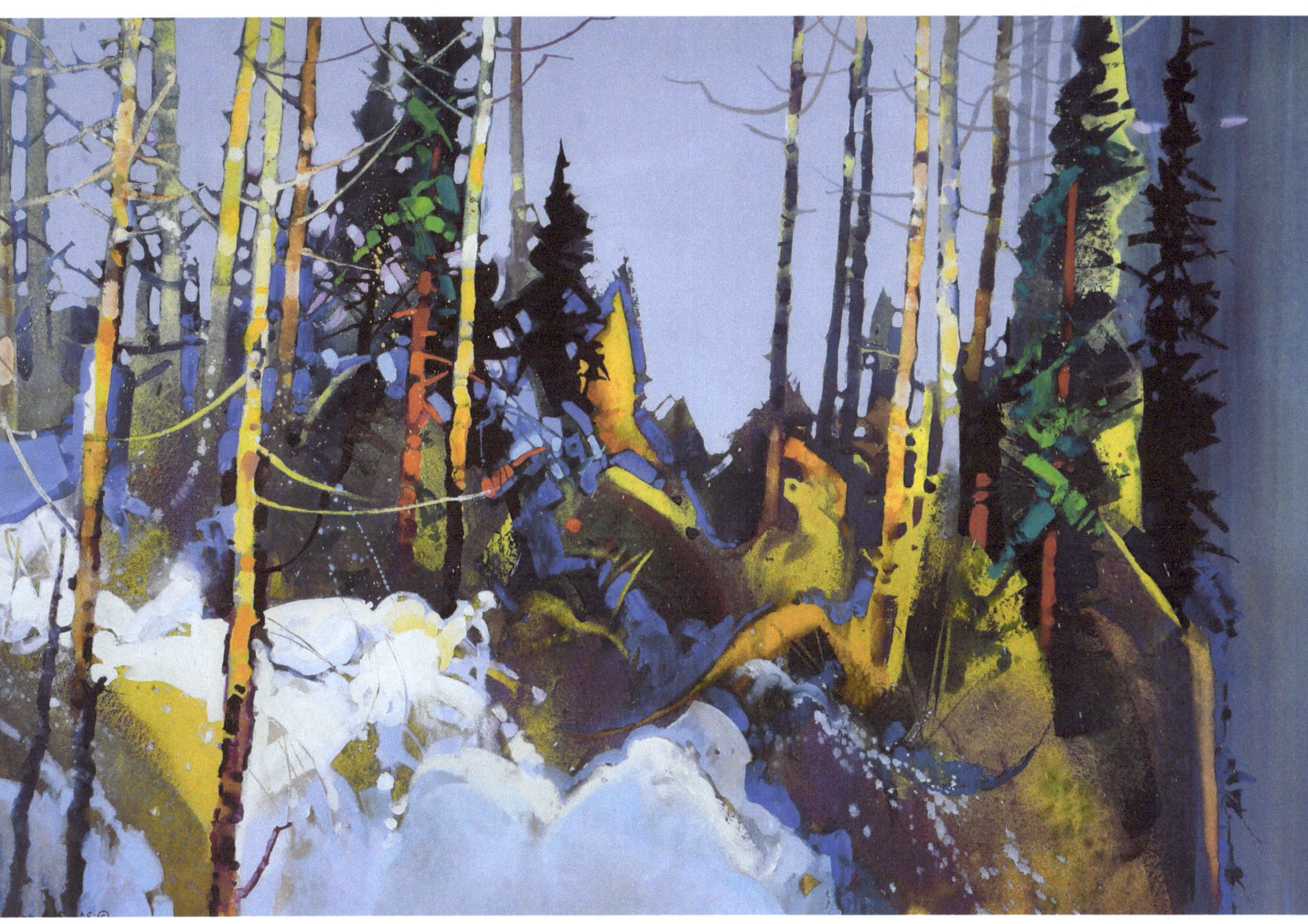

I was inspired for this painting while I was skiing down a hillside. Out of the corner of my eye I "felt" a flickering light and shadow shimmering through the trees. I climbed back up the hillside and took some notes and brief sketches. I didn't want detail but rather an impressionistic quality. Back in the studio I washed a transparent layer of yellow to yellow-orange acrylic on the paper. Once it was dry, I brought out my casein palette and began painting. Most of the casein color is in the red orange to yellow range, with some of the under color showing through. The upper negative sky area is an opaque neutral gray. I have added the few blue violet notes as a complementary color to enhance the predominant yellow families.

COMPLEMENTARY UNDER COLOR

Referring to the casein color wheel on page 29, find the complement of the color family that you will use for the painting. For instance, if it's a rocky mountain scene with predominantly neutral blues and violets applied for the rocks and cliffs, the under color can be a transparent yellow to yellow-orange acrylic. If it is a summer landscape with yellow greens to blue-greens for the meadows and vegetation, the undertone will be red-violet.

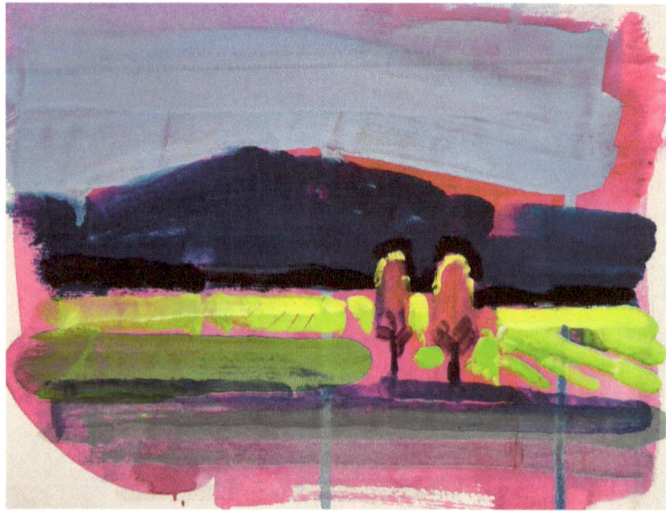

In this study I used quinacridone violet transparently with acrylic as the underlay. I then proceeded with casein in yellow greens to blue greens, letting the under color radiate through.

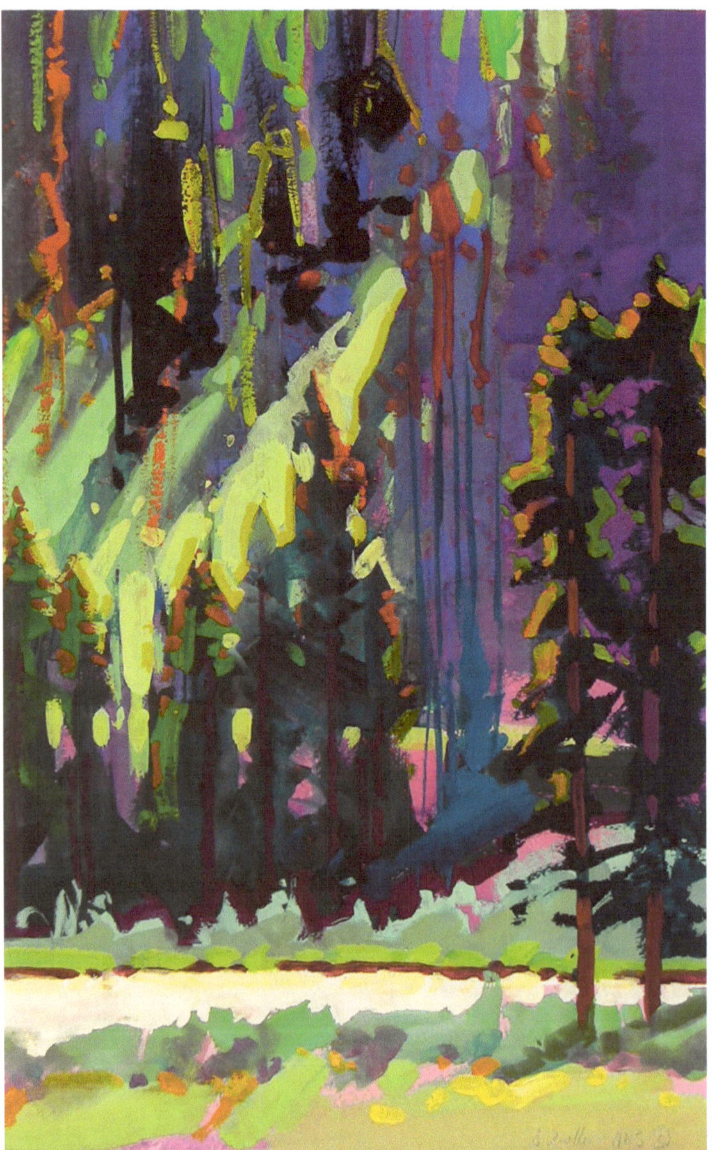

I did this painting on an early morning in the high country at 11,000 feet elevation. It was cool and crisp as the sun peeked over the high mountain, casting diagonal light and shadows down the hillside. Sunlight reflecting from the beaver pond seemed almost a brilliant yellow-white. Like the study above, I started with the transparent red-violet acrylic undertone and then painted with casein. The complementary color family was in the yellow-greens to deep blue-greens.

High Meadow by Equity
2005
casein with transparent red violet acrylic underlay
17" x 11"
Private Collection

From my studio deck, I see interesting, gnarly blue spruce that punctuate the view of the downstream Rio Grande River. They have such character. They are like elderly but lively, shiny-eyed people that we know in our lives. I've painted these trees many, many times and still cannot get enough of them.

I began this panel with a transparent red-orange acrylic under wash. With casein I then painted the dark structure of the trunk, foliage, and branches of the trees. With the color family of green, blue-green and blue, I then began painting negatively around the spruce in high key tones. I allowed some of the red-orange to be left exposed while I painted translucently with soft blue-greens in the foreground water. A bit of the red-orange undertone radiates through. Last, I did go out of the color scheme with a soft yellow band in the upper middle of the painting to create a highlight.

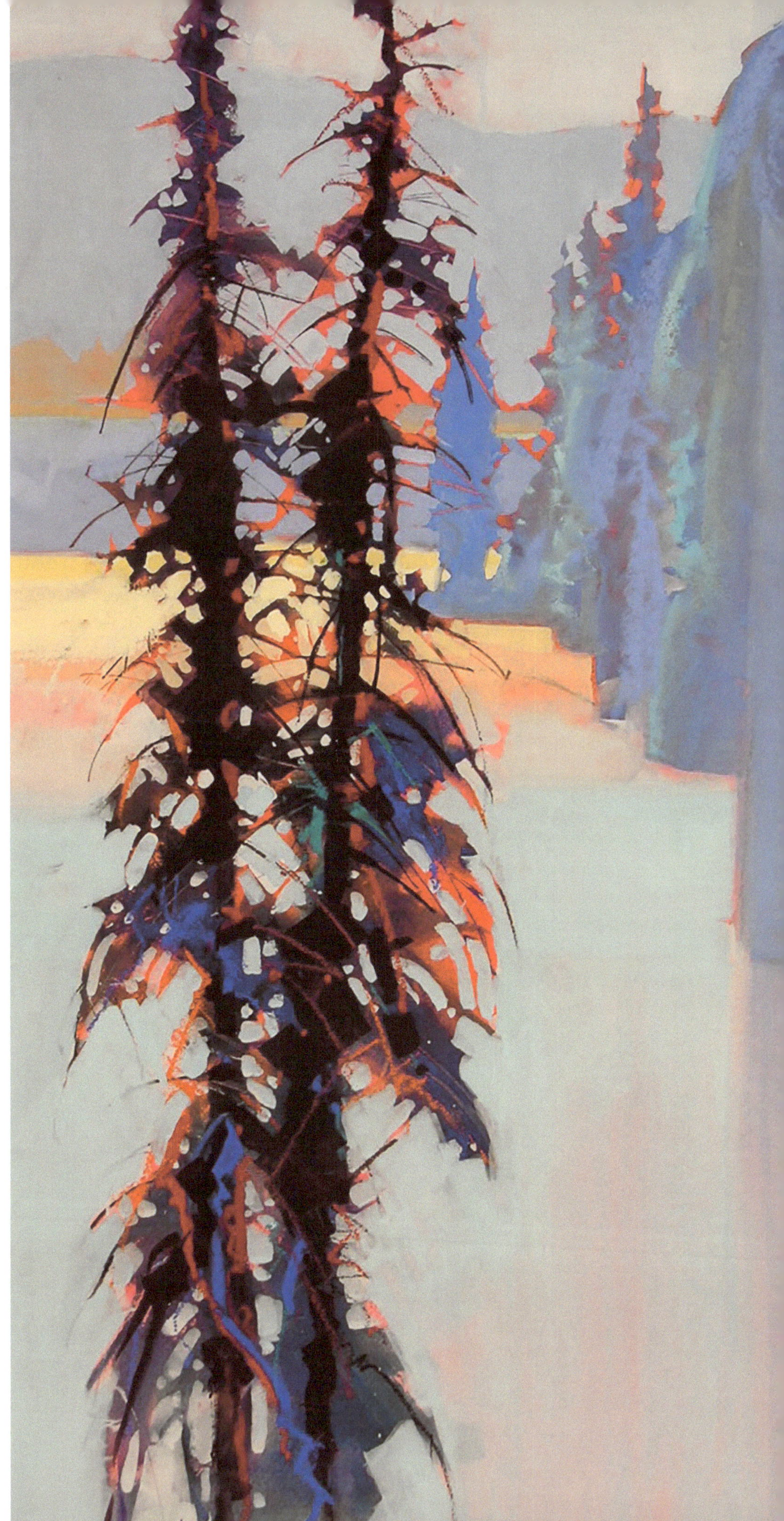

Black Spruce,
View From the Studio
2009
casein over transparent red-orange acrylic
29" x 15"
Private Collection

ATMOSPHERE OR MOOD

This approach can be loosely interpreted. The under color is selected for the mood or atmosphere that the painting needs. For example, the strong transparent acrylic under wash of yellow to yellow-orange could be selected if the painter wants a strong feeling of sunlight. The overpainting in casein needs to allow some of the underpainting to peek and radiate through, influencing the feeling of the painting as a whole.

The underpainting can be turquoise and the overpainting can create the feeling of early evening, allowing some of the under color to show through.

One could start with a gestural underpainting of yellows to yellow-oranges. This could then be followed by casein to create a field and close up of sunflowers.

The underpainting could be selected if you want to do a gray atmospheric mood or deep blue violet shadows of a summer beach scene.

Blue violets and violets, being the most spiritual of colors, could be used as an underpainting for some sort of a regal, cathedral forest scene. With your imagination, it is limitless what can be done for your personal expression.

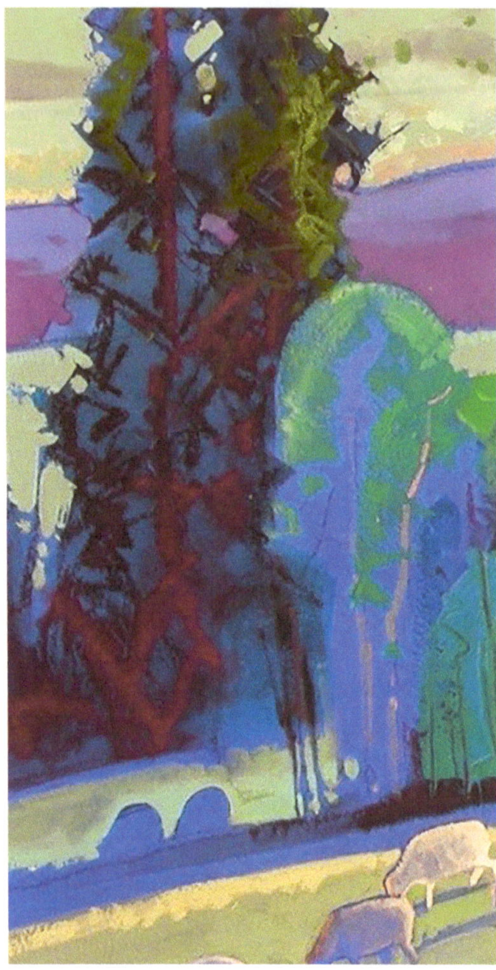

This is a detail of " Sheep Drive, San Juan's", the finished painting on page 107. The the ultramarine blue that you see in the shadow of the aspen tree and the sheep shapes is the undertone acrylic wash that I started to painting with. All the color surrounding the deep blue is painted with translucent and opaque casein. The velvety matte visual quality of the casein brings out the luminous blue of the undertone.

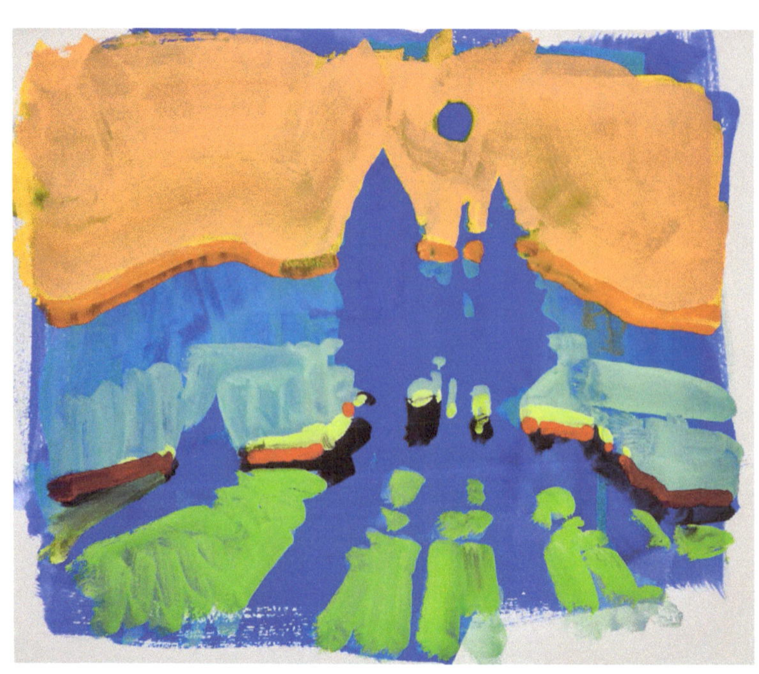

The acrylic under wash for this study is ultramarine blue deep. This, like the finished painting on page 107, creates a feeling of shadow. With casein I then painted negatively around the shapes to create the tree forms and shadows.

Sheep Drive, San Juans *2003*
casein over ultramarine blue deep acrylic underlay, 26" x 34"
Artist's Collection

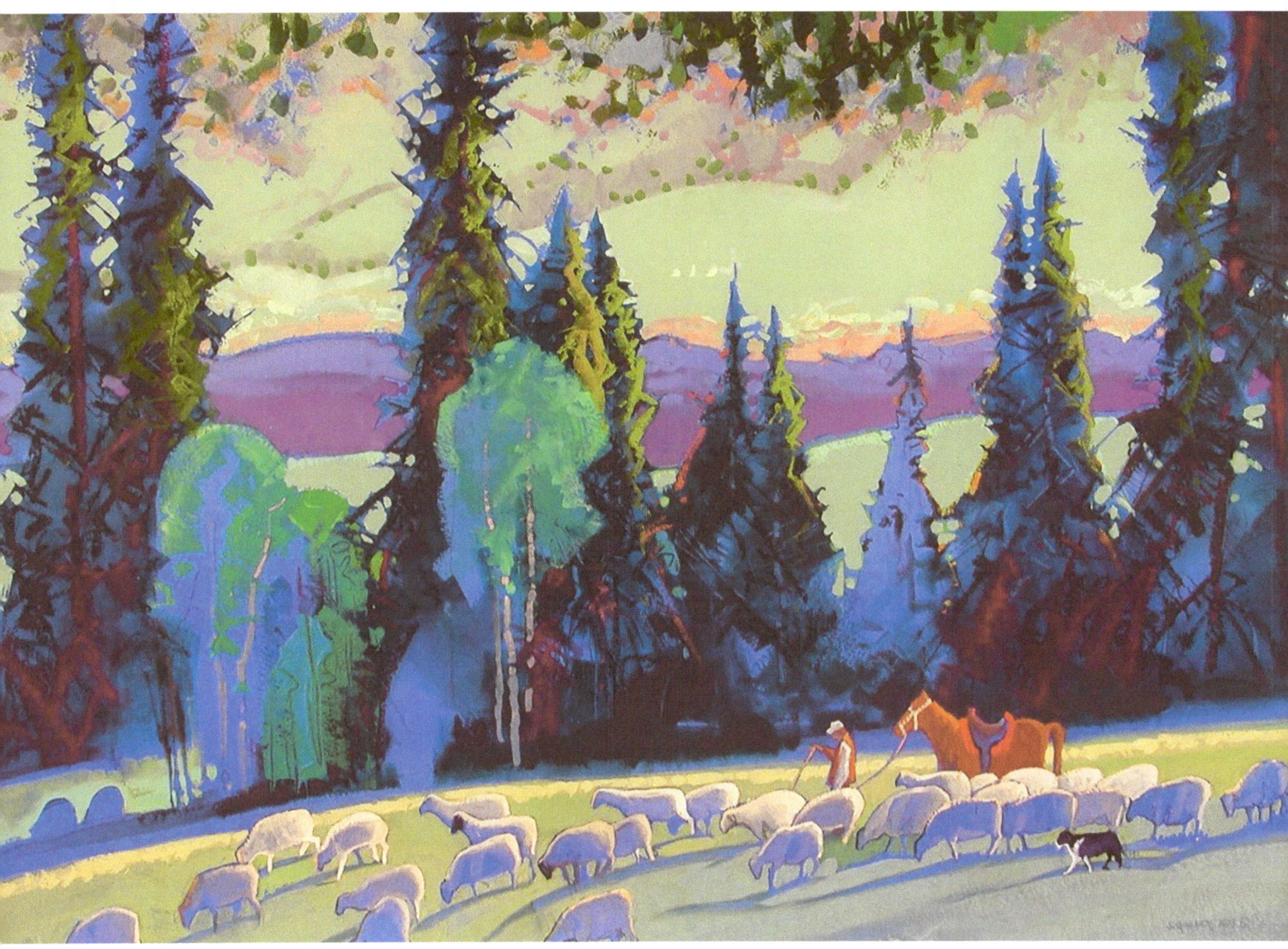

On this particular late June day I followed the sheep drive not far from my studio. I took my sketchbook and camera, as the sheep were moving at a slow pace. I've actually done quick watercolor studies as the sheep moved toward me in the canyon. I began by coating my watercolor paper with rich ultramarine blue acrylic, for the essence of summer and deep shadow. In this painting, wherever you see the blue, it is the exposed acrylic, such as in the trees and the shadows of the sheep. I then used casein to capture the feeling of the heat, the stillness, and the dryness of the summer day. The Basque sheepherder, horse and sheepdog were also important elements in the composition.

MULTICOLOR UNDER PAINTING

This can be used if the artist chooses to have a warm to cool gradation, a multicolored floral pattern, or a festive mood. Obviously, this approach could be used very beautifully with abstract painting. First, dive in with multicolored bright acrylic worked transparently on a rigid support. Once it is dry, apply the casein both translucently and opaquely, leaving some of the shapes of the under color exposed. While it is still damp, scrape into the casein to expose the under color or lift into soft shapes. In some areas leave translucent passages. It can be exciting and quite beautiful.

Another example could be the painting of a loose bright floral arrangement in transparent acrylic using red-violets, roses, red-orange to yellow-orange and white. Then, paint negatively around the flower shapes in opaque casein, using the vegetation colors. I particularly like painting the opaque casein around bright acrylic transparent color. The light reflects off the rich, transparent luminous acrylic, contrasting with the velvety-matte opaque casein.

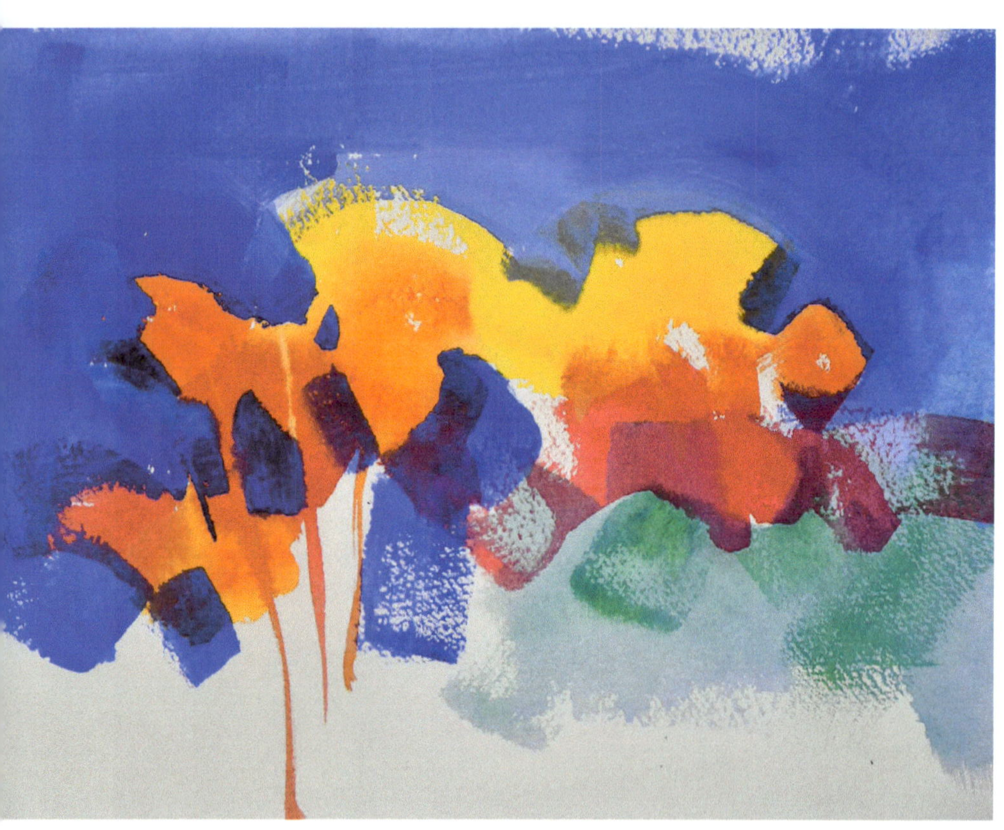

Gladioli, France
2002 (right)
Multicolored red-orange to yellow-orange transparent acrylic floral pattern underlay with casein
29" x 21"
Private Collection

This study is a good example of a multicolored underlay in transparent acrylic. First I charged in yellow, yellow-orange, and red transparent acrylic shapes. When it was dry, I came in with ultramarine blue deep casein mixed with some white, painting opaquely around the brilliant acrylic color.

I spent an extended period of time with my family painting in France. One day I purchased an array of gladioli, daisies, and iris, and set them up on a picnic table in our yard. I started with acrylic transparently and painted in the floral shapes. Some of the white gladioli and daisies were simply the white of the watercolor paper. I did the rest of the painting completely with casein. I love how the opaque color surrounds the white and orange transparent shapes, bringing them to life.

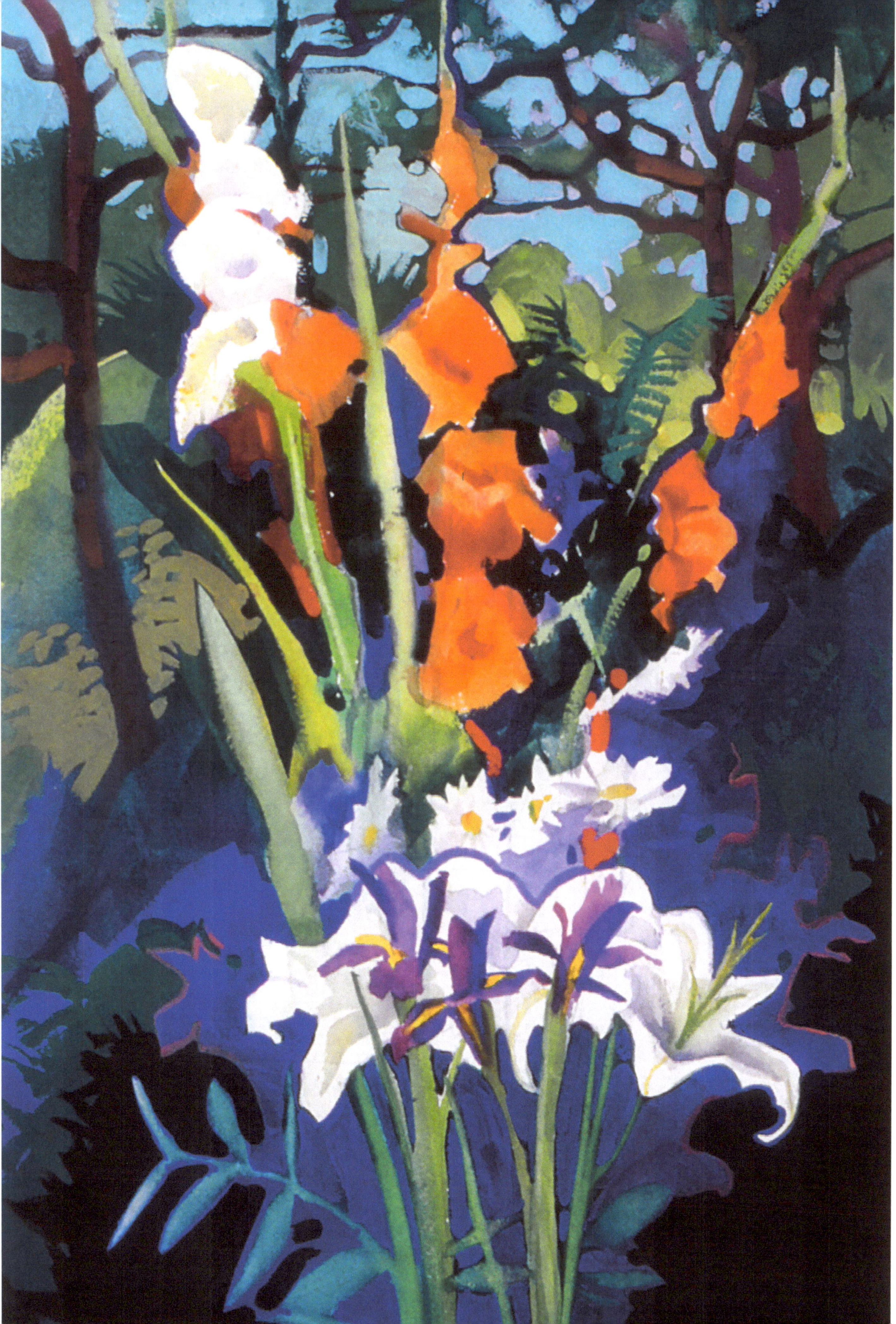

EN GRISAILLE METHOD

I referred to this method in the introduction to this chapter. Working in this manner, the acrylic transparent undertone is all in neutrals. The lighter and darker color is built on a middle value surface. The casein around the neutral tone will influence how you see the gray. It will influence the mood. This could well be used for a gray atmospheric coastal day or a stormy mountain scene.

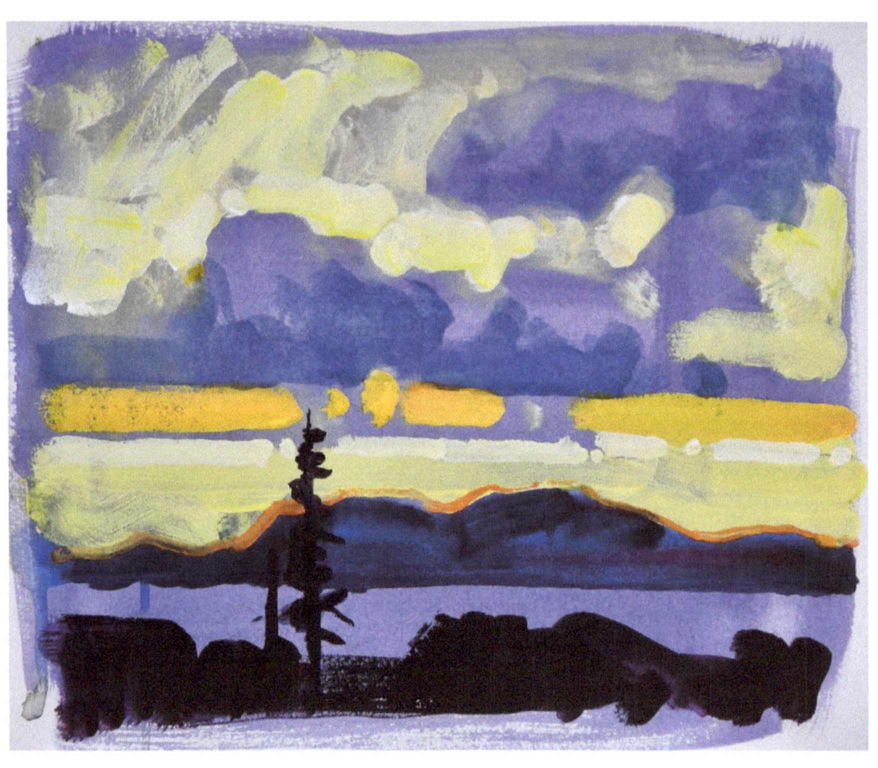

In this study I simply started by washing in a neutral, to the violet side, transparent acrylic. When it was dry, I built the light yellow to yellow orange sky around the cloud patterns, the dark hill, and the foreground island and tree. Beginning with the neutral tone, the artist needs to think of value, building to the light and pushing to the darks.

Cloud Shadows
2015 (right)
transparent acrylic neutral tone with casein overlay.
24" x 18"
Private Collection

I often fly on a "puddle jumper" from Denver, passing over the Sangre de Cristo Mountains, and land in the San Luis Valley. I get many of my ideas from these flights. On this particular day the clouds were socked in and I literally could not see any landforms. However, as we approached the airport, the clouds opened and revealed the mountains, field patterns and cloud shadows below. This was inspiration for a painting. I began with the neutral gray transparent acrylic wash on the watercolor board. Then I finished the painting, building the color and value using the neutral gray as the key element from which to work.

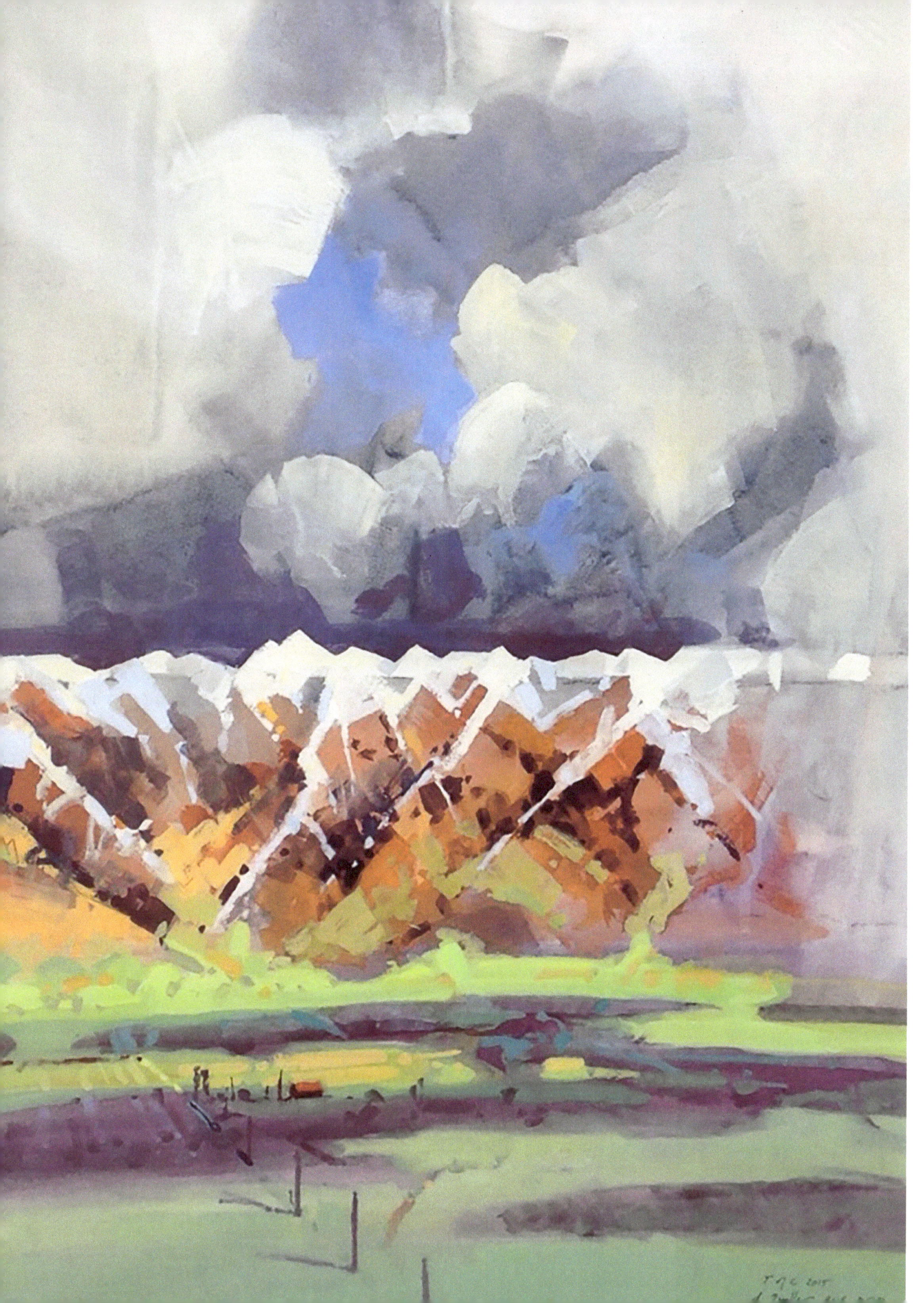

Casein with Transparent Acrylic and Granulating Watercolor

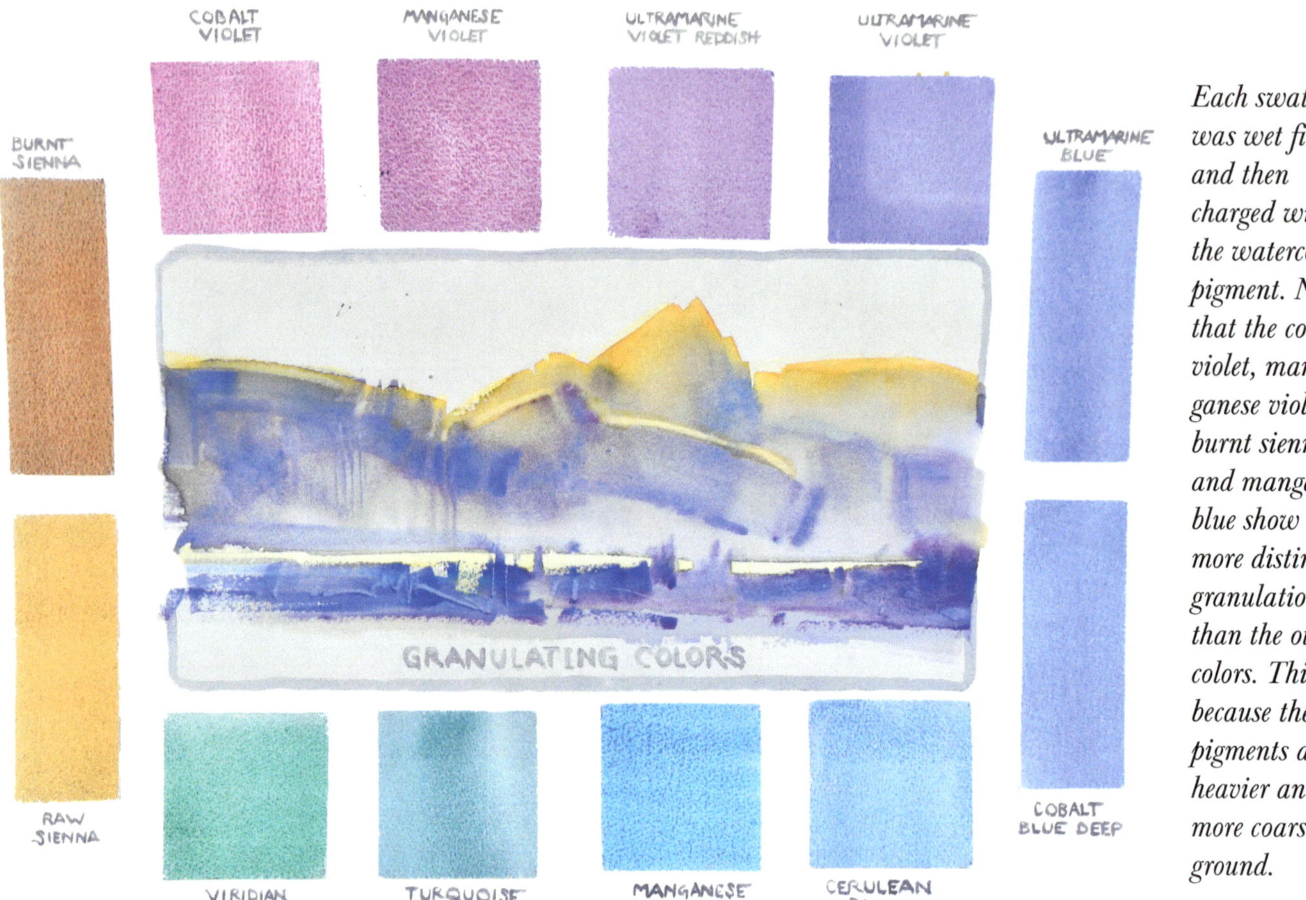

Each swatch was wet first and then charged with the watercolor pigment. Notice that the cobalt violet, manganese violet, burnt sienna and manganese blue show a more distinct granulation than the other colors. This is because their pigments are heavier and more coarsely ground.

My life's work has predominantly been about color and water media. For over 40 years I've experimented with the different water media, their handling characteristics and visual qualities. In this section I want to talk about an approach that I've been using for the last few years and find it extremely exciting. Painting in this direction I actually use three different water media, each to their advantage. Although I've been playing with this direction for a while, I feel I'm only scratching the surface. Earlier I demonstrated working with transparent acrylic as an underlay. I use this technique for two reasons. First, it is very luminous and intense when used transparently, and the under color radiates through the overlay. Second, the acrylic paint will not lift once it is totally dry. I will be using this method to start the following studies and paintings. I will discuss the granulating watercolor paint, as this will be a very important part of this painting process.

GRANULATING WATERCOLOR PIGMENTS

Watercolor is another water medium but it is very different in its visual qualities and handling characteristics from casein and acrylic. I want to use this medium to its advantage. First of all, watercolor can be lifted after it is totally dry. With this medium you can soften the edges, lift back to the near white paper and glaze over, using it for painterly approaches.

There are basically two kinds of pigments used in every medium, whether it be watercolor, acrylic, or casein. I'm interested here with the mineral and earth pigments in watercolor. These pigments are a heavier density and are ground more coarsely than the transparent, staining organic pigments. This means that the pigments sink quickly in the water and are also more coarsely ground. They tend to sit on the surface of the support rather than infiltrate and stain the fibers of the paper, watercolor board or clay coated surface. Above is a granulating pigment chart.

Here is some key information to achieve this granulating visual effect. First, the paper needs to be a very rough texture. I have found the Hahnemuhle German paper to be extraordinary. Second, the paper should be almost horizontal to allow the pigment to sink into the pockets of the paper. Third, the paper should be very wet to allow the heavy and course pigments time to sink.

Notice the sharp edges contrasting against the wet granulating marks. When these strokes are damp or dry, I can come back and lift with the damp clean brush back to the white paper.

STUDY #1

In this study I simply wet the paper and charged in the granulating watercolor and let it rest. I used cerulean blue and some ultramarine blue deep. When this paint is damp to totally dry, it can be lifted. Notice the distinct character of the granulating pigments sinking to the pockets of the rough paper.

STUDY #2

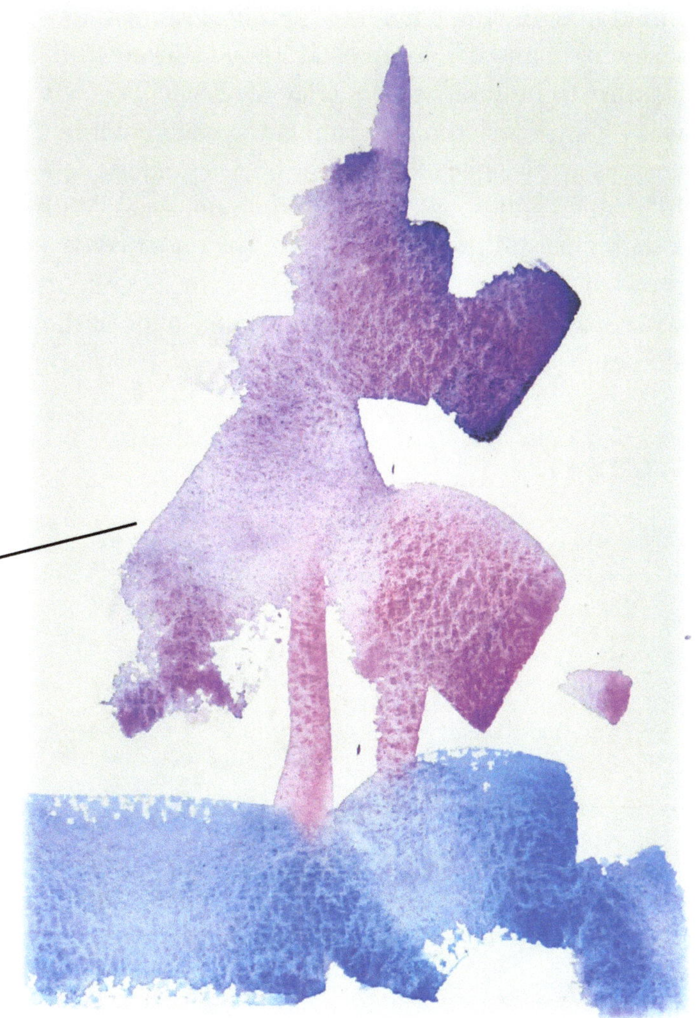

Contrasting to the last study, I did this work on dry paper. The key here again is that the paper needs to be almost horizontal and the brush has to be very wet and loaded with granulating color. With this juicy, wet, highly charged pigmented brush I can put down spontaneous marks on dry paper. The brush marks will allow the granulating pigment time to sink on the rough paper. Here I used ultramarine violet, cobalt violet, and cerulean blue watercolor.

COMBINING THESE MEDIA TOGETHER

Here are two studies that demonstrate the combination of the three media of acrylic, granulating watercolor, and casein. In each study I started with a transparent luminous underlay of acrylic. When it was totally dry, I applied granulating watercolor in various areas while allowing the acrylic undertone to be open and not painted over in some areas. With a damp brush I then lifted back to the under color through the granulating watercolor. Last, I came in with opaque casein and painted around some of the shapes to set them off.

STUDY #1

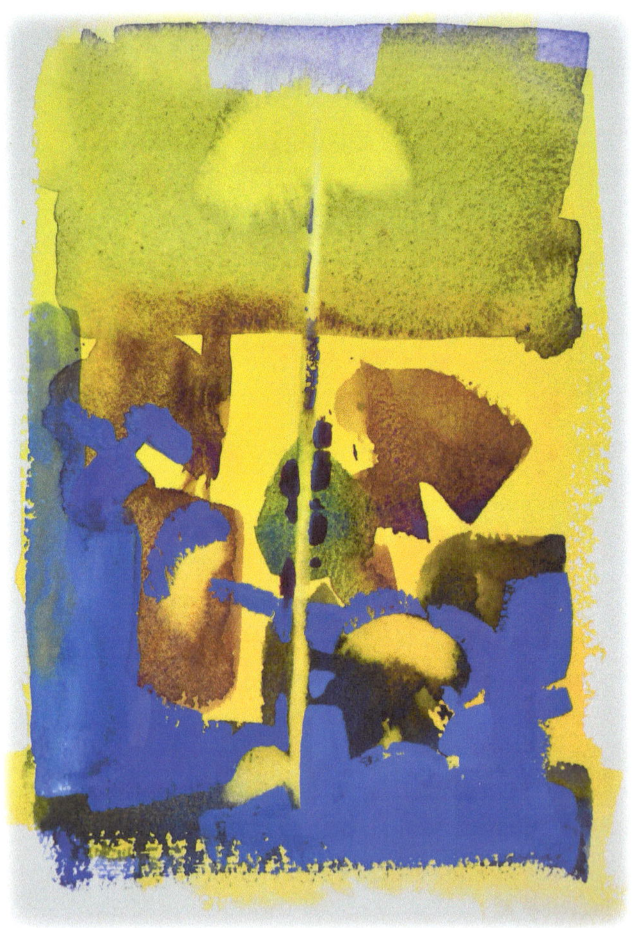

I applied yellow transparent acrylic on the rough watercolor paper and let it dry. I then washed in the granulating watercolors ultramarine violet and manganese violet, leaving some of the yellow untouched. I then came in with opaque ultramarine blue deep casein to set off the shapes and accentuate the transparent visual quality.

STUDY #2

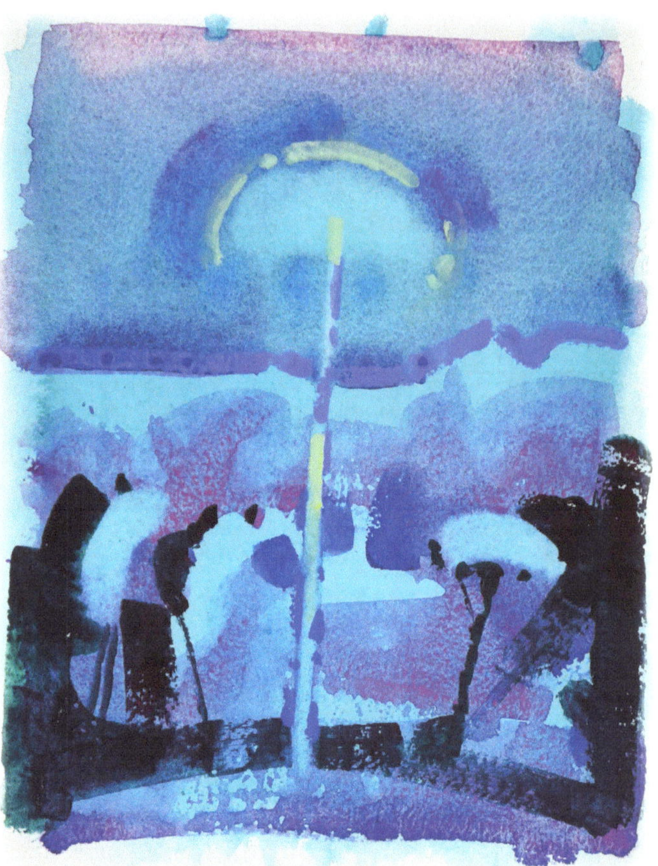

I started with a transparent turquoise wash of acrylic and let it dry. I then used cobalt violet, cerulean blue, and ultramarine blue deep granulating watercolor, and charged in the various wet passages. When the paper was slightly damp I lifted with a clean damp brush in some areas to expose the under color. Finally, I came in with the dark, opaque casein mix of Shiva green and quinacridone violet, and painted around some of the shapes.

Evening Star, Moon Shadows 2005

transparent acrylic, granulating watercolor and casein, 23 ¾" x 36"

Collection of Erick Mann

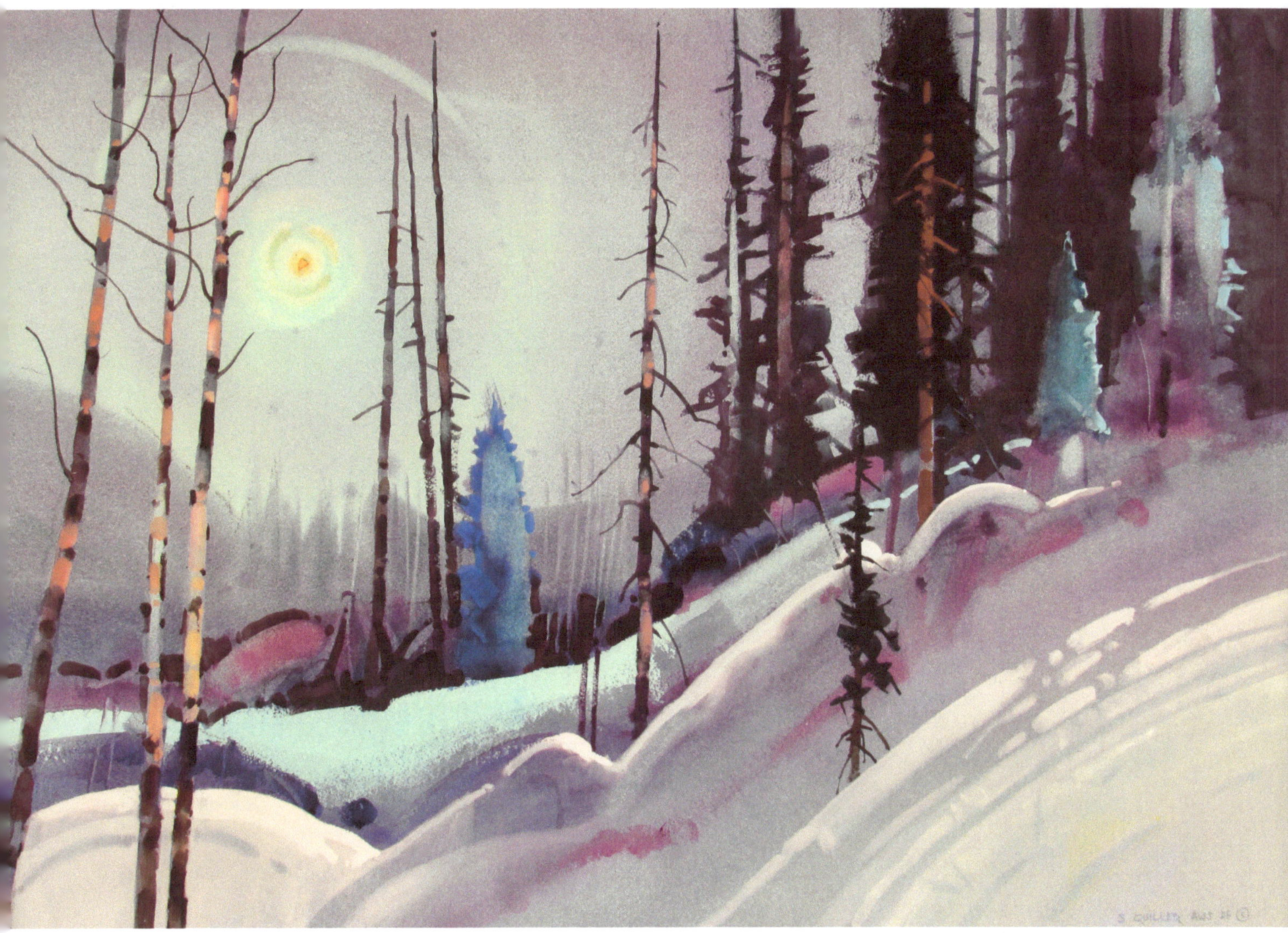

I was inspired for this image while I was on a moonlight ski. It was a full moon, casting shadows, and I could see Venus shining ahead while I skied. The shadows moved rhythmically from left to right. I began with with a teal transparent acrylic underlay. I then wet the paper and charged in cobalt violet, manganese violet, and cerulean granulating watercolors, and lifted back to the star's radiant aura. I applied the opaque passages of casein, forming the dark trees at upper right which flowed down to the three vertical aspen on the left. The casein punctuated and set off the rest of the painting.

Inspiration comes when I least expect it. I truly believe that the best ideas find me rather than me seeking them! I was on a late afternoon ski with friends. I was not looking for painting material but just enjoying the day. While I was skiing down a gentle slope, my friend who was behind me exclaimed "Steve, did you see the snow bow?" I turned around and skied back to his location and there it was! I've been skiing in these mountains for decades and never experienced this. The crystals hanging in the sunshine projected the snow bow. I jotted down a few lines and made some mental notes to return the next day at the same time to capture the essence of the light and shadow.

Back in the studio on a rough sheet of 300# watercolor paper I washed an undertone of transparent yellow. Once it was dry, I rewet the paper and charged in the granulating watercolors of manganese violet and cerulean blue, and then I gradually painted in the sun and snow bow in the sky, some of the dark patterns of the trees, and the ice blue negative opaque notes behind the trees in opaque casein. With the same medium I put in the lower white horizontal band at the base of the trees. Finally, I lifted around the shadows for the radiant light on the snow.

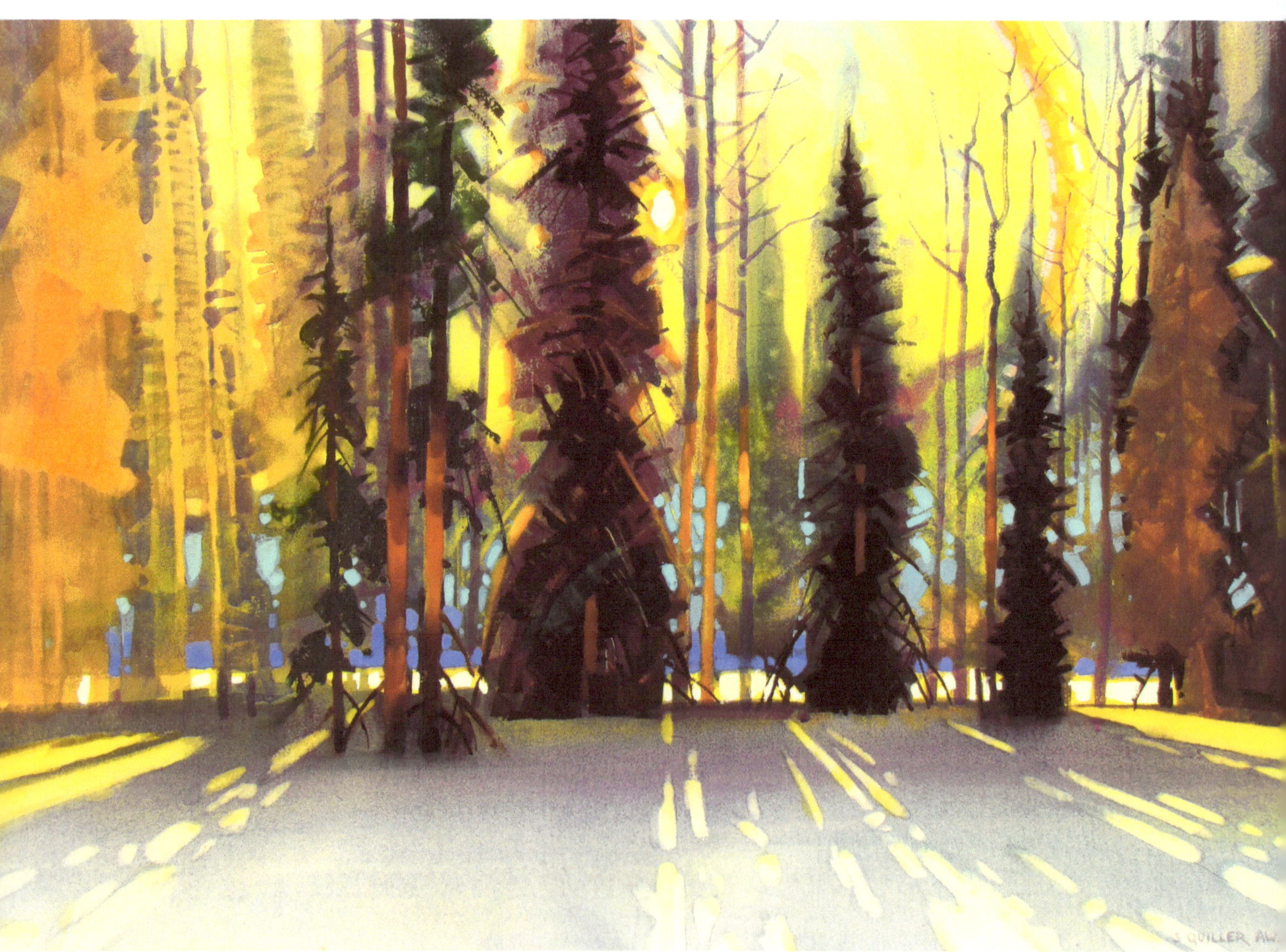

Snow Bow 2003
transparent acrylic, granulating watercolor and casein, 23 ½" x 34"
Collection of Dorothy Sander

Pulsating Night Sky
2008
transparent acrylic, granulating watercolor, and casein
36" x 24"
Collection of Pete and Lindsey Leavell

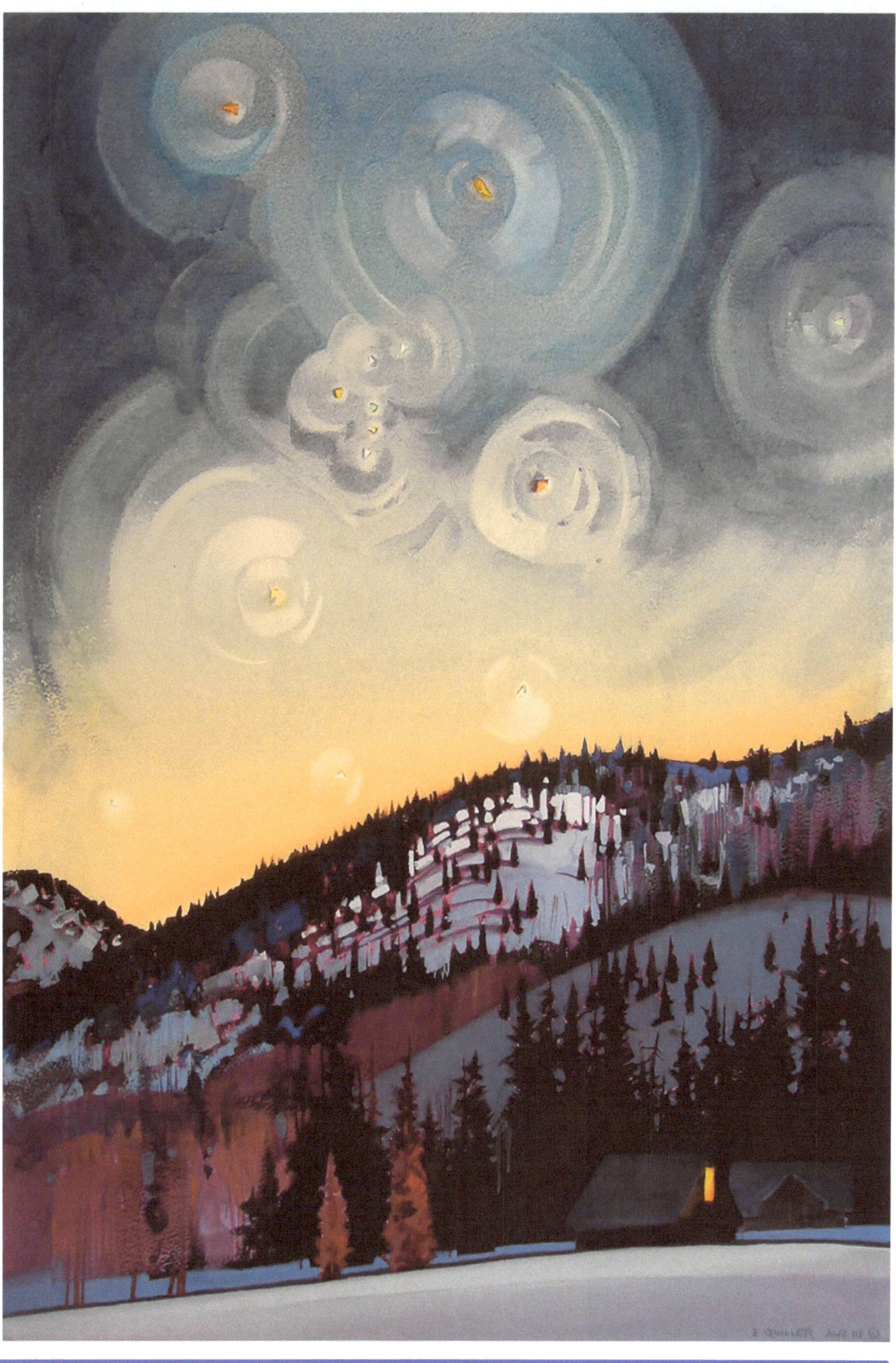

I live in a rural region of the San Juan Mountains in southern Colorado. We have almost no light pollution in our dark skies. On moonless nights we witness the Milky Way and constellations. As I returned to the house from my studio one late evening I saw Orion lit up in the sky, and nearby was a lone cabin with one light on, a bright yellow-orange against the contrast of black. I sensed a red-violet underlay on the mountain forms.

I washed in a transparent yellow orange in the sky, moving to a red-violet acrylic wash on the mountain foreground. Once it was dry, I played with the granulating watercolors cerulean blue, ultramarine, and manganese violet, and lifted back to the undertone, delicately glazing over with watercolor. I then painted with opaque casein to build solid mountain forms and snow, light and shadows, and dark tree patterns. Last, I painted the black cabin to set off the transparent yellow orange light in the window, and the foreground snow.

Casein with Charcoal

Casein is compatible with drawing media. The dry velvety visual quality of the medium works well with charcoal. There is an earthiness about it. The charcoal can be applied before or during the casein painting process, or later on top of the paint. There are no rules, and the artist is free to experiment. This could go well with any subject. I can imagine it combined with figure drawing. Below is one example of a painting that I completed using these two media. It is important to note that when the painting is complete, four or five coats of a pastel varnish is necessary.

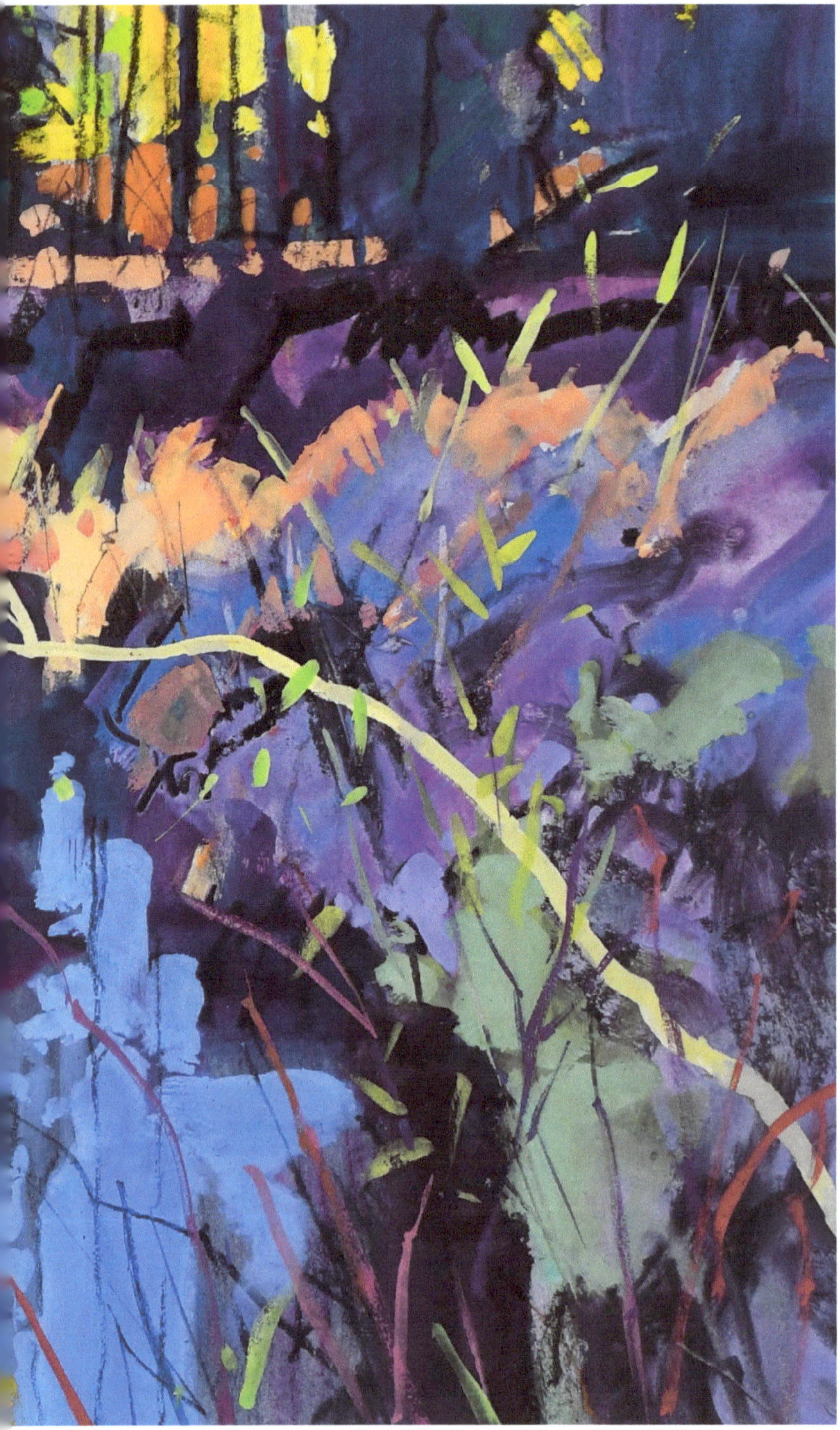

This detail demonstrates how the charcoal drawing medium can integrate and be compatible with casein. At the lower right I took my thumb and smudged the charcoal into the casein. In other areas I used line for a crisp mark. In all areas I found the compressed charcoal to be the best drawing tool compared to the natural willow charcoal.

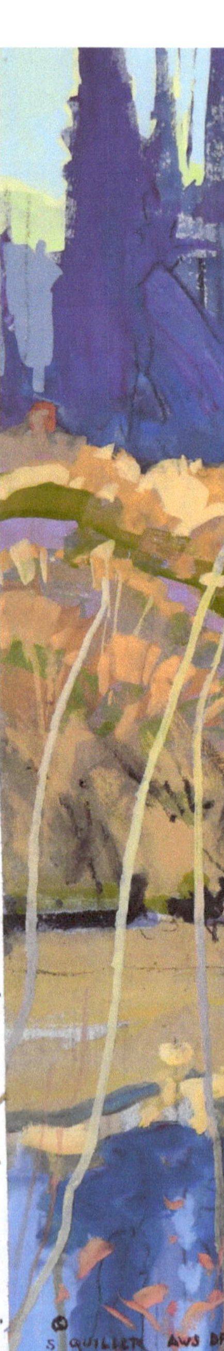

Moose were introduced to our area Colorado in the 1990s and have adapted well! I see them often when I am out painting. Although I am not known as a wildlife painter, from time to time I have the urge to introduce an animal or animals into my painting. This is one of those times. However, in this painting I wanted to capture the mud, the dirt, and the earthiness of this animal as a part of the landscape. I felt it important to use charcoal to emulate this feeling along with the casein. After working out the color and composition in a way similar to the paintings in Chapter 3, I started this work on Crescent cold press watercolor board. This surface was important because the paper has a nice tooth to accept the charcoal drawing.

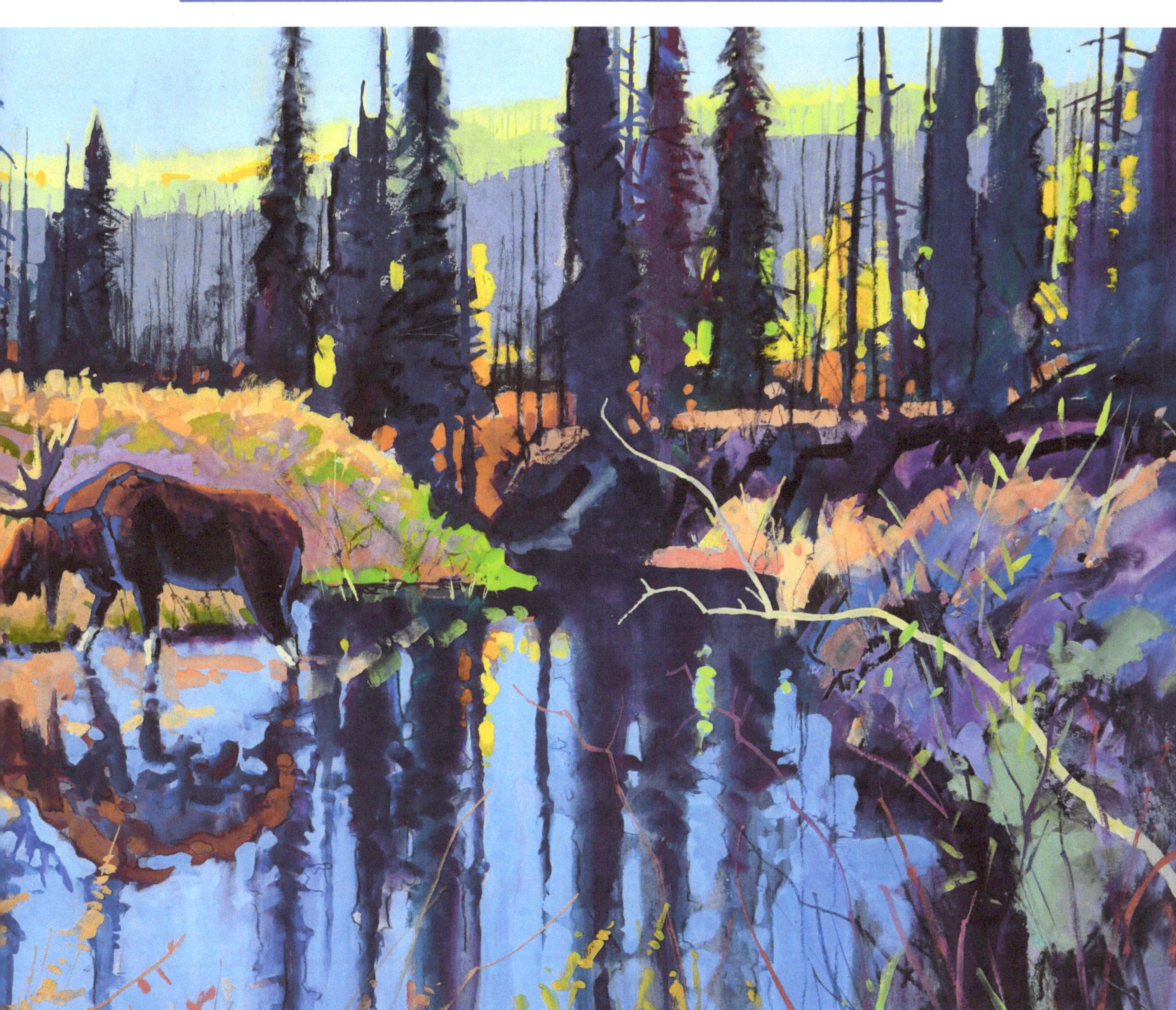

Moose, Deer Lakes 2009
casein and charcoal, 20" x 30"
Private Collection

Casein with Pastel

I've never seen two mediums that are more compatible than casein and pastel. The velvety, chalky, dry visual quality of casein has the same visual quality of the dry marks of pastel. Edgar Dégas built layer upon layer of pastel, wetting the medium and varnishing with a mixture that is not known to this day. They even estimate that one third of his pastel paintings have a ghost of a monotype underneath. He was not afraid to experiment. If you have some pastels, bring them out and experiment with them along with layers of casein. Remember to use a pastel fixative on the finished painting. I would suggest working with a cold press watercolor board. The surface has a nice tooth to accept the pastel drawing.

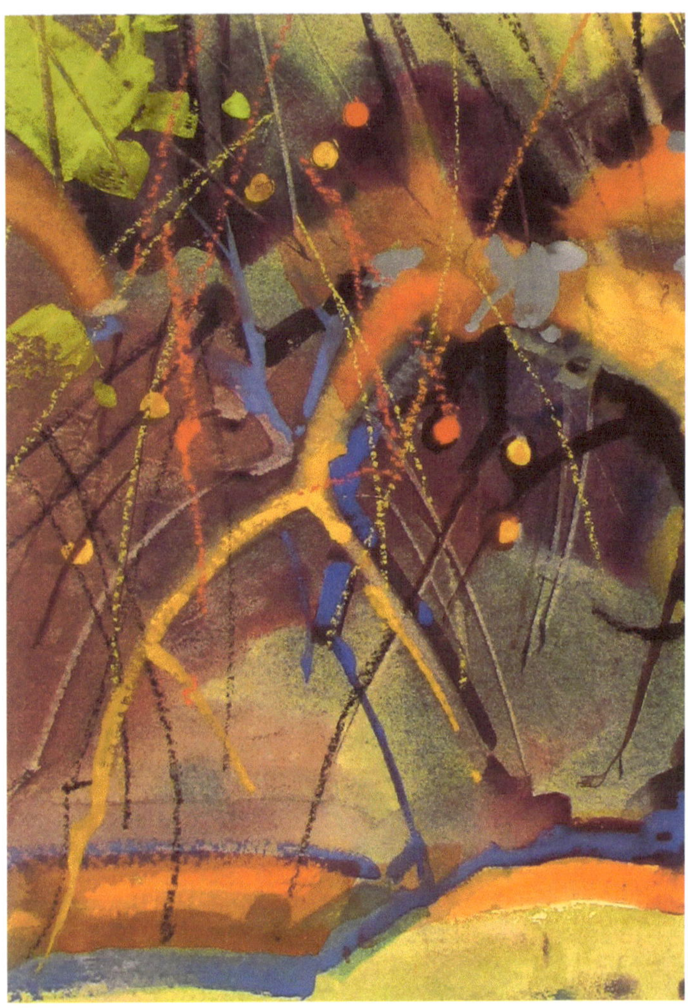

This detail shows the extent of my experimentation. First I layered the transparent warm yellow acrylic on a rough 300# watercolor paper. Then I wet the paper and washed in granulating watercolor. I lifted back to the undertone and applied casein notes in and around the branch forms as well as the apples. Finally, I came back with the dry pastel marks over the rough paper to create the textural line of the branches.

I've used this this ancient apple tree, with its strong character, in a number of my paintings. I found this tree while exploring some of the backcountry in Taos, New Mexico. I spent the day drawing this tree from different angles. There were sheep in the field next to this iconic tree. Although normally when I work with casein and pastel, I use cold press watercolor board, for this piece I also used granulating watercolor, and the rough paper was important. I used casein to paint in the yellow background negatively around the granulating watercolor, and I also added in the cool and warm marks of the shadow and sunlight of the tree with the dark passages behind. The ultramarine blue deep casein links the foreground, the sheep and the tree. The bright yellow to orange opaque apples add syncopated notes to the composition. Finally, the sweeping linear marks of the pastel add a whimsical carefree feeling to the composition.

Exercise #1 Paint a bright colorful underpainting using transparent yellow orange, orange and red acrylic on cold press watercolor board, emulating floral patterns. When dry, paint around the flower shapes with transluscent and opaque casein, to make the flowers pop!

Exercise#2 On a sheet of rough, 300# watercolor paper, wash a bright transparent yellow acrylic tone. When dry, re-wet and charge in granulating watercolor using manganese violet and ceurelean blue. When dry, lift back to the yellow undertone and accentuate shapes using translucent and opaque casein.

Exercise#3 On a sheet of cold press watercolor board or Aquabord®, paint some loose floral or autumn foliage shapes. When dry, draw in some marks and patterns with pastel to go along with the underpainting.

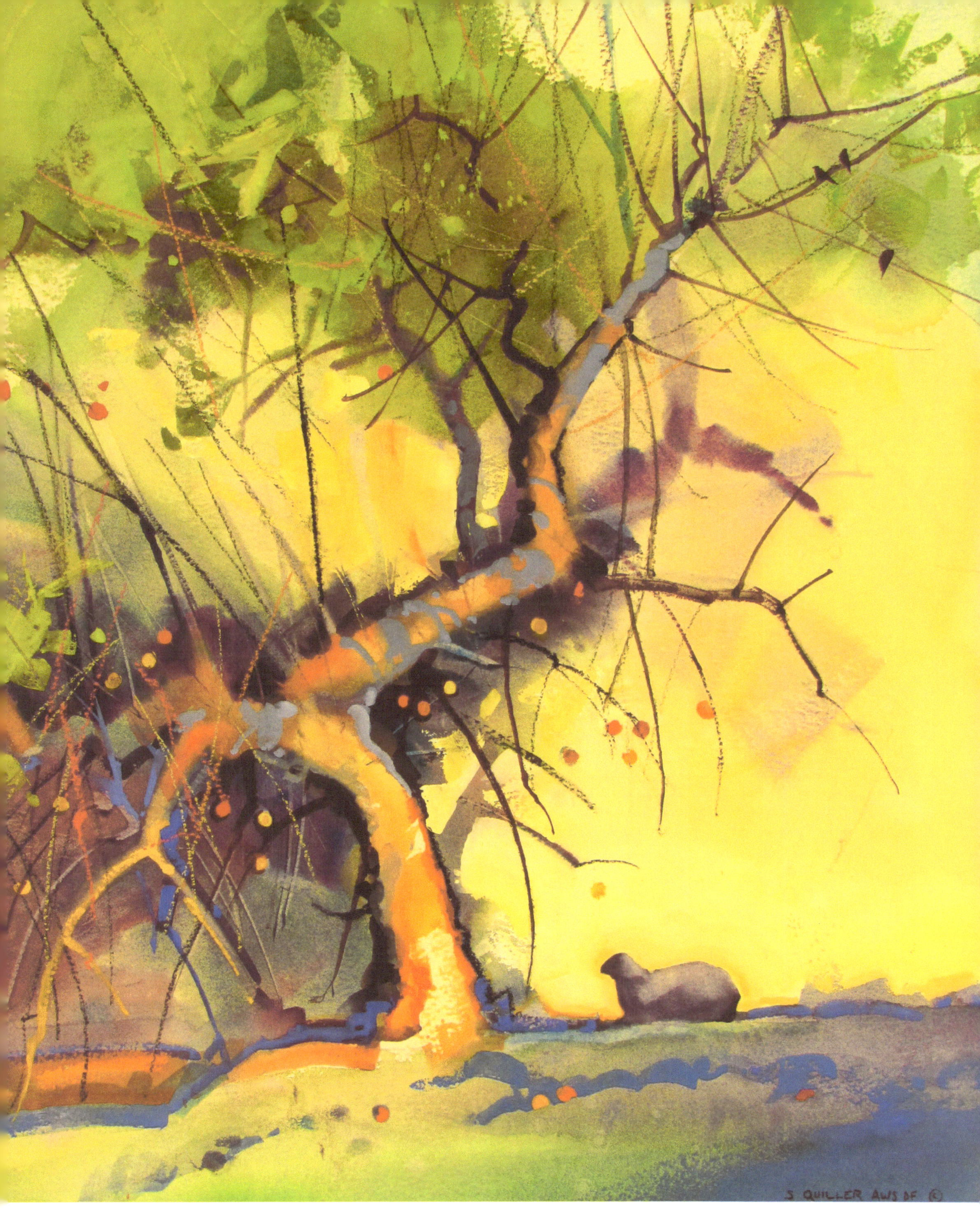

Sheep With Yellow Apples 2011
acrylic, watercolor, casein with pastel, 21 ½" x 19"
Private Collection

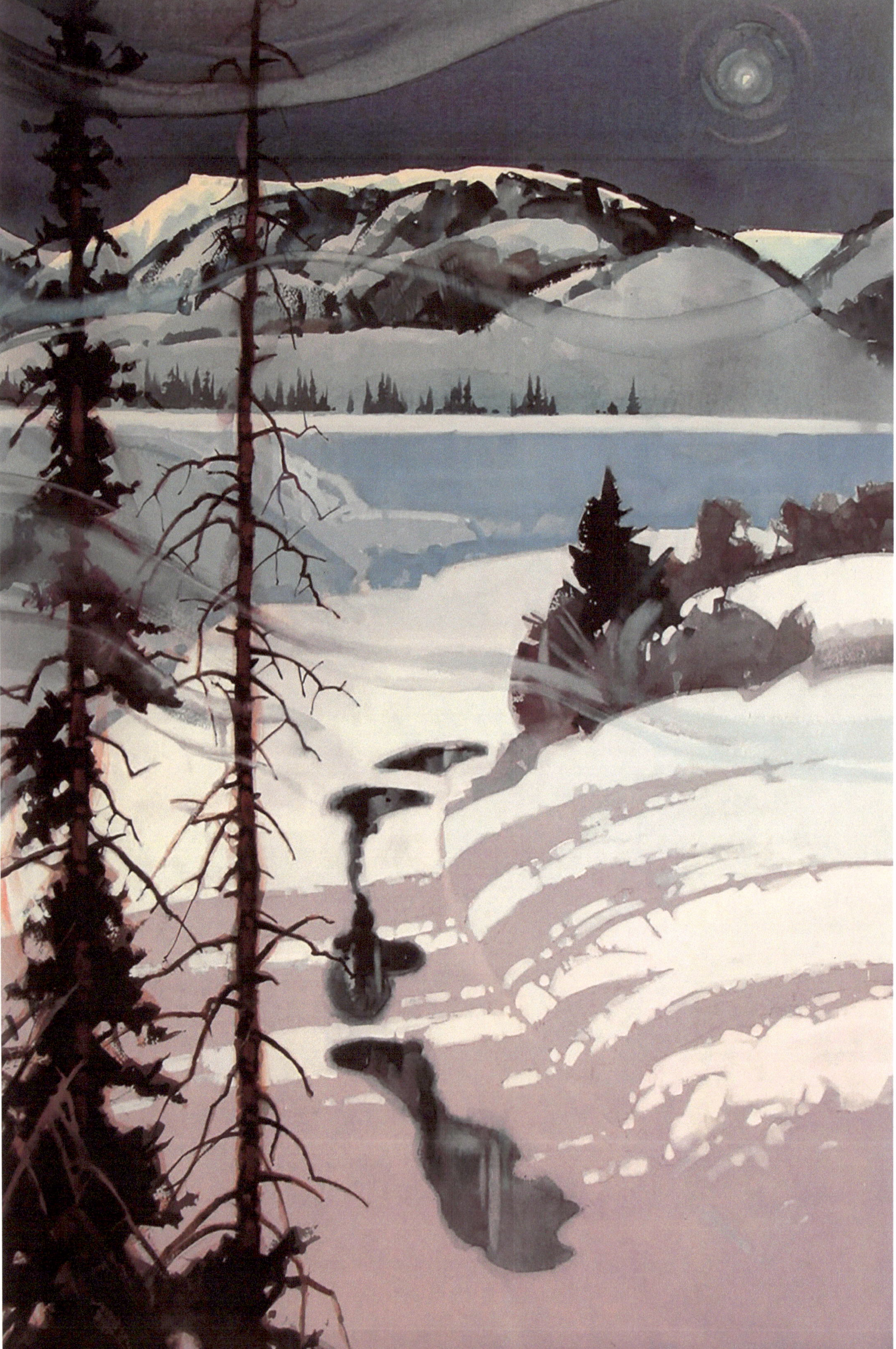

6 A Gallery "Symphony" of Casein Paintings

Night Breeze
(left) 2010
watercolor and casein, 28" x 28"
Diane and Jim Knutson

For many years I've kept journals, recording many thoughts from an artist's perspective. I have divided these thoughts into six categories:

Living life as an artist
Painting
Spiritual
Teaching art and workshop stories
Nature
Mentors and Masters: Museums and Study.

In this chapter I would like to blend a "symphony" of my work with some of my journaling thoughts and excerpts. I will display the selection of paintings dating from the 1970s up to the present, and journal excerpts from the early 90s.

May 22, 2005

In late July of 1967, I connected my 1950 Studebaker to a small teardrop trailer with a mattress inside, along with my painting gear, and headed for the Tetons and Jackson Hole. I painted there for a few days, sleeping in the trailer and hosing myself down occasionally. I had been introduced the year before to the work of Conrad Schwiering, a painter living in this Jackson Hole area, and wanted to meet him. One day I got directions and headed to his home. In retrospect, this is what being young and naive can do. I went to his home and he was out painting. But his wife was gracious and did show me around their home and studio. What I remember is that his studio, in the valley of the Tetons, had an incredible view of the majestic peaks. I thought that this has to be the ultimate life! Now I look across the valley floor to the San Juans and the La Garita range and realize that the thought I had in 1967 was put out into the universe and has come back many, many times over. My view is of an older range, softer, rounded, wizened sage-like mountain forms, so beautiful and easy to live with. I have material for a life time!

May 11, 1996

I notice that many times I have used and continue to use a band of the river that flows through my compositions. It is a compositional device that weaves and connects many of the elements in the composition, while connecting and repeating color as well. However, as I drive down to South Fork, CO today on my way to Taos, NM to teach a workshop, it dawns on me that this compositional device, this tool, is really basically part of my being. I have been a part of this river for over twenty five years and it has weaved through every part of my being. I drive this road weekly if not more often and watch this silver band of the river wind slowly through my mountains and through the valley, sometimes light and sometimes dark, sometimes fast or slow, sometimes clear and sometimes muddy, sometimes open and sometimes frozen. This water moves on endlessly, each droplet different, yet the flow never ends. I am so fortunate to be a part of this river and to observe it for the short time I am here.

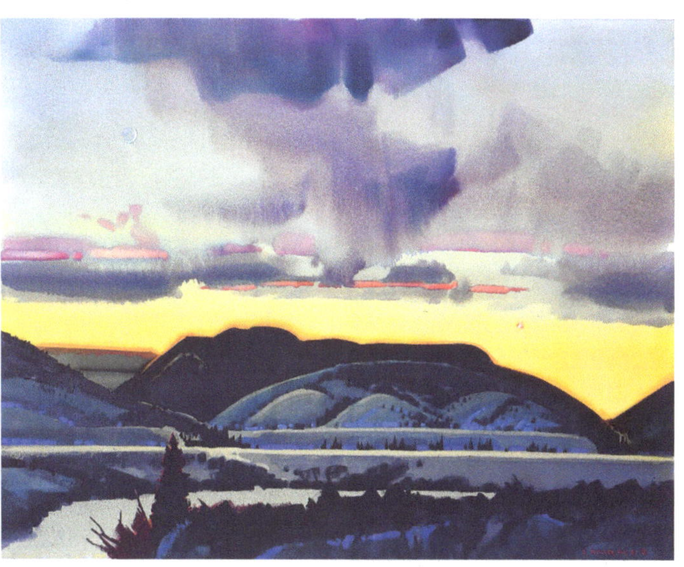

New Moon, Evening Star 2019
watercolor and casein, 28" x 38", Private Collection

A SERIES OF FOUR PAINTINGS I DID WITHIN TWO WEEKS OF EACH OTHER AT CATHEDRAL WOODS

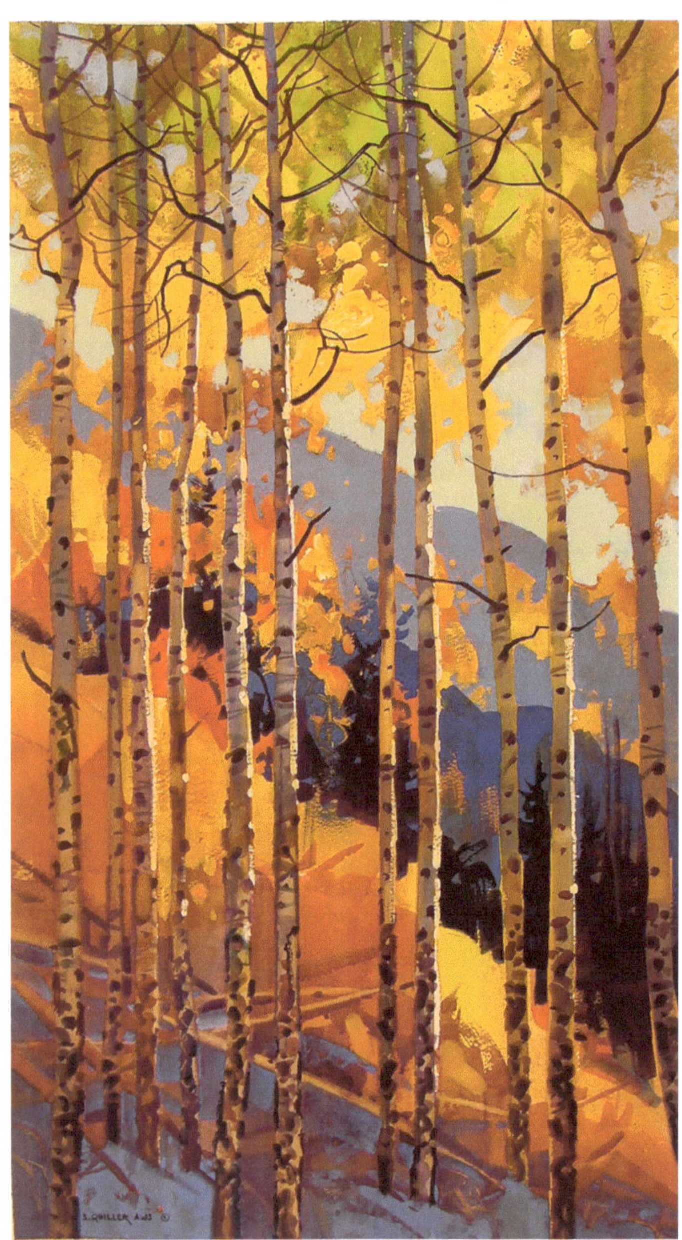

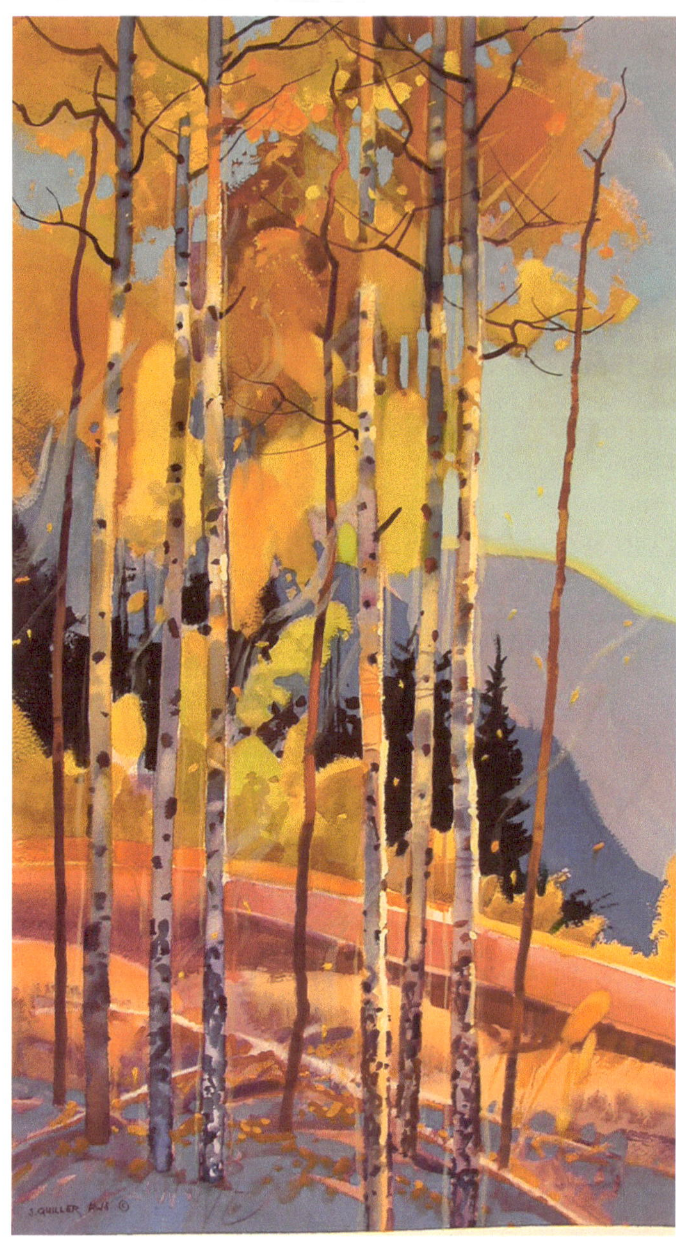

Cathedral Woods, October
(p. 124, left) **2003**
transparent acrylic under wash, watercolor and casein, 34" x 24"
Private Collection

Falling Leaf Contrails, October
(p. 124, right) **2003**
transparent acrylic under wash, watercolor and casein, 34" x 24"
Collection of Jim and Ginny Neece

Wind Gust, Cathedral Woods
(p.125, left) **2003**
watercolor and casein, 34" x 24"
Private Collection

Light & Shadow, Forest Sounds
(p.125, right) **2003**
watercolor and casein, 34" x 24"
Private Collection

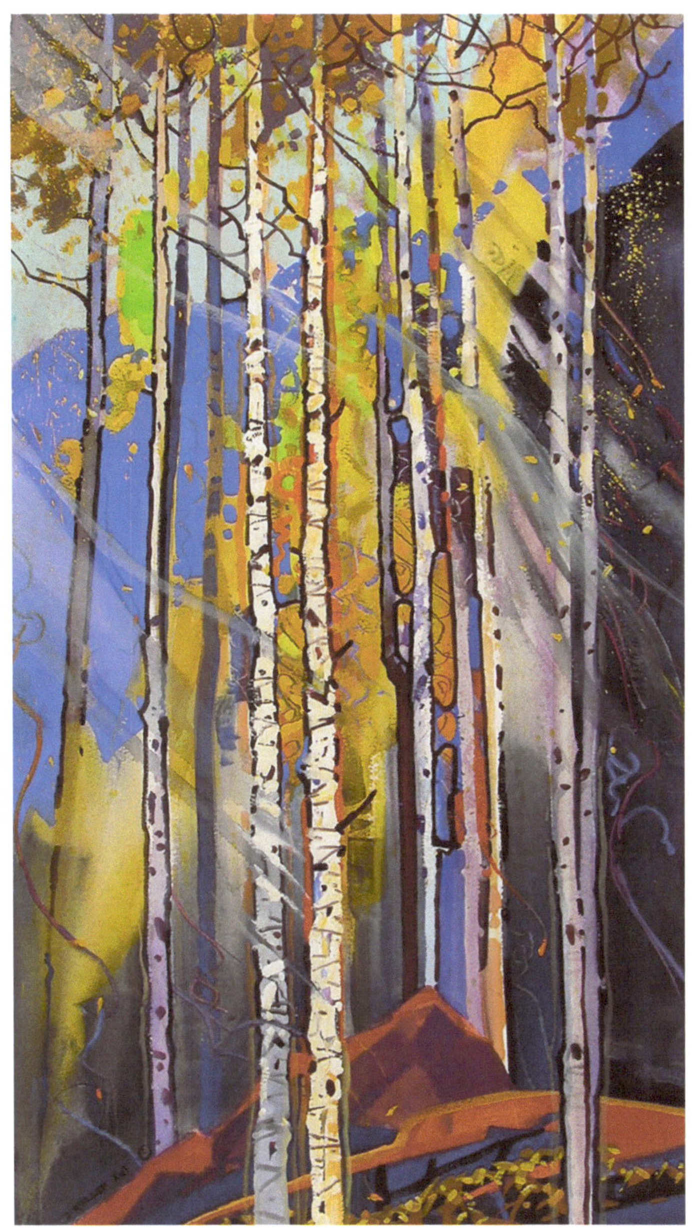

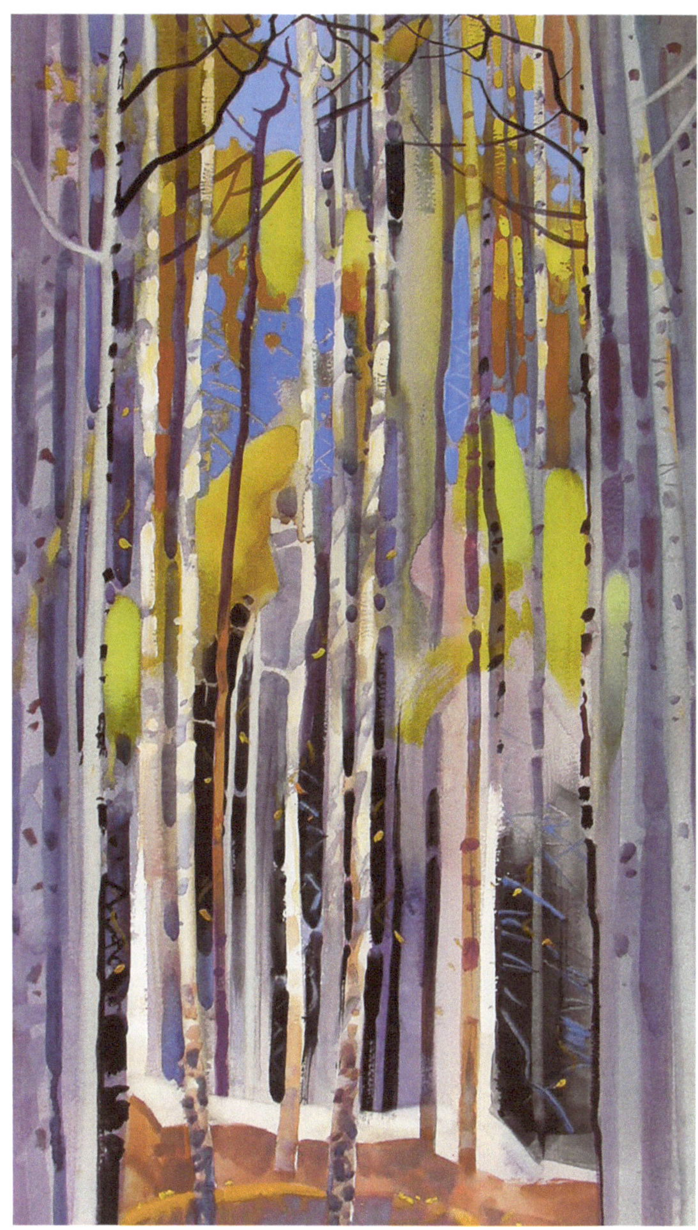

October 9, 2010

I have been painting autumn since mid-September when I returned from Scotland. Autumn starts in the high country above where I live with late summer yellow-green aspen and a few dots of yellow. Gradually the yellows take over and their color family range from the same yellow-green to orange with all shades and intensities in between. These colors are punctuated with dark spruce notes. The leaves are lost while some foliage hangs on. This leaves the soft gray-violet bare stands of aspen against a still bright yellow to orange. To catch more autumn I travel down river to lower elevations and milder climate. Fall can hang on until mid October. There are days painting in the woods that are seemingly timeless. The stillness, warmth and dry autumn smells permeate my being, and it feels as if this experience will last forever. A few leaves land on my palette; a crow caws overhead and a sluggish bee explores my paint, sensing the honey in the color. One day after a short meditation I stood to begin my painting. I was confronted by a startled five-point bull elk, just 40 yards away. Then one evening it rains and is followed by a cold snap. The yellow leaves turn brown and strong gusts of wind strip the aspen of their leaves and I am left only with some paint on paper, and a memory.

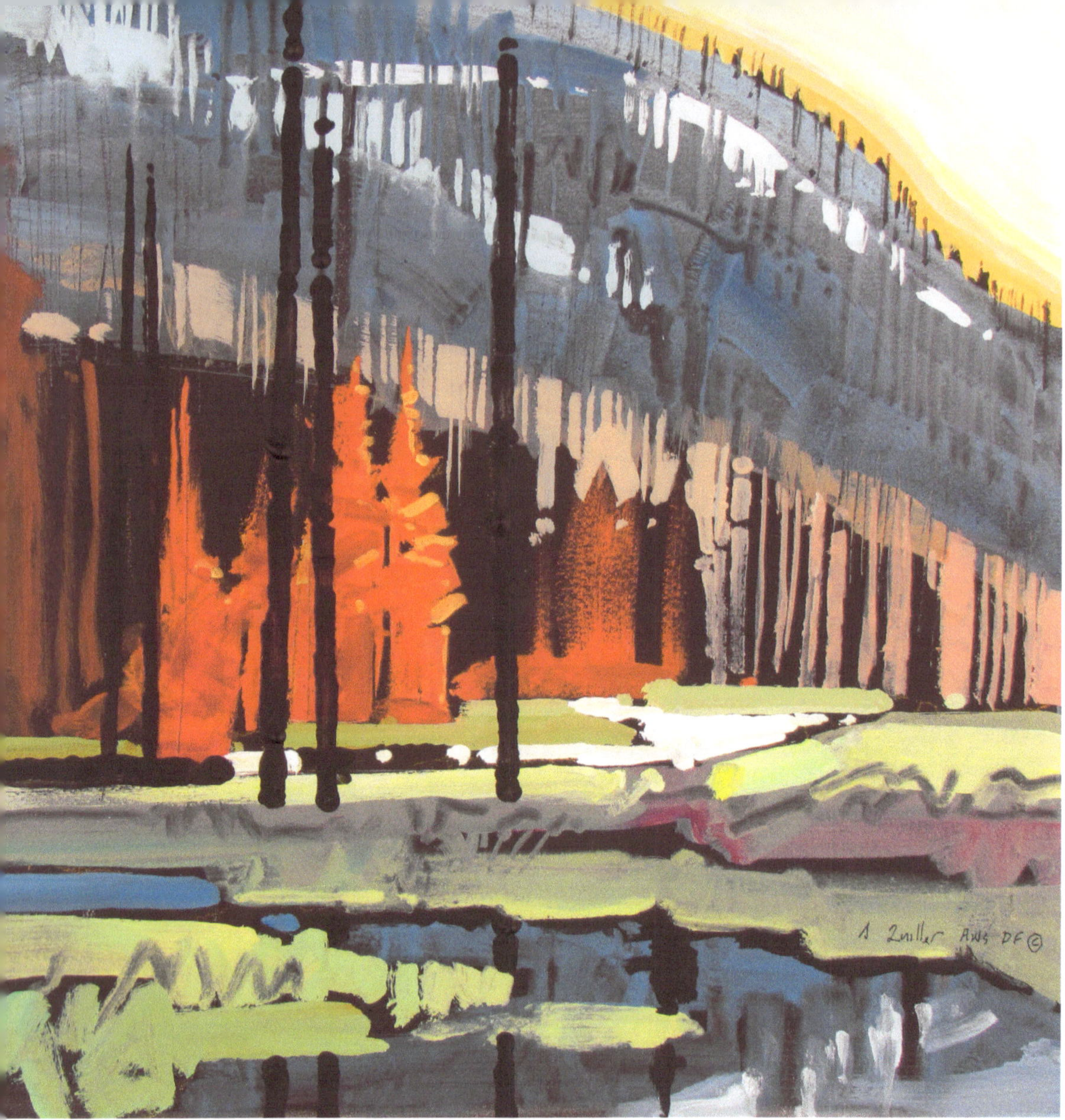

By Little Squaw
(left) 2015
casein on black paper, 28" x 28"
Private Collection

Autumn Off Fern Creek Road
(right) 2018
casein en plein air
18 ½" x 13 ½"
Private Collection

In mid June of 2013, two fires broke out in our area: the West Fork Fire and the Papoose Fire. For three weeks our town was closed off and many of the guest ranches and summer homes were evacuated. In total 110,000 acres burned, leaving a black scar on the land. It was also devastating to the local economy and our community's lives.

October 10, 2013

When the smoke cleared and my denial had lifted, I felt compelled to paint "The Burn." I began scouting the various back roads to experience the heart of the burn.

In the process I have come to some major realizations. The majority of our forests covered with the "beetle kill spruce" was already dead. The fire in a sense was a cleansing to open up and give room for new growth. In some of the most heavily burned areas, new fresh aspen saplings are sprouting everywhere. These aspen roots have lain dormant forever, waiting to emerge after a fire. Wildflowers are bursting into the black and gray landscape. Magenta fireweed are hip-high along the stream's edge with new yellow-green grass covering the banks.

I walk gently on this fresh wound blanketed with burnt spruce needles and charcoal ash. Yet I am a part of this wound, nature's wound. This land that I have come to know in a certain way over the last forty or more years will not be the same in my lifetime.

It takes fresh eyes to see that there is in fact beauty in the burn. And so I go out to paint every day using a palette unlike any I have ever used. I have gone through more ivory black and Payne's gray in the last few weeks than I have used in a lifetime. I am exploring so many different ways to express. Painting outside, I am working on black paper and with casein. In the studio I am experimenting with gold and black gessoed Aquabord® panels and painting in acrylic. Sometimes I lift back with Q-tips or a brush using rubbing alcohol. I plan to do collage pieces using the actual ash and burnt spruce needles for texture.

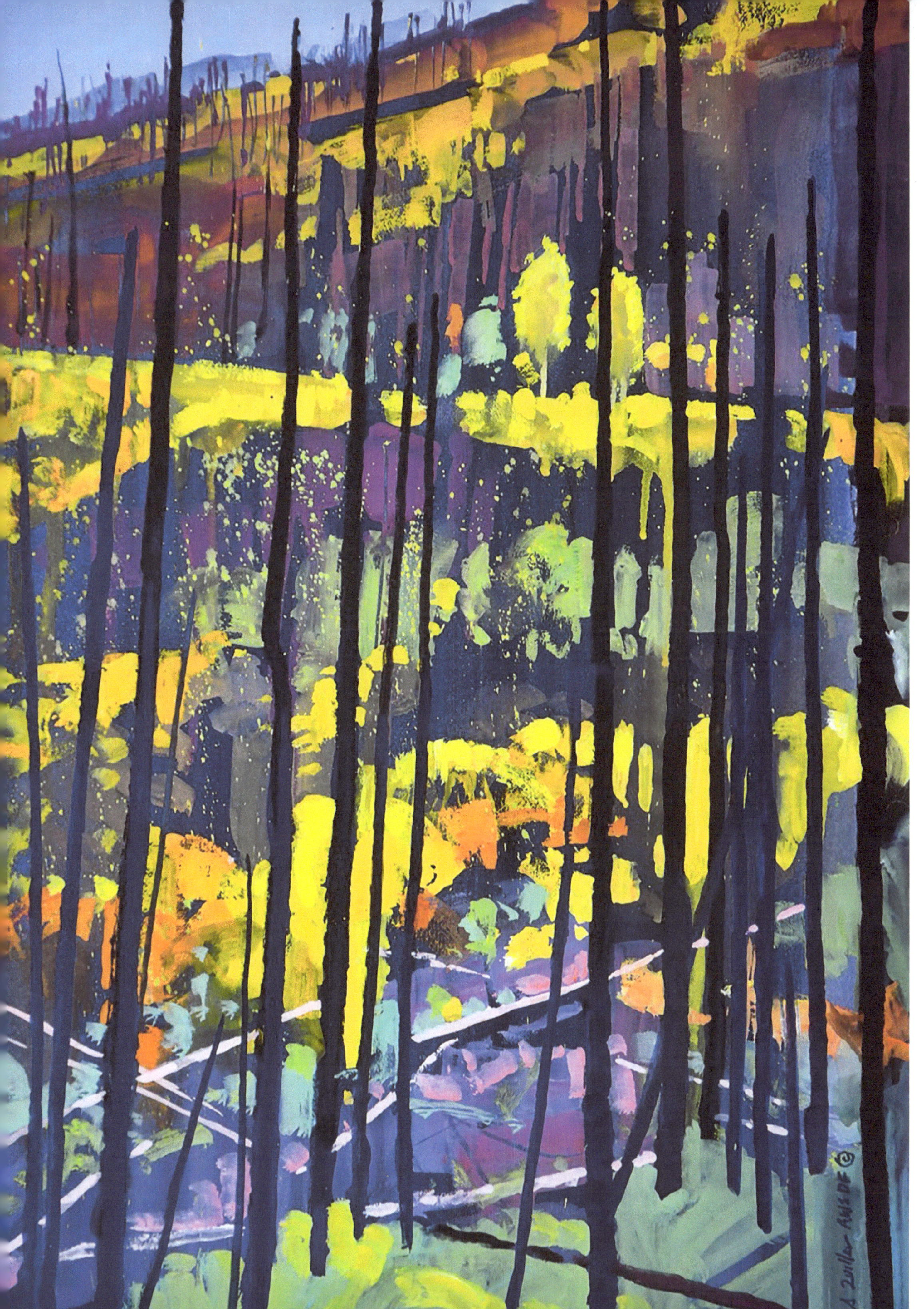

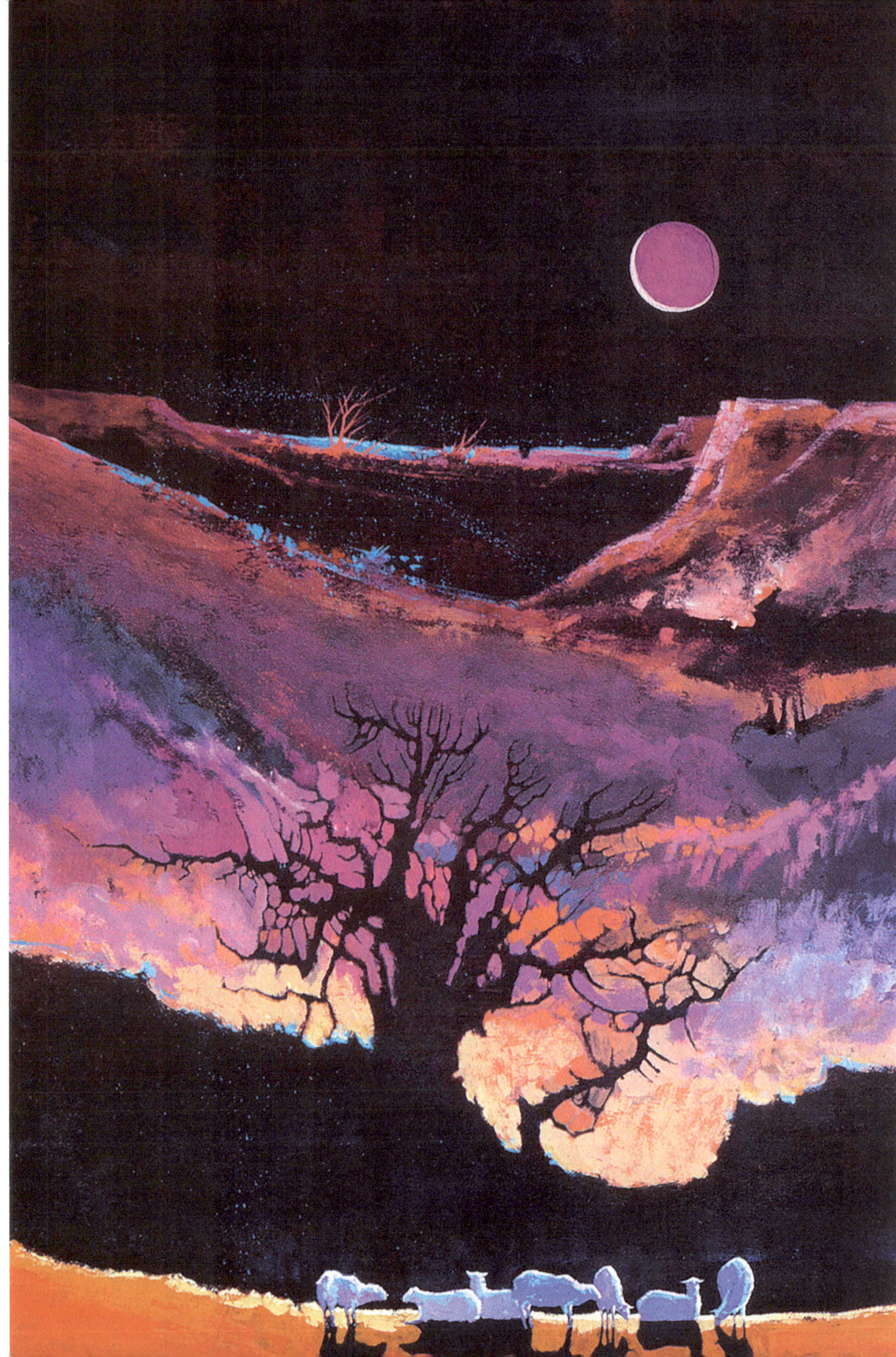

April, 1999

I visited the Chicago Art Institute in late April 1999, returning from a workshop in Toronto, Ontario. There happened to be a Gustav Moreau exhibition that deeply touched me. I had just been reading a biography of Henri Matisse's early years and it mentions Moreau as his teacher. The following are two quotes from Gustav Moreau:

"All that I have sought, I have found, in small proportions no doubt, but informs perfectly pure and flawless, for I have never looked for dream and reality or for reality in dream. I have allowed my imagination free play, and I have not been led astray."

"To be modern does not consist of searching for something outside of everything that has been done ... It is on the contrary, the question of coordinating all that the preceding ages have brought us, to make visible what our century has accepted of this heritage and how it makes use of it."

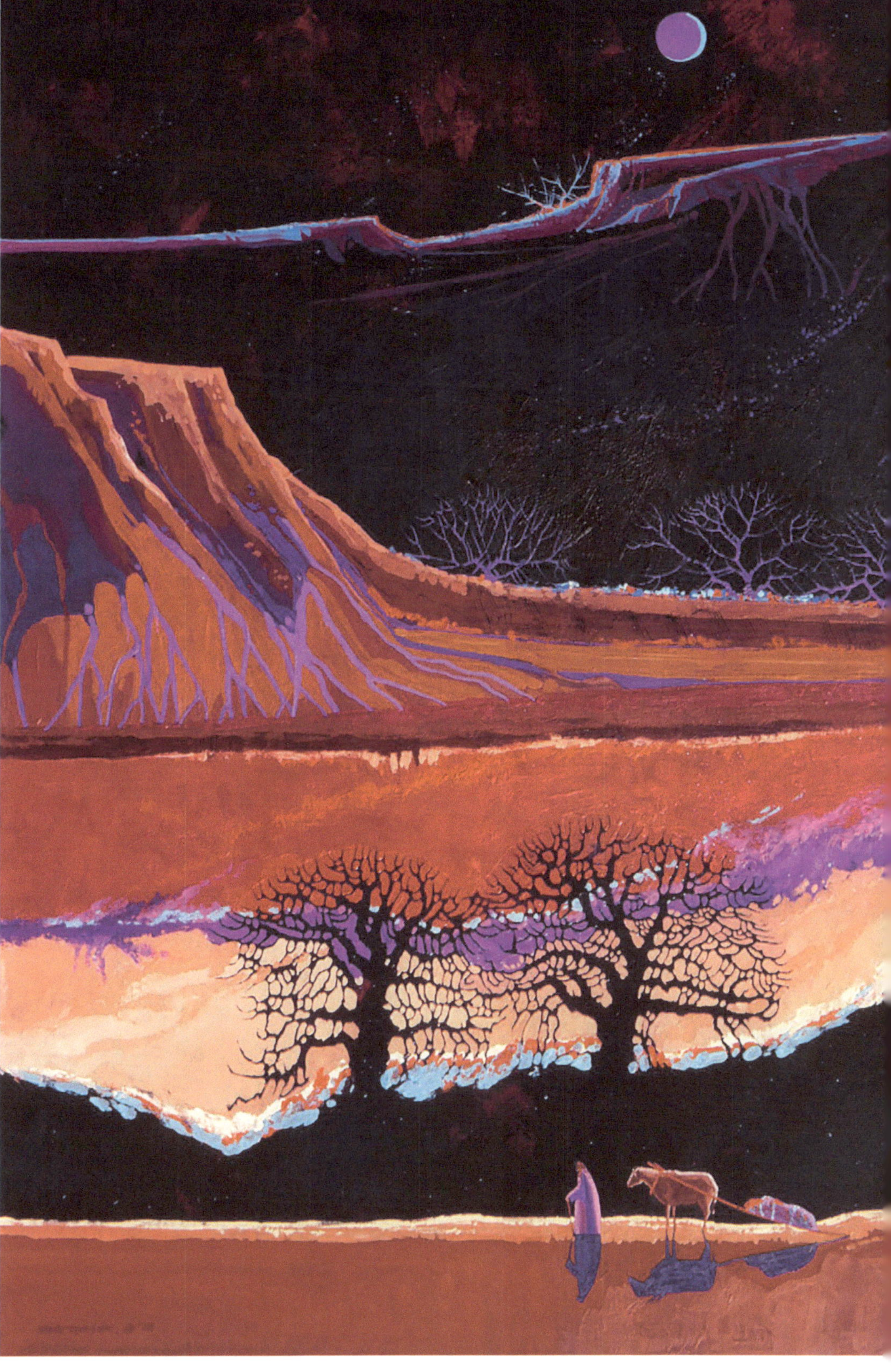

Travois *1978*
casein, 28" x 38",
Collection of Darlene Zarosinski estate

Southwest Textures
(left) 1977
casein, 30" x 20"
Private Collection

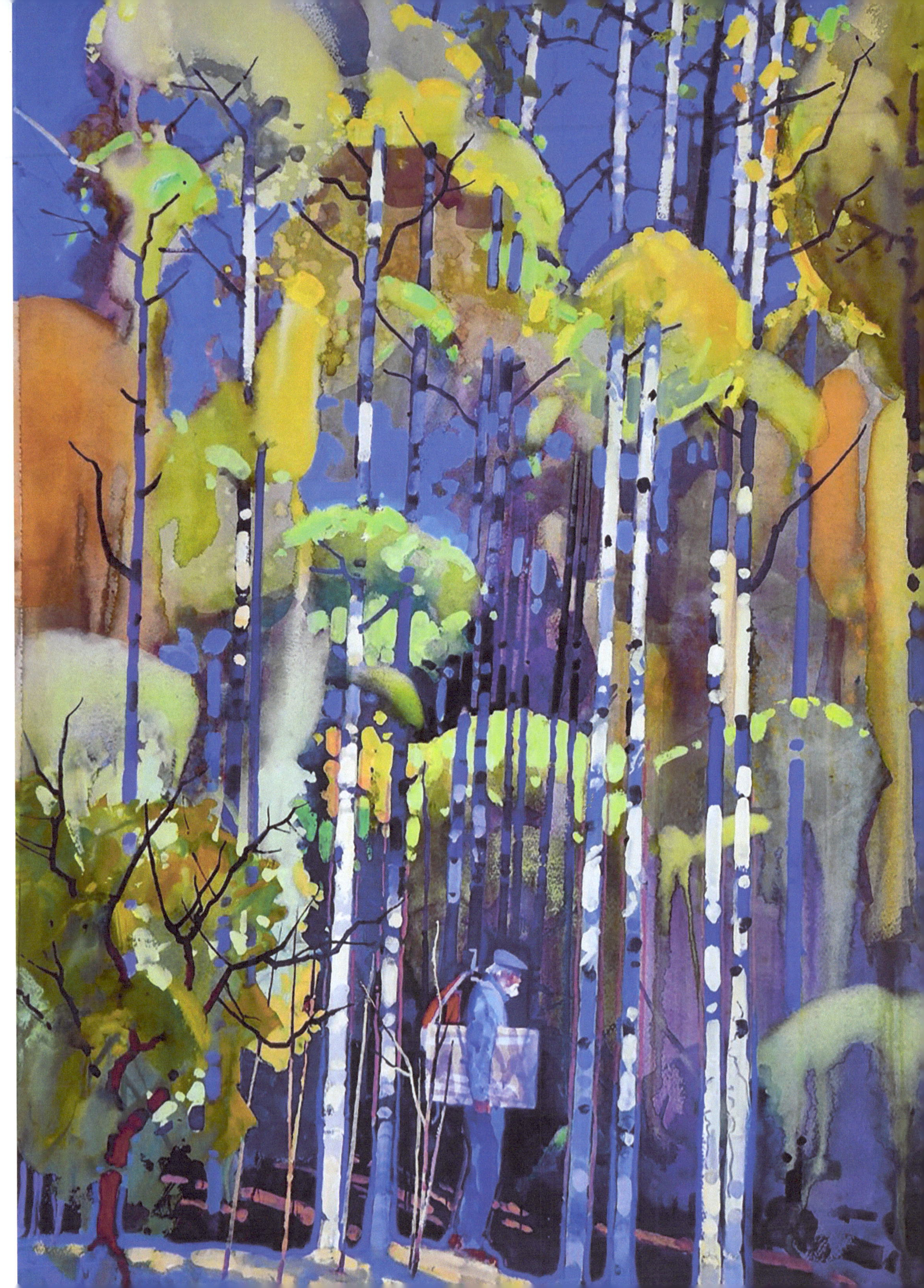

January 31, 2006

I love the blue, blue-violet and violet color range and use these notes extensively in my painting. Many times I use these colors as a thread running subordinately through my compositions; these are the base notes in my painting. In a classical musical composition, the base notes are the foundation from which everything else is built. I see these "deep" colors providing the same foundation in many of my paintings.

Interconnectedness, Autumn Aspen Walk
(left) 2019
watercolor and casein, 34" x 24"
Artist's Collection

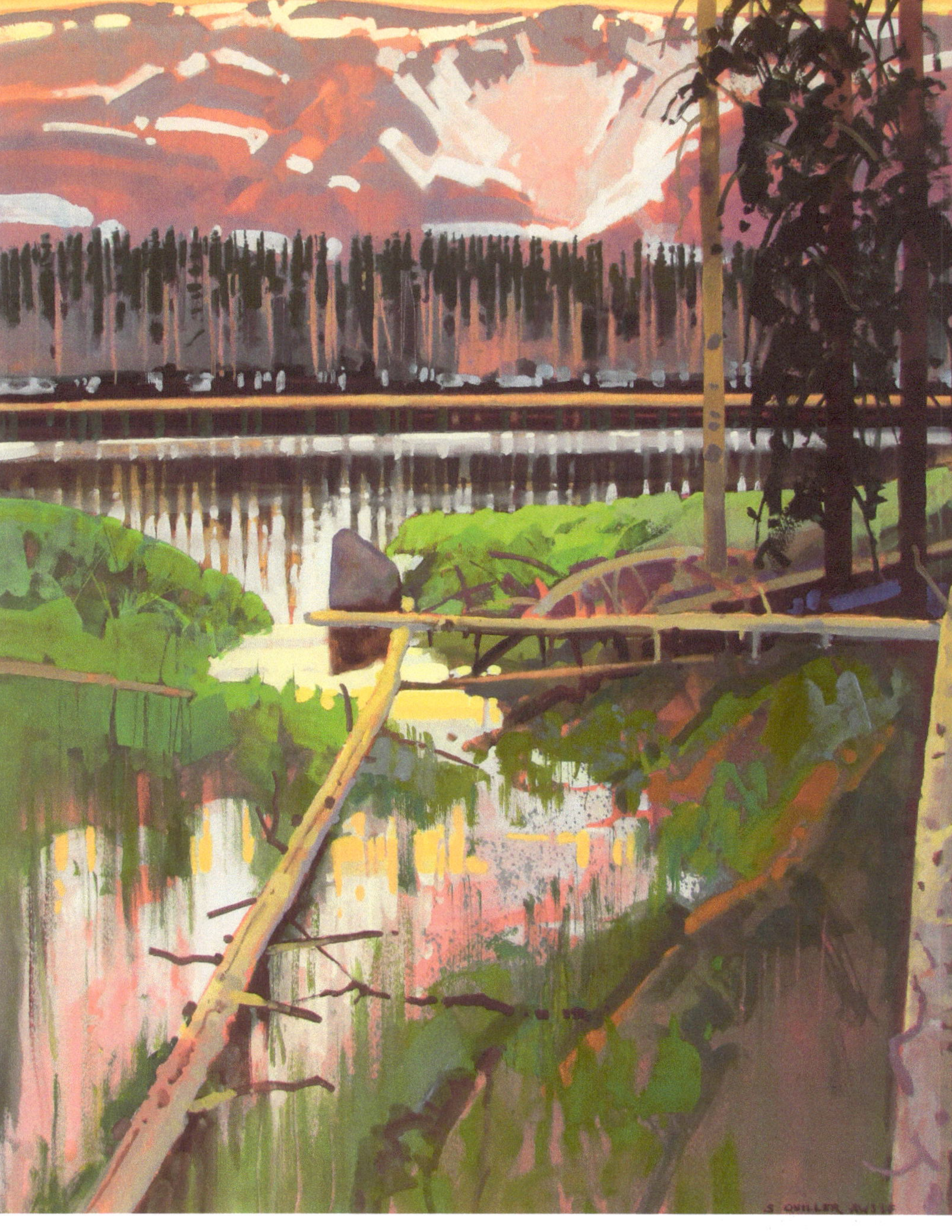

Reflections, Hunter's Lake
1977
casein, 34" x 23"
Collection of Bill Bieber

March 9, 2006

I feel that landscape painting can be the most abstract, painterly and freeing of all representational directions. I can move the mountain, shift the trees (or leave them out) and fully express in a variety of ways. There is freedom in knowing this, as the subject can be merely the excuse to express. A figure painter has a more difficult time moving eyes, arms, legs, and emphasizing or changing color.

However, it seems to me that there are fewer and fewer true water media landscape painters today, and I wonder if we as a society are losing touch with nature as we are involved with our computers, internet, tv, media, and phones. We are becoming an indoor culture and getting out in nature is not part of our present day routine.

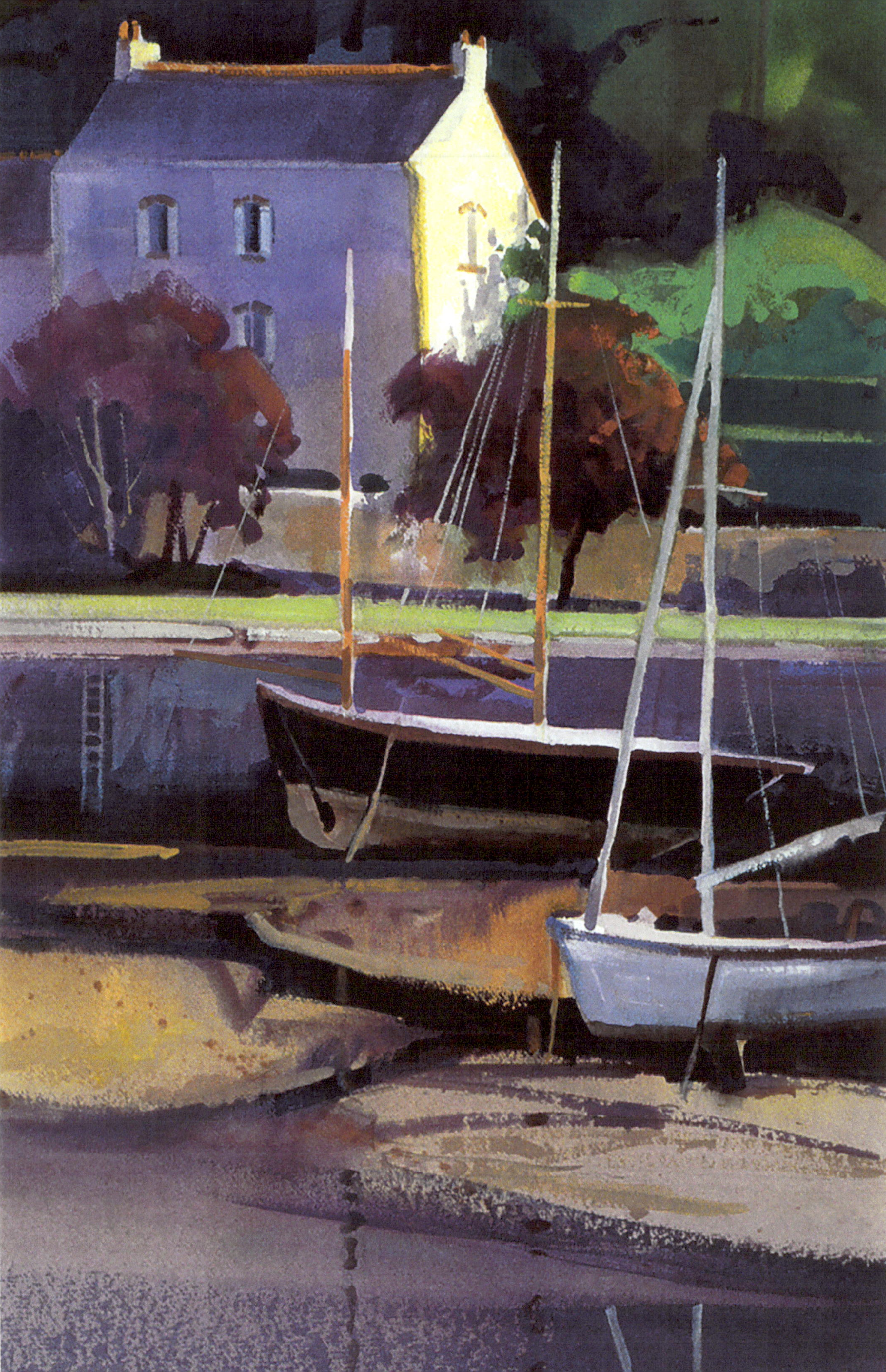

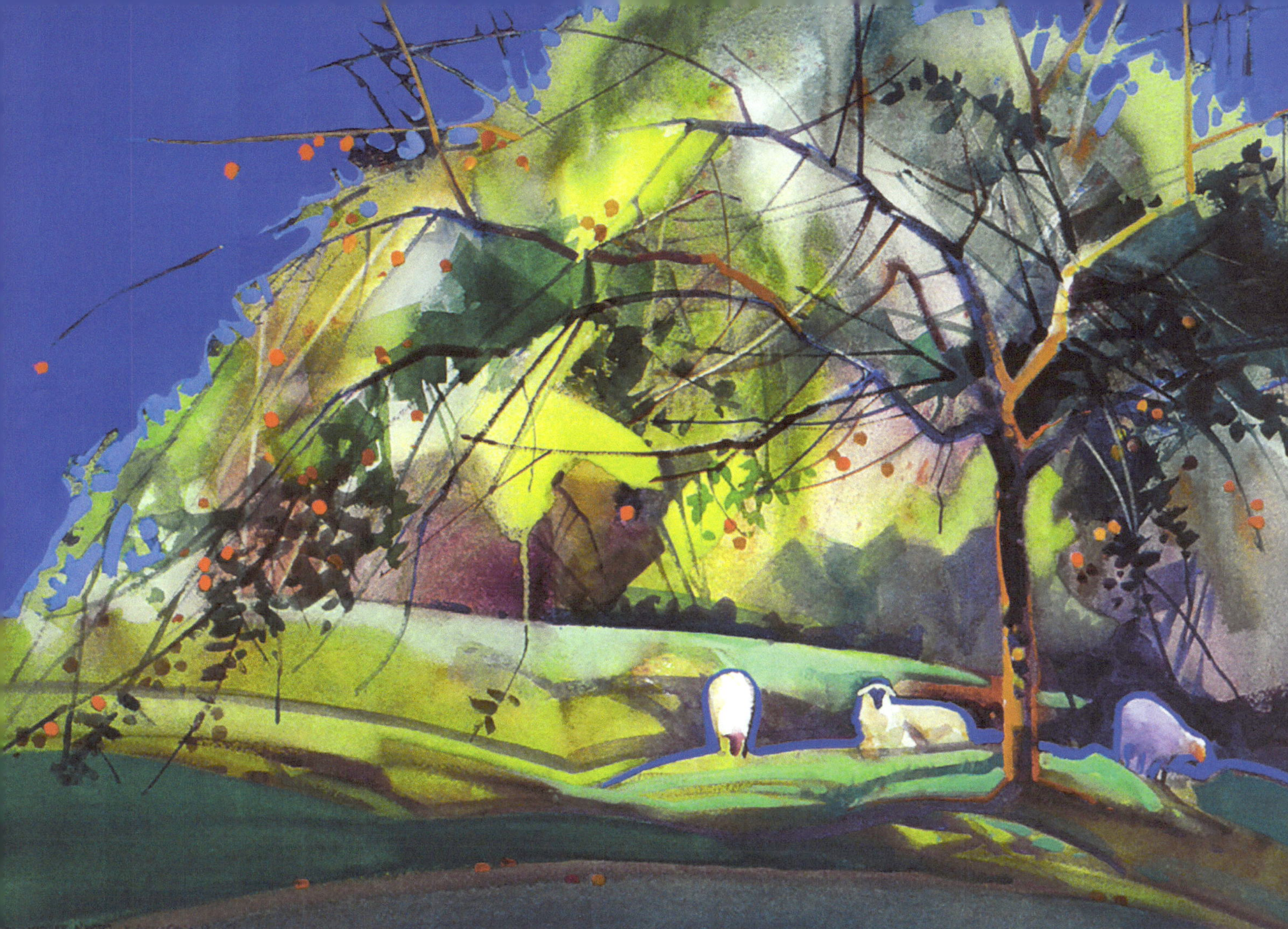

Sheep and Apple Tree, Chambre d'Hotes, Foix 2002
watercolor and casein, 21" x 29", Private Collection

September 20, 2002

We arrive in Pont Aven, a town of 3000 and the home of the Synthesist School of painters: Gauguin, Bernard, Vallatton, Denis, and Serieurs. We find a very interesting charming hotel called Minosas and we will stay three nights.

The next morning I begin by painting a boat by the hotel at low tide. I begin this piece but then Marta and I decide to go on a wander to find the wood sculpture that Gauguin was inspired by when he painted "The Yellow Christ." We walk to the Chapelle de Tremalo. The sanctuary is 1 ½ miles from the hotel, up a hill through some woods. Entering the small church I find this beautiful sculpture and sit down to pay homage and sketch it. Over one hundred years before, Paul Gauguin had done the same.

September 25, 2002

We drive all day and arrive at our destination in Foix. We explore the town and finally find a place to stay outside of the village, a "chambre d'hotes." This is a beautiful country farm hotel called Caussou. It is very lovely and quiet, with sheep and apple trees, and panoramic views. We decide to stay three nights and I hope to paint. Our evening meal is part of the experience on this farm as everything we eat was grown here. We have dinner with a friendly couple from Belgium. Breakfast, and then up for painting! I decide to paint an apple tree and some sheep in watercolor and casein.

Harbor, Pont Aven
(left) 2002
casein, 29" x 21"
Private Collection

On Rena Rosequist, 1967- 2019

Finding Rena has been life-changing for me. Back in the late 70s and early 80s I would go to her gallery in Taos to view Doel Reed's aquatint prints. He was a master printmaker who I later got to know, and I now have a good collection of his work. In the autumn of 1983 I moved to Taos. The following winter I walked the back streets of Taos smelling piñon smoke in the cool wintry air. Occasionally I would go to the Mission Gallery and spend some time conversing with Rena. Later she found out that I was an artist and asked to see my work. She then invited me to show at her gallery. In all the years I exhibited at the Mission Gallery, Rena always encouraged me to bring my latest work and was excited to see growth and change.

Throughout the last 34 years we have become great friends. Every other year she has given me a one-man show and the paintings and etchings have sold very well. However, that has always been just the excuse to spend time with Rena. She is now 87 years old and needs to close the gallery. This has been her life since 1962. At least four to six times a year Marta and I have traveled to Taos to deliver paintings, to ship paintings from our gallery, and mainly to be with Rena. Her knowledge of Southwest art history is unsurpassed. Her mind is still as acute as ever. I will miss this experience very much.*

**(Rena Rosequist 1931-2019, age 88)*

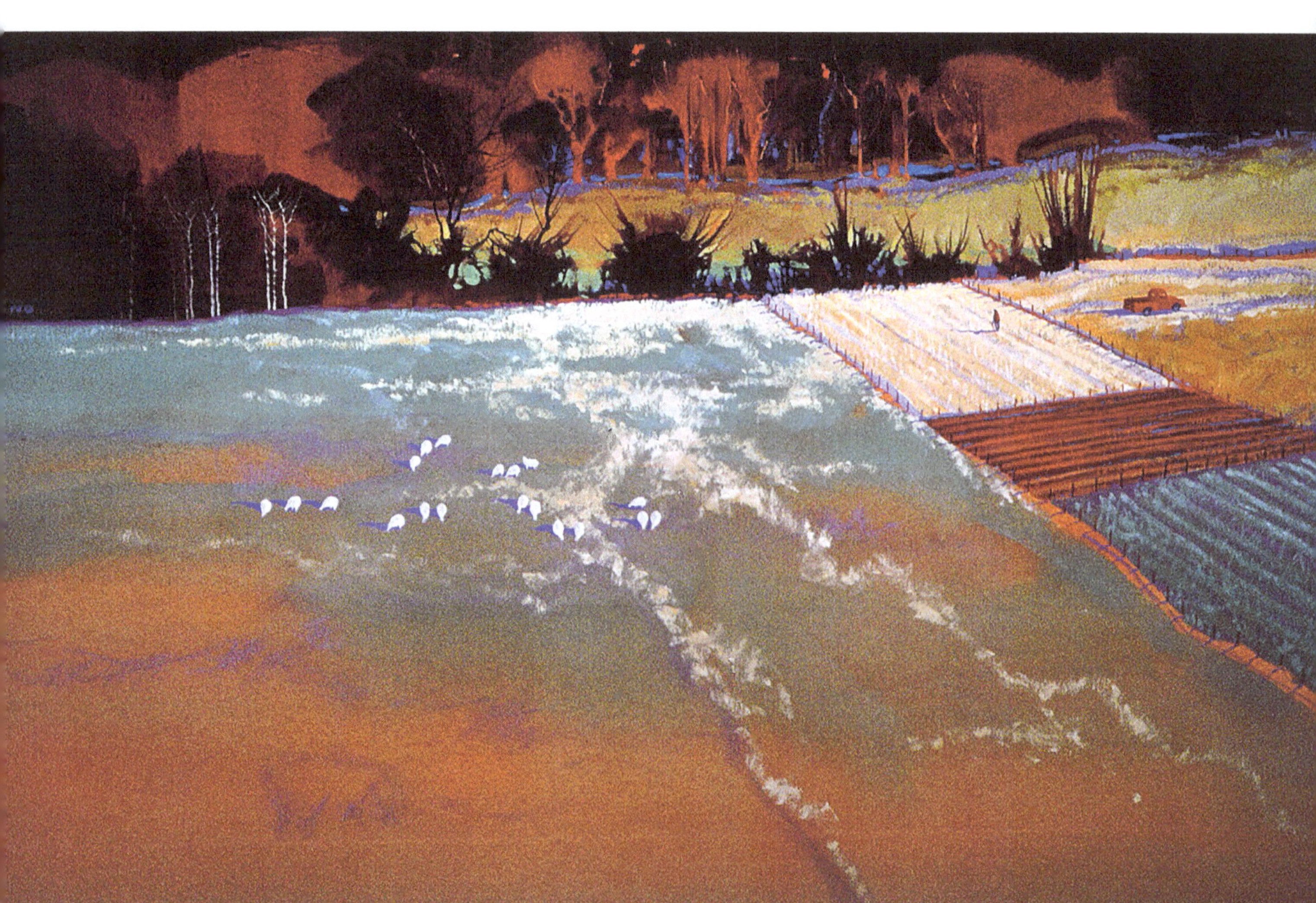

Late Autumn Field Patterns, Valdez 1984

transparent acrylic underlay with casein, 21" x 29"

Private Collection

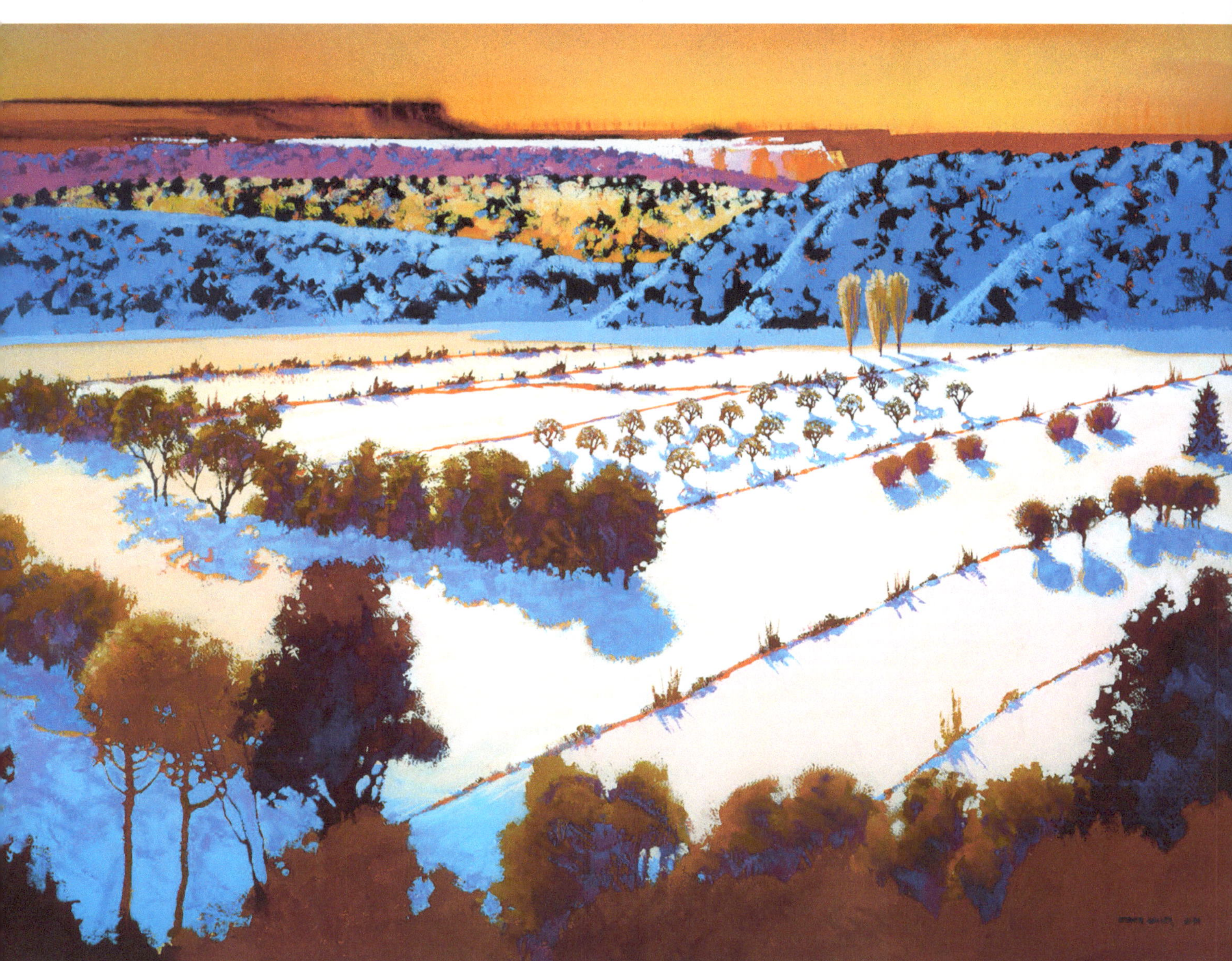

Winter Field Patterns, Valdez *1984*
transparent acrylic underlay with casein, 28" x 40"
Artist's Collection

November 11, 2009

I look at the Taos field pattern paintings that I did in the mid-80s, the color and vision that I had at the time, as well as what I was going through personally, and today I could not recreate those paintings. I have changed and I'm not the same person. However, if I am lucky with my health and mind, my last works will be a culmination of a life in art, the culmination of knowledge, craft and my spirit.

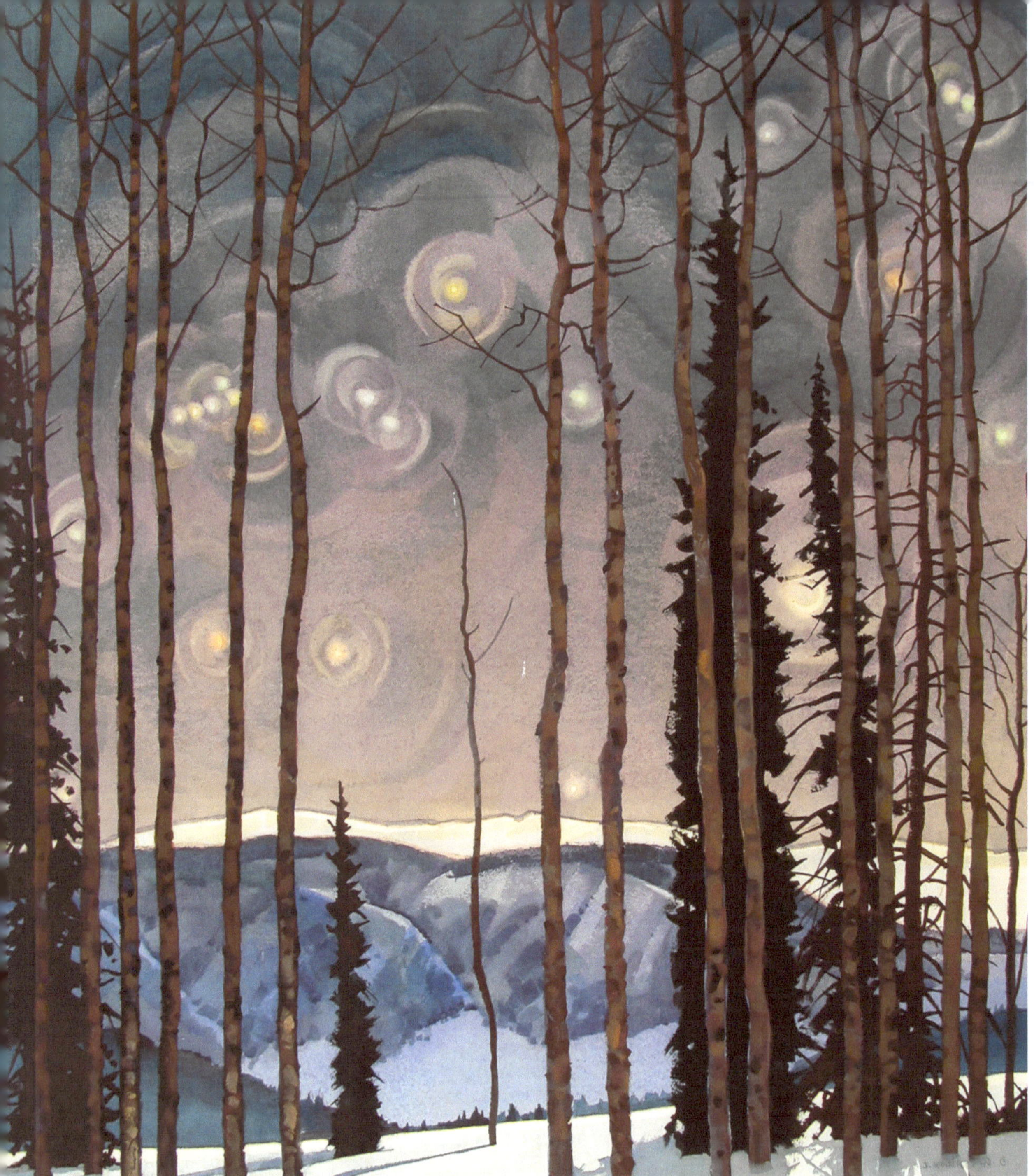

Winter, Night Sky, View From Bachelor
2002
watercolor and casein, 38" x 30"
Collection of Cary Bush

October 11, 1997
Early on I learned to meditate. This has made all of the difference for me. However, this to me is not a formula for success. It is a special time daily to pause, give thanks, reflect, and be a part of the universe. This is what keeps me centered. Sometimes life gets hectic and complicated: traveling and doing workshops, seminars, lectures, meeting new people, writing new books. But if I take time to meditate, there is peace for me, and I then enjoy following this life course.

September 3, 2012
I walk, late evening, from my studio in the moon shadow and experience the Milky Way splashed across the sky. I think of how minuscule and fleeting life can be. Yet even these moments and one's "mark" can be left, and it can bring joy to those who encounter it.

May 20, 2000

I watch the sun slowly fall
Behind the mountain
While listening to Ravel's "Adagio Assai".
The silver waves staccato dance
Moves with the piano riffs.
I look to my right and see
Myself cross country skiing on my trail
And look back to the water
For the silhouette of my rhythmic casts.
Life is rich. Life is good.

Evening Star 2020
transparent acrylic underlay with casein, 28" x 44"
Collection of Ralph Nagel

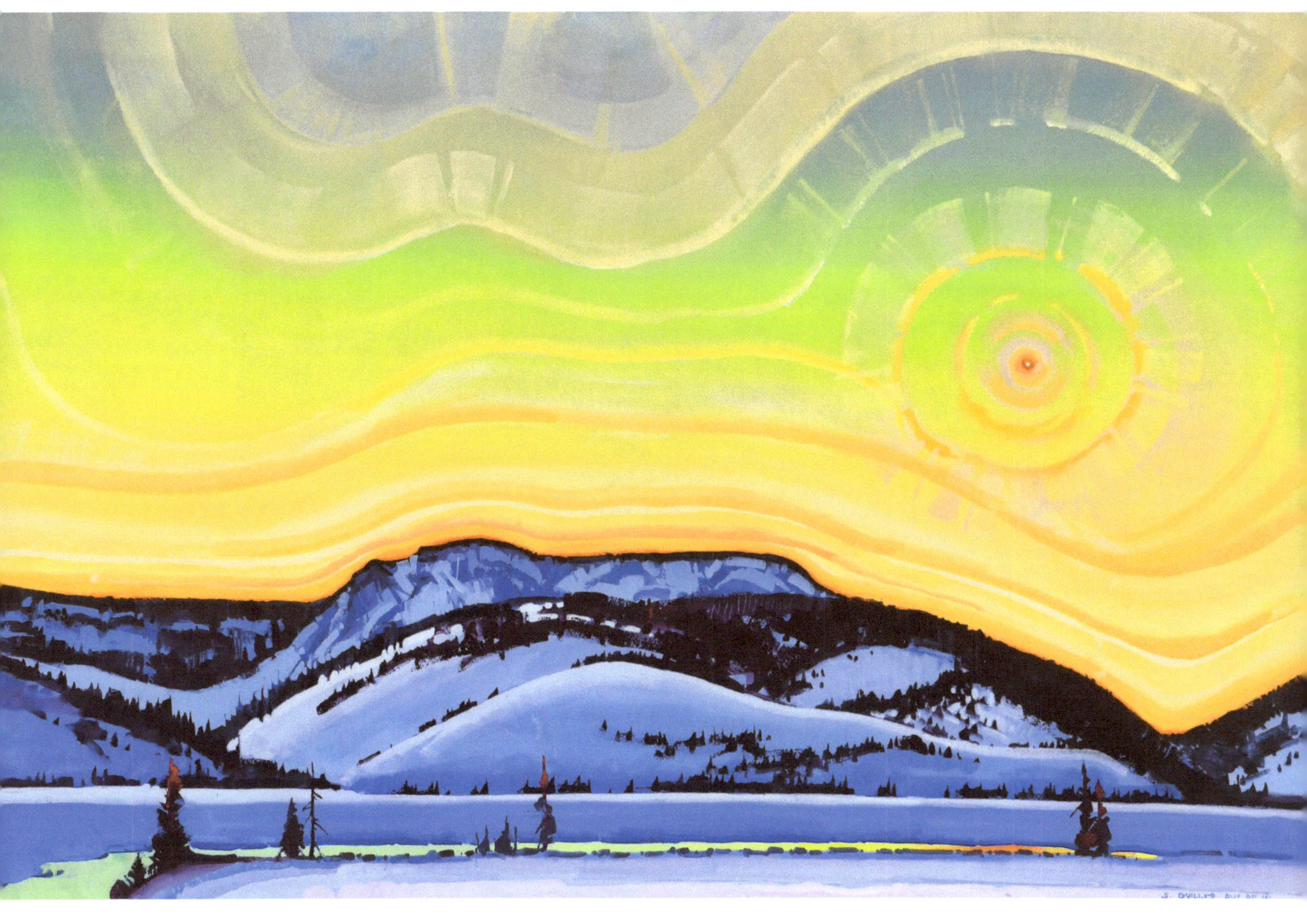

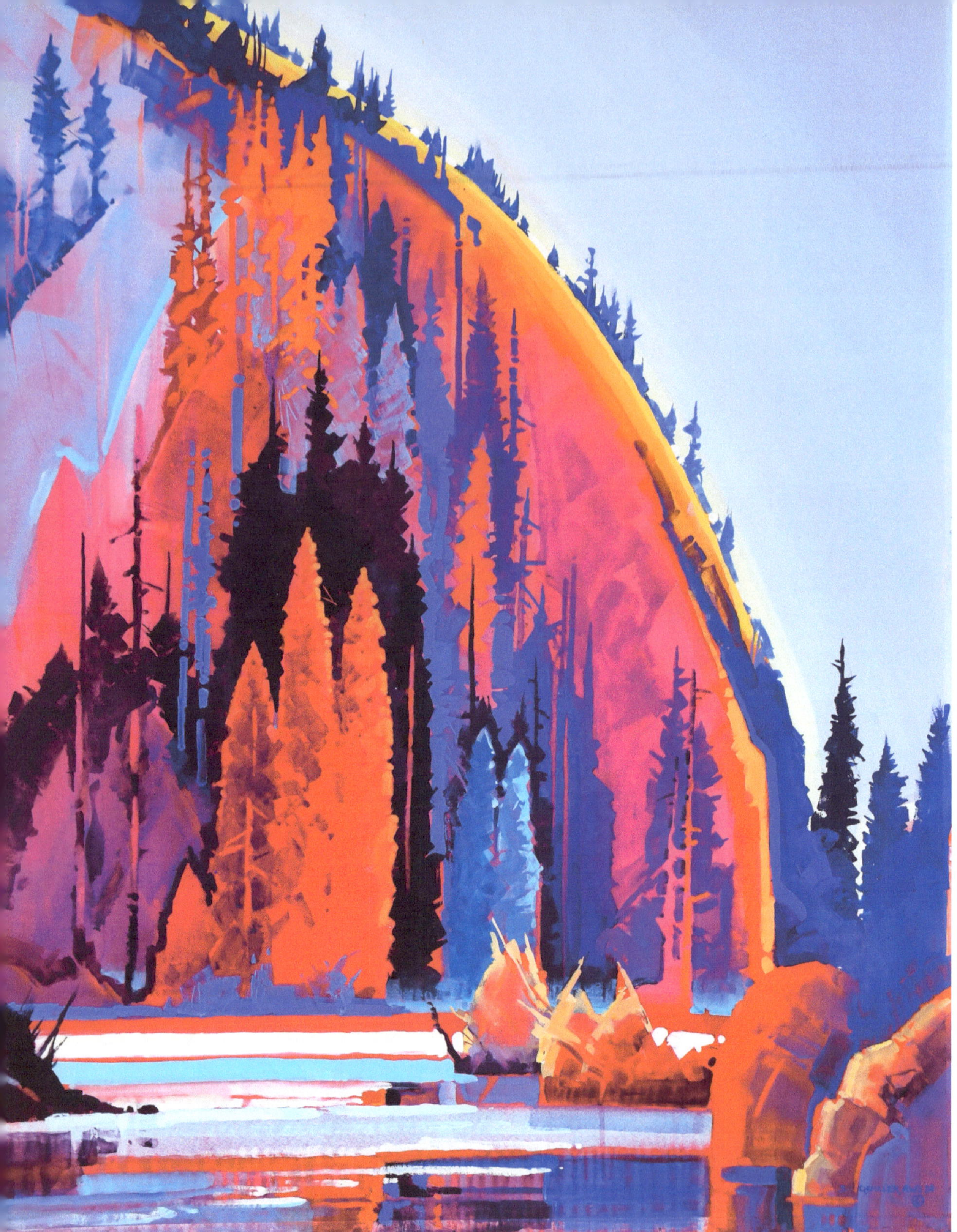

Three Red Spruce
2018
casein with transparent acrylic under wash
36" x 24"
Collection of Jim Stievater and Mai Nguyen

1993

One of my favorite things to do is to go to art museums. And, as I go through the various rooms, enjoying the work, knowing something about the various artists and their time, their philosophy and their approach to painting (some much more than others), occasionally there is a piece that jumps out and grabs me. There is no way that I could miss this work. In fact it holds me and I will spend much time with it. I walk around the room but come back, being drawn to that particular painting. I may leave and then come back later the same day and if I return to the same museum years later, I will look forward to seeing the work. It is a living energy radiating from that painting to which I have connected.

Winter could possibly be my favorite time. Of course then there is spring, summer and autumn. But the quiet time with Marta, the "holing up" and working in the studio is the best. The late afternoon skis are what I think about all summer, and there are a few of those times that I live for. One of these happened a couple of weeks ago. There were two fresh inches of snow covering the trail and large snow flakes were softly falling, almost enough to feel like a translucent blanket or veil that enveloped me. The glide of my ski was like floating on a cloud. I could feel my heart beat, my breathing, and almost hear the silent sound of the snow fall. It was like I could feel the heart beat of nature. I have recently been reading about "entrainment" through a Depak Chopra book. It is the idea that one can be immersed in nature and actually become one with its rhythm and soul.

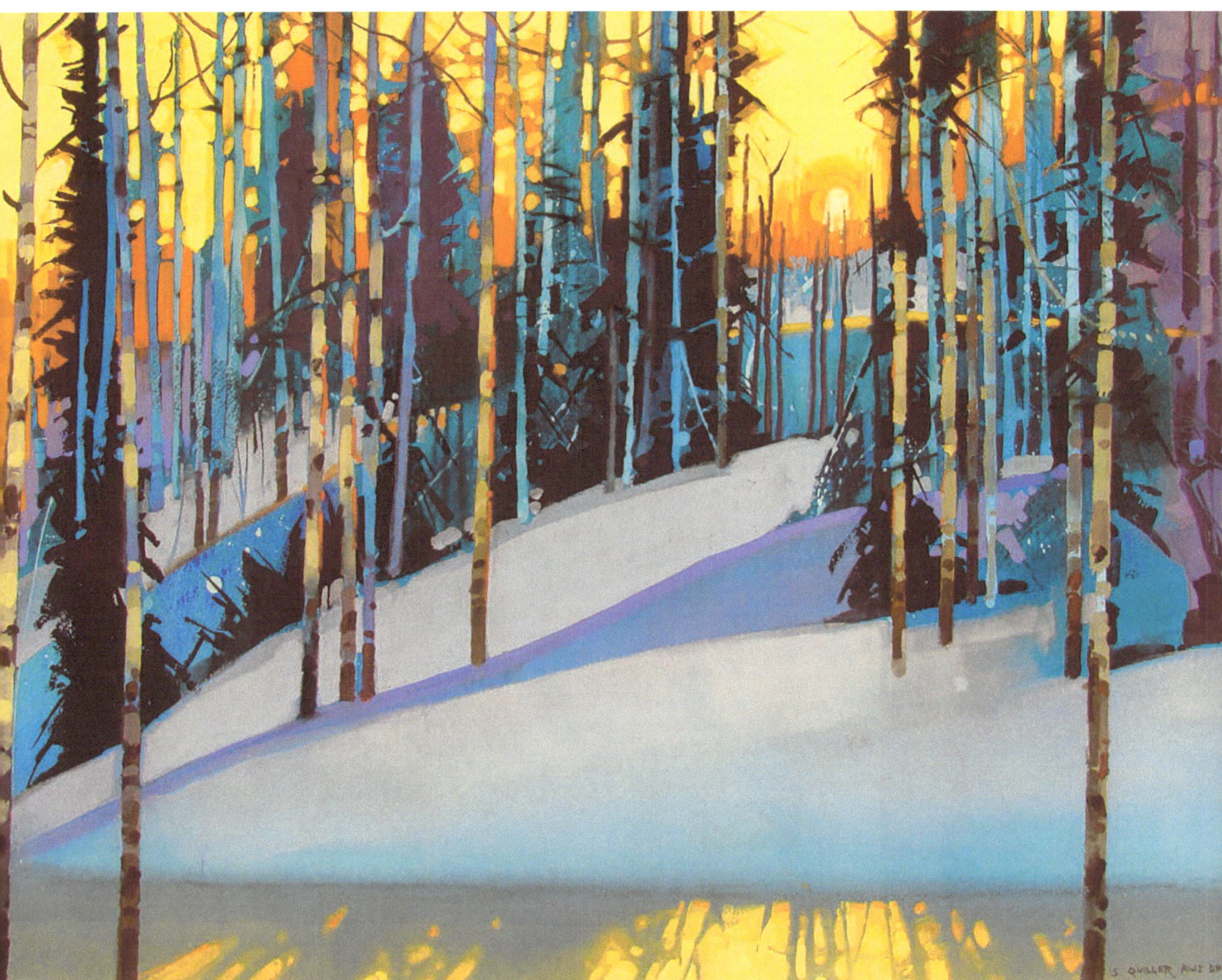

Flickering Light Along the Ridge Trail 2016
transparent acrylic underlay with casein, 22 ½" x 30"
Artist's Collection
Silver Medal of Honor, American Watercolor Society, 2018

Winter Crows at the Vesper Hour *2018*
transparent acrylic underlay, granulating watercolor, casein, 36" x 60"
Artist's Collection

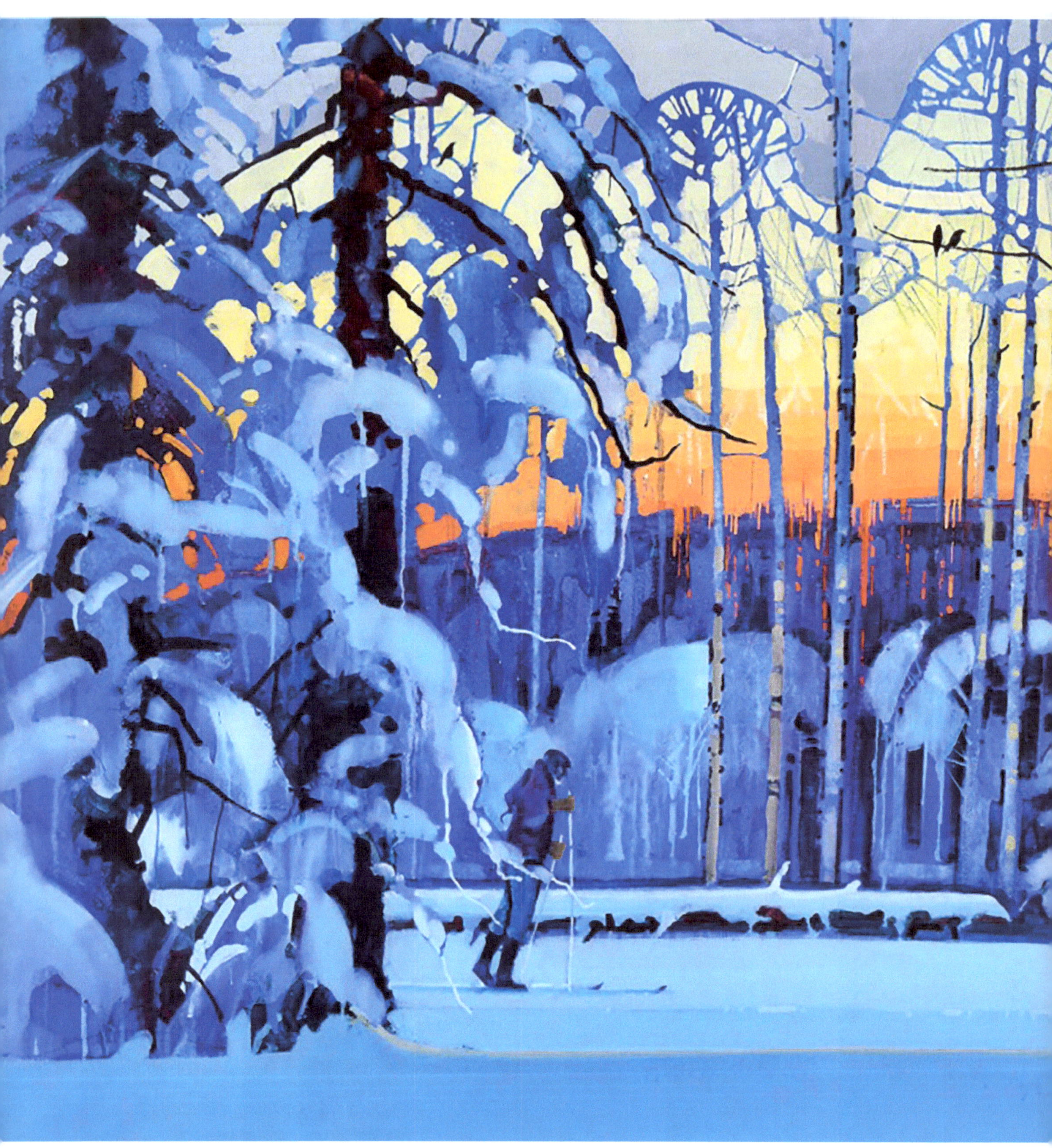

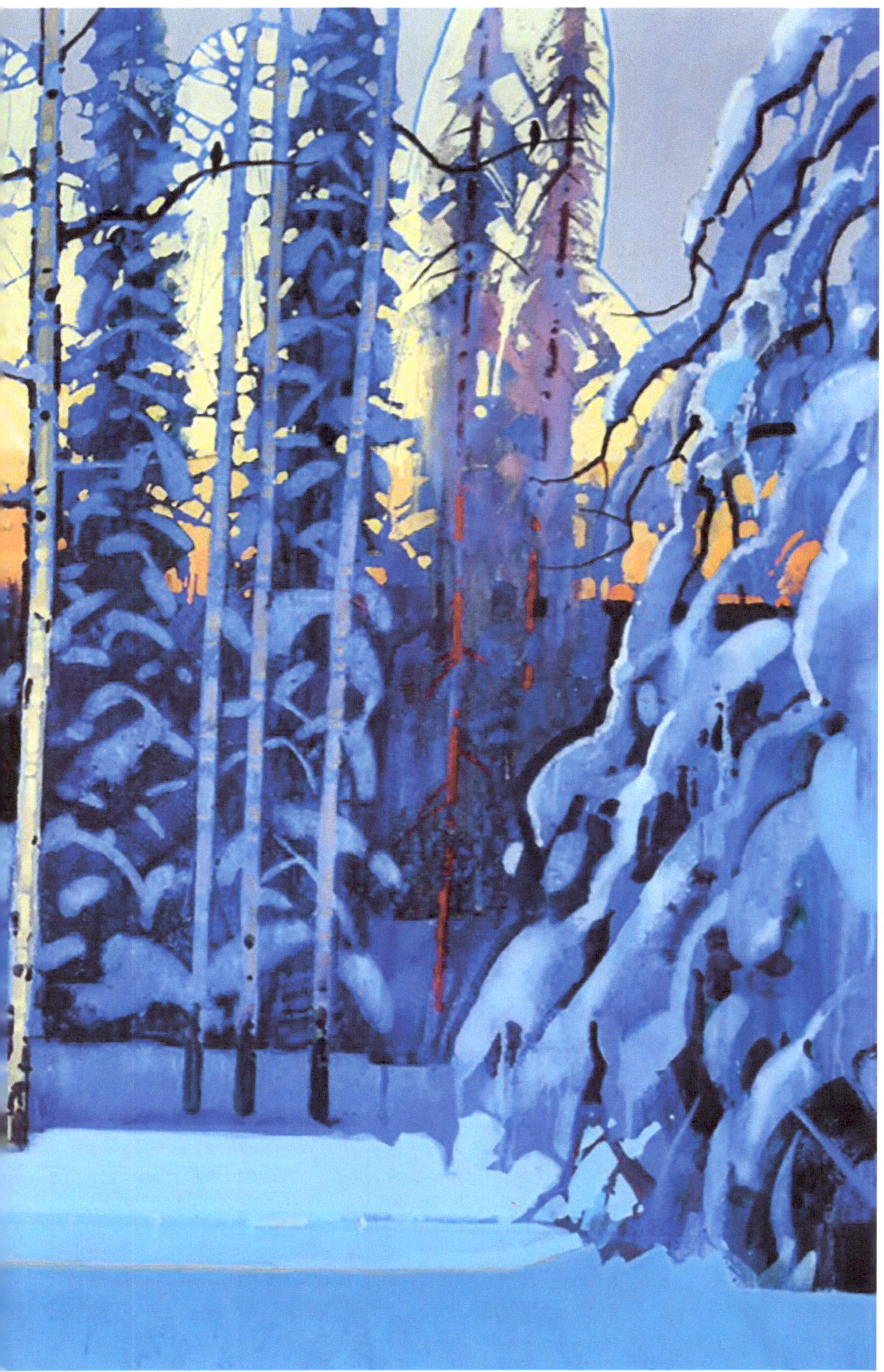

January 25, 2019

During the winter I get much of my painting material from my crosscountry skiing experiences. Most of the time I slip up to my trails at the end of the painting day when the light is retreating. I call it the Vesper Hour, the lighting of the lamps, the hour of prayer. This painting is an example of that time of day.

April, 1995

In the high country where I live there are distinct color harmonies that emerge during the seasons of the year.

Spring: yellow-green and red violet and their color families

Summer: deep greens, violets and blue violets and their families

Autumn: yellow orange to yellow-green / rose violets to violets

Winter: blue and orange and their color families

Early May Snow *1990*
watercolor and casein, 21" x 29"
Private Collection

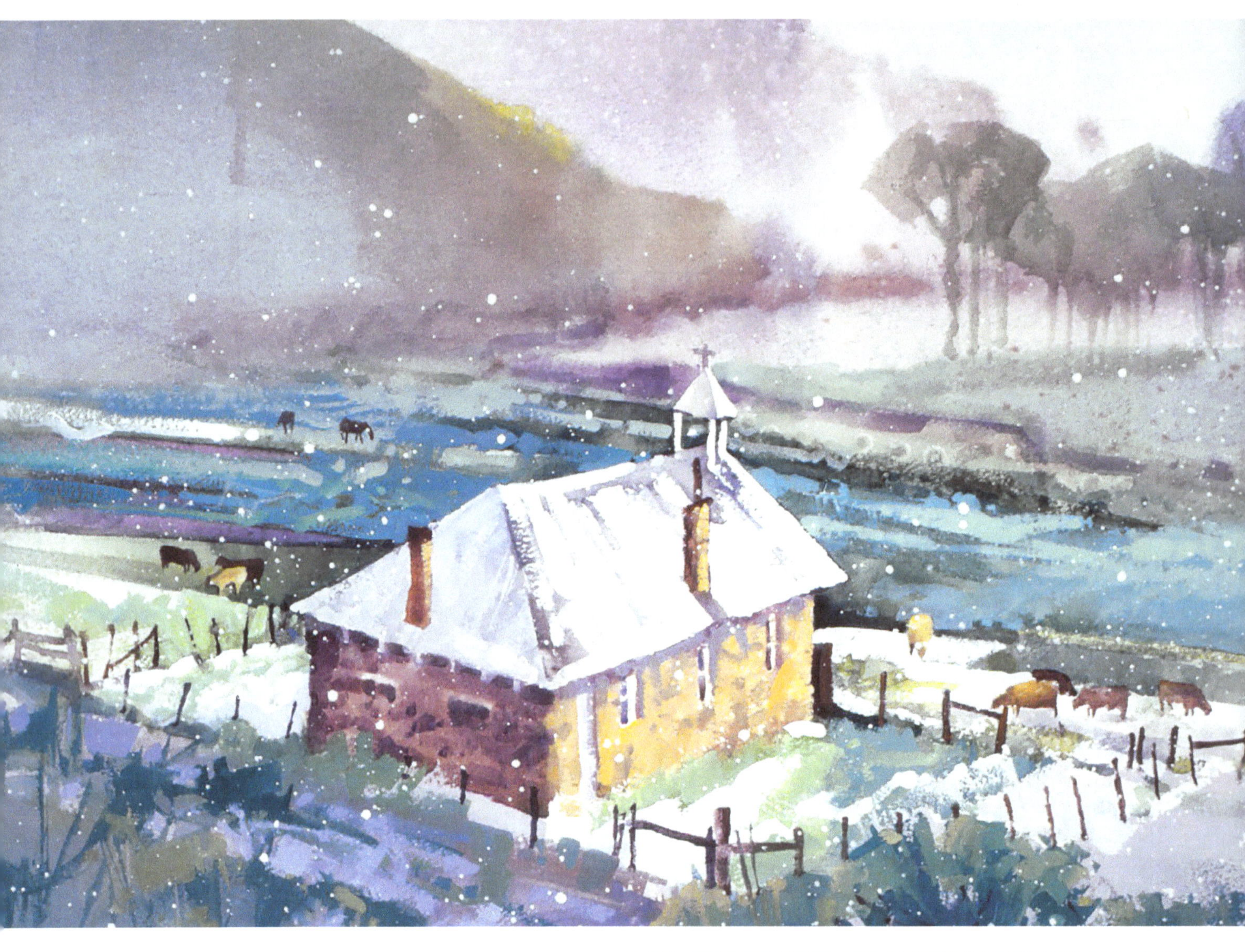

May, 1990

I was with two painting companions, Charlie Ewing and Roger Williams, on this early May day. We drove 18 miles up a corrugated dirt road to find a small Hispanic community with a beautiful church and cows roaming in the meadows. Part way through my painting, which I had started in transparent watercolor, large snowflakes began softly sinking vertically from the sky. I planted a large Yarka umbrella, centered it to cover my painting and my body, and continued on. Casein was the perfect medium to capture this moment. By the time I finished, there were 3 inches of snow stacked on my umbrella. This is what on location painting is all about and days like this are ones that are etched in my soul.

Epilogue

SKIING WITH STEVE

At first every tree will seem the same, every aspen and spruce indistinguishable from another. The sloping crowns of the mountains too, until Steve stops in a clearing to name them - Bristol Head, thick with pines, another you will know only by the color of the shadow cast along its side, a purple blue darker than the sky but its sister. Then gradually the snow path will guide you to places you can find again - the field of stumps, stalwart survivors of a fire a hundred years before, the patch of pines good for sketching and the steep drop of the trail down to the logging road. Other markers will disappear. The big-toe prints deep in the snow and so far apart. A bear? A big cat loping, chasing something that has, you think, climbed the tree? And those little prints with tiny toenail finger claw back and forth, back-and-forth, finding or hiding food, you don't know which. If you are the first to break the drifts the wind pushed across the trail the night before, you will see this all as if you were alone, the discovery. And when you have completed the wondering snow-bound loops and find yourself standing again at the top of the only world you wish to know, don't worry. It won't matter if you can only remember a few of the names, recognize only one tree or mountain. Just stand a while in the place you find yourself. Look carefully in every direction. The song that is this stillness is a long one, the aspen radiant really in any light. Even the river, which you cannot see, icebound or not, will be there when you return. It is only important to know a right place to begin. Here probably, where you can see the start of the changing path ahead.

—Dyan Sublett, 2007

www.ingramcontent.com/pod-product-compliance
Lightning Source LLC
LaVergne TN
LVHW070124110826
845147LV00002B/182
* 9 7 8 1 6 3 5 6 1 9 6 5 2 *